INJUNCTIONS AGAINST INTERMEDIARIES IN THE EUROPEAN UNION

In the European Union, courts have been expanding the enforcement of intellectual property rights by employing injunctions to compel intermediaries to provide assistance, despite no allegation of wrongdoing against these parties. These prospective injunctions, designed to prevent future harm, thus hold parties accountable where no liability exists. Effectively a new type of regulatory tool, these injunctions are distinct from the conventional secondary liability in tort. At present, they can be observed in orders to compel website blocking, content filtering, or disconnection, but going forward, their use is potentially unlimited. This book outlines the paradigmatic shift this entails for the future of the Internet and analyzes the associated legal and economic opportunities and problems.

Martin Husovec is a Slovak-born lawyer and academic. He is Assistant Professor at Tilburg University (Netherlands), appointed jointly by the Tilburg Institute for Law, Technology, and Society (TILT) and the Tilburg Law and Economics Center (TILEC). Husovec holds a PhD (awarded *summa cum laude*) from the Max Planck Institute for Innovation and Competition and Ludwig Maximilian University (Munich). He is also an Affiliate Scholar at Stanford Law School's Center for Internet and Society.

T0370552

CAMBRIDGE INTELLECTUAL PROPERTY
AND INFORMATION LAW

As its economic potential has rapidly expanded, intellectual property has become a subject of front-rank legal importance. *Cambridge Intellectual Property and Information Law* is a series of monograph studies of major current issues in intellectual property. Each volume contains a mix of international, European, comparative and national law, making this a highly significant series for practitioners, judges and academic researchers in many countries.

Series editors
Lionel Bently, *Herchel Smith Professor of Intellectual Property Law,*
University of Cambridge
Graeme Dinwoodie, *Professor of Intellectual Property and Information Technology Law,*
University of Oxford

Advisory editors
William R. Cornish, *Emeritus Herchel Smith Professor of Intellectual Property Law,*
University of Cambridge
François Dessemontet, *Professor of Law, University of Lausanne*
Jane C. Ginsburg, *Morton L. Janklow Professor of Literary and Artistic Property Law,*
Columbia Law School
Paul Goldstein, *Professor of Law, Stanford University*
The Rt Hon. Sir Robin Jacob, *Hugh Laddie Professor of Intellectual Property, University*
College, London
Ansgar Ohly, *Professor of Intellectual Property Law, Ludwig Maximilian University of*
Munich, Germany

A list of books in the series can be found at the end of this volume.

Injunctions Against Intermediaries in the European Union

ACCOUNTABLE BUT NOT LIABLE?

MARTIN HUSOVEC

Tilburg University Institute for Law, Technology, and Society
Tilburg Law and Economics Center

CAMBRIDGE
UNIVERSITY PRESS

University Printing House, Cambridge CB2 8BS, United Kingdom

One Liberty Plaza, 20th Floor, New York, NY 10006, USA

477 Williamstown Road, Port Melbourne, VIC 3207, Australia

314-321, 3rd Floor, Plot 3, Splendor Forum, Jasola District Centre, New Delhi - 110025, India

79 Anson Road, #06-04/06, Singapore 079906

Cambridge University Press is part of the University of Cambridge.

It furthers the University's mission by disseminating knowledge in the pursuit of education, learning and research at the highest international levels of excellence.

www.cambridge.org
Information on this title: www.cambridge.org/9781108400213
DOI: 10.1017/9781108227421

© Martin Husovec 2017

First published 2017
First paperback edition 2018

A catalogue record for this publication is available from the British Library

Library of Congress Cataloging in Publication data
Names: Husovec, Martin, author.
Title: Injunctions against intermediaries in the European Union : accountable but not liable? | Martin Husovec.
Description: Cambridge [UK] ; New York : Cambridge University Press, 2017. | Series: Cambridge intellectual property and information law ; 41 | Includes bibliographical references and index.
Identifiers: LCCN 2017034605 | ISBN 9781108415064 (hardback)
Subjects: LCSH: Injunctions – European Union countries. | Provisional remedies – European Union countries. | Intellectual property – European Union countries. | Intellectual property infringement – European Union countries. | Torts – European Union countries. | Interdict (Civil law) | BISAC: LAW / Intellectual Property / General.
Classification: LCC KJE3954 .H87 2017 | DDC 346.2404/8 – dc23
LC record available at https://lccn.loc.gov/2017034605

ISBN 978-1-108-41506-4 Hardback
ISBN 978-1-108-40021-3 Paperback

Cambridge University Press has no responsibility for the persistence or accuracy of URLs for external or third-party internet websites referred to in this publication, and does not guarantee that any content on such websites is, or will remain, accurate or appropriate.

To beings of no flesh but of playful spirit, whose colour was once beige and eternity is their living.

– Anonymous

Contents

Foreword		*page* xiii
Preface		xv
Acknowledgments		xvii
Abbreviations		xix

PART I. SOCIAL AND ECONOMIC CONTEXT

1	**Introduction to the Problem**	3
	1.1 A Societal Problem	3
	1.2 From Liable "Infringers" to Accountable "Innocent Third Parties"	9
2	**Enforcement Economics**	16
	2.1 Proximate and Remote Services	16
	2.2 Injunctions Against (Mostly) Remote Services	21
	2.3 Solution A: Right to Assistance	25
	2.4 Solution B: Voluntary Assistance	33
	2.5 Comparison of Solutions	35

PART II. EUROPEAN FRAMEWORK

3	**Historical Legislative Developments**	41
	3.1 Design Directive (1996)	42
	3.2 E-Commerce Directive (2000)	42
	3.3 InfoSoc Directive (2001)	45
	3.4 Enforcement Directive (2004)	46
	3.5 Agreement on a Unitary Patent Court (2013)	48

4	**European Intermediary Liability Framework**	50
	4.1 Union and National Safe Harbors	51
	4.2 Injunctions Against Intermediaries	57
	4.3 Secondary Liability	64
	4.4 New Legislative Developments	70

PART III. ACCOUNTABLE BUT NOT LIABLE: INJUNCTIONS
FOR ASSISTANCE

5	**Right to Third-Party Information**	75
	5.1 Conditions	76
	5.2 Scope and Limitations	78
	5.3 Costs	85
6	**Conditions for Injunctions Against Intermediaries**	87
	6.1 "Intermediary"	87
	6.2 "Whose Services Are Used by a Third Party"	90
	6.3 "To Infringe an Intellectual Property Right"	92
	6.4 National Implementation	94
7	**Scope of Injunctions Against Intermediaries**	104
	7.1 Correction and Prevention	104
	7.2 Goal of Injunctions	107
	7.3 Role of Preliminary Measures	111
8	**Limits of Injunctions Against Intermediaries**	112
	8.1 Secondary Law: General Limitations	113
	8.2 Secondary Law: Safe Harbors	116
	8.3 Secondary Law: Illegal General Monitoring	117
	8.4 Primary Law: Human Rights Limits	122
	8.5 A New Approach	137
	8.6 Costs	138

PART IV. LEGAL TRADITIONS

9	**Injunctions in Civil Law: Germany**	145
	9.1 Roman Influence	145
	9.2 German Civil Code in the Making	150
	9.3 From the Civil Code to Today's Principles	156
	9.4 Age of Internet Cases	166
	9.5 Information Disclosure	174
	9.6 Costs of Compliance	175
	9.7 Duty to Review	179

10 **Injunctions in Common Law: England** 184

    10.1 Court's Powers 185
    10.2 Assisting by Information Disclosure 189
    10.3 Assisting by Blocking Websites 195
    10.4 Costs of Compliance 200
    10.5 Equitable Duty 206

PART V. OUTLOOK AND CONCLUSIONS

11 **Global Context** 213

    11.1 International Public Law and Its Shifts 213
    11.2 New Global Movement? 217

12 **Conclusions** 222

    12.1 Two Traditions, One Innovation 223
    12.2 The European Union: To Reform or Rethink? 225
    12.3 Regulating Self-Regulation: The Problem of Voluntary
        Agreements 229

Table of Legislation 235
Table of Cases 237
References 249
Index 269

Foreword

The problem of issuing injunctions against intermediaries has arisen in the case law of European judiciary in the recent years in three instances. Even though it does not stem from the title of the book, it is clear that the real problems of liability of intermediaries emerged with the development of Internet services. Professor Martin Husovec correctly points out in the introduction to his book that his intention is to encapsulate two main stories: the website-blocking story and the password-locking story.

From this point of view, one may say that this volume constitutes a journey into terra incognita. Indeed, several decisions of the Court of Justice and, not substantially more, of national jurisdictions of the Member States do not explain all the problems pertaining to responsibility of Internet intermediaries. I would even dare to assert that the most sensitive aspects of Internet intermediaries are still to be identified and resolved.

It is true that the conditions of liability of Internet intermediaries in Europe are to some extent harmonized on the EU level. On one hand, the possibilities to issue injunctions have their legal base in Article 8(3) of the InfoSoc Directive and Article 11, third sentence, of the Enforcement Directive. On the other hand, the E-Commerce Directive provides for the limitation of intermediary liability – but does not shield from injunctions. Despite this harmonization, many of the cases in which national courts apply these provisions do not reach the Court of Justice. My impression is that national judges are not always aware that the rules on Internet intermediaries' liability they apply constitute the implementation of the relevant EU Directives. It is for this reason that the Court of Justice had so far only a few possibilities to rule on the interpretation of these Directives in the context of the liability of Internet intermediaries.

Another problem at the level of EU law which is closely linked to the liability of Internet intermediaries concerns the uncertainties related to the concept of striking a fair balance between fundamental rights, especially those enshrined into the EU Charter of Fundamental Rights. As the decisions in *UPC Telekabel*, *Scarlet Extended*, and *McFadden* show, the task of balancing conflicting fundamental rights is particularly challenging.

I would not disclose any secret by saying that the cases that have reached the Court of Justice were not easy ones. Indeed, each of them presented a new challenge. They invited the Court to delve into novel technological concepts and, moreover, contributed to controversial societal debates. It is sufficient to recall that in probably the most important decisions on the subject, the Court of Justice did not follow opinions of Advocates General. The judges were not entirely convinced by arguments put forward by my learned colleagues Cruz Villalón and Wathelet in, respectively, the cases of *UPC Telekabel* and *GS Media*. Nor was the Court of Justice wholly persuaded by my humble submissions in the case of *McFadden*. In this context I cannot resist a temptation to express my thanks to the author that despite discrepancies between opinions of Advocates General and the actual rulings of the Court of Justice, he asked one of the former to write the foreword for his book – a book in which he duly presents the issues from the perspective of both the Opinions of Advocates General and the actual rulings of the Court of Justice.

The problems pertaining to liability of Internet intermediaries are not of course limited to EU law. The author lays a particular emphasis on English and German law. The challenges that the he had to face were twofold. First, procedural instruments that could potentially be qualified as "injunctions" vary from one country to another. Second, one has to bear in mind that we are dealing here with a very special type of injunction that can be addressed to intermediaries who are not considered directly or indirectly liable for infringements in question – innocent parties, as described by the author. Moreover, concerning some situations where secondary liability is invoked, it is clear for every comparative private lawyer how complex and divergent rules on secondary liability are.

Professor Husovec's book addresses the most complex, difficult, and innovative aspects of liability of Internet intermediaries. His analyses take into account not only legal aspects but also social and economic considerations. He demonstrates excellent analytical skills as well as an impressive clarity in his study. The final proposals of the book, based essentially on the distinction between "remote" and "proximate" services, are very well argued. They confirm the author's awareness of practical consequences and show his attention to the influence of technological development.

I am deeply convinced that this volume will substantially enrich the doctrinal debate on the liability on Internet intermediaries. It will also constitute a useful tool of argumentation for practicing lawyers. Last, but not least, the book will serve as a source of inspiration for judiciary, including Advocates General.

Maciej Szpunar, Advocate General of the Court of
Justice of the European Union

Preface

The newspaper headlines are full of them. They are hard to avoid, and equally hard to regulate. Internet intermediaries – the symbols of how innovation can improve our well-being while at the same time put it at risk.

Since the 2000s, we have grown accustomed to the basic social contract. They were legally obliged to be reactive and only morally obliged to be proactive. Not anymore. Intellectual property law is just one of the areas where this is changing. The legal obligations to prevent third-party wrongdoing before it takes place are on the rise. In the European Union, injunctions against intermediaries are the symbol of this shift. Based on Article 8(3) of the InfoSoc Directive and the third sentence of Article 11 of the Enforcement Directive, these injunctions do not primarily target bad actors. They address by-standers who often comply with the law. The question asked is not what the intermediary did wrong but how it can help. The measures thus seek accountability where no liability exists. And there are signs that these instruments are going global.

The book that you are reading conceptualizes this shift and looks at novel problems that it creates. It breaks the phenomenon into pieces in order to tell the story of these injunctions, from yesterday to tomorrow. While doing this, the European Union law, its case-law and implementation, remains at the center of the debate. At the same time, in order to offer the view of law in action, the book also explores the developments of two jurisdictions – Germany and the United Kingdom. As the prototypes of different systems, the countries also serve as two case studies of the historical foundations on which the European and domestic concepts of today operate. By contrasting two jurisdictions and their recent practice in the area, the book also highlights how a similar tool can take on itself different goals, if put into a different setting. It also demonstrates how universal, nevertheless, some of the considerations remain.

The book argues that we are witnessing the emergence of a new type of regulatory tool distinct from the conventional secondary liability in tort. It appears next to primary and accessory liability as a third category. Depending on its design, it can complement the two but also compete with them. The tool's goal is to achieve more targeted intervention oriented toward future wrongdoing. Unlike tort law, where the decision about standards of care necessarily triggers an entire avalanche of consequences, injunctions governed by courts allow for tailor-made responses framed as specific forms of enforcement assistance. However, exactly because these injunctions do not use a weight of damages to force private parties to arrive at socially optimal levels of care, they pose new challenges for the cost and benefit analysis.

This is why the economics of enforcement plays a central role in this book and is offered to the reader right after the introduction. Economic analysis helps in suggesting how to rethink and redesign the tool, if we aspire to benefit from it beyond the world of "nice gestures." I offer a simple modeling of the interactions to improve our understanding of how and when we risk wasting the resources for symbolic enforcement that is of no economic value, since such enforcement does not deliver anyone with better justice.

However, economics doesn't capture the full breadth of the social problems. Therefore, even welfare-maximizing injunctions should not be automatically endorsed. Economic gain is not always social bargain. Unsupervised injunctions against intermediaries can strip citizens of their fundamental rights or circumvent political processes where they are inconvenient. To prevent this from happening, we have to pay attention to their limitations, safeguards, and rule of law. The book explains how.

Naturally, I could not address everything. One of the underdeveloped areas is how to optimally regulate voluntary agreements that often result from the enforcement of rights. As a necessary by-product, they deserve much more of our attention. In order to sketch the issues that I see, I offer brief remarks on the subject in the concluding section.

I wish you an enjoyable and informative read and hope that the book will, at the very least, bring more clarity into our collective thinking about these issues.

Maciej Szpunar, Advocate General of the Court of
Justice of the European Union

Acknowledgments

It is 2007 in Košice, a little picturesque town in eastern Slovakia. A young second-year law student decides to found a start-up and thereby invest his earned scholarship, but not just any start-up! Its name roughly translates into "I do not go to lectures dot sk." Its main purpose is to create an online space for students to share their notes from university lectures. The students should not be forced to attend boring lectures just to be able to study, goes the motto. The website booms. The number of law students attending boring lectures plummets. Selected law professors are outraged, which means that the young entrepreneur has a problem – a legal one. Are such notes protected by teachers' copyright? And if so, is the entrepreneur liable for his users' actions? He needs to find out.

A decade later, in the Netherlands, the young man becomes a full member of the Law Faculty. To his surprise, he finds himself still reading about the same issues. Hopefully his lectures are not boring.

Naturally, founders of start-ups do not turn into law professors overnight. It takes a regiment of excellent teachers to inspire a young mind and a supportive family to nurture it. I am extremely lucky to have all of that.

Radim Polčák's pioneering books were the first I touched. Ivo Telec's advanced lectures propelled me to read more. Annette Kur, a true giant of intellectual property scholarship, accepted to be my doctoral supervisor and then became the best mentor one could wish for. Ansgar Ohly, my lecturing hero, thought that my never-ending comments amounted to something and was always ready to offer his feedback. Jeremy Phillips thought it was a good idea to give a chance to a young Slovak blogger. Jennifer Granick warmly welcomed me at Stanford University and opened doors to many Silicon Valley firms to understand the industry. Graeme Dinwoodie, an endless source of inspiration on many fronts, always had advice for me when I needed it. Arthur van Martels and Fabian Hafenbrädl, two of my closest friends and doctoral peers, always encouraged me to enter academia. Lucia, my beloved wife, had commitment that was not shaken by the prospect of marrying an academic with seven-league boots. And finally, Marianna and Viktor Husovec, the best parents under the sun, always supported me in all my pursuits, regardless of how crazy they were, and taught me never to act without a plan and to easily give up on it.

Over the years, I also became indebted to an ever-increasing number of scholars, who became my colleagues and sometimes close friends. I keep learning from them every day. In particular, I owe gratitude to my "intermediary liability crowd," Christina Angelopolous, Miquel Peguera, Daphne Keller, Eleonora Rosati, and Sophie Stalla-Bourdillon, whose excellent insights keep me convinced that the area of research probably never dries out. Moreover, I certainty couldn't have written this book without formative discussions with Richard Arnold, Annemarie Bridy, Robert Cooter, Henri de Belsunce, Thomas Dreier, Josef Drexl, Niva Elkin-Koren, Giancarlo Frosio, Eric Goldman, Patrick Goold, Dietmar Harhoff, Reto Hilty, Franz Hofmann, Mrinalini Kochupillai, Matthias Leistner, Mark Lemley, Robert Merges, Sylvie Nérisson, Jan Nordemann, Pamela Samuelson, Pekka Savola, Graham Smith, Jennifer Urban, and many other brilliant minds. They all engaged with my ideas and influenced my thinking.

Finally, yet importantly, I would like to thank Advocate General Maciej Szpunar, who, despite his much more important tasks at the Court of Justice of the European Union, generously agreed to write the foreword for this book. I also owe thanks to Matt Gallaway and his colleagues from Cambridge University Press for bringing the book into the reader's hands. Therefore, dear reader, the thinking, I definitely did not do alone, only the writing and mistakes, those are my own.

Abbreviations

AG	Advocate General
Art 11(III) Enforcement Directive	Article 11 sentence 3 *Directive 2004/48/EC*
Art 8(3) InfoSoc Directive	Article 8 paragraph 3 *Directive 2001/29/EC*
BGB	The German Civil Code
BGH	The German Federal Supreme Court
CJEU	The Court of Justice of the European Union
E-Commerce Directive	*Directive 2000/31/EC*
Enforcement Directive	*Directive 2004/48/EC*
EU Charter	Charter of Fundamental Rights of the European Union
InfoSoc Directive	*Directive 2001/29/EC*
OGH	The Austrian Supreme Court
The Convention	The European Convention on Human Rights
TRIPS	The Agreement on Trade-Related Aspects of Intellectual Property Rights

PART I

Social and Economic Context

1

Introduction to the Problem

1.1 A SOCIETAL PROBLEM

The following collection of stories best encapsulates the problems that this book tries to resolve.

The website blocking story. In autumn 2010, in-house lawyers of British Telecommunications (BT) received an unusual request. The Motion Picture Association was asking whether it would agree to block access to a copyright-infringing website. The company replied that it would require a court order to block a service; otherwise, it would face business exposures, including potential legal liabilities. A week before Christmas of the same year, a notification of the lawsuit arrived. BT decided to oppose.

Justice Arnold, the judge hearing the case, had an important task before him. Although the legislator already created a legal basis for injunctions against intermediaries, it still had to decide on many open issues. How effective must such an injunction be to justify its grant? How should such orders look? Should they be flexible to allow for their re-updating? What technology is appropriate? Can someone challenge them ex post? What happens in case of abuse? And who shall bear the costs of what?

These questions weren't answered at once. It took the brilliant judge and his other esteemed colleagues several years and hundreds of hours of hard work on dozen of decisions until most of the principles materialized into settled practice. How much did the rightholders benefit? It is hard to say, as the evidence seems conflicting.[1]

---

[1] Ofcom, "Site Blocking to Reduce Online Copyright Infringement: A Review of Sections 17 and 18 of the Digital Economy Act" (2010), 48, http://stakeholders.ofcom.org.uk/binaries/internet/site-blocking .pdf, accessed 13 January 2015 (comparing costs and benefits of various techniques); Brett Danaher and others, "The Effect of Piracy Website Blocking on Consumer Behavior" (SSRN, 2015), http://ssrn.com/abstract=2612063, accessed 1 July 2015 (blocking 19 different major piracy sites caused a meaningful reduction in total piracy and subsequently led former users of the blocked sites to increase their usage of paid legal streaming sites, such as Netflix, by 12 percent on average); Luis Aguiar and others, "Online Copyright Enforcement, Consumer Behavior, and Market Structure" (European Commission, 2015),

But given that they still keep applying for the new injunctions, they must at least believe that they benefit beyond their own (limited) expenses. How much did it cost society? At least several hundred thousand euros of direct expenses.[2] And was the money well spent? We don't know. It depends on whether the overall costs are offset by the obtained benefits, and those remain unknown. Will we ever know? In addition, what happens if measures become ineffective after some time? Will they be discontinued?

The password-locking story. In autumn 2006, rightholders of the song "Sommer unseres Lebens" (Summer of our life) detected that the Internet connection of a private person was used for filesharing. They decided to sue. In the course of the proceedings, it was found that the owner of the connection didn't commit any infringement himself and that the infringement was likely committed by an unknown third party using his open WiFi. The question thus arose: should the owner of the connection have done something about it prior to any notification? And with what tools?

Four years later, the German Federal Supreme Court provided its answers. It held that a private operator of an open WiFi network should assist rightholders in enforcing their rights by sufficiently password locking the network's connectivity in order to prevent possible misuse. The court undertook a balancing exercise by comparing the costs and benefits to private users and rightholders. It observed that password locking is very cheap and easy for a user to implement and that it might even increase the user's security and arguably reduce the opportunities for potential infringers to hide their identities. Unlike in the English story, the costs and benefits thus seemed to have been clear. But were they?

After the ruling, password-protected WiFi connections became the de facto standard in Germany. Because even prelitigation efforts are financially compensated, citizens generally comply prior to any lawsuit. Two years after the judgment, the reputed magazine *Der Spiegel* summarized the state of affairs in the article "Silence on the Sidewalk," which criticized the fact that, in the aftermath of the decision,[3] citizens can hardly find public Internet access. According to a study conducted in 2014, there were only 1.87 open hotspots per 10,000 inhabitants in Germany, while in Sweden, the number is 9.94, in the United Kingdom, it is 28.67, and in South Korea, it is 37.35.[4]

---

https://ec.europa.eu/jrc/sites/default/files/JRC93492_Online_Copyright.pdf, accessed 1 July 2015 (finding the relative effectiveness of blocking led to limited substitution for legal sources of consumption); Joost Poort and others, "Baywatch: Two Approaches to Measure the Effects of Blocking Access to The Pirate Bay" (2014) 38 Telecommunications Policy, 383–392 (no lasting net impact is found on the percentage of the Dutch population downloading from illegal sources).

[2] See *Cartier International AG & Ors v. British Sky Broadcasting Ltd & Ors* [2016] EWCA Civ 658 [18], [19].

[3] Rosenbach Marcel and Schmundt Hilmar, "Funkstille auf dem Bürgersteig" *Der Spiegel* (1 July 2013), 128–130.

[4] Eco, "Verbreitung und Nutzbarkeit von WLAN, WLAN-Zugangspunkten Sowie öffentliche Hotspots in Deutschland" (2014), www.eco.de/wp-content/blogs.dir/eco-microresearch_verbreitung-

It appears that the court failed to foresee one particular type of cost – wireless technologies as a source of new innovation and competition. The judges were too influenced by their perception of WLAN as a carrier of private, community, or corporate local networks. Although, in the past, it might have seemed that 3G and WiFi address completely different needs, in distinct, nonoverlapping markets, the opposite is nowadays true.[5] WiFi access has become an alternative to substantially slower, limited, and more expensive mobile access. This has motivated some foreign carriers, such as RepublicWireless, to start offering subscription plans where public WiFi is the primary channel for phone calls and cellular technology only serves as a backup in its absence. Low barriers to entry, no rights over the spectrum, and wide diffusion of technology make it inherently very competitive.[6] Moreover, the ease of sharing of Internet access over WiFi, facilitated by cheap router equipment, with its scalability and speed of implementation, has made it a more viable alternative to Internet distribution in places where fixed-line access would be expensive to establish.[7] The court failed to see the full innovative potential. Unwittingly, it silenced WiFi on the German sidewalk, thinking that it was doing the right thing.

The social value of open WiFi has also become apparent in emergency situations. For instance, during the 2012 earthquake in northern Italy, local authorities requested the general public to remove passwords from their private WiFi networks in order to allow the widest possible emergency access to communications networks.[8] Similarly, in 2007, when a 40-year-old bridge in Minneapolis collapsed into the river, WiFi played an important role in managing the response and recovery efforts.[9] The untapped potential of WiFi technology is greater still. Its user-centric, decentralized approach is more conducive to innovation – the development of the

---

und-nutzung-von-wlan1.pdf. See also the recent consumer survey from Bitkom, "Öffentliche WLAN-Zugänge fristen Nischendasein" (2015), www.bitkom.org/de/presse/8477_82493.aspx, accessed 1 July 2015 ("Trotz einer insgesamt guten Versorgung mit mobilen Internetzugängen *bremst die geringe WLAN-Nutzung die digitale Entwicklung. Ein Grund dafür sind die restriktiven gesetzlichen Haftungsregeln*, die viele potenzielle Hotspot-Betreiber, zum Beispiel Café- oder Restaurant-Besitzer, abschrecken").

5 William Lehra and Lee W. McKnight, "Wireless Internet Access: 3G vs. WiFi?" (2003) 27 Telecommunications Policy 356; also Paul S. Henry and Hui Luo, "WiFi: What's Next?" [2002] IEEE Telecommunications Magazine 66–72 ("Extension of WiFi from the Office Environment to Wide-Area Coverage Opens New Vistas for WiFi Technology and Will Likely be a Key Driver of Its Future Growth").

6 William Lehra and Lee W. McKnight, 'Wireless Internet Access: 3G vs. WiFi?' (2003) 27 Telecommunications Policy 365.

7 Ibid.; Eric Schmidt and Jared Cohen, *The New Digital Age: Reshaping the Future of People, Nations and Business* (Knopf 2013), 4.

8 Editorial, "Authorities Call for WiFi to Be Open after Deadly Italy Quake" *Famagusta Gazette* (29 May 2012), http://famagusta-gazette.com/authorities-call-for-wifi-to-be-open-after-deadly-italy-quake-p15591–69.htm, accessed 27 November 2014.

9 US Fire Administration, "Technical Report Series, I-35W Bridge Collapse and Response" (2007), 45, http://berec.europa.eu/doc/publications/consult_add_cable_netw_chapter/dt.pdf, accessed 27 November 2014.

unknown.[10] The opportunities of peer-to-peer communication, such as between autonomous cars and pedestrians in order to avoid car accidents, or between drones and their operators, are endless.

So was the German Court wrong in its analysis after all? It depends on your reference point. Password locking of WiFi hotspots may really have made all the parties better off, however, only back then, with the existing state of technology and its uses. In the meantime, WiFi has grown from a local personal network into an important competitive technology for delivering "last mile" Internet access. It has turned into a blossoming source of numerous innovations – benefits that cannot be fully reaped when everybody has to engage in password locking. The advances in the use of the technology over recent years have gradually mounted the evidence that the ruling might actually be a break on social progress. It is very plausible that it costs society more than it benefits rightholders.

So how can the rule change? The public outcry in Germany went so far that the Bundestag, the German Parliament, tried to step in to correct the decision of the court.[11] This begs the following question: is this a new model of technological governance, when the legislator has to step when the courts get their standard setting wrong? Is this approach sufficiently fast and institutionally future-proof? Do judges ever have enough information to be entrusted with such activity? Can we expect them to predict use of technology that the markets cannot predict?

The graduated-response stories. In 2009, the French Parliament, after lengthy political discussions, enacted a so-called graduated copyright enforcement regime and entrusted it to a newly minted authority – HADOPI. The rationale of the law was that access providers could notify their users who are found to be infringing on copyright, and after some escalation, further steps could be taken to fine or even temporarily disconnect those subscribers.[12] In 2013, the system was redesigned. Although it was found to improve the behavior of consumers,[13] the change in their use was probably not substantial enough to offset the system's maintenance costs. The

---

[10] William Lehra and Lee W. McKnight, "Wireless Internet Access: 3G vs. WiFi?" (2003) 27 Telecommunications Policy 359.

[11] Bundesministerium für Wirtschaft und Energie (BMWi), "Entwurf eines Zweiten Gesetzes zur Änderung des Telemediengesetzes (Zweites Telemedienänderungsgesetz – 2. TMG ÄndG)" (2015), www.bmwi.de/, then adopted as Zweites Gesetz zur Änderung des Telemediengesetzes (2016) Teil I Nr. 36, 1766.

[12] See generally about the French experiment Eldar Haber, "The French Revolution 2.0: Copyright and the Three Strikes Policy" (2011) 2(2) Harvard Journal of Sports & Entertainment Law 297.

[13] Brett Danaher and others, "The Effect of Graduated Response Anti-Piracy Laws on Music Sales: Evidence from an Event Study in France" (2014) 62(3) Journal of Industrial Economics 541–553 (meta-study of various studies); Brett Danaher, Michael D. Smith, and Rahul Telang, "Government-sanctioned and market-based anti-piracy measures can both mitigate economic harm from piracy" (2017) 60(2) ACM 68–75 (finding positive changes following HADOPI); Alexis Koster, "Fighting Internet Piracy: The French Experience with the HADOPI Law" (2012) 16(4) International Journal of Management & Information Systems 327 (reports show some modest positive changes in the behavior of French Internet users).

government admitted to having spent 12 million euros and the time of 60 civil servants to generate 1 million e-mail-first notifications, 99,000 second notifications, and only 134 prosecution cases.[14] French culture minister Aurélie Filippetti described the system as "unwieldy, uneconomic and ultimately ineffective."[15]

In 2015, a judge of the Irish Commercial Court created a similar scheme with the stroke of a pen.[16] The legal basis for injunctions against intermediaries was used to impose an entire three-strikes notification scheme upon Internet access providers. The cost was divided among the parties. The rightholders have to cover 20 percent of the capital expenditure, capped at 940,000 euros, and the number of notices to be processed is limited at 2,500 per month.[17] Upon sending a third notification, the plaintiffs can seek identity disclosure concerning the subscribers and also an order to terminate their access. Such applications will not be opposed by access providers, and no costs will be sought. Although the scheme has not yet entered into force, as the case is still pending before the Irish Court of Appeal, it is striking that what requires a lot of political debate in one country is created by a single judge in another without any public discussion. Are injunctions against intermediaries really so limitless? And if so, can they so easily circumvent the political process? What else can they impose?

Consider yet another case. Just a few days before Christmas 2013, it was decided that Juan Carlos,[18] an unknown citizen, must be cut off from the Internet. Juan wasn't a terrorist or a dangerous offender, nor did he stop paying his broadband bill. An IP address assigned to Juan was, however, found to have fileshared some copyright-protected materials. Juan never received any prior notice warning him that this might happen. In fact, Juan might have read about his case in the newspapers. He could have learned that a local association of Spanish music producers had brought a private copyright action against his Internet access provider in court, demanding that he be *forever* disconnected from the Web – at least, with this particular provider.

The court proceedings before the Barcelona court were very Kafkaesque. In Juan's absence, without his provider raising a single objection, the court readily issued an injunction ordering his provider to disconnect him from the World Wide Web. Nobody asked Juan or gave him the opportunity to defend himself against the allegation of copyright infringement, to dispute the admissibility and veracity of the antipiracy firm's evidence, or to prove that he could not use the filesharing client

---

[14] Music Updates, "French Count the cost of HADOPI" (2012), www.musiclawupdates.com/?p=5092.

[15] Ibid.; *Le Nouvel Observateur*, "Aurélie Filippetti: 'Je vais réduire les crédits de l'Hadopi'" (2012), http://obsession.nouvelobs.com/high-tech/20120801.OBS8587/aurelie-filippetti-je-vais-reduire-les-credits-de-l-hadopi.html.

[16] *Sony Music Entertainment (Ireland) Limited v. UPC Communicaitons Ireland Limited (No 1)* [2015] IEHC 317.

[17] Gerard Kelly, "A Court-Ordered Graduated Response System I Ireland: The Beginning of the End?" (2016) 11(3) Journal of Intellectual Property Law and Practice 183, 184.

[18] Audiencia Provincial Barcelona *Promusicae v. X* (2013) 470/2013 (the name is a fictional one).

or explain that his Internet access was probably misused. Nobody even asked him if he considered disconnection to be a proportionate measure, given the needs of his professional and private life. And nobody gave him a chance to defend against a disconnection without any expiration period.[19]

Shouldn't individuals have a say in copyright enforcement measures directed against them? Who will respect their right to a fair trial if only their providers are sued? And how is it possible that while the French graduated-response scheme only foresaw a temporary disconnection for a maximum of one month, the Spanish court–granted injunction terminates access without limitation in time? Where are the bounds of rule of law?

The Irish and Spanish cases show that injunctions against intermediaries grant rightholders unprecedented powers. They allow them to propose solutions that would otherwise have to be legislated in a tedious and costly political process. Where are the limits of such injunctions? And where is the guarantee that they will be abandoned by rightholders when they become wasteful enforcement practices? The French example shows that government-funded enforcement schemes will be reevaluated if they don't constitute the bang for the buck. The US example of the voluntary graduated-response scheme, the Copyright Alert System, shows that even private ordering schemes will be reevaluated.[20] Can we say the same about court-imposed systems? If not, aren't we at risk of indefinitely wasting society's resources on ineffective enforcement?

All these stories have one thing in common – their legal basis. The European legal basis for these enforcement measures is set out in several provisions (Article 8(3) of the InfoSoc Directive, Article 11(III) of the Enforcement Directive) that are very brief in their wording but, as can be seen, potentially far-reaching in their consequences. They address intermediaries of different kinds who are "best placed" to prevent the infringing activities of third parties. It is believed that the intermediaries can most cheaply prevent the wrongs of others. Hence they should be obliged by injunctions to assist the rightholders, irrespective of their own liability. These injunctions make individuals and companies *accountable* and oblige them to some acts of cooperation, even if they are *not* liable for damages. Hence they are *accountable but not liable*. This research looks into the history, economics, and application of such "forced cooperation" in order to answer the social problems that were mentioned earlier.

At the time when Article 8(3) of the InfoSoc Directive and Article 11(III) of the Enforcement Directive were enacted, only a few would have predicted their

---

[19] Fortunately, the user will probably never be disconnected from the Internet, as the Spanish ISP could not match the IP address with a particular subscriber. It is also perfectly possible that he changed his ISP before this decision was even issued. Moreover, the court applied the measure to only one of many Spanish ISPs named by the plaintiff. This, however, does not reduce the worrisome picture painted by the case.

[20] EFF, "It's the End of the Copyright Alert System (as We Know It)" (2017), www.eff.org/deeplinks/2017/02/its-end-copyright-alert-system-we-know-it.

present-day consequences. A single sentence prescribing the Members States to legislate "an injunction against intermediaries whose services are used by a third party to infringe" developed into a full-fledged concept reaching its protective hand far beyond regular concepts of liability. As of now, the provision "obliges Member States to ensure that an intermediary whose services are used by a third party in order to infringe an intellectual property right may, regardless of any liability of its own in relation to the facts at issue, be ordered to take measures aimed at bringing those infringements to an end and measures seeking to prevent further infringements."[21]

Its expansive reach didn't go unnoticed in the industry. Yahoo! commented on the state of affairs during a debate about an amendment to the Enforcement Directive, arguing that "for online intermediaries, legal liability per se is not key, but rather the effect of injunctions on their business."[22] This is a remarkable statement for the "old world" of intermediary liability, which concerned telling who is a good and who is a bad actor. The reassurance of being a good actor seems of no comfort when imposed orders of assistance lead to significant costs. Increasing accountability of innocent third parties thus should not be of lesser concern than liability as such. It has an economic impact, and, although by different means, it affects the allocation of responsibility. We should question when and how it advances the goals of exclusive rights.

This book argues that the policy of intermediary liability is becoming increasingly multifaceted. Instead of simplistically answering when actors turn bad, today's map of interactions is more complex. It calls upon good actors as much as on those who misbehave. In European Union (EU) intellectual property law, by far the biggest development has been injunctions against intermediaries. This book unpacks the phenomenon and explains that we are witnessing an entirely separate type of policy intervention.

1.2 FROM LIABLE "INFRINGERS" TO ACCOUNTABLE "INNOCENT THIRD PARTIES"

The Internet makes social interactions easier, but also more complex. The usual e-spoken word has to involve dozens of intermediaries to carry it to its recipient. As in the physical world, the spoken word can sometimes hurt and infringe somebody else's rights. However, because the Internet is, by default, anonymous and global, enforcing otherwise ordinary torts becomes less straightforward. The rightholder often needs to engage not only the speakers of the words, but also some by-standing intermediaries that could assist him in enforcing his right.

---

[21] Case C-494/15 *Tommy Hilfiger Licensing and Others* [2016] ECLI:EU:C:2016:528, para. 22.
[22] See European Commission, "Public Hearing on Directive 2004/48/EC and the Challenges Posed by the Digital Environment" (7 June 2011), http://ec.europa.eu/internal_market/iprenforcement/docs/conference20110607/hearing-report_en.pdf, accessed 1 March 2015.

In a democratic society, individuals are born equal. This means that one individual may never force others with self-help to do things they do not want to. Even if a legal title exists for some conduct (e.g., a claim for contractual performance), one still needs to go to court to force the other party to fulfill its obligation. If somebody commits a tort, an enforceable legal obligation is created, which entitles its creditor (victim) to ask for specific acts from a debtor (injurer). Without someone being a debtor in this sense, the victim is released to his mercy. Such by-stander can provide voluntary help, but also might not. The victims can invoke morals or social responsibility or leverage its market power, but have no legally enforceable way how to hold the person to account.

For most of the 1990s and early 2000s, the legal debates and court cases in intellectual property law focused on answering the question when someone becomes an infringer. The infringer, whether primary or secondary, was seen as the only way how to become legally indebted to a victim. All big cases of the period, *Amstrad*, *Napster*, *Grokster*, and *Viacom v. YouTube*, were of this kind.[23] They all focused on the conditions of attribution of user's actions with full consequences of joint and several liability. This book analyzes a different response of the European law. Partly because of the institutional setup,[24] the attention in the last few years was shifted from delineating the wrongful conduct and its full attribution to platforms, to a discussion of possibilities that by-standers have in helping out the rightholders. This accountability without liability, as I call it, became a main driver of the modern online enforcement in Europe.

Traditionally, wrongful conduct is determined by the system of rules known as tort law. It outlines when somebody is liable for his conduct or can be attributed that of others. The system provides for causes of actions, legal rights, against those who committed such a blameworthy act, a tort, or a wrong. These persons are then referred to as tortfeasors or wrongdoers, which include primary infringers as well as their accessories. Traditions of civil and common law, however, also recognize cases when a person who is not found to be a wrongdoer also needs to assist a rightholder in the enforcement of his right. These cases are about cooperation, not sanctions. This third party (nonwrongdoer) is herewith held accountable for some help, but not liable for the acts of the wrongdoer. Despite a successful lawsuit against it, it remains a lawful actor. In this work, I refer to this third party as an "innocent third

---

[23] *A & M Records, Inc. v. Napster, Inc.* 239 F.3d 1004, 1022 (9th Cir. 2001); *Metro-Goldwyn-Mayer Studios Inc. v. Grokster Ltd.*, 125 S. Ct. 2764 (2005); *CBS Songs Ltd v. Amstrad Consumer Electronics Plc* [1988] UKHL 15 (12 May 1988); *Viacom International Inc et. Seq. vs. Youtube*, 718 F. Supp. 2d 514 (SDNY 2010).

[24] Today, most noncontractual obligations are still an issue of the national civil laws of the Member States of the EU. Union law, thus so far, regulates only very specific sector issues such as unfair commercial practices, intellectual property rights, and their enforcement, without ambition to be comprehensive. Despite numerous academic projects, the European Civil Code is still far from reality. As a consequence, missing accessory liability is being dispersed among primary liability and accountability without liabity in order to avoid reference to nonharmonized piece of the puzzle.

party" or an "innocent intermediary." Alternatively, one could also use the term "noninfringer."

This is *not* meant to imply any judgment of fairness,[25] although undeniably for many civil law lawyers the term will likely sound this way.[26] I have taken the term from its common usage in the English case-law.[27] As early as 1871 in *Upmann v. Elkan*, the English courts would talk about an "innocent" party that was "mixed up with the transaction" when describing the position of a forwarding agent who unknowingly forwarded a case of trademark-infringing cigars and was then ordered by the court to remove the signs from the goods.[28] This development continued[29] until a landmark case from 1974, in which the House of Lords held that a disclosure by a relief granted against the British Customs authority is possible, irrespective of the fact that authority's conduct was "entirely innocent."[30] In the recent case-law of the common law courts, the term "innocent third party" has become clearly settled in its meaning as referring to nonwrongdoers in the context of equitable injunctive relief.[31]

[25] Mark MacCarthy, "What Payment Intermediaries Are Doing about Online Liability and Why It Matters" (2010) 25 Berkeley Technology Law Journal 1037, 1056 (arguing that burdening innocent people is unfair).

[26] German scholars would not usually refer to a nonliable person serving such an injunction as "an innocent third party" or a "nonwrongdoer," despite the fact that historical examination shows that legal basis of injunctions was meant to address also those who did not act wrongfully. An additional reason might be that in the current German intellectual property jurisprudence, injunctions outside of tort law also serve cases which could be solved by a more developed the negligence rule. So it is counterintuitive to label these parties as innocent.

[27] Steven C. Bradford, "Shooting the Messenger: The Liability of Crowdfunding Intermediaries for the Fraud of Others" (2015) 83 University of Cincinnati Law Review 371, 379 (using the term "innocent intermediary" for a nonliable intermediary); Ronald J. Mann and Seth R. Belzley, "The Promise of Internet Intermediary Liability" (2005) 47 William & Mary Law Review 239, 276 (using the term "innocent third parties"); Mike Conradi, Liability of an ISP for allowing access to file sharing networks (2003) 19 Computer Law & Security Report 289, 292 (noting that "the Ashworth case shows that it is likely that an English court would be willing" to make an disclosure order against an innocent Internet access provider); European Observatory on Counterfeiting and Piracy, "Injunctions in Intellectual Property Right" 17, http://ec.europa.eu/internal_market/iprenforcement/docs/injunctions_en .pdf (uses the term "innocent intermediaries" in its questionnaire).

[28] *Upmann v. Elkan* [1871] 7 Ch App 130.

[29] Viscount Dilhorne in *Norwich Pharmacal Co. & Others v. Customs and Excise Commissioners* [1974] AC 133 [75] says: "In Orr v. Diaper Diapers were involved, so were Elkans in Upmann v. Elkan, L.R. 12 Eq. 140, so was the East India Company in Moodalay v. Morton, 1 Bro.C.C. 469 and it matters not that the involvement or participation was *innocent* and in ignorance of the wrongdoing."

[30] *Norwich Pharmacal Co. & Others v. Customs and Excise Commissioners* [1974] AC 133 [10].

[31] *JSC BTA Bank v. Ablyazov & 16 Ors* [2014] EWHC 2019 [72], [75] ("where the third party has become mixed up in the wrongdoing of the defendant, however innocently, he is under a duty to assist the claimant" and "the innocent third party"); *Ashworth Hospital Authority v. MGN Ltd* [2002] HRLR 41 House of Lords [36] ("innocent third parties"); *British Steel Corporation v. Granada Television Ltd* [1981] A.C. 1096 House of Lords 1183 ("These passages show that the House was unanimous in thinking that an action for discovery would lie against an innocent person involved in the tortious acts of another and that an order could properly be made requiring him to name the wrongdoers"); *Interbrew SA v. Financial Times Ltd* 2002 WL 237064 Court of Appeal [12] ("a person who, albeit innocently, facilitates

An injunction is usually understood as an order requiring the person to whom it is directed to perform a particular act or to refrain from carrying out a particular act. This conventional definition of injunction addresses a person who acts against the law – an infringer – and should be stopped from doing so. Such a person acts in a way that the rights of other people prohibit. Seeking an injunction is thus nothing but the request of a rightholder to an authority (court) for the individual compliance of a particular person with the abstract letter of the law. Injunctions against intermediaries, based on Article 8(3) of the InfoSoc Directive and Article 11(III) of the Enforcement Directive, however, do not target such persons. They address by-standers who (also) comply with the law. The basis for this kind of injunction is thus not an act of disrespect toward the rights of others, but the mere existence of circumstances giving hope to rightholders, that if they are assisted by such a person, they will be better off. Put differently, such injunctions against innocent third parties want to achieve better enforcement by seeking a help of intermediaries who can do more, but do not have to, as they did all the law required from them in order to avoid liability in tort. The ensuing responsibility to assist is what I call accountability without liability, which is also referred to as "injunctive liability" or "intermediary liability" stricto sensu.[32]

Because the term is repeatedly used in this work, I wish also to outline my own working definition of what is meant by such an entity here, in this book, focusing on its three elements: (1) an injunction, (2) innocence, and (3) a third party.

"An injunction" is understood as a court order by which an individual is required to perform, or is restrained from performing a particular act (for instance provide information, implement technical features, refrain from providing service to some-body). The term "injunction" in this work therefore refers to a separate cause of action in the *private law*, regardless of whether it is understood as material law, or as a procedural entitlement.[33]

---

the tortious act of another must co-operate in righting the wrong by disclosing the wrongdoer's identity to the wronged party, and can be made by the court to do so if no other expedient is available. The basis of the newly asserted jurisdiction being the old equitable bill of discovery, the power does not run against a mere witness; but it runs in respect of equitable as well as common law wrongs"); Irish case *EMI Records & Ors v. Eircom Ltd* [2010] IEHC 108 [35] ("Injunctions are granted by the court where it 'just and convenient.' That is the basis for all equitable relief formalised by the Supreme Court of Judicature (Ireland) Act 1875. I interpret the Copyright and Related Rights Act 2000 as extending to the making of an injunction against an innocent third party in order to block"); *Equustek Solutions Inc. v. Jack* [2014] BCSC 1063 [156] ("Google is an innocent by-stander but it is unwittingly facilitating the defendants' ongoing breaches of this Court's orders"); In the United States and Canada, these orders also take form of ancillary orders known as "innocent non-party injunctions" (*Equustek Solutions Inc. v. Google Inc.* [2015] BCCA 265); Cartier International AG & Ors v. British Sky Broadcasting Ltd & Ors [2016] EWCA Civ 658 [166] ("innocent third parties").

[32] Martin Husovec, "Is There Any Union Wide Secondary Liability?" (*Huťko's Technology Law Blog*, 2012), www.husovec.eu/2012/11/is-there-any-union-wide-secondary.html (speaking of intermediary liability); Jaani Riordan, *The Liability of Internet Intermediaries* (Oxford, 2016) (speaking of injunctive liability).

[33] For comparative work on nature of remedies – see Franz Hofmann, *Der Unterlassungsanspruch als Rechtsbehelf* (Mohr Siebeck 2017).

The "innocence"[34] is judged from the perspective of the tort law system of a particular country. If a party's conduct falls outside of the category of wrongdoer, then he is innocent. It might well be that he still infringes a right. What is crucial, however, is that such a person is not tortiously responsible for the infringement. Everybody who is not liable in such a way is therefore innocent. It is the opposite of tortfeasance. Hence, if a blogger, despite all his efforts diligently publishes a copyright-infringing content in a country with negligence based liability for damages, he will be innocent. However, such a journalist is still *not* subject of this book which looks into the obligations imposed on innocent *third parties*.

A "third party" is broadly understood in this work as anybody else than a person who himself acts against the scope of a right. I also refer to this person as a "nonactor." The blogger may be innocent, but is not a third party (nonactor) because he himself acted against the scope of a right (published the content). A third party has to be a by-stander, somebody who is not directly acting in a way that the rights of others prohibit (a direct infringer). As a matter of tort law, third parties are also regulated by a branch of tort liability known as "secondary"[35] or accessory liability. The requirement of their *innocence*, however, demands that the third parties are *not* even secondarily liable under tort law.

In summary, the term "injunction against innocent third party" means (1) a separate private cause of action by which an individual is required to perform, or is restrained from performing a particular act, (2) against a person who did not commit a tort, thus bears no compensatory burden, and (3) did not act against the scope of the right. As an alternative, one can talk about injunctions against "noninfringers," provided that the term "infringer" includes both primary, as well as secondary, infringers.[36]

---

[34] An another frequently used understanding of innocence is one limited to situations of nonfault conduct, regardless of the resulting liability for damages. For instance an "innocent infringer" is seen as someone who did not act in fault, but infringed copyright and is held liable for such acts – see Dane S. Ciolino and Erin A. Donelon, "Questioning Strict Liability in Copyright (2001–2002)" 54 Rutgers Law Review 351.

[35] The term is used here because of its wide usage not only among scholars, but also in the case-law of the CJEU – see Case C-324/09 *L'Oréal and Others* [2010] ECLI:EU:C:2010:757, Opinion of AG Jääskinen, para. 55.

[36] See Michel M Walter and Dominik Goebel, "Enforcement Directive" in Michel Walter and Silke von Lewinski (eds.), *European Copyright Law: A Commentary* (OUP 2010) Art. 8 (as for information claims, they include both direct and secondary infringers in the scope of the term); Martin Husovec and Miquel Peguera, "Much Ado about Little – Privately Litigated Disconnecting Injunctions" [2015] IIC 10, 13 (discussing the issue of primary and secondary infringers). This term could be misleading, especially in the German setting, because there does not seem to be an agreement about whether an interferer/disturber who is not liable for damages should be understood also as a noninfringer. This debate has legal relevance in the context of a right to information, where the law makes a distinction between a person who wrongfully infringed a right (e.g. § 101(1) UrhG) and other persons, such as providers whose services were used by a third party to infringe (e.g. § 101(2) UrhG); see Thomas Dreier and Gernot Schulze, *Urheberrechtsgesetz: UrhG* (4th ed., C. H. Beck 2013) § 101, para. 4ff.; In favor of the understanding as a "noninfringer" e.g. Annette Kur, "Rough Start Happy Landing" [2004] IIC 821, 826 (noting that "already at present, national laws may allow in certain instances to direct claims for

Surprisingly, it was not the Internet that made the pure tort law rules of negligence and strict liability an imperfect explanation of how we enforce rights. As will be shown, both civil law and common law already had earlier developed systems where even innocent parties that "got mixed up" with the third-party wrongdoing needed to assist the rightholders. The occurrence of "accountable but not liable" actors is thus by no means consequences of the digital age. Its exponential rise in the recent years, however, can well be.

Although this work makes a distinction between *liability* and much broader *accountability*, this is a somewhat rhetorical exercise. It is only meant to suggest that imposing obligations upon those who did nothing wrong should be broadly distinguished from dealing with those who "legally misbehaved." I openly admit that both common law and civil law would describe such obligations as a form of liability.[37] After all, by no means all the noncontractual obligations enforceable by law have wrongful conduct as their prerequisite; unjust enrichment would be a typical example.

The scholarship might further try to explain these injunctions as some atypical form of secondary liability – a tort liability without damages and wrongfulness. From the recently published important works, for instance, Angelopoulos, argues that injunctions against intermediaries should best be viewed "not as existing outside of the ambit of all liability, but simply as (occasionally) extending it beyond personal misconduct."[38] Although I understand the reasons, I don't think such conceptualization advances our understanding of the issue. Collapsing injunctions against innocent intermediaries and situation of infringers in one conceals their true nature and design. It blurs the notion of what is wrongful to do and prevents us from seeing that, for better or worse, we witness emergence of a new separate regulatory tool.

To be sure, injunctions against innocent third parties are a form of liability – Angelopoulos is right in that regard. But that, by itself, doesn't say anything about them, similarly as it says nothing about unjust enrichment claims. These injunctions stand nearby tort law and have important interactions with it. They are even unthinkable without someone's wrongdoing which needs to be remedied. However,

---

injunction etc. against non-infringers, e.g. in German law on the basis of the so-called 'Störerhaftung,' Sec. 1004 of the Civil Code (only applying under narrow conditions)").

[37] *Norwich Pharmacal Co. & Others v. Customs and Excise Commissioners* [1974] AC 133 [4] (Lord Reid noting that "the question therefore now is whether the respondents are in law *liable* to make discovery of the names of the wrongdoers who imported the patented substance"). In German law, *Störerhaftung* literally translates as the *liability* of a disturber. Similarly even an obligation to surrender information about users would be labeled as "liability" – see Gerald Spindler and Joachim Dorschel, "Auskunftsansprüche gegen Internet-Service-Provider" [2005] Computer und Recht 341, 343 ("haftet nunmehr auch jeder Dritte auf Auskunft").

[38] Christina Angelopoulos, *European Intermediary Liability in Copyright: A Tort-Based Analysis* (Kluwer Law International 2017) 22.

neither historically, nor as a matter of policy, are they the same.[39] They even aren't just another regular injunctions. The label of "injunctions" can be misleading. As I will explain in the upcoming pages, unlike tort law or regular injunctions, they seek different goals and use different means. But before I get there, let's have a look at the economics to understand the enforcement dynamics.

[39] Riordan seems to come to same conclusion for the UK part – see Jaani Riordan, *The Liability of Internet Intermediaries* (Oxford, 2016) 76 ("Assistance without more is not tortious, but it is often sufficient for disclosure. Disclosure is in reality a no-fault response to conduct causing harm, even if that conduct otherwise creates no liability") 71 (noting that although equitable jurisdiction "bears some similarities to the various species of secondary liability examined elsewhere in this work – because it derives from an independently caused primary wrong – but it is conceptualy and historically distinct").

2

Enforcement Economics

What *is* the law and what *ought* to be the law are two separate questions. The legal methodology of analyzing case-law, statues, and literature is a method of understanding what *is* the law, be it that of Germany, England, or the EU. However, in order to formulate what *ought* to be the law, the law has to often rely on other disciplines, such as economics, sociology, and other social sciences. In this part, I explore what simple economic analysis could tell us about the injunctions against intermediaries. There is a reason why this normative part, exploring what *ought* to be the law, *precedes* the discussion of what *is* the law in the later descriptive parts of the book. The lawyers tend to hide their normative judgments into the *is*-analysis. By "outposting" normative suggestions, I try to be more transparent in the legal analysis and with respect to my conclusions. Because this part could easily fill up a book by itself, I have decided to only condense some basic arguments here.[1]

2.1 PROXIMATE AND REMOTE SERVICES

The services of online intermediaries today could be conceptually divided into two groups, depending on how closely they predetermine the infringing activity of users. The first group of services, let's call them (1) *proximate* services, are on the top of the application-level regulation. The second group of services, (2) *remote* services, is on the bottom of the application-level regulation.

Proximate services are applications such as YouTube, eBay, Dropbox, Facebook, cyberlockers, advertisement providers, search engines, and Web forums, among others. These services are often involved in *intermediating content* – whether it is actual files, Web streams, hyperlinks, or other references such as search results or

---

[1] For more elaborate discussion, see Martin Husovec, "Accountable, Not Liable: Injunctions Against Intermediaries" (2016, TILEC Discussion Paper No. 2016-012).

magnet links. Remote services, on the other hand, are services such as domain name registration systems, online payment systems, and Internet access. These services are involved in *intermediating architecture* for access to the content.

Conventionally, liability of most of the *proximate services* in intellectual property is triggered by an appropriate notice sent to a provider (notice-based liability). Of course, many countries also outline other reasons when liability might be triggered even prior to such a notice, such as constructive knowledge and evidence of intent. Liability of most of the *remote services*, on the other hand, isn't often triggered even after a notice is received. Usually an act of more close cooperation is required, such as intentional assistance or inducement. Some countries even exclude liability of such services altogether.

Most of the legislative regimes of intermediary liability today, such as the American DMCA, European E-Commerce Directive and Chinese Tort Law,[2] incorporate some form[3] of *statutory negligence standard*, in L&E literature also called negligence *per se*.[4] *Proximate services* such as the hosting of third-party information, the provision of information location tools or similar services[5] are often subject to liability only upon obtaining a knowledge either from notice, and/or other sources. Under such a system, responsibilities are placed on the shoulders of both rightholders and intermediaries. The former should assist by identifying the infringing content and the latter by examining requests and taking the content down if necessary. This two-stage process can be well-explained by the negligence rule of so-called joint-care scenarios.[6]

---

[2] 17 U.S. Code § 512; Article 12-15 of the E-Commerce Directive; Article 36 of the Chinese Tort Law; The United States include safe harbors regularly into BTAs: see the overview compiled by Daniel Seng, "The State of the Discordant Union: An Empirical Analysis of the State of DMCA Takedown Notices" (2014) 18 Virginia Journal of Law and Technology 369, 373; similarly the EU included safe harbors into its BTAs. For China, see Jie Wang, *Regulating Hosting ISPs' Responsibilities for Copyright Infringement The Freedom to Operate in the US, EU and China* (PhD Thesis 2016).

[3] William M. Landes and Douglas Lichtman, "Indirect Liability for Copyright Infringement: An Economic Perspective" (2003) 16 Harvard Journal of Law and Technology 395, 405 (noting that DMCA safe harbors negligence standard); Mark A. Lemley, "Rationalizing Internet Safe Harbors" (2007) 6 Journal of Telecommunications and High Technology Law 101, 118 (describing European approach as negligence based); Jonina S. Larusdottir, "Liability of Intermediaries for Copyright Infringement" (Stockholm Institute for Scandianvian Law paper 2010) 476ff. (safe harbors and fault based liability); Ronald J. Mann and Seth R. Belzley, "The Promise of Internet Intermediary Liability" (2005) 47 William & Mary Law Review 239, 250 ("the existing liability regimes, which are largely fault-based").

[4] Robert Cooter and Ariel Porat, *Getting Incentives Right: Improving Torts, Contracts and Restitution* (Princeton University Press 2014) 6.

[5] BGH *Autocomplete* (2013) VI ZR 269/12 (Google suggestion tool is liable only upon notice); Paula Vargas, "Argentine Supreme Court Decides Landmark Intermediary Liability Case" (*Stanford CIS Blog*, 5 November 2014), https://cyberlaw.stanford.edu/blog/2014/11/argentine-supreme-court-decides-landmark-intermediary-liability-case.

[6] See more: Martin Husovec, "Accountable, Not Liable: Injunctions Against Intermediaries" (2016) TILEC Discussion Paper No. 2016-012, 25.

There are recent attempts to move from *notice and takedown system* to a *notice–and–stay down system*.[7] Notice and stay down essentially collapses a two-stage, two-person process into a single responsibility of an intermediary. It requires him to prevent reappearance of the same content. It is beyond the ambition of this work to comment on social desirability of this rule. I have argued elsewhere that standardized notice and takedown system is superior to a notice–and–stay down rule in number of ways.[8] In the context of this work, this is also matters. Rightholders have previously attempted to reverse notice and takedown by imposing stay down onto selected platforms on the bases of Article 8(3) InfoSoc and Article 11(III) of the Enforcement Directive. In Germany, they even succeeded.[9]

I think it is a bad approach to redesign notice and takedown by means of other instruments, regardless of the solution sought. Injunctions against proximate providers, that is providers who are already regulated by tortious liability upon notice, should not be re-regulated by injunctions. If tortious framework is flawed, e.g., because notice and takedown is not scalable enough, then changes should be implemented within its design, not by outside measures such as injunctions.[10] Providing "policy plug-ins" by means of injunctions isn't a good way forward.

Moreover, a close reading of Union law doesn't support imposition of stay-down (see Chapters 7 and 8). It is limited to a possibility to seek an injunction to avoid "new infringements of the same nature by the same" infringer. At most, therefore, such injunctions can be read as instituting the repeat-infringer policies. Countries like Germany, which go beyond this rule, are in my view in violation of the Union law.[11]

Apart from the stay-down attempts, the proximate providers are not the primary targets of these injunctions. In Europe,[12] the United States,[13] and many other countries, we recognize existence of intermediaries that are cleared of any copyright, trademark, or other similar liability *even after* they receive a notice about a particular infringing website, domain name, or financial transaction.[14] These *remote providers*

---

[7] See Section 4.4.

[8] See more: Martin Husovec, "Accountable, Not Liable: Injunctions Against Intermediaries" (2016) TILEC Discussion Paper No. 2016-012, 43.

[9] See Section 9.4.

[10] See more: Martin Husovec, "Accountable, Not Liable: Injunctions Against Intermediaries" (2016) TILEC Discussion Paper No. 2016-012, 15 et seq.

[11] See Section 8.3.   [12] Article 12 of E-Commerce Directive.

[13] See for domain name authorities in the trade mark context: 15 U.S.C. § 1114(2) (Lanham Act); Internet access providers in the copyright context: 17 U.S. Code § 512(a) (Digital Millennium Copyright Act); and payment intermediaries in the gambling context: 31 U.S.C. § 5365(c) – see more: Mark MacCarthy, "What Payment Intermediaries Are Doing about Online Liability and Why It Matters" (2010) 25 Berkeley Technology Law Journal 1037, 1041.

[14] The credit card companies are not liable for infringements committed by their customers (*Perfect 10, Inc. v. Visa Int'l Serv. Ass'n*, 494 F.3d 788, 798 (9th Cir. 2007)); domain name registries for infringing domain names (*Lockheed Martin Corp. v. Network Solutions, Inc.* 141 F. Supp. 2d 648 (N.D. Tex. 2001)); Internet access providers for copyright infringements of its users (17 U.S. Code § 512(a)); See

include access providers, domain name authorities, and payment intermediaries.[15] In some jurisdictions, the condition is that they did not collaborate with the infringer,[16] or that they terminate access for repeat infringers.[17] However, in general, they don't have to act upon a received notice.

Unlike services such as search engines or video platforms, remote intermediaries provide a more general-purpose technical infrastructure. Their services are more *distant* from the user who is committing the infringements. In the prenotice period, like other intermediaries, their burden of identifying content, determining its status, and subsequently intervening would generally be prohibitively high. This, of course, changes after receiving the notice, for instance about an infringing website. Internet service providers who received a notice might potentially be in a position to cheaply block access to a website and thus reduce some, but certainly not all or even most, of the harm the website causes to the rightholder. These intermediaries often *can* influence the expected loss of rightholders on their platforms using a fraud policy, bandwidth sanctions, or a quick dispute resolution system. Despite this, the law often does not require such an action in tort law. Why?

Consider following example. A car driver, A, crashes into traffic lights at high speed on a very busy crossroads. This triggers a massive traffic jam. A second car driver, B, is caught in this traffic jam and decides to cut his waiting time by driving over a nearby grass verge in order to turn. Should driver A be liable for the lost time/opportunity of all the drivers waiting in the tailback? And if so, should he be also liable for damage on the grass verge? It is clear that without his action, there would be no traffic jam and thus also no need for driver B and others to drive over the grass verge (retrospective causality). It is also clear that driver A was negligent in

---

also Annemarie Bridy, "Graduated Response and the Turn to Private Ordering in Online Copyright Enforcement" (2010) 89 Oregon Law Review 81, 89 (noting that notice does not impose take down obligations).

[15] Other examples can be providers of Internet browsers, computer hardware, operating systems, routers, etc.

[16] The Internet access providers are generally not liable for copyright, trademark or other kinds of third-party infringements (Article 12 of the E-Commerce Directive); liability of payment intermediaries is left to the law of the Member States, but there are no known cases of such liability being imposed; liability of domain name authorities is also outside of Union law as domain name authorities do not qualify for any of the safe harbors. The Member States generally refrain from imposing liability in tort on these intermediaries.

[17] In the US, mere conduit intermediaries are subject to 17 U.S. Code § 512(i) obligations for repeat infringers (see *Perfect 10, Inc. v. CCBill LLC*, 481 F.3d 751, 758 (9th Cir. 2007) (stating that "[t]o be eligible for any of the four safe harbors at §§ 512(a)–(d), a service provider must first meet the threshold conditions set out in § 512(i)"); this will be explicitly tested in the pending case of *BMG Rights Management and Round Hill Music v. Cox Communications*. The jury of the first instance court found Cox was liable for contributory infringement (*BMG Rights Management (US)LLC et al v. Cox Enterprises, Inc. et al.*, No. 1:2014cv01611 – Document 703 (E.D. Va. 2015). For more discussion of obligations of mere conduits under US law – see Annemarie Bridy, "Graduated Response and the Turn to Private Ordering in Online Copyright Enforcement" (2010) 89 Oregon Law Review 81, 89–90.

causing his accident. But should the risk of lost time/opportunity of all the drivers, and their subsequent actions be attributed to a driver A? Though doctrinal reasons might differ, many jurisdictions would probably answer "no" to both claims for compensation (loss of opportunity in the tailback and damage to the grass verge).[18]

Schäfer points out that imposing liability would be *inefficient* because advantages to individuals driving over the grass verge cannot be assessed by the court.[19] An alternative explanation could be that denying compensation in both cases is necessary, as otherwise the average cost of accidents would sky-rocket. This could make driving cars very expensive and thus greatly reduce the uncompensated public benefits which society obtains by the widespread use of cars, such as the improved distribution of goods or freedom of movement of individuals.[20] If viewed from the macro-perspective, the time loss of drivers is always relative to the state of technological development. Their time loss would have been substantially higher in a parallel world where the technology did not exist or was not used as widely. In other words, the individual opportunity cost to drivers arising from traffic jams is always substantially lower that it would have been had they not used automobiles in the first place. The cost of technology cannot be compared to its ideal without flaws, but to a world without such technology or without its current diffusion. Limiting the liability radar, for instance by causality, can thus serve as a moderator of excessive emphasis on static effects and a promoter of dynamic effects. Where positive externalities are so highly disproportionate that accepting *any* duty of care can heavily endanger them, the law could relocate such activity beyond the line of legal causality and thus immunize it from any care.

Or consider a different story. According to current epidemiological research,[21] the operation of trains was crucial in the dissemination of the HIV-1 virus around the African continent. Had there been no trains, disease would probably not have spread so exponentially. But if trains are such an important conductor, should their operators be responsible for the health risks imposed by their passengers on others? Making them liable for enabling such infections would pose similar risks to public transport as our traffic jam example. Yet it shows more clearly that the inherent risk of technological progress can be unavoidable, and must be fought by different means than liability in tort.

The main policy reasons behind excluding remote providers from the list of potential tortfeasors is thus a societal need for stable and not excessively expensive

---

[18] For the German law – see Hans-Bernd Schäfer and others, *The Economic Analysis of Civil Law* (Edward Elgar 2004) 202 (as to second); the first type of damage would be rejected as pure economic loss.

[19] Hans-Bernd Schäfer and others, *The Economic Analysis of Civil Law* (Edward Elgar 2004) 202.

[20] Arthur Cecil Pigou, *The Economics of Welfare* (first published 1920, Macmillan 1932) 183; Ronald Coase, "The Problem of Social Cost" (1960) 3 Journal of Law and Economics 1, 28, 32–33.

[21] Nuno R. Faria and others, "The Early Spread and Epidemic Ignition of HIV-1 in Human Populations" (2014) 346 Science 56–61.

infrastructure.[22] One can also argue that human rights dimension of actions taken by these actors is much more intensive. Excluding remote services from potential liability, however, does *not* mean that other, non–tort law means of constraining undesired activities cannot be developed. It just means that exposing the infrastructure to the same tortious incentives as hosting and similar platforms could lead to lot of instability and even bigger abuse.

This means that preventive systems could and should be still used, but tort law or liability in general is just the *wrong tool*. The domain name system is a perfect example of this. In the early 1990s when the Internet became popular as a tool of commerce, fraudulent and blocking registrations of domain names (so-called cybersquatting) became omnipresent, since the registration was cheap and based on a first-come-first-served principle. As a response, soft-law systems of alternative dispute resolution (ADR) such as the UDRP were gradually developed. This system of adjudication was not binding and its decisions could still be challenged before the courts. But it nonetheless proved to be very influential. It offered the rightholders a limited, but very quick and cheap, remedy against cybersquatting.

The system was not pushed by tort law.[23] On the contrary, imposing notice-based liability on domain name registrars would have had grave consequences for the Internet commerce. And it would have hardly solved the situation. ADR, which started as a government-pressured voluntary effort by domain name authorities, and was later even implemented as a statutory regime in some parts of the world, such as in the top level domain name of the EU,[24] proved to be much more successful. Today's injunctions against intermediaries in the EU could prescribe such UDRP.

2.2 INJUNCTIONS AGAINST (MOSTLY) REMOTE SERVICES

Any self-interested rightholder naturally wants to enforce his rights *as much as possible* if he or she does not bear the real costs of such litigious behavior.[25] But this is at odds with societal interest in enforcing their rights only *as much as necessary* to provide for sufficient incentives. Since courts face information asymmetry and many societal uses and their benefits are hard to predict or grasp, they tend to support

[22] In the German case of *ambiente.de* the German Federal Supreme Court rejected the imposition of obligations on a domain name authority, citing the public interest in the cheap DNS infrastructure (BGH *ambiente.de* (2001) I ZR 251/99).

[23] The System is a consequence of governmental pressure – see Jessica Litman, "DNS Wars: Trademarks and the Internet Domain Name System" (2000) 4 J. Small & Emerging Bus. L. 149, 160 ("One of the terms of the handoff-one of the things the government has told ICANN that it must do-is a commitment to a dispute resolution process that meets trademark owners' perceived needs").

[24] Regulation (EC) No 733/2002 of the European Parliament and of the Council of 22 April 2002 on the implementation of the .eu Top Level Domain [2002] OJ L 113.

[25] Mark MacCarthy, "What Payment Intermediaries Are Doing about Online Liability and Why It Matters" (2010) 25 Berkeley Technology Law Journal 1037, 1055.

the claims presented by rightholders. Often, they simply assume that because the rightholders apply for such measures, they most likely also need them.[26] The courts then see their role not in accepting and rejecting certain practices, but rather as a moderator of abuse.

This perspective is, however, misleading. It must be emphasized that resolving the question of whether or not to grant assistance at all is not a binary choice of doing something or doing nothing. It is a choice between rightholders that are entitled to such assistance, and rightholders that need to negotiate it through voluntary agreements. In other words, it is a question of *allocating the entitlement* to either rightholders or intermediaries.

Under Coase theorem[27] such allocation is irrelevant as long as barriers to negotiations are zero, because whichever party values it more would bypass the legal rule and simply purchase it from the other. However, barriers in the form of transaction costs are rarely zero. And sometimes such costs are even asymmetrically distributed among the parties. As explained earlier, if an entitlement to enforcement assistance is allocated to rightholders (right to assistance), intermediaries need to contract with all of them in order to secure the possibility of running a service without such enforcement measures. So, for instance, Internet access provider would need to contract with all the rightholders whose rights might be infringed upon by users of its service, to be able to opt-out of website blocking measures. Such negotiations are clearly impossible, given the number of rightholders. On the other hand, if an entitlement is allocated to intermediaries (voluntary measures), rightholders would need to contract into such enforcement measures with the intermediaries. Unlike intermediaries, however, they would not necessarily need to contract with all of them, since they can target only those intermediaries who they consider critical. Moreover, remote intermediaries such as domain name authorities, Internet access providers, and payment intermediaries tend to exist in smaller numbers. So, for instance, a handful of rightholders can already negotiate the website blocking of a particular website or a new antifraud policy with most of the major ISPs or payment intermediaries.

---

[26] One very interesting case study is provided in the example of keyword advertising. In the 2000s, many rightholders decided to chase those competitors who were bidding on their branded keywords. They assumed that it was hurting their brand, otherwise they would have not pursued these litigations. Recent empirical studies, however, suggests that such branded keyword advertising might do little if any harm – see Thomas Blake and others, "Consumer Heterogeneity and Paid Search Effectiveness: A Large Scale Field Experiment" [2014] Working paper, http://faculty.haas.berkeley.edu/stadelis/Tadelis .pdf (noting "As an extreme case, we show that brand-keyword ads have no measurable short-term benefits"); Stefan Bechtold and Catherine Tucker, "Trademarks, Triggers, and Online Search" (2014) 11(4) Journal of Empirical Legal Studies 718–750 ("For trademark owners, this means that a keyword advertising policy that does not allow third-party use of trademarked keywords is not necessarily better, as trademark owners may lose traffic from non-navigational searchers and the negative effects they suffer from navigational searchers may be limited").

[27] Ronald Coase, "The Problem of Social Cost" (1960) 3 Journal of Law and Economics 1.

This could, however, be more difficult if remote service providers also become plentiful, as is the case with WiFi operators. Contracting into password protection or other enforcement measures might either require negotiating with all such operators, or negotiation with the producers of routers or standard-setting bodies. If rightholders have an entitlement, shopping malls or airports that want to provide open WiFi would need to seek the consent of all the rightholders to opt-out. If WiFi operators receive an entitlement, then rightholders need to opt-in into password locking by negotiating with each operator.

If transactions costs impede negotiations, the question is who should initially receive an entitlement? Coase does not provide an answer.[28] The neoclassical solution advocated by Posner is to assign it to the party which we expect to have the higher valuation.[29] The idea is that fewer people will need to trade on the market, and thus fewer transactions will need to occur. Even if we were to accept this view, it is difficult to see who that party might be in our context. Do rightholders value such assistance more than intermediaries do their freedom from such assistance? Or the other way round? Moreover, does their valuation change according to who holds the entitlement?[30] We don't know. And it is difficult to find out, given that such a valuation might differ among various remote services and types of rightholders.[31] Therefore it would be difficult to use higher valuation as a guide to allocation, even if we were to accept this neoclassical guiding rule.

A more holistic approach is offered by Calabresi, who notes that economic efficiency is not the sole reason which induces a society to allocate an entitlement.[32]

---

[28] Steward J. Schwab, "Coase Defends Coase: Why Lawyers Listen and Economists Do Not" (1989) 87 Michigan Law Review 1171, 1195–1196.

[29] According to Schlag, Posner gives Coase's insigh a right-wing normative gloss (Pierre Schlag, "Appreciative Comment on Coase's the Problem of Social Cost: A View from the Left" [1986] Wis. L. Rev. 919, 921) in his work (Richard Posner, *The Economics of Justice* (Harvard University Press 1981) 48ff.).

[30] This is a result of the so-called endowment effect, i.e. the hypothesis that people ascribe more value to things merely because they own them – see Daniel Kahneman and others, "Experimental Tests of the Endowment Effect and the Coase Theorem" (1990) 98 Journal of Political Economy 1325–1348.

[31] If lobbying expenses for SOPA and PIPA, the legislation promoting some of such enforcement measures, could be seen as a proxy of such valuation, the higher valuing party would be the rightholders. But such a proxy is problematic from many angles and it does not unveil valuation in a conversed situation (if intermediaries were to lobby for repeal they would likely need to invest more to "move the legislator"). See Jeffrey E. Friedman, "Sponsors of SOPA Act Pulled in 4 Times as Much in Contributions from Hollywood as from Silicon Valley" (*Map Law*, 1 May 2009), http://maplight.org/content/72896 (calculating that "the 32 sponsors of the bill have received almost 4 times as much in campaign contributions from the movie, music, and TV entertainment industries ($1,983,596), which support the bill, as they have received from the software and Internet industries ($524,977), which believe the language goes too far"); it is impossible to calculate precisely "how much of the money spent on lobbying was directly connected to SOPA and PIPA, since the reporting forms don't require that level of detail" (Viveca Novak, "SOPA and PIPA Spur Lobbying Spike" (*Open Secrets*, 26 January 2012), www.opensecrets.org/news/2012/01/sopa-and-pipa-create-lobbying-spike/).

[32] Guido Calabresi and Douglas A. Melamed, "Property Rules, Liability Rules, and Inalienability: One View of the Cathedral" (1972) 85 Harvard Law Review 1089, 1097; Guido Calabresi, *The Costs of Accidents* (Yale University Press 1970) 20.

And that (static) efficiency analysis is not conclusive, since there might be other distributional goals the society could follow, such as dynamic efficiency or considerations of justice.[33] Calabresi himself offers several approaches for achieving efficient allocation, namely, (1) allocating according to the overall costs and benefits of granting or withholding certain entitlements; if this is not possible, due to uncertainty; (2) allocating so that we impose costs on the party that can best carry out such analysis; and lastly, if this is still not possible due to uncertainty, (3) allocating so that we impose costs on the party that can, with lower transaction costs, act to correct an error in entitlements by bargaining.[34] They all represent only reformulations of the general cost-benefit analysis.

These guidelines are, in fact, very intuitive. Our primary concern is comparing costs and benefits. If uncertainty arises about either of the two, we try to "outsource" such a decision to the party that is best positioned to do it for us. And if we cannot find this person or it would conflict with some other policy considerations, we try to allocate it to the party that can most easily correct our errors. Since the primary (economic) consideration of "crafting [legal rules] ought to be minimization of transactions costs,"[35] if we cannot determine *when* the entitlements are inefficiently allocated,[36] we can at least make it easier to bypass our allocation.[37] Calabresi

---

[33] Guido Calabresi and Douglas A. Melamed, "Property Rules, Liability Rules, and Inalienability: One View of the Cathedral" (1972) 85 Harvard Law Review 1089, 1098; this approach makes it easier to incorporate the thoughts of philosophers of law such as Rawls (John Rawls, *A Theory of Justice* (Harvard University Press 1971) or Dworkin (Ronald Dworkin, "What Is Equality? Part 2: Equality of Resources" (1981) 10 Phil. & Pub. Aff. 283).

[34] Guido Calabresi and Douglas A. Melamed, "Property Rules, Liability Rules, and Inalienability: One View of the Cathedral" (1972) 85 Harvard Law Review 1089, 1097; Guido Calabresi, *The Costs of Accidents* (Yale University Press 1970) 20.

[35] Niva Elkin-Koren and Eli Salzberger, *The Law and Economics of Intellectual Property in the Digital Age: The Limits of Analysis* (Routledge 2013) 74.

[36] Guido Calabresi and Douglas A. Melamed, "Property Rules, Liability Rules, and Inalienability: One View of the Cathedral" (1972) 85 Harvard Law Review 1089, 1097, 1093; Guido Calabresi, *The Costs of Accidents* (Yale University Press 1970) 24–33, 150–151 ("if the initial loss bearer chosen is not in fact the cheapest cost avoider, we have minimized the obstacle transaction costs impose on the market's finding and influencing the behavior of the cheapest cost avoider"); this costs includes finding who to transact with (p. 151).

[37] Ronald Coase, "The Problem of Social Cost" (1960) 3 Journal of Law and Economics 1, 11 ("even when it is possible to change the legal delimitation of rights through market transactions, it is obviously desirable to reduce the need for such transactions and thus reduce the employment of resources in carrying them out"); Guido Calabresi and Douglas A. Melamed, "Property Rules, Liability Rules, and Inalienability: One View of the Cathedral" (1972) 85 Harvard Law Review 1089, 1096–1098 (advocate for "economic efficiency standing alone would dictate that set of entitlements which favors knowledgeable choices between social benefits and the social costs of obtaining them, and between social costs and the social costs of avoiding them" as a primary consideration. In this respect, this is a natural cost-benefit analysis of granting or withholding entitlements. They suggest other two criteria before they proceed to the best-briber criterion, but those are not easily implementable in our context, since the question of who is the cheapest cost avoider cannot be resolved by pointing to one single party – see more in: Martin Husovec, "Accountable, Not Liable: Injunctions Against Intermediaries" (2016) TILEC Discussion Paper No. 2016-012).

calls the party who can act more cheaply to correct the initial allocation the "best briber."[38]

In our context, since we are uncertain about the benefits of coerced assistance to the rightholders and thus whether it is worth its costs to society, we can follow Calabresi's suggestion to allocate the costs of such assistance to the party best located to make such a cost-benefit analysis.[39] This would mean granting the assistance to rightholders, but coupling it with full imposition of its costs. Alternatively, since the costs of correcting a wrong allocation are asymmetrically higher for intermediaries than for rightholders, we could withhold the assistance from rightholders, and try to make it as easy as possible for rightholders to correct it. Calabresi's suggestion thus isn't conclusive and can support both systems – with and without injunctions.

As a consequence, there seem to be two possible ways of approaching the initial question. First, we could allocate an entitlement to rightholders, but design incentives so that they have to make a full cost evaluation *before* they apply for new measures. This way, we ensure that the outcome of the proposed measures enriches rightholders *more* than it costs others at a particular point in time (Kaldor-Hicks improvement).[40] This can be achieved, for instance, by making the entitlement of one of the parties conditional upon payments of its observable direct costs. Potential dynamic inefficiencies, however, still stay hidden. The second option is to allocate legal entitlements to those who have lower transaction costs when reaching agreements on the market. This would speak in favor of allocating the entitlement with intermediaries, since it is generally easier for rightholders to opt-in to increased enforcement measures than to opt-out of the imposed ones for intermediaries.

2.3 SOLUTION A: RIGHT TO ASSISTANCE

Right to assistance could impose the same levels of care as the negligence rule, without exposing intermediaries to the risks of compensation.[41] It allows the courts to come up with specific standards of assistance. However, proper adjudication requires the courts to have enough information about best-technology-standards, their effectiveness, and their overall costs. A general possibility to impose any enforcement measures turns the courts hearing such claims into *standard-setting bodies*. The right

---

[38] Guido Calabresi, *The Costs of Accidents* (Yale University Press 1970) 150.

[39] Guido Calabresi and Douglas A. Melamed, "Property Rules, Liability Rules, and Inalienability: One View of the Cathedral" (1972) 85 Harvard Law Review 1089, 1096.

[40] Mark Lemley and Anthony R. Reese, "Reducing Digital Copyright Infringement Without Restricting Innovation" (2004) 56 Stanford Law Review 1345, 1374; Ronald Coase, "The Problem of Social Cost" (1960) 3 Journal of Law and Economics 1, 28 (noting that "there is a real danger that extensive government intervention in the economic system may lead to the protection of those responsible for harmful effects being carried too far").

[41] Hamdani also recognized this option, but had a legislator in mind as a standard setter (Assaf Hamdani, "Who's Liable for Cyberwrongs" (2002) 87 Cornell L. Rev. 901, 934–935 ("legislator might impose specific monitoring standards instead of damages liability")).

to assistance by means of an injunction could remedy all the individual cases where enforcement is suboptimal. This presumes, first, that the situation of the rightholder would substantially improve with the proposed measure, and second, that the situation for the rest of society, including that of intermediaries and users, will worsen to a lesser extent (the so-called Kaldor-Hicks or potential Pareto improvement).[42] How to screen for those cases?

The problem is that it is unrealistic to hope that courts will ever be in a position to completely see the full costs and benefits of the proposed measures.[43] The parties are generally better positioned than courts to make such estimates since they possess private information about their costs and benefits, which the courts first somehow need to acquire.[44] The courts will thus always be less informed than intermediaries or rightholders.[45] Therefore, if the claims for assistance are permitted, the system must incorporate sufficient incentives for rightholders to carry out the cost-benefit analysis *before* they apply for such measures. This follows from the Calabresi's approach as previously described – allocate costs of instituting an entitlement to those who can best carry out the cost-benefit analysis. This way, rightholders will basically vote with their applications, if and when such an entitlement pays off for society.

Generally, the cost equation is not only about *direct* expenses incurred by the rightholders in requesting and administering the measures (C^1), by the intermediaries in developing and implementing them (C^2), and by the state in moderating and administering them (C^3),[46] but also *indirect* and not so easily observable expenses

---

[42] Martin Husovec, "Injunctions Against Innocent Third Parties: Case of Website Blocking" (2013) 4 JIPITEC 116, 12.

[43] Mark MacCarthy, "What Payment Intermediaries Are Doing about Online Liability and Why It Matters" (2010) 25 Berkeley Technology Law Journal 1037, 1060 ("precision in the estimate of costs and benefits is unlikely in this area"); Even Arnold J in his *Cartier* decision (*Cartier International AG & Ors v. British Sky Broadcasting Ltd & Ors* [2014] EWHC 3354 (Ch)) admitted that he was not aware of full effects at the time of his first website blocking decisions. Only ex post, he is now able to fully evaluate the costs of such measures; Jerry Green, "On the Optimal Structure of Liability Laws" (1976) 7(2) The Bell Journal of Economics 553–574 ("However, courts are usually not disposed to making such fine continuous judgments about care, since in actuality it is a multidimensional and highly complex entity not really expressible in a single number. Courts seem to be much more comfortable with decisions about whether or not an individual has met some predetermined due-care standard").

[44] Louis Kaplow and Steven Shavell, "Property Rules versus Liability Rules: An Economic Analysis" (1996) 109 Harvard Law Review 713–790; Assaf Hamdani, "Who's Liable for Cyberwrongs" (2002) 87 Cornell L. Rev. 901, 914.

[45] Steven Shavell, "Liability and the Incentive to Obtain Information about Risk" (1992) 21(2) The Journal of Legal Studies 259, 270; Jerry Green, "On the Optimal Structure of Liability Laws" (1976) 7(2) The Bell Journal of Economics 553–574 ("However, courts are usually not disposed to making such fine continuous judgments about care, since in actuality it is a multidimensional and highly complex entity not really expressible in a single number. Courts seem to be much more comfortable with decisions about whether or not an individual has met some predetermined due-care standard"). Robert Cooter and others, "Liability Rules, Limited Information, and the Role of Precedent" (1979) 10(1) The Bell Journal of Economics 366–373 ("The situation may be inefficient efficient at a point in time [owing to lack of information], but it tends towards efficiency [over time]").

[46] Richard Posner, *Economic Analysis of Law* (Aspen Publishers 2003) 171 (on administration costs).

incurred by the rest of the society in foregoing certain benefits from legitimate activities that are being blocked (C^4).[47] If you consider WiFi password locking, the overall cost equation includes not only the direct litigation costs of rightholders requesting the measure (C^1), the implementation costs of all the WiFi operators (C^2), and the state's costs of court supervision (C^3), but also the costs of innovation, such as accident avoidance, that can not materialize due to the existence of the measure (C^4). The first three costs ($C^1+C^2+C^3$) are relatively easily observable or roughly estimated at the time of the decision, the last one (C^4) is not. It often becomes apparent only with time.

Costs C^1, C^2, C^3 only take into account a static picture. Society might also lose in the long run, if development of a certain technology and its associated positive benefits (C^4) are foreclosed by solutions that appeared to maximize welfare at the time. Take, as an example, our WiFi case. Password protection of WiFi hot spots might be of little cost to their operators, but can prevent new technological uses from being deployed due to enforcement restraints. If, for instance, widespread use of open WiFi could help to force down the price of mobile Internet access, then any foregone consumer surplus is also a cost of enforcement of password locking. Or, if open WiFi could reduce number of road accidents, thanks to its use as a signaling technology between pedestrians and cars or among cars themselves, the cost of accidents which would have been avoided also constitutes foregone benefits (C^4).

Under this option, the rightholders would need to pay the full implementation costs of proposed enforcement measures (self-funding). The underlying idea is that rightholders, faced with the potential costs of enforcement measures, are encouraged to analyze the measures' effectiveness for their business model will pay off (benefit them). Such a cost would be, however, always incomplete, since rightholders could bear only easily observable direct costs ($C^{1,2,3}$). From this perspective, it is not important if this money would serve as a reimbursement to intermediaries, or as a fee to the state.

However, the problem is that if the costs are not paid to the intermediaries, the social costs of such measures are actually raised, because implementation costs are suddenly duplicated. First they would be paid for by rightholders, and then by the intermediaries who do not get compensated. Even though a lack of reimbursement could be very useful as an incentive for intermediaries to reduce the costs of implementation, the duplication of costs removes a major advantage of the self-funded measures: that any application of the rightholders for assistance is a rationale choice

---

47 These costs do not seem to be captured by the framework of Calabresi. It should be noted that this last category of costs includes both costs at the time of the granting of the measures, as well as costs that became known later. We, however, assume that C^4 costs are not easily observable or even often not present at the time of decision. C^4 thus includes all costs of other persons than rightholders, intermediaries, and the state, regardless whether they are known at the time of decision, or become known only at some later stage.

only when the expected benefit is higher than all its observable direct costs. For these reasons, the compensation should be part of the system, but made subject to the discretion of judges, in order to guard against any inflation of the implementation costs by intermediaries.

Self-interested rightholders would thus *apply* for measures only if the anticipated benefit for their business is higher than the expected sum of costs ($C^{1,2,3}$), that is it is at least a (static) Kaldor-Hicks improvement. If the expected benefit is below the sum of the known costs, e.g., because reducing the number of infringements is insignificant for the business model of a rightholder, he will not apply for such measures. What remains nevertheless hidden from rightholders calculations are other possible societal benefits (C^4) which are blocked by the enforcement practice in the long run.

One of the roles of the judges, namely, to oversee the effectiveness of the proposed measures, would thus be "outsourced" to rightholders. An application for a measure by rightholders before the judge would indicate its effectiveness. The judges would thus examine only the other aspects of such measures, such as compliance with human rights limits and other public policies. Injunctions prescribing assistance would then be issued on the condition that rightholders keep paying the implementation costs ($C^{1,2,3}$). If rightholders stop paying, injunctions dissolve. This would also introduce more flexibility to the system, since various measures can be tried out and abandoned if not successful. This would bring a much needed in-built time limitation to such measures,[48] which is important given that technologies become obsolete very quickly. Moreover, under this system, it is also easier to negotiate away such measures, because intermediaries need to contract only with those rightholders who would really benefit from the measures.

Furthermore, this could also solve another possible abuse of these measures, namely, that such fees would make claims for cooperation more attractive than usual tortious claims. It has already been observed[49] that rightholders also use claims for cooperation (1) to avoid resistance and enforcement against certain parties or (2) because they are cheaper than claims in tort, where they would need to argue about numerous conditions. From the economic standpoint, the tendency to circumvent the parties for whom it would be cheaper to act is particularly problematic (e.g., suing an Internet access provider instead of a domain name holder in a regular domain name dispute).[50] From the human rights perspective, it is a tendency to

---

[48] Mr. Justice Arnold recently imposed a sun-set clause, which has time limitation of two years (*Cartier International AG & Ors v. British Sky Broadcasting Ltd & Ors* [2014] EWHC 3354 (Ch)); Torrentfreak, "The Pirate Bay Must Be Blocked in Sweden, Court of Appeal Rules" (2017), https://torrentfreak.com/the-pirate-bay-must-be-blocked-in-sweden-court-of-appeal-rules-170213/ (reporting that the Swedish Patent and Market Court also required a three year limit to injunctions).

[49] Martin Husovec, "Injunctions Against Innocent Third Parties: Case of Website Blocking" (2013) 4 JIPITEC 116.

[50] The Danish case of Home A/S v. Telenor A/S (Retten på Frederiksberg *Home A/S v. Telenor A/S* (2012)), where the Spanish-owned property site called HomelifeSpain.com was blocked in Denmark

circumvent due process of nondefendants.[51] Unlike negligence, these claims have no cap on the optimal level of care. This could, driven by a desire to save on enforcement, lead to overburdening at the expense of remote services instead of the closer proximate services. Conditional injunctions prevent this as long as the benefit from such circumvention is not higher than the cost that is due to be paid ($C^{1,2,3}$).

Under the prevailing European praxis, rightholders can apply for assistance from intermediaries and usually only need to pay their own costs (C^1) and possibly also the costs of the state (C^3). This means that self-interested rightholders apply anytime the benefit from proposed measures is higher than the cost ($E(\pi) > C^1 + C^3$). However, even from the static perspective, there are other direct costs, namely, those incurred by intermediaries (C^2). If an injunction is granted by the court, there can easily be no improvement in the allocation of existing resources (if $E(\pi) - C^2 < C^1 + C^3$),[52] since an improvement would occur only if rightholders are better off accounting for the static costs in general ($E(\pi) - C^2 > C^1 + C^3$). If rightholders would have to bear the full direct cost of their measures, they would *only* apply when such a situation *is* a Kaldor-Hicks improvement (if $E(\pi) > C^1 + C^2 + C^3$). Or in other words, when benefits of such measures outweigh the (static) costs.

To illustrate this, suppose that the cost of applying for a blocking order (legal services, gathering of evidence, etc.) is a flat sum of 7.000 EUR (C^1), regardless of the number of providers sued and that the state's cost of granting (court fees) and supervising it (subsequent submission of IP addresses) is 5.000 EUR (C^3). The cost of implementation is 10.000 EUR for each of two larger access providers (C^2) and 20.000 EUR for each of three smaller providers (C^2). Under currently prevailing praxis, a rightholder would apply for an injunction if his benefit from blocking is higher than 12.000 EUR ($C^1 + C^3$). For society, however, such blocking imposed on two big access providers and three small ones would be waste of resources unless it yields benefit of at least 92.000 EUR ($C^1 + C^2 + C^3$). Rightholders under current system do *not* have any incentive to apply only when the measures benefit society, i.e., when the benefit is higher than 92.000 EUR.

Now suppose that blocking by each big provider yields a benefit ($E(\pi)$) of 30.000 EUR, and blocking by each small one 10.000 EUR. If the rightholder were to carry the full costs of such blocks, they would apply for an injunction against both bigger providers, since a benefit of 60.000 EUR is higher than cost of 32.000 EUR

after the Danish site home.dk, as the owner of the word mark "home" applied and received the remedy of the website being blocked for Denmark – see more at Glyn Moody, "Danish Court Orders Spanish Site Blocked Because It Uses Trademarked English Word 'Home' as Part of Its Name" (*Techdirt* 2012), www.techdirt.com/articles/20121228/09275521510/danish-court-orders-spanish-site-blocked-because-it-uses-trademarked-english-word-home-as-part-its-name.shtml.

[51] Martin Husovec and Miquel Peguera, "Much Ado about Little – Privately Litigated Disconnecting Injunctions" [2015] IIC 10.

[52] This cannot simply be solved by requiring an efficiency of at least C^2. It is almost impossible for the judges to forecast correctly the efficiency of the measures before they grant them. This debate is as old as the law of negligence itself.

$(E(\pi) > C^1 + C^2 + C^3)$. They would not, however, apply for injunctions against smaller providers, since a benefit of 30.000 EUR is smaller than the cost of 72.000 EUR (if applied for separately). As a consequence, the rightholders themselves do *not* apply for wasteful measures.

In order for the system to work, the costs of intermediaries need to be reimbursed on margin. This means that if a measure requires a huge up-front fixed investment (sunk cost), the first enforcement measure of its kind would be responsible for the required infrastructure investment.[53] This would motivate rightholders to work together on the first cases,[54] since they can share these costs, and also to consider if future payoffs from such measures outweigh the initial investment and subsequent marginal costs. Otherwise, we cannot prevent rightholders from experimenting with measures requiring huge up-front investments, but which are unlikely to pay out sufficiently. The risk of effectiveness of the measures is thus born by the rightholders.

The problem with this system, however, is that it does not entirely prevent inefficiencies from happening in the long run, since the full social cost is never accounted for (C^4). In other words, cases like password locking of WiFi won't be prevented, because the observable direct costs of $C^{1,2,3}$ are very low, so the measure is easily a static Kaldor-Hicks improvement. The system thus does not prevent enforcement measures that are statically efficient, but which can become an obstacle to the growth of tomorrow. If court-imposed measures have no time limits, there is not even an opportunity for the courts to realize this change of costs and benefits. Alternatively to time limits, one could think of a sort of "innovation clause" or "clausula rebus sic stantibus," under which a third party could achieve annulation of the measures upon proving change in the societal benefits that are being blocked. If established, any related constraining enforcement obligations could be terminated at any point in time. Admittedly, however, the solution is still not too comforting.

The entire above discussion assumes that such injunctions would be always granted only by the courts. The same outcome, with one notable exception, also applies to effects on voluntary agreements. A threat of an injunction have an important impact on what intermediaries offer on "voluntary grounds." In Germany, for instance, the debt (obligation) of an injunction addressee is formed *before* he applies to the court to force compliance. Injunction-addressees are thus expect to comply without court interference. One of the consequences of such a setup is that the rightholders might request compensation of the pretrial costs.[55] This amount, together with other procedural costs, creates additional incentives to comply with

---

[53] Compare the approach of Arnold J in *Cartier International AG & Ors v. British Sky Broadcasting Ltd & Ors* [2014] EWHC 3354 (Ch), [239]–[247].

[54] Coordination would most likely be easier given that the group of rightholders would be smaller and bigger rightholders can easily have sufficient expected benefits to initiate the group-formation or even sue on their own. On general theory of groups and collective action see Mancur Olson, *The Logic of Collective Action: Public Goods and the Theory of Groups* (Harvard University Press 1974).

[55] See Section 9.6.

requests before any lawsuit. This is significant when the cost of implementation is very low, for instance password protection of private wireless. In those cases, intermediaries rather save costs by avoiding a lawsuit by complying upon request.

In contrast, when compliance costs are not insignificant, the outcomes is different. Recall our example of website blocking injunctions against two large and three small access providers. The website blocking assistance is granted only against the defendants in the suit. However, since the plaintiff will derive benefit only from blocking against two large providers, he will not sue the three small ones. They are left without any obligation, which is good for society, as any blocking imposed on them would just be waste of resources. An obligation to compensate forces to do the same kind of assessment also in the out-of-court negotiations regarding voluntary actions. As long as the cost-split from litigation is *not* used as a template for out-of-court demands against smaller providers, the rightholder would need to pay the actual higher costs to them. In effect, he would thus never ask them to institute the blocking, as its costs exceed the benefits.

This means that for the administration of the system, a court determination is not necessary. As long as the costs of compliance are set independently, the intermediaries would be compensated according to their costs, whether they await or not the court order. However, this is not to say that such blocking without court interference might not sill be a problem from the innovation and human rights perspective which may require independent supervision of the measures.

In addition, the system of self-financing avoids one other problem, namely, that costly enforcement assistance might become a way of disadvantaging smaller competitors among intermediaries. Large intermediaries possess bigger scale, and thus can not only implement better and more expensive solutions, but can also do so more cheaply.[56] In 2006, the Industry Canada estimated the processing cost of one notification under the Canadian notice-to-notice system, a system of forwarding notices to the subscribers who were found to be engaging in copyright infringements, to be $11.73 CAN for large ISPs, but $23.73 CAN for smaller ISPs.[57] The cost difference in the case of more expensive enforcement measures, such as website blocking by Deep Packet Inspection might be even higher.[58] Unlike in the case of voluntary measures, if costs were not to be reimbursed, the courts would inadvertently be increasing barriers to entry. It is possible to imagine scenarios where larger intermediaries, when they have no other choice, might be in favor of more expensive types of assistance,

---

[56] Arnold J assumes opposite in *Cartier International AG & Ors v. British Sky Broadcasting Ltd & Ors* [2014] EWHC 3354 (Ch) [252] ("Clearly it is important that none of the ISPs should gain a competitive advantage over the others, but this is ensured by the fact that they are all required to take approximately equivalent measures").

[57] See Michael Geist, "The Liberal Roundtable on the Digital Economy: My Comments" (*Geist Blog*, 11 February 2010), www.michaelgeist.ca/content/view/4787/125/.

[58] See the costs estimates for website blocking injunctions in the UK (*Cartier International AG & Ors v. British Sky Broadcasting Ltd & Ors* [2014] EWHC 3354 (Ch)).

as they would have the effect of excluding their own competitors. Self-financing prevents this, because the rightholders reimburse the costs.

The proposed solution of self-financing assistance is not so unusual. It appears to be similar to the so-called Rule Four of Calabresi and Melamed. This is a scenario, where the court enjoins pollution by a polluter only provided that injured party pays "damages" to a polluter. So that polluter can be stopped from certain activity only if he is compensated by a victim of such pollution.[59] Moreover, the UDRP system created as a voluntary scheme for domain name issues is an example of a self-financing enforcement scheme. Trademark holders apply for dispute resolution only if the expected benefit is higher than the fee, which incorporates the cost of processing the complaint. The system is thus financially self-sustaining. One can easily imagine that if the system of domain name dispute resolution were financed by domain name authorities, its use by rightholders would be much more intensive, and probably abusive. This would, in turn, naturally result in more expensive domain name infrastructure for consumers.

One problem of self-financing, however, is that if costs are fully reimbursed by rightholders, intermediaries have no incentive to reduce the operational costs of such measures. Worse still, intermediaries could employ various strategies to either inflate the costs to make it less attractive to rightholders, or just avoid developing cheaper solutions.[60] The court could, however, employ several tactics to prevent this. For instance, the court could lower the compensation which is due, if the rightholders demonstrate that the same or an equivalent solution can be implemented in a cheaper way. Alternatively, the court could oblige the intermediary to arrange auctions for the required technical solutions or punish for inflated prices. Such auctions would then assure that the price is competitive and nonabusive. Since sometimes the most efficient and cheapest solutions can be developed in-house, intermediaries themselves should also be allowed to bid on the solutions sought.

This framework also has an immediate impact on voluntary measures. It provides for minimal conditions for any such negotiated scheme under which any payoff above the cost of the measures $(C^1 + C^2 + C^3)$ goes to the rightholder. So when

---

[59] In *Spur Industries v. Del Webb* (In *Spur Industries, Inc. v. Del E. Webb Dev. Co.*, 494 P.2d 700 (Ariz. 1972)), Del Webb, an Arizona real-estate developer of retirement communities, sued for an injunction against Spur Industries, the owner of a feedlot whose activities resulted in an alleged nuisance to the encroaching retirement community (causing Del Webb difficulties in selling properties close to the feedlot). Spur Industries already operated their feedlot before Del Webb came to build a retirement community. The Supreme Court of Arizona ruled that Spur Industries' activities did create a nuisance, but Del Webb had brought its unwitting retirees to this existing environment. The court ruled that Spur Industries would be forced to move, but that Del Webb had to indemnify for the related business troubles.

[60] Interestingly enough, this seems to be happening even when rightholders are not paying the bill of such measures. In a recent *Cartier* decision (*Cartier International AG & Ors v. British Sky Broadcasting Ltd & Ors* [2014] EWHC 3354 (Ch)), the rightholders were complaining that intermediaries could block websites more cheaply [202].

the benefit of measures outweighs their costs, intermediaries are presented with two options: either to consent to them in voluntary schemes with flexible conditions out of court, or to have them imposed by the court. This alternative creates what economists call a "credible threat" and thus additional incentives for voluntary measures.

2.4 SOLUTION B: VOLUNTARY ASSISTANCE

In order to maximize the likelihood that errors in allocation will be corrected by the market, we should allocate rights in a way which will make it easier (and thus more likely) for parties to re-organize their affairs according to their relative valuation. Since transactions are asymmetrically smaller for rightholders, intermediaries facing higher transaction costs will be given the entitlement. This basically means that rightholders would need to negotiate each and every instance of assistance with the intermediaries providing remote services. Many countries, such as the United States and Canada, seem to operate under this system today where no such right to general assistance exists or at least is being used.

But negotiations do not always result in voluntary agreements. It is, however, necessary to distinguish between two situations. First of all, when socially *wasteful* enforcement measures do not materialize. Because their expected benefit $(E(\pi))$ is lower than the costs to both parties, neither of the parties is willing to pay the other party to make it a profitable arrangement. So, for instance, if an enforcement measure of filtering has an expected benefit $E(\pi)$ of 100 EUR, but the costs are 200 EUR to each intermediary, the rightholder is willing to offer less than 100 EUR, which does not even cover the costs. The intermediary thus will not accept any offer made by rightholders, since even the highest offer of 100 EUR would cause the intermediary to lose 100 EUR.

The consequence, i.e., that these socially wasteful measures do not materialize, is actually a good thing, since they are, after all, welfare decreasing. We should, however, be more concerned when welfare maximizing deals $(E(\pi) - C > 0)$ do not materialize. But deals are welfare maximizing exclusively when they account for all associated costs, either statically $(E(\pi) - C^1 - C^2 > 0)$[61] or dynamically $(E(\pi) - C^1 - C^2 - C^4 > 0)$. At the moment, there is a very little empirical evidence mapping the claimed inefficiencies in negotiating these kind of agreements. So we do not really know whether there is some real problem ongoing, or not. In theory, however, there can be numerous reason why even these negotiations fail.

One explanation can be a *misalignment of business perspectives*. If rightholders emphasize long-term benefits, but an intermediary is myopic, he might be unwilling to trade existing benefits for uncertain future ones. For instance, an advertising

---

[61] C^3 does not appear when parties are negotiating out of court since the state does not need to grant the measures.

network that is asked to cut off its infringing customers can lose a great deal of revenue by terminating cooperation with infringing websites. At the same time, preventing infringing websites from using its service can have a positive effect on the reputation of the network, minimize other types of abuses within the advertising network and potentially even improve the conversion rate of its advertising and thus value of the advertising. Since these are only uncertain future benefits, myopic intermediaries will not consider them.

Another explanation attacks the *rationality assumption*. Coase theorem assumes that if two individuals find themselves in a position to strike a mutually advantageous bargain, they will always do so.[62] But reality is sometimes different. Consider what economists call the "ultimatum game."[63] In this bargaining game, one party (the proposer) is asked to split a certain amount of money between itself and another party (the responder). The responder then has a possibility to either accept the split, in which case everybody receives their own share, or to reject it, in which case nobody receives anything. Experimental evidence has shown that humans will reject certain splits (rational choices), even if they would derive a net benefit from it, just to punish the proposer for his unfair offer. This rejection then signals the necessity of a certain level of mutual fairness for future transactions. In a way, it sets the standards for the future negotiations. It is possible that the same notion of fairness prevents parties from agreeing about higher enforcement measures. Rightholders could reject offers that provide them with net benefits just to avoid a precedent for the future. For instance, some rightholders could view it as unfair when it is proposed that they reimburse part of the implementation costs of intermediaries. In their view, intermediaries are the cause of all their problems, so they do not see why they should compensate them for anything. As a consequence, they reject or don't propose even well-fare maximizing offers.

Despite possible impediments to negotiations and lack of legal incentives, we can still see a number of voluntary initiatives in countries with no entitlement to assistance. Examples include the US Copyright Alert system and Canadian notice-to-notice system[64] negotiated with major access providers, the UDRP system with most of the domain name providers, or the IAB Quality Assurance Guidelines with advertising intermediaries,[65] and the Principles of the Center for Safe Internet Pharmacies negotiated with payment, domain name, and advertising

---

[62] Elizabeth Hoffman and Matthew L. Spitzer, "The Coase Theorem: Some Experimental Tests" (1982) 25 Journal of Law and Economics 75.

[63] Werner Güth and others, "An Experimental Analysis of Ultimatum Bargaining" (1982) 3 Journal of Economic Behavior & Organization 367–388 (using the game for the first time); since then it was applied in several other settings – see Richard H. Thaler, "Anomalies: The Ultimatum Game" (1988) 2 The Journal of Economic Perspectives 195–206; Martin A. Nowak and others, "Fairness Versus Reason in the Ultimatum Game" (2000) 283 Science 289, 1773.

[64] Lilian Edwards, "Role and Responsibility of Internet Intermediaries in the Field of Copyright and Related Rights" (WIPO report, 2009) 29, www.wipo.int.

[65] See www.iab.net/QAGInitiative/overview/quality_assurance_guidelines.

intermediaries.[66] The cost-splits of these system are very different. The UDRP system, in particular, has had a very significant impact, despite the fact that its dispute resolution is not legally binding. UDRP is financed by dispute resolution fees paid by claimants. The costs of the Canadian notice-to-notice system, on the other hand, were reported to be shared: the costs of sending out warnings to subscribers are born by ISPs and costs of notification by rightholders.[67] Such cost-splits and other exact conditions are mutually agreed in negotiations, which prevents the occurrence of inefficient rules for negotiating parties. Of course, voluntary measures do not prevent dynamically inefficient solutions. But, unlike when they are imposed as legal obligations, the participants of such agreements will have the possibility to discharge themselves from such contractual obligations, as their competition, which is not bound by them, will otherwise take advantage of it.

2.5 COMPARISON OF SOLUTIONS

Both of the systems have their advantages and disadvantages. Even if the system of *mandatory assistance* is self-financed by rightholders, which we have concluded is necessary in order to prevent waste of resources, the danger is that the courts could unwittingly be involved in prescribing assistance that stifles economic growth. And the assistance could be even misused in competition fights over old and new generation business models. The open-ended possibilities of assistance also create uncertainties as to what kind of demands rightholders can have on the proximate services of intermediaries.

Some of these disadvantages can be mitigated to a certain extent by the negotiation of industry voluntary agreements which would be facilitated by the state, for instance, under the condition of mutual litigation cease-fire or standards with legal effects.[68] But these agreements can be very fragile if nonparticipating rightholders could demand more assistance from participating intermediaries using civil lawsuits. Such strategic behavior could easily undermine any value of agreements. For these reasons, it would be advisable for courts not to impose higher standards than those that were already agreed upon in the industry agreements. This would also give an incentive to discuss these measures at the negotiation table rather than have them imposed by the courts.

[66] Participating payment intermediaries obliged themselves, for instance, to employ technologies to proactively monitor the Internet for merchants that attempt to process illegitimate Internet pharmacy transactions and to conduct due diligence on their agents in order to ensure compliance with the payment system operator's policies and procedures regarding the online sale – see www.safemedsonline.org/who-we-are/principles-participation/.

[67] Lilian Edwards, "Role and Responsibility of Internet Intermediaries in the Field of Copyright and Related Rights" (WIPO report, 2009) 29.

[68] Such state-mediated schemes would fix the assistance for a while and would help by codifying expectations in the industry. The external pressure by the state motivates by creating a threat of possible regulation.

At the same time, this system clearly creates stronger incentives for intermediaries to engage in voluntary agreements. This is because the litigation path with self-funded measures by rightholders can be seen as a template for voluntary measures that can be imposed by the courts, despite the resistance of intermediaries. This creates an instrument of credible threat and thereby promotes negotiations by moving the bargaining frontier for the benefit of a rightholder.

The imminent threat of obstacles to future economic growth can be partially mitigated by the time limitation of such injunctions and an innovation clause, which should both introduce a periodical review to the measures. So if, for instance, car makers want to unlock the password-locked WiFi of operators who were previously sued (for instance university campuses), the judge could consider these potential benefits in the review of the measures. The innovation clause would provide an extra opportunity to challenge the measures at any point in time, also for any third parties. In both cases, of course, it is impossible to prove or even calculate the exact blocked benefits.[69] What is being blocked was not put in use in that setting, and thus cannot be quantified. The probability should therefore suffice. As stated above, this still does not appear too satisfactory.

This type of review is, however, only possible if measures are only granted by the authorities, which can also anytime discharge the intermediaries from such obligations. The same problem of dynamic inefficiency also arises under the system of voluntary agreements which can also impede innovation in progress. The latter, however, could be remedied by competition law in some cases.

A system of *voluntary agreements*, on the other hand, still motivates remote intermediaries to enter into negotiations only as far as it serves their own interests, as explained in Section 2.2. But even when most of the industry is self-motivated to assist rightholders sufficiently, some of the players might exploit exactly the gap in the market that the rest of the industry has left. This is well-illustrated by the functioning of advertising networks in the infringing ecosystem of cyberlockers. More than 17 out of the 30 most widely used cyberlockers were reported to rely on one single nonmainstream advertising network.[70] This is no coincidence. It is often not enough that most of the industry uses better enforcement techniques, when several players can easily take their place and serve the demand stemming from rogue websites.

In some cases, this strategy might work, though, especially when consumers are very cautious with the service providers they choose or when it is not so easy to launch new services (for instance the industry is concentrated or has high barriers to

---

[69] It is often difficult to quantify potential benefits even when they are currently tested in the society – see Paul Milgrom, and others, "The Case for Unlicensed Spectrum" (2011), http://ssrn.com/abstract=1948257 ("Again, it is difficult to place an exact number on the value created by having Wi-Fi connectivity on mobile phones").

[70] Net Names, "Behind the Cyberlocker Door: A Report on How Shadowy Cyberlocker Businesses Use Credit Card Companies to Make Milions" (*Net Names*, 2014) 4.

entry[71]), for instance. An example of this kind are payment intermediaries. Shortly after both Visa and MasterCard stopped processing payments for allofmymp3.com, its popularity plummeted.[72] The website tried to secure income by selling vouchers, but this attempt was prevented by the police.[73] It is clear that a substitution of payment processing in this case was very difficult.[74]

On the other hand, a clear advantage of the system of voluntary measures is that rightholders cannot impose obligations which might undermine the future innovative uses of technologies. If they are agreed upon, there are strong market incentives to relinquish them. But unless the parties to an enforcement agreement feel the *indirect costs* (C^4), at least partly, as their own (for instance the impossibility to launch certain products or services), they also have no reason to take them into account. If the indirect costs (C^4) gradually outgrow the private benefit to rightholders reduced by the cost of self-funded measures ($C^4 > E(\pi) - C^1 - C^2$), then the enforcement agreements again become socially wasteful. These deals could potentially be a target for antitrust law, since they are vertical or horizontal agreements that can easily have as their effect the restriction or distortion of competition by limiting technical development. An example could be an industry agreement of payment intermediaries with the rightholders that excludes an entire technological class, such as peer-to-peer services, from their payment systems.

To sum up, the choice between the two systems is hard to answer in abstract and without solid data.[75] One can surely tilt the debate with distributional goals. If the distributional preference is to give more resources to innovate or create to rightholders, one would recommend the solution A. If the preference is to give more resources to innovate to intermediaries, one would recommend solution B. However, if one does not want to resort to the distributional goals,[76] the answer to

---

[71] Ronald J. Mann and Seth R. Belzley, "The Promise of Internet Intermediary Liability" (2005) 47 William & Mary Law Review 239, 241.

[72] Mark MacCarthy, "What Payment Intermediaries Are Doing about Online Liability and Why It Matters" (2010) 25 Berkeley Technology Law Journal 1037, 1094.

[73] IFPI, "Police Dawn Raid Stops allofmp3.com Pirate Vouchers Scheme" (Enforcement Bulletin, 2007) 3, www.ifpi.org/content/library/enforcement-bulletin-34.pdf.

[74] Rogue websites use different alternative strategies, such as pretending to accept regular methods of payment and then asking consumers to transfer the money to a bank account directly or by other means (see *Cartier International AG & Ors v. British Sky Broadcasting Ltd & Ors* [2014] EWHC 3354 (Ch), [206]). These strategies can be also fought by freezing accounts or targeting alternative methods of payment.

[75] The question is in its essence empirical. This is how Coase perceived the question of allocation of frequencies in his work (Ronald Coase, "The Federal Communications Commission" (1959) 2 Journal of Law and Economics 1–40); see Steven G. Medema, "Legal Fiction: The Place of The Coase Theorem in Law and Economics" (1999) 15 Economics and Philosophy 209, 211.

[76] Choice of the default rule has, however, an impact on the distribution of the resulting resources. This is well-recognized by the contract theory (Ronald J. Mann and Seth R. Belzley, "The Promise of Internet Intermediary Liability" (2005) 47 William & Mary Law Review 239, 279; Ronald J. Mann, "Contracts-Only with Consent" (2004) 152 University of Pennsylvania Law Review 1873, 1896–1901) and also finds its expression in many debates about the Coase theorem, where it is argued that, although

the question of choice seem to be only a very "Machlupian" one:[77] based on present knowledge, if a country does not have a system of general accountability in form of the claims for assistance, one cannot conclusively recommend instituting it. But if it has one, neither can one recommend removing it. What one can do, however, is to shape either of the two systems to deliver better results using the insights of the above analysis.

> efficiency can be served the same regardless of the allocation of entitlements, the resulting distribution of resources is different depending on the default allocation (Steven G. Medema, "Legal Fiction: The Place of the Coase Theorem in Law and Economics" (1999) 15 Economics and Philosophy 209, 218).
>
> [77] Machlup ended his review of the US patent system with famous quote: "If we did not have a patent system, it would be irresponsible, on the basis of our present knowledge of its economic consequences, to recommend instituting one. But since we have had a patent system for a long time, it would be irresponsible, on the basis of our present knowledge, to recommend abolishing it" (see Fritz Machlup, "An Economic Review of the Patent System" (Study of Commission on Judiciary, Subcommittee on Patents, Trademarks, and Copyrights, 1958) 80).

PART II

European Framework

3

Historical Legislative Developments

The basic structure underlying the system of injunctions against innocent inter-mediaries is contained in Article 8(3) of the InfoSoc Directive and Article 11 third sentence (III) of the Enforcement Directive, which provide that

> Member States shall ensure that rightholders are in a position to apply for an injunction against intermediaries whose services are used by a third party to infringe [a copyright or related right/ an intellectual property right].

Some other provisions targeting innocent third parties are included in Article 8 (claim for third-party information), Article 9(1)(a) (preliminary injunctions against intermediaries) and Article 10 (right to recall and destruction of goods) of the Enforce-ment Directive. Recently, the provisions of the Enforcement Directive were further extended to the international agreement executing the Unitary Patent system, the Agreement on a Unified Patent Court (the UPC Agreement).[1] This includes provi-sions on preliminary (Article 62) and permanent injunctions against intermediaries (Article 63), as well as the right to third-party information (Article 67).

The provisions of Article 8(3) of the InfoSoc and Article 11(III) of the Enforcement Directive led to a tectonic change in enforcement on the Internet. It is therefore worth exploring what, historically, are their conceptual underpinnings and goals. In this section we explore how the Union law developed a rule like Article 8(3) of the InfoSoc Directive for copyrighted works, which was later extended to all other intellectual property rights by virtue of the Enforcement Directive, and from there further exported as an enforcement standard not only to other instruments of Union law, but also numerous EU free trade agreements. It all started, surprisingly, with another directive.

---

[1] Agreement on a Unified Patent Court, Brussels, 19 February 2013.

3.1 DESIGN DIRECTIVE (1996)

The first provision on injunctions against innocent parties in Union law appeared in 1996, in the proposal for the Directive on legal protection of designs.[2] Article 16a, proposed by the Commission at the suggestion of Parliament,[3] envisaged a right to third-party information about an infringement of a design right.[4] Liability of the addressee of such a claim was *not* a precondition. The corresponding Recital 16e argued that this is necessary in order to "reinforce effective action against the infringement of design rights" and that "any effective fight against product counterfeiting makes it necessary (. . .) that this remedy is (. . .) available by court order, where appropriate, even before final judgement in an infringement case." The provision was eventually abandoned because it was feared that it might endanger the fragile compromise that had been reached on other issues.[5] As a result, the Green Paper on Combating Piracy, which was presented shortly after the adoption of the Directive, expressly proposes that the right to third-party information should be subject to further discussion.[6]

3.2 E-COMMERCE DIRECTIVE (2000)

In 1998, the European Commission announced[7] that, in order to "eliminate existing legal uncertainties and to avoid divergent approaches at Member State level," it will introduce a law which would establish "an exemption from liability *for intermediaries where they play a passive role as a "mere conduit" of information* from third parties *and* limit service providers" liability for other "intermediary" activities such as the storage of information." It promised that the proposal "strikes a careful balance between the different interests involved in order to stimulate co-operation between different parties and so reduce the risk of illegal activity on-line." One month later, it officially published its proposal for what was to become the E-Commerce Directive.

In the first proposal,[8] the legislative text already contained the present safe harbors for mere conduits, caching and hosting, and also outlawed general monitoring.

---

[2] Amended proposal for a European Parliament and Council Directive on the legal protection of designs [1996] OJ C 142/07.

[3] Annette Kur, "'Freeze Plus; Melts the Ice – Observations on the European Design Directive" [1999] IIC 620, 621; Annette Kur, "The Enforcement Directive – Rough Start, Happy Landing?" [2004] IIC 821, 822.

[4] Article 16a was proposed as follows: "(. . .) if the person in question: (a) has been found in possession, for commercial purposes, of such goods, or (b) has been identified by a person under (a) as being the origin or a link in the route for the commercial distribution of such goods" (amended proposal for a European Parliament and Council Directive on the legal protection of designs [1996] OJ C 142/07)a.

[5] Annette Kur, "The Enforcement Directive – Rough Start, Happy Landing?" [2004] IIC 821, 822.

[6] Ibid.

[7] European Commission, "Electronic Commerce: Commission Proposes Legal Framework" (press release, 18 November 1998), http://europa.eu/rapid/press-release_IP-98-999_en.htm?locale=en.

[8] Proposal for a European Parliament and Council Directive on certain legal aspects of electronic commerce in the internal market [1999] OJ C 30/04.

The important difference from today's wording, however, was that the safe harbors section did not contain a separate paragraph enabling injunctions, but rather all three anticipated injunctions appear directly in the main wording, as follows:

> Where an information society service is provided that consists of (. . .), Member States shall provide in their legislation that the provider of such a service shall not be liable, *otherwise than under a prohibitory injunction*, for (. . .), on condition that (. . .)[9]

Surprisingly, apart from this change, one alteration in the wording concerning actual knowledge[10] and an exception to prohibition on general monitoring obligation,[11] the text is remarkably similar to the final Directive. This proposal was welcomed by the Economic and Social Committee, which noted that:

> With regard to liability, the introduction of a graduated system of exemptions and restrictions establishes a common framework, allowing the diverse activities of internet providers to *be assessed separately*; assessment is *based on providers' degree of involvement with the content* transmitted and their scope for monitoring content. The Committee welcomes efforts to establish clear rules on the responsibility of service or information society providers and shares the view that the "manufacturer" of information should bear primary responsibility for its content.[12]

After the opinion from the European Parliament, the Commission presented the second, amended proposal for the Directive in 2000.[13] The provisions on intermediaries remained unchanged. Subsequently, the Council proposed in its common position[14] that the phrase "not be liable, otherwise than under a prohibitory injunction"[15] should be substituted with a separate paragraph in each of the safe harbors stating that the applicability of a safe harbor "shall not affect the possibility

---

9 Proposal for a European Parliament and Council Directive on certain legal aspects of electronic commerce in the internal market [1999] OJ C 30/04 (emphasis mine).

10 The proposed Article 14 read, "The provider does not have actual knowledge that the activity is illegal." Existing Article 14 reads, however, "The provider does not have actual knowledge of illegal activity or information."

11 The proposed Article 15(2) read: "Paragraph 1 shall not affect any targeted, temporary surveillance activities required by national judicial authorities in accordance with national legislation to safeguard national security, defence, public security and for the prevention, investigation, detection and prosecution of criminal offences."

12 Opinion of the Economic and Social Committee on the Proposal for a European Parliament and Council Directive on certain legal aspects of electronic commerce in the internal market [1999] OJ C 169/36 (emphasis mine).

13 Amended proposal for a European Parliament and Council Directive on certain legal aspects of electronic commerce in the Internal Market [2000] OJ C 248E/69.

14 Common Position (EC) No 22/2000 of 28 February 2000 adopted by the Council, acting in accordance with the procedure referred to in Article 251 of the Treaty establishing the European Community, with a view to adopting a Directive of the European Parliament and of the Council on certain legal aspects of information society services, in particular electronic commerce, in the internal market (directive on electronic commerce) [2000] OJ C 128/32.

15 In the German text, this was expressed, "Außer im Falle einer Unterlassungsklage."

for a court or administrative authority, in accordance with Member States' legal systems, of requiring the service provider to terminate or prevent an infringement." The Council also proposed to change the wording of actual knowledge and the exception to the prohibition of general monitoring, as well as the addition of Recitals 42–45. Recital 42, in particular, which stated that exemptions apply only where the activity of the provider is limited to the technical and passive process, later caused a great deal of confusion.

The Commission eventually accepted these proposals noting that:

> *The conditions to be met in order to benefit from the exemptions from liability for intermediary service providers are explained in new recital 42.* New recital 43 further explains the conditions for the exemptions for "mere conduit" and "caching" whereas new recital 44 underlines that a service provider who deliberately collaborates with a recipient of his service in order to undertake illegal activities, cannot benefit from these exemptions. *The possibility of injunctions against service providers in respect of infringing activities is further explained in new recital 45.*[16]

It is surprising that the Commission either did not realize the shift in meaning, or did not want to defend its initial proposal, which arguably expected passivity only from the mere conduits[17] and not from the hosting providers. As to why the Council proposed the above recitals, one can only speculate. Maybe the Council wanted to cover only mere conduits, as the language of activities suggests, and was simply not aware of the general language it had chosen, or maybe it inserted such broad language deliberately. The change, however small, has become crucial today, because the CJEU in the meantime potentially limited the applicability of all the safe harbors, relying exactly on Recital 42 and its alleged requirement of passivity.

In the end, the European Parliament approved the final version and asked "the Commission to ensure rapid and rigorous implementation of this Directive in the Member States," especially in regard to "the establishment of efficient notice and take-down procedures by interested parties, and to prevent any interpretation of Articles 12 to 15 which would call into question the balance achieved in those articles." Whether the CJEU also acted on this advice will be shown in Chapter 4.

---

[16] Commission, "Communication from the Commission to the European Parliament pursuant to the second subparagraph of Article 251 (2) of the EC Treaty concerning the Council common position on the proposal for a Directive on certain legal aspects of Information Society services, in particular electronic commerce, in the Internal Market" COD (2000) 0386 (emphasis mine).

[17] See first the European Commission, "Electronic Commerce: Commission Proposes Legal Framework" (press release, 18 November 1998), http://europa.eu/rapid/press-release_IP-98–999_en.htm? locale=en, and compare it with the Opinion of the Economic and Social Committee on the Proposal for a European Parliament and Council Directive on certain legal aspects of electronic commerce in the internal market [1999] OJ C 169/36. Passiveness was arguably meant to be embodied in the condition that an intermediary can not initiate a transmission or that it does not collaborate.

3.3 INFOSOC DIRECTIVE (2001)

The second, and this time successful attempt, to introduce injunctions against innocent third parties came in 2000 when the Council in its common position before the
second reading,[18] of what was to become the InfoSoc Directive, added a new paragraph 3 to Article 8 of the proposal,[19] foreseeing injunctions "against an intermediary
who carries a third party's infringement." This paragraph was supplemented with an
explanatory Recital 58, which justified the amendment with the argument that intermediaries are best placed to put an end to the increasing number of infringements
online. The Commission very eagerly welcomed this addition stating that:

> the provision obliges Member States to ensure that rightholders are in a position
> to apply for an injunction against intermediaries whose services are used by third
> parties to infringe a copyright or related right. Such a possibility *may not be made
> dependent on the lawfulness of the acts of intermediaries*. The Commission welcomes
> this useful clarification.[20]

The Parliament's Committee on Legal Affairs and the Internal Market suggested
changing the wording to "intermediary whose services are used by a third party
to infringe" and also the wording of the recital before the second reading.[21] The
interesting suggested addition to the recital was the following text:

> However, such injunctions must be specific, proportionate, and feasible and relate
> only to the infringement against which the injunction was applied for, and must in
> any case respect the principles of free movement of goods and services as well as
> the principle of freedom of speech.[22]

The Committee argued[23] that there is a need to be consistent with only the recently
passed E-Commerce Directive, which, in its own words, requires that "injunctions
based on Article 8(3) always have to be specific" and that "the Article should *not*

---

18 Council of the European Union, "Common position adopted by the Council with a view to the
    adoption of a Directive of the European Parliament and of the Council on the harmonisation of
    certain aspects of copyright and related rights in the information society" COD (1997) 0359.
19 "The Council also added a new paragraph 3 to Article 8, which calls upon Member States to provide
    for the possibility of rightholders to apply for an injunction against intermediaries carrying third parties'
    infringements, even where the relevant intermediaries' acts fall under the exception provided for in
    Article 5(1). This new paragraph is accompanied by new recital 58." Ibid.
20 Commission, "Communication from the Commission to the European Parliament pursuant to the
    second subparagraph of Article 251 (2) of the EC Treaty concerning the common position of the
    Council on the adoption of a Directive of the European Parliament and of the Council on the
    harmonisation of certain aspects of copyright and related rights in the information Society" COM
    (2000) 1734 final (emphasis mine).
21 Committee on Legal Affairs and the Internal Market, "Recommendation for second reading on the
    Council common position for adopting a European Parliament and Council Directive on the har-
    monisation of certain aspects of copyright and related rights in the Information Society" (9512/1/2000-
    C5-0520/2000).
22 Ibid.   23 Ibid.

be interpreted in such a way as to enable the imposition of general monitoring and filtering requirements on ISPs and intermediaries, which are in contradiction with Article 15 of the E-Commerce Directive." As is known from the present wording of the provision, these suggestions were not accepted in the end.

3.4 ENFORCEMENT DIRECTIVE (2004)

Another initiative that included injunctions against innocent third parties came in 2003 with the debate about the Enforcement Directive. The very first proposal of the Commission contained Article 15(2) which read:

> Member States shall ensure that right holders are able to apply for an injunction to be addressed to intermediaries whose services are used by third parties to infringe an intellectual property right.

This provision, however, unlike injunctions targeting infringers (Article 15(1)),[24] did not include any noncompliance fines. Interestingly, the accompanying explanatory memorandum did not contain any *specific* justification or explanation for Article 15(2). A general justification can be found in the introduction, where the Commission mentions that apart from the main objective of removing barriers on the internal market, the proposal also furthers the aims of "promoting innovation and business competitiveness" and "preservation and development of the cultural sector." Interestingly, the Commission even stated[25] that in order for "businesses, universities, research organisations and the cultural sector (. . .) to be able to innovate and be creative under good conditions," especially, "the free movement of information should (. . .) be ensured and access to the Internet not made more difficult or costly by, for instance, imposing excessively heavy obligations on Internet intermediaries."

It is very surprising that the Commission instead of justifying its choice for "special injunctions," warns itself of the possible consequences of the instrument. Apart from Article 15 (preventive measures), the other relevant provisions of the proposal providing for injunctions *also* against innocent third parties were Article 9 (right of information), Article 10 (provisional measures), Article 13 (right of recall) and Article 14 (right to destruction of goods). The proposal was followed by the report of the

---

[24] Commission, "Proposal for a Directive of the European Parliament and of the Council on measures and procedures to ensure the enforcement of intellectual property rights" COM (2003) 46 states: "Member States shall lay down that, when a judicial decision has been taken finding an infringement of an intellectual property right, the judicial authorities may serve the infringer with an injunction aimed at prohibiting the continuation of the infringement. Non-compliance with an injunction shall be punishable by a fine accompanied, where applicable, by a recurring fine, with a view to ensuring compliance."

[25] Commission, "Proposal for a Directive of the European Parliament and of the Council on measures and procedures to ensure the enforcement of intellectual property rights" COM (2003) 46.

Committee on Legal Affairs and the Internal Market.[26] The Committee suggested changing the wording of Article 15 and Article 10 by inserting following words to Article 15:

> (1) Member States shall lay down that, when a judicial decision has been taken finding an infringement of an intellectual property right, the judicial authorities may serve the infringer with an injunction aimed at prohibiting the continuation of the infringement. (2) *The measures referred to in Articles 10* [provisional measures] *and 15* [preventive measures] *shall be available against intermediaries where the conditions set out there are met and where this Article does not provide otherwise.* (3) *However, in respect of intermediary service providers Articles 12 to 15 of Directive 2000/31/EC shall apply.* (4) Non-compliance with an injunction shall be punishable by a fine accompanied, where applicable, by a recurring fine, with a view to ensuring compliance.[27]

This means that the Committee firstly suggested making injunctions against intermediaries dependent on the same criteria as those against infringers. Secondly, it was suggested that noncompliance fines be extended to cover also intermediaries. And lastly, the intermediaries that are shielded by any of the E-Commerce Directive's safe harbors were probably meant to be exempted from the injunctions entirely. Despite the lack of concrete justifications for this change, the above interpretation is also supported by the suggestion of a new Recital 23a, which anticipated that "this Directive creates no other liability for information society services and intermediaries than is provided for in Directive 2000/31/EC," and also by the amendment to Article 2, where it was suggested that:

> This Directive shall not in any way affect Directive 2000/31/EC, and in particular the provisions in Articles 12 to 14 of the Directive. Thus, for the purpose of the present Directive, intermediary service providers whose role is limited to the activities specified in Articles 12 to 14 of Directive 2000/31/EC shall not be considered as infringers, or participants in an infringement.[28]

This amendment was justified on the basis that it "clarifies the relationship between the present Directive and the E-Commerce Directive," since the "E-Commerce Directive's provisions on intermediary liability are the result of detailed and lengthy discussions and a careful compromise that should not be reopened." Hence, it seems that the Committee was trying to prevent any change in the *status quo* for intermediaries. And this might be despite the fact that the E-Commerce Directive does *not* substantially limit injunctions. The other evidence for taking the E-Commerce

---

[26] Committee on Legal Affairs and the Internal Market, "Report on the proposal for a directive of the European Parliament and of the Council on measures and procedures to ensure the enforcement of intellectual property rights" (COM(2003) 46-C5-0055/2003-2003/0024(COD)).

[27] Committee on Legal Affairs and the Internal Market, "Report on the proposal for a directive of the European Parliament and of the Council on measures and procedures to ensure the enforcement of intellectual property rights" (COM(2003) 46-C5-0055/2003-2003/0024(COD)) (emphasis mine).

[28] Ibid.

Directive into account beyond its actual scope was a proposed amendment to Recital 21, in which the Committee suggested adding the following to the right to third-party information: "this should not constitute a general obligation to monitor third parties." As a justification, it was stated that such a clarification was needed in order "to establish consistency with Directive 2000/31/EC" and in order to "emphasise that the extent of the duty of vigilance in favour of third parties remains clearly limited." This quite cautious approach of the Committee was underlined even in the explanatory memorandum.[29]

However, the final text, adopted on 9 April 2004 after the first reading in the Parliament, no longer contained most of these suggestions. Small, but relevant changes were also introduced in Article 8 [right of information], where, by inserting "infringer and/or any other person," their broad applicability was made even clearer. Furthermore, Article 9 [on provisional measures] now stipulated that "an interlocutory injunction may also be issued, under the same conditions [as against the infringer], against an intermediary whose services are being used by a third party to infringe an intellectual property right." Last but not least, Article 11 was basically passed in its initially proposed form. The cautious approach of the Committee was expressed in one recital (Recital 15) and one article (Article 2(2)), which continued to stress that the Enforcement Directive shall not affect the E-Commerce Directive framework.

3.5 AGREEMENT ON A UNITARY PATENT COURT (2013)

A more recent addition to the enforcement framework is the Agreement on a Unitary Patent Court (the UPC Agreement). The agreement is neither part of primary, nor of secondary Union law, but has the form of an international intergovernmental treaty, a so-called *inter se* treaty,[30] membership of which is open only to the Members States of the EU. It is unclear to what extent, if at all, the Court of Justice of the European Union even has jurisdiction to interpret the issues of substantial patent law *in general*.[31] However, in the case of remedies specifically the subject

---

[29] Ibid. ("Bearing in mind the concerns of the telecommunications and access supply industries and in the interest of legal certainty the rapporteur believes it is worth spelling out explicitly that the directive does not affect the provisions concerning Directive 2000/31/EC, particularly those relating to the liability of service-providers").

[30] See Steffen Hindelang, "Circumventing Primacy of EU Law and the CJEU's Judicial Monopoly by Resorting to Dispute Resolution Mechanisms Provided for in Inter-se Treaties? The Case of Intra-EU Investment Arbitration" (2012) 39 Legal Issues of Economic Integration 179–206.

[31] Substantive patent law was, to a great extent, transferred to the UPC Agreement. These provisions are thus provisions of international public law, but not of Union law (Case C-146/13 *Spain v. Parliament and Council* [2015] ECLI:EU:C:2015:298, para. 30). Provisions of substantive law thus appear in two constellations: (1) where they represent an international agreement building upon the harmonization at the EU level (e.g., remedies) and (2) where they extend beyond such existing harmonization (e.g., scope of rights). There is little doubt that the former is part of the Union law, and will need to be interpreted by the CJEU. As to the latter, the situation is more difficult, since strictly speaking the provisions are not part of Union law. However, they complement two other instruments of Union law –

matter still remains to be covered by Union law, which also binds the new Unitary Patent Court.[32] Therefore, unlike for the other provisions of substantive patent law,[33] fundamental rights guaranteed by the EU Charter remain clearly applicable as the national law implementing the UPC Agreement is at the same time implementing the Enforcement Directive (Article 51(1) of EU Charter). The difference, however, is to what extent national conditions and modalities within the context of injunctions against innocent third parties are still permissible under the framework of the UPC Agreement.

As mentioned earlier, the provisions of the Enforcement Directive were copied into the UPC Agreement. The provisions on preliminary (Article 62) and permanent injunctions against intermediaries (Article 63), as well as the right to third-party information (Article 67) thus also became provisions of international public law. Regardless of whether they form part of Union law, they become autonomous legal rules subject to the interpretation rules of the Vienna Convention on the Law of Treaties.[34] This could mean that the Member States have, unlike in the Enforcement and InfoSoc Directive context, less or even zero room for making these measures subject to their own conditions.[35] The only *minimal* conditions for issuing such injunctions, going beyond the Enforcement Directive, are thus regulated by the UPC Agreement itself. In other words, the UPC Agreement can remove the "domestication option" otherwise available under the Union framework.[36] The *maximal* ceiling, however, still remains set by Union law, including the EU Charter.

two regulations relating to the UPC system; see Thomas Jaeger, "Shielding the Unitary Patent from the ECJ: A Rash and Futile Exercise" [2013] IIC 389 (noting that the harmonization of substantive patent law is introduced only through the back-door of international law); Milosz Malaga, "The European Patent with Unitary Effect: Incentive to Dominate?" [2014] IIC 621 (noting that the judicial system will fall out of the scope of the EU's legal order); Josef Drexl, "The European Unitary Patent System: On the 'Unconstitutional' Misuse of Conflict-of-Law Rules" [2015] Max Planck Institute for Innovation & Competition Research Paper No. 15, 18 (outlining the possibility, in response to AG's Bot opinion in Case C-146/13 *Spain v. European Parliament and Council*, that the CJEU could open doors for the Union law by "climbing" upon Article 5(3) of the UPP Regulation, which, in AG's Bot opinion, obliges the Member States to adhere to the UPC Agreement based on the principle of loyalty enshrined in Article 4(3) of the TEU); Tuomas Mylly, "Constitutional Perspective" in Justine Pilla (ed.) *The Unitary EU Patent System* (OUP 2014) 77 et seq.

[32] Article 21 of the UPC Agreement.

[33] See discussion Josef Drexl, "The European Unitary Patent System: On the 'Unconstitutional' Misuse of Conflict-of-Law Rules" [2015] Max Planck Institute for Innovation & Competition Research Paper No. 15, 15ff., fn. 56 (an obligation to respect the Convention could be based on Article 24(1)(d) UPC Agreement).

[34] In particular Articles 31, 32, 33 of the Vienna Convention on the Law of Treaties.

[35] There are no equivalents of Recital 58 of the InfoSoc Directive and Recital 23 of the Enforcement Directive in the context of the UPC Agreement.

[36] See Section 6.4.

4

European Intermediary Liability Framework

The general legal framework of noncontractual liability of Internet intermediaries is provided in the E-Commerce Directive. The Directive, by outlining so-called safe harbors, guarantees that selected types of intermediaries will not be exposed to most forms of liability in the domestic law of the Member States,[1] if they behave in a prescribed way. The E-Commerce Directive, contrary to common misinterpretation, does *not* establish any liability itself,[2] not even when the safe harbors are inevitably lost. The Directive is thus akin to a conditional liability-free zone, in which you can move freely as long as you respect its predefined boundaries. What happens outside this zone, however, is still mostly, but not entirely, in the hands of the Member States.

Apart from the E-Commerce Directive, Union law is usually said to leave to the discretion of the Member States how they set up their own accountability schemes for intermediaries. But this is only partially true. Injunctions against intermediaries under Article 8(3) of the InfoSoc Directive and Article 11 of the Enforcement Directive are a massive limitation on this discretion, as are other general provisions of the Enforcement Directive. Therefore, in truth, the regulation of intermediaries in Europe is a rather complicated jigsaw, composed of various puzzles from several pieces of Union law. Since the Directives always claim not to amend each other, these pieces need to fit together with each other and build up a single undistorted

---

[1] The Directive takes a so-called horizontal approach (Case C-324/09 *L'Oréal and Others* [2011] ECLI:EU:C:2010:757, Opinion of the Advocate General, para. 132; Recital 16 of the InfoSoc Directive). This means that the aim of the directive cuts through all types of liabilities existing in national law, irrespective of their source. Since the process of harmonization influences the legal order as a whole (Case C-397/01 to C-403/01 *Pfeiffer and Others* [2001] ECLI:EU:C:2004:584, para. 115), the impact is also very broad.

[2] Case C-324/09 *L'Oréal and Others* [2010] ECLI:EU:C:2010:757, Opinion of AG Jääskinen, paras. 136, 150 (noting that it is more a clarification or a restatement and therefore does not need to be interpreted restrictively); Case C-324/09 *L'Oréal and Others* [2011] ECLI:EU:C:2011:474 para. 107.

picture. In a situation where a central part of the jigsaw, the accessory liability, is missing, however, any gap in the Union law is also influencing the neighboring pieces.

4.1 UNION AND NATIONAL SAFE HARBORS

The three *union* safe harbors[3] – mere conduit, caching, and hosting – which the E-Commerce Directive foresees, cover only some of the services usually provided in the information society.[4] Article 21(2) obliges the Union legislator to consider the need for other safe harbors, especially for activities such as "hyper-links and location tool services." Despite the lack of an explicit provision to this end, several Member States inserted, in the course of their implementation of the E-Commerce Directive, additional *national* safe harbors for these two activities into their legal systems.[5]

Today, however, it is questionable to what extent such national safe harbors are still compatible with Union law in the absence of their harmonization.[6] What happens when Austrian law[7] protects a person who unknowingly creates a hyperlink to infringing content up to the point when he obtains such knowledge, but the InfoSoc regards this as a form of communication to the public? The national safe harbor, especially in relation to financial compensation prior to such notification, would most likely be *preempted* in its application by the InfoSoc Directive, since such provisions are only optional for the Member States.

The safe harbors cover certain types of technical activities and they are meant to be business model neutral.[8] If the overall business activity of a provider steps out

---

[3] On their compatibility with the TRIPS Agreement, see Frederic Ufer, *Die Haftung der Internet Provider nach dem Telemediengesetz* (Kovač 2007) 28ff.; Gerald Spindler et al., *Teledienstegesetz* (C. H. Beck 2004) 5.

[4] See more Andreas Rühmkorf, "The Liability of Online Auction Portals: Toward a Uniform Approach?" (2010) 14(4) Journal of Internet Law 3–10; Anne S. Cheung and Kevin K. Pun, "Comparative Study on the Liability for Trade Mark Infringement of Online Auction Providers" (2009) 31(11) European Intellectual Property Review 559–567.

[5] Spain and Portugal have opted for the model of Article 14 both for search engines and hyperlinks, whereas Austria and Liechtenstein have opted for the model of Article 12 for search engines and of Article 14 for hyperlinks (see Commission, "Report from the Commission to the European Parliament, the Council and the European Economic and Social Committee – First Report on the application of Directive 2000/31/EC of the European Parliament and of the Council of 8 June 2000 on certain legal aspects of information society services, in particular electronic commerce, in the Internal Market (Directive on electronic commerce)" COM (2003) 0702 final).

[6] This is because the national safe harbors may *not* conflict with other areas of harmonized EU legislation. The most pressing question in this context is the conflict of possible national hyperlinking safe harbors and a communication to the public right which, under some circumstances, regards the creation of a hyperlink as a case of direct infringement – see Case C-466/12 *Svensson and Others* [2014] ECLI:EU:C:2014:76; Case C-160/15 *GS Media* [2016] ECLI:EU:C:2016:644; Case C-348/13 *BestWater International* [2014] ECLI:EU:C:2014:231.

[7] See § 17 of the Austrian E-Commerce-Gesetz (ECG).

[8] Case C-324/09 *L'Oréal and Others* [2010] ECLI:EU:C:2010:757, Opinion of AG Jääskinen, paras. 147, 148 (noting that they should not be understood as watertight compartments).

of the realms of exempted technical activity, the question arises how to treat the otherwise exempted activity. To illustrate the question consider what happens if one and the same information is exposed to two different activity treatments (passive and active) in two separate parts of the service. Does the more active one contaminate the safe harbor also for the passive one?

The Advocate General in *L'Oréal v. eBay* suggested that various activities should be split and treated separately.[9] The approach adopted by CJEU seems to say that certain activities beyond the safe harbor can *contaminate* its availability even for otherwise exempted activities with respect to the same information.[10] This means the information is denied a safe harbor, regardless of potential separability of two situations. On the other hand, the Court confirmed that denying of the safe harbor applies only to contaminated information that was exposed to an active intervention and not for all information on a service in general.[11] This approach is confirmed also by the national case-law.[12]

From the three union safe harbors, mere conduit and hosting are the most relevant.

A "mere conduit" activity "consists of the transmission in a communication network of information provided by a recipient of the service, or the provision of access to a communication network," such as provision of Internet access by providers, WiFi operators, etc. Providers of such the services may "not [not be held] liable for the information transmitted," on the condition that the provider (1) is passive, (2) does not initiate the transmission, (3) does not select the receiver of the transmission, (4) does not select or modify the information contained in the transmission, and (5) does not deliberately collaborate with one of the recipients of his service in order to undertake illegal acts.[13] This safe harbor is thus a typical liability regime for providers we termed remote service providers in the Chapter 2.

A "hosting" activity, on the other hand, represents a service, or its part, consisting of "the storage of information provided by a recipient of the service," such as video-sharing or trading platforms, discussion forums, social networks, Web-hosting services etc. Providers of such services are "not liable for the information stored at the request of a recipient of the service," on the condition that the provider (1) is passive, (2) does not have actual knowledge of illegal activity or information and,

[9] Case C-324/09 *L'Oréal and Others* [2010] ECLI:EU:C:2010:757, Opinion of AG Jääskinen, para. 147–150.

[10] Case C-324/09 *L'Oréal and Others* [2011] ECLI:EU:C:2011:474 para. 116.

[11] Ibid. ("Where, by contrast, the operator has provided assistance which entails, in particular, optimising the presentation of the offers for sale in question or promoting those offers, it must be considered not to have taken a neutral position between the customer-seller concerned and potential buyers but to have played an active role of such a kind as to give it knowledge of, or control over, *the data relating to those offers for sale*. It cannot then rely, *in the case of those data*, on the exemption from liability referred to in Article 14(1) of Directive 2000/31"; emphasis mine).

[12] *Kaschke v. Gray & Anor* [2010] EWHC 690 (QB); *Mulvaney & Ors v. The Sporting Exchange Ltd trading as Betfair* [2009] IEHC 133.

[13] Recitals 42, 44 and Article 12 of the E-Commerce Directive.

as regards claims for damages, is not aware of facts or circumstances from which the illegal activity or information is apparent, (3) upon obtaining such knowledge or awareness, the provider acts expeditiously to remove or to disable access to the information, and (4) the recipient of the service is not acting under the authority or the control of the provider.[14] Hosting safe harbor is thus a typical liability regime for the providers we termed proximate service providers.

Unlike the DMCA,[15] the E-Commerce Directive does not harmonize the ways in which the hosting providers may obtain their knowledge. The case-law of the CJEU only requires[16] that the perspective of a "diligent economic operator" is decisive.[17] The constructive knowledge can be obtained in any situation,[18] including, as a result of an investigation undertaken on the provider's own initiative, as well as a situation in which the operator is notified of the existence of such activity or information, but perhaps not sufficient to constitute actual knowledge.[19] General awareness, however, would not be sufficient.[20] Actual knowledge is, without doubt, triggered when the provider receives a sufficiently precise or adequately substantiated notice. The unanswered question is whether infringement recidivism of the same person upon the same right is to be considered as one or two infringements.[21] If the latter is the case, then actual knowledge would extend to repeated double identity infringements and hence open to proactive duty of care.

Union law thus does not regulate procedure of receiving the necessary knowledge, but leaves it up to the Member States. As a consequence, there are numerous diverging solutions present on the national level, which leads to little legal certainty. The European Commission is therefore currently considering a new directive, the so-called Notice and Action Directive,[22] which would harmonize the procedure of how hosting providers obtain knowledge, process and evaluate it, and eventually act upon it.

Despite the lack of harmonization of the notice and take-down procedure, the Member States are not completely at liberty to implement their own systems.

---

[14] Recital 42 and Article 14 of the E-Commerce Directive.

[15] Digital Millennium Copyright Act, 17 U.S. Code § 512.

[16] Case C-324/09 *L'Oréal and Others* [2011] ECLI:EU:C:2011:474 paras. 121, 122.

[17] Case C-324/09 *L'Oréal and Others* [2010] ECLI:EU:C:2010:757, Opinion of AG Jääskinen, para. 161 (suggesting that the two types of knowledge are mutually exclusive).

[18] Case C-324/09 *L'Oréal and Others* [2011] ECLI:EU:C:2011:474, para. 121.   [19] Ibid., paras. 121, 122.

[20] Case C-324/09 *L'Oréal and Others* [2010] ECLI:EU:C:2010:757, Opinion of AG Jääskinen, para. 163 ("It is not enough that the service provider ought to have known or has good reasons to suspect illegal activity"). Some authors seem to argue that general awareness leads to constructive knowledge – Aleksandra Kuczerawy, "Intermediary Liability & Freedom of Expression: Recent Developments in the EU Notice & Action Initiative" (2014) ICRI Research Paper No. 21, 10.

[21] Case C-324/09 *L'Oréal and Others* [2010] ECLI:EU:C:2010:757, Opinion of AG Jääskinen, para. 167, fn 77 (arguing for autonomous meaning of the term "infringement" that would also include continuation of double identity infringements).

[22] See Aleksandra Kuczerawy, "Intermediary Liability & Freedom of Expression: Recent Developments in the EU Notice & Action Initiative" [2014] ICRI Research Paper No. 21.

Although Recital 46 provides that "the removal or disabling of access has to be undertaken in the observance of the principle of freedom of expression and of procedures established for this purpose at national level" and that "this Directive does not affect Member States' possibility of establishing specific requirements which must be fulfilled expeditiously prior to the removal or disabling of information." After the Lisbon Treaty has now come into effect[23] together with the EU Charter, there is no question now that the local regulations on hosting safe harbors, including the notice and take-down procedure, amount to the implementation of Union law which is subject to its human rights standards.

As will be discussed in Section 8.4, the guarantees of freedom of expression in the EU Charter subsequently became the decisive standard.[24] Therefore, it might no longer always be possible for the Member States to keep all their higher or lower standards of the freedom of expression guarantees.[25] Fortunately, it seems that some members of the CJEU are recognizing this problem and are willing to require, as a matter of Article 11 of the EU Charter, that the alleged infringer has an interest in defending the information posted by him.[26] If this is perceived as a positive obligation of the state, there is a room for revisiting some national notice and take-down schemes or judicial praxis that does not guarantee this to users.

A universal precondition for the applicability of the safe harbors is that of *passivity of providers*. This requirement stems from Recital 42, which, as a result of the Commission-Council legislative ping-pong, paved the way for this ambiguous requirement to enter the case-law. In *Google France*,[27] the CJEU confirmed that it is a general requirement for the *entire* liability-free zone.[28] Although some of the Advocates General later objected to this reading,[29] the CJEU did not change its view,[30] but only slightly modified the arguments used to support it.[31] It therefore became

---

[23] Of course, even before the EU Charter became binding, the had CJEU already applied so-called general principles that included human rights considerations – see discussion of the *Promusicae* case in Chapter 8.

[24] Case C-324/09 *L'Oréal and Others* [2010] ECLI:EU:C:2010:757, Opinion of AG Jääskinen, paras. 156, 157 (listings on a trading platform are protected under Article 11 of the EU Charter in the notice and take down context).

[25] In Finland, for example, national legislation provides, for constitutional reasons (Constitutional Law Committee of the Finnish Parliament, Opinion PeVL 60/2001 vp), that a hosting service provider is required to remove information stored in his system only after having received a court order to that effect in the case of a trademark infringements and upon notice in the case of an alleged infringement of copyright or related rights – Case C-324/09 *L'Oréal and Others* [2010] ECLI:EU:C:2010:757, Opinion of AG Jääskinen, para. 159.

[26] Case C-324/09 *L'Oréal and Others* [2010] ECLI:EU:C:2010:757, Opinion of AG Jääskinen, para. 158.

[27] Cases C-236/08 to C-238/08 *Google France and Google* [2010] ECLI:EU:C:2010:159.

[28] Ibid., paras. 114, 120.

[29] Case C-324/09 *L'Oréal and Others* [2010] ECLI:EU:C:2010:757, Opinion of AG Jääskinen, paras. 139–142, 146 (noting that this reading seriously endangers the objective of the Directive and its framework).

[30] Case C-324/09 *L'Oréal and Others* [2011] ECLI:EU:C:2011:474 para. 116.

[31] The CJEU attempted to defend its position by generally alluding to the "intermediary character" of the services that may be covered (ibid., paras. 111–113) and omitting to mention the critical recital.

crucial to enquire about passivity in order to resolve whether hosting providers such as video-sharing platforms or trading platforms are still entitled to safe harbor.[32]

The condition of passivity, to which the CJEU also refers as a "neutrality condition," is tested by asking whether "[an] operator has not played an active role allowing it to have knowledge or control of the data stored."[33] An instance of such a role, according to the Court, could be when the operator of a trading platform "provides assistance which entails, in particular, optimising the presentation of the offers for sale in question or promoting them."[34] At the same time, however, "the mere fact that the operator of an online marketplace stores offers for sale on its server, sets the terms of its service, is remunerated for that service and provides general information to its customers cannot have the effect of denying it the exemptions from liability."[35]

The issue of neutrality/passivity is key for two reasons. First, the intermediaries not qualifying as passive providers do not qualify for safe harbor of any kind and are thus thrown into the uncharted waters of many national laws. As the recent case of *Delfi v. Estonia*[36] shows, this could also mean landing in the waters of strict liability for acts of third parties. Second, it exponentially increases legal uncertainty because safe harbors, especially for hosting, are built on very easily moving foundations.[37]

Despite this, the condition of passivity also has a potential to improve the Union framework. However, if the CJEU construes passivity very broadly as technical noninteractivity, which is distant from the current business models of most hosting providers,[38] it can essentially empty much of the liability-free zone and make any safe harbor useless for new innovations. The potential, on the other hand, is if the CJEU would use it rather as a filtering tool for what constitutes "third-party information." The latter requires some explanation.

The liability-free zone hinges entirely on the determination of what is "information provided by a recipient of the service." Some countries, such as Germany,

---

[32] Tribunale di Milano, *Reti Televisive Italiane S.p.A. (RTI) v. Yahoo! Italia S.r.l. (Yahoo!) et al.* (2011) Case No. 3821/11 (denying the hosting safe harbor to Yahoo! due to the alleged active character of the service); reversed on appeal Corte d'Appello di Milano, *Reti Televisive Italiane S.p.A. (RTI) v. Yahoo! Italia S.r.l. (Yahoo!) et al.* (2015) Case No. 3821/2011; see also Sophie Stalla-Bourdillon, "Internet Intermediaries as Responsible Actors? Why It Is Time to Rethink the E-Commerce Directive as Well . . . ." in Luciano Floridi and Mariarosaria Taddeo, *The Responsibilities of Online Service Providers* (Springer 2016) 275–293 (discussing the question of active vs. passive hosting).

[33] Case C-324/09 *L'Oréal and Others* [2011] ECLI:EU:C:2011:474 para. 113; Cases C-236/08 to C-238/08 *Google France and Google* [2010] ECLI:EU:C:2010:159, paras. 114 and 120.

[34] Case C-324/09 *L'Oréal and Others* [2011] ECLI:EU:C:2011:474, para. 116.   [35] Ibid., para. 115.

[36] *Delfi AS v. Estonia*, App no. 64569/09 (ECHR, 16 June 2015).

[37] Ansgar Ohly, "Urheberrecht in der digitalen Welt – Brauchen wir neue Regelungen zum Urheberrecht und dessen Durchsetzung?" in Gregor Bachmann (ed.) *Verhandlungen des 70. Deutschen Juristentages* (C. H. Beck, 2014) F 112 (noting the same).

[38] These attempts are currently central in the attempts of the International Federation of the Phonographic Industry to curtail the safe harbors. IFPI claims that the safe harbors cause services such as YouTube to pay less on licensing fees compares to streaming services. See IFPI, "Digital Music Report 2015" (2015), www.ifpi.org/downloads/Digital-Music-Report-2015.pdf.

use a rule according to which "adopted content" of third parties is also treated as intermediary's own.[39] Other countries, such as Estonia, do not shy away from holding a forum provider to be a publisher of third-party comments.[40] For these countries, the presented cases do not involve information provided by a recipient, and so they do *not* apply safe harbors. This is not necessarily incorrect, but one needs to be mindful that in order for the E-Commerce Directive to be effective, and to remove the possibility of the Member States undermining Union law, what constitutes "information provided by a recipient of the service" needs to be *autonomous*. Otherwise classification in the national law can lead to avoidance of the entire Union framework. And this is where the passivity criterion, if applied carefully, could be of assistance.

In other words, passivity precondition could morph into a horizontal test for "third-party information."[41] In the recent case of *Papasavvas*, the Court arguably used the test to this end. The CJEU held that a newspaper may not benefit from the hosting safe harbor vis-à-vis its own articles because, in respect to them, it played an active role which allowed it to have knowledge or control of the data stored.[42] Similarly, in *L'Oréal v. eBay* it could be argued that this criterion served to distinguish between storage and processing of third-party ads on the one hand, and their promotion by own advertising on the other.[43] If the passivity criterion is used to filter out these kinds of cases, then it can even be of benefit to the entire framework.

---

[39] This category of content first appeared in the decision of the German Federal Supreme Court in *marions-kochbuch.de* case (BGH *marions-kochbuch.de* (2009) I ZR 166/07); the test was later summarized in the *RSS-Feed* case (BGH *RSS-Feed* (2013) VI ZR 211/12), in which the Court held that an intermediary "usually makes a third party statement his own when he identifies himself with it and incorporates it into his own chain of thought in such a way that it appears as his own" ("Der Verbreiter macht sich eine fremde Äußerung regelmäßig dann zu eigen, wenn er sich mit ihr identifiziert und sie so in den eigenen Gedankengang einfügt, dass sie als seine eigene erscheint" (§ 19 *RSS-Feed*)). This distinction seems to be brought from media law (Karl Wenzel et al., *Das Recht der Wort- und Bildberichterstattung: Handbuch des Äußerungsrechts* (5th ed., Otto Schmidt 2003) Chapter 4, para. 102ff.; Daniel Holznagel, *Notice and Takedown Verfahren als Teil der Providerhaftung* (Mohr Siebeck 2013) 99ff.), where media would need to distance themselves from the information in order not to be liable for it. In the recent literature, Prof. Ohly, mindful of the potential conflict with "information provided by a recipient of the service," suggested incorporating the doctrine of adopted content into the safe harbor system (see Ansgar Ohly, "Urheberrecht in der digitalen Welt – Brauchen wir neue Regelungen zum Urheberrecht und dessen Durchsetzung?" in Gregor Bachmann (ed.) *Verhandlungen des 70. Deutschen Juristentages* (C. H. Beck, 2014) F 111). The latest case-law develops further this concept (BGH (2016) VI ZR 34/15, para. 17; BGH *Posterlounge* (2015) I ZR 104/14, para. 48).

[40] See facts in *Delfi AS v. Estonia*, App no. 64569/09 (ECHR, 10 October 2013); but also *Metropolitan International Schools Ltd. (t/a Skillstrain and/or Train2game) v. Designtechnica Corp (t/a Digital Trends) & Ors* [2009] EWHC 1765 (QB) (discussing whether a search engine can qualify as a publisher in common law).

[41] In this direction also Georg Nolte and Jörg Wimmers, "Wer stört? Gedanken zur Haftung von Intermediären im Internet – von praktischer Konkordanz, richtigen Anreizen und offenen Fragen" [2014] GRUR 16, 20ff.

[42] Case C-291/13 *Papasavvas* [2014] ECLI:EU:C:2014:2209, paras. 44, 45.

[43] Case C-324/09 *L'Oréal and Others* [2010] ECLI:EU:C:2010:757, Opinion of AG Jääskinen, para. 144.

Moreover, after the early criticism by the Advocate General Jääskinen,[44] the CJEU attempted to defend its position by generally alluding to the "intermediary character" of the services that may be covered and omitting to mention the critical recital.[45] This would also support the position presented here that the rationale of passivity requirement is to draw a division line between one's own and third-party content, and not to narrow down the hosting safe harbor.

Such use of the criterion could allow the Court to better signal the Directive's breadth to the Member States, and also to synchronize the safe harbors with the Union direct infringement tests, such as one for communication to the public.[46] The notion of "third-party information" in the E-Commerce Directive could also act as a mold for direct attribution of acts in copyright law. Thus the persons co-intervening in the communication to the public would be construed as not processing third-party information, but already adopting the information as their own. AG Szpunar recently proposed a step in this direction.[47]

4.2 INJUNCTIONS AGAINST INTERMEDIARIES

To understand the legal framework concerning injunctions against intermediaries, one needs to first look into the structure of the E-Commerce Directive. The Directive provides that the "Member States shall ensure that the service provider is not liable for the information" of third parties that it stores (Article 14(1)) or transmits (Article 12(1)). However, some forms of liability are not exempted because each safe harbor includes a legislative carve-out for a "possibility for a court or administrative authority, in accordance with Member States' legal systems, to require a service provider to terminate or prevent an infringement."[48] As was explained in Chapter 3, this was added as a substitute for the initially proposed "shall not be liable, otherwise than under a prohibitory injunction" wording. The interplay of the general exclusions of "liability" and their carve-outs for authorities is not a simple one and co-defines the role of injunctions against intermediaries.

---

[44] Ibid., paras. 139–142, 146 (noting that this reading seriously endangers the objective of the Directive and its framework).

[45] Case C-324/09 *L'Oréal and Others* [2011] ECLI:EU:C:2011:474 paras. 111–113.

[46] English courts have already interpreted the communication to the public right to include also intermediaries who *intervened* in the distribution of the content of their users – see *Twentieth Century Fox Film Corporation & Anor v. Newzbin Ltd* [2010] EWHC 608 (Ch).

[47] Case C-610/15 *Stichting Brein* [2017] ECLI:EU:C:2017:99, Opinion of AG Szpunar, para. 53 ("The intervention of those operators therefore meets the conditions of being necessary and deliberate, laid down in the case-law of the Court. Those operators should therefore in my view also be considered, simultaneously and jointly with the users of the network, as originating the making available to the public of works that are shared on the network without the consent of the copyright holders, if they are aware of that illegality and do not take action to make access to such works impossible").

[48] Art. 12(2), Art 13(2) and Art 14(3) of the E-Commerce Directive.

Since the Directive addresses any possible consequences, including administrative and criminal, it prescribes broadly that the "liability" is to be prevented,[49] if the conditions of the safe harbors are met. Only the hosting safe harbor of Article 14(1)(a) specifies that "as regards claims for damages," certain more relaxed conditions are applicable. For private law, "liability" (*Verantwortlichkeit*), in this context, equals to noncontractual obligations. And those come in many forms:[50] injunctions, damages, unjust enrichment, negotiorum gestio, culpa in contrahendo and other obligations arising out of tort/delict, for instance the right to an apology or information. What form "liability" is, then, exempted by means of a "carve-out"?

In the case-law of the CJEU, but also in the scholarly literature, there seems to be little doubt that the court-imposed injunctions should fall under this carve-out.[51] A carve-out of the obligation resulting from right to third-party information[52] is further supported by Article 15(2) of the E-Commerce Directive. The dividing line between a "possibility of requiring to prevent an infringement" (carve-out) and

---

[49] Art. 12(1), Art 13(1) and Art 14(1) of the E-Commerce Directive.

[50] See the typology in the Regulation (EC) No 864/2007 of the European Parliament and of the Council of 11 July 2007 on the law applicable to noncontractual obligations (Rome II) [2007] L 199/40.

[51] Christina Angelopolous, "Filtering the Internet for Copyright Content in Europe" [2009] IRIS Plus 5; Darren Meale, "NewzBin2: The First Section 97A Injunction against an ISP" (2011) 6 Journal of Intellectual Property Law & Practice 854–857; Miquel Peguera, "Internet Service Providers' Liability in Spain: Recent Case Law and Future Perspectives" (2010) 1 JIPITEC 151, 154, 160; Helmut Koziol, "Providerhaftung nach ECG und MedienG" in Walter Berka, Christopher Grabenwarter and Michael Holoubek (eds.) *Persönlichkeitsschutz in elektronischen Massenmedien* (Manz Verlag, 2012) 41–55; Halldórsdóttir Hjördis, "Enforcement of Copyright" (2004) 47 Scandinavian Studies in Law 168; Sandfeld Jakobsen, "Injunctions Against Mere Conduit of Information Protected by Copyright – A Scandinavian Perspective" (2011) IIC 151; Sandfeld Jakobsen, "Mobile Commerce and ISP Liability in the EU" (2011) 1 International Journal Law Information Technology 46; Christopher Czychowski and Jan Nordemann, "Grenzenloses Internet – entgrenzte Haftung?" [2013] GRUR 986, 987; Jörg Reinbothe, "Die EG-Richtlinie zum Urheberrecht in der Informationsgesellschaft" [2001] GRUR Int 733, 743; Gerald Spindler, "Europäisches Urheberrecht in der Informationsgesellschaft" [2002] GRUR 105, 119; Thomas Dreier, "Die Umsetzung der Urheberrechtsrichtlinie 2001/29/EG in deutsches Recht" [2002] ZUM 28, 41; Christian Czychowski, "Auskunftsansprüche gegenüber Internetzugangsprovidern „vor" dem 2. Korb und 'nach' der Enforcement-Richtlinie der EU" [2004] MMR 514, 516; Stefan Freytag, "Verantwortlichkeit für rechtswidrige Inhalte nach der E-Commerce-Richtlinie" [2000] CR 600, 605; Arndt Berger and Ruth Janal, "Suchet und Ihr werdet finden? Eine Untersuchung zur Störerhaftung von Online-Auktionshäusern" [2004] CR 917–925.

[52] For the German debate on the conflict of right to third-party information and the safe harbors, see Gerald Spindler and Joachim Dorschel, "Vereinbarkeit der geplanten Auskunftsansprüche gegen Internet-Provider mit EU-Recht" [2006] CR 341, 345 (arguing that an obligation to surrender information does not constitute "liability"); Gerald Spindler, "Europäisches Urheberrecht in der Informationsgesellschaft" [2002] GRUR 105, 119; Jörg Reinbothe, "Die EG-Richtlinie zum Urheberrecht in der Informationsgesellschaft" [2001] GRUR Int 733, 743; Thomas Dreier, "Die Umsetzung der Urheberrechtsrichtlinie 2001/29/EG in deutsches Recht" [2002] ZUM 28, 41; Stefan Freytag, "Verantwortlichkeit für rechtswidrige Inhalte nach der E-Commerce-Richtlinie" [2000] CR 600, 605; Christian Czychowski, "Auskunftsansprüche gegenüber Internetzugangsprovidern 'vor' dem 2. Korb und „nach" der Enforcement-Richtlinie der EU" [2004] MMR 514, 516; Ulrich Sieber and Frank Michael, "Drittauskunftsansprüche nach § 101a UrhG gegen Internetprovider zur Verfolgung von Urheberrechtsverletzungen" [2004] MMR 575, 580; Volker Kitz, "§ 101 a UrhG: Für eine Rückkehr zur Dogmatik" [2005] ZUM 298, 301.

absence of "liability" (safe harbor) is conventionally interpreted as a general green light for nonpecuniary claims, even for providers in the liability-free-zone. This characterization is, however, too simplified.

If all noncontractual claims fall under the term "liability," but all "nonpecuniary" claims are excluded by means of the exception, this would mean, for instance, that the coercion fines for disrespecting a court-imposed injunction are barred by a safe harbor, whereas a court-imposed prohibition of exercising specific professional activity is exempted by it. Even though a coercion fine is clearly pecuniary, if it is targeted at enforcing "carve-out" measures, it serves only enforcement of already accepted justice. On the other hand, even a nonpecuniary obligation, e.g., prohibition of the entire professional activity can effectively amount to a sanction for conduct. Although it is not calculated in money, it certainly has an effect equivalent to any other criminal or administrative pecuniary liability. Therefore, the division between pecuniary and nonpecuniary "liability" cannot hold.

In *Mc Fadden*, the Court confirmed that monetary character is not a decisive one in order to qualify for the legislative "carve-out." The Advocate General suggested to hold that "[the] limitation of liability extends not only to claims for compensation, but also to any other pecuniary claim that entails a finding of liability for copyright infringement with respect to the information transmitted, such as a claim for the reimbursement of pre-litigation costs or court costs."[53] The mere conduits, in his view, "may incur liability only after a specific obligation contemplated by Article 12(3) of E-Commerce Directive has been imposed on him" and thus not before the safe harbor is lost or an injunction granted.[54] This proposition wouldn't limit posttrial compliance costs, however.

The Court did not follow the advice. It ruled that although both pretrial costs and litigation costs are form of "liability" in sense of Article 12(1), given that the injunctive relief granted by court or an administrative authority is exempted by Article 12(3), also the costs associated with it should be.[55] Putting other possible consequences aside, this means that nonpecuniary character is not the decisive one when assessing the extent of the carve-out from the safe harbors. What is it then?

The dividing line, it is submitted, should be rather in the nature of the remedy sought. If the remedy aims to sanction a person for the acts of third parties, it should remain covered by the safe harbor, since it imposes legal consequences for its own acts. If it aims to secure cooperation against the acts of third parties, it should, also as a form of "liability," be able to rely on the carve-out, since it asks for assistance to "terminate or prevent an infringement."[56] One might object that this

---

53 Case C-484/14 *Mc Fadden* [2016] ECLI:EU:C:2016:170, Advocate General Szpunar, para. 74.
54 Martin Husovec, "Holey Cap! CJEU Drills (Yet) Another Hole in the E-Commerce Directive's Safe Harbors" (2017) 12(2) Journal of Intellectual Property Law & Practice 115–125 (discussing the broader consequences).
55 Ibid., 119; Case C-484/14 *Mc Fadden* [2016] ECLI:EU:C:2016:689, para. 101.
56 Czychowski and Nordemann also suggest that penalties are covered (Christopher Czychowski and Jan Nordemann, "Grenzenloses Internet – entgrenzte Haftung?" [2013] GRUR 986, 987: "Die

merely translates the problem into a new sanction versus cooperation distinction. The problem is that, given the horizontal nature of the Directive, it is hardly possible to draw any clear-cut boundaries. Eventually, the interpretation needs to be strictly teleological, thus following the very aim of the Directive. This framing, in my view, offers a lot of guidance.

It disarms the criticism that *Mc Fadden* might open doors too widely for the monetary claims.[57] The "sanction-cooperation" distinction allows the Court to moderate acceptance of remedies on the level of their exact consequences. Pretrial or procedural costs can be restricted to their reasonable nondissuasive amounts. Injunctions can be restricted to nonsanctioning forms of assistance in enforcement.[58]

If one reads the central part of the jigsaw, the E-Commerce Directive, in this way, it is also easier to understand the concept of injunctions against intermediaries. Such injunctions should then serve as a cooperation tool only, never as a tool of sanction. Several "injunction-internal" arguments can be offered in support of this. First, the legislative history of both Article 8(3) of the InfoSoc Directive and Article 11 of the Enforcement Directive. Second, it is the systematic argument of the InfoSoc and the Enforcement Directive. And third, coherence of the Union legal order created by the InfoSoc, Enforcement, and E-Commerce Directives.

To begin with, the legislative history supports this reading, since the attempt of the Committee on Legal Affairs and the Internal Market to amend the provisions of the Enforcement Directive as overlapping rules (which would be targeting only intermediaries who are "infringers") was eventually rejected. This shows an interpretation maintaining the mutual exclusivity of the two. In the resulting text of Article 11 of the Enforcement Directive, the obligation to provide a recurring penalty payment for noncompliance with an injunction is systematically limited to proceedings against infringers, as was initially proposed, thus indicating different treatment. Even clearer is the Commission's reply to the Council from 2000, concerning the newly proposed Article 8(3) of the InfoSoc Directive:

> the provision obliges Member States to ensure that rightholders are in a position to apply for an injunction against intermediaries whose services are used by third parties to infringe a copyright or related right. *Such a possibility may not be made dependent on the lawfulness of the acts of intermediaries.* The Commission welcomes this useful clarification.[59]

Privilegierung gilt nur für Schadensersatzansprüche (und damit zusammenhängende Ansprüche wie sie vorbereitende Auskunftsansprüche) und für bußgeld- sowie strafrechtliche Sanktionen, aber nicht für Unterlassungsansprüche"); Case C-70/10 *Scarlet Extended* [2011] ECLI:EU:C:2011:255, Opinion of AG Villalón, fn 36 (suggesting that the penalties are understood as a sanction).

57 Martin Husovec, "Holey Cap! CJEU Drills (Yet) Another Hole in the E-Commerce Directive's Safe Harbors" (2017) 12(2) Journal of Intellectual Property Law & Practice 115, 119.

58 Sir Robin Jacob in *Samsung Electronics (UK) Ltd v. Apple Inc* [2012] EWCA Civ 1339 [81] (the point is not to punish the party by a publicity order).

59 Commission, "Communication from the Commission to the European Parliament pursuant to the second subparagraph of Article 251 (2) of the EC Treaty concerning the common position of the

This again indicates that the legislator intended the distinction between infringing intermediaries on the one hand, and noninfringing on the other.[60]

From a systematic point of view, both Article 8(3) InfoSoc Directive and Article 11(III) of the Enforcement Directive deal with injunctions against intermediaries *after* remedies against infringers. In the InfoSoc Directive, injunctions against intermediaries appear after Article 8(1), which deals with "sanctions and remedies in respect of infringements of the rights and obligations."[61] In the Enforcement Directive they appear after the first sentence of Article 11, which refers to the power of "the judicial authorities [to] issue against the infringer an injunction."

A similar position on the nature of injunctions is presented by the European Commission itself. In the official report on the application of the Enforcement Directive, it states:

> Injunctions against intermediaries are *not intended as a penalty* against them, but are simply based on the fact that such intermediaries (e.g., internet service providers) are in certain cases in the best position to stop or to prevent an infringement. This interpretation is confirmed by Articles 12(3), 13(2) and 14(3) and by Recital 45 of the e-commerce Directive and Recital 59 of Directive 2001/29/EC on the harmonization of certain aspects of copyright and related rights in the information society.[62]

The CJEU slowly developed this position as well. In *L'Oréal v. eBay*, the Court rephrased the question of the referring court as asking "[whether the] provision requires the Member States to ensure that the operator of an online marketplace may, *regardless of any liability of its own* in relation to the facts at issue, be ordered to take, in addition to measures aimed at bringing to an end infringements of intellectual property rights brought about by users of its services, measures aimed at preventing further infringements of that kind." The CJEU then used a contextual reading of Article 11 to point out that injunctions against intermediaries *differ* from "injunctions

---

Council on the adoption of a Directive of the European Parliament and of the Council on the harmonisation of certain aspects of copyright and related rights in the information Society" (2000) 1734 final (emphasis mine).

[60] Similar can be inferred from: Commission, "Staff Working Document: Analysis of the application of Directive 2004/48/EC of the European Parliament and the Council of 29 April 2004 on the enforcement of intellectual property rights in the Member States" COM(2010) 779 final, 13, 16, 17.

[61] Article 8 of the InfoSoc Directive appears under the heading of "Sanctions and remedies."

[62] Commission, "Staff Working Document: Analysis of the application of Directive 2004/48/EC of the European Parliament and the Council of 29 April 2004 on the enforcement of intellectual property rights in the Member States – accompanying document to the Report from the Commission to the Council, the European Parliament and the European Social Committee on the application of Directive 2004/48/EC of the European Parliament and the Council of 29 April 2004 on the enforcement of intellectual property rights" COM(2010) 779 final (emphasis mine); European Observatory on Counterfeiting and Piracy, "Injunctions in Intellectual Property Right," http://ec.europa.eu/internal_market/iprenforcement/docs/injunctions_en.pdf ("despite the fact that under the IPRED, injunctive relief is not conditional on the intermediary being liable").

which may be obtained against infringers of an intellectual property right,"[63] thus suggesting that Article 11(III) covers *only* noninfringing intermediaries. This also reflects the more articulated position of Advocate General Kokott in *Frisdranken* who opined that "in contrast to the sanction applicable where an intermediary infringes a trademark, the third sentence of Article 11 of Directive 2004/48 does not provide for damages, these can be obtained in accordance with the national provisions governing participation in a tort or delict."[64] In her view, the referring court "appears to presume that claims against the service provider presuppose such an infringement," which is "incorrect."[65] The Advocate General here clearly agrees that assuming a prerequisite of an infringement is incorrect and also, that injunctions against intermediaries have to be contrasted with the "sanction applicable where an intermediary infringes."

In *UPC Telekabel Wien*, the Court, then refers to an Internet access provider as someone who "is not the author of the infringement of the fundamental right of intellectual property which has led to the adoption of the injunction"[66] and, in *Tele2*, it says that the dispute in a lawsuit against a provider is "not [about] whether [it] has infringed."[67] And finally, in *Tommy Hilfiger*, the Court explicitly summarizes its own case-las as follows:

> It is settled case-law that the third sentence of Article 11 of Directive 2004/48, like Article 8(3) of Directive 2001/29 to which it refers, obliges Member States to ensure that an intermediary whose services are used by a third party in order to infringe an intellectual property right may, *regardless of any liability of its own in relation to the facts at issue*, be ordered to take measures aimed at bringing those infringements to an end and measures seeking to prevent further infringements.[68]

The third argument in favor of this reading is Recital 16 of the InfoSoc Directive which provides that "this Directive should be implemented within a timescale similar to that for the implementation of the Directive on electronic commerce, since that Directive provides a harmonized framework of principles and provisions relevant inter alia to important parts of this Directive" and that the "Directive is without prejudice to provisions relating to liability in that Directive." Similarly, Recital 15 of the Enforcement Directive states that "this Directive should not affect (. . .) Directive 2000/31/EC." This means that the Union legislator did not intend

---

[63] Case C-324/09 *L'Oréal and Others* [2010] ECLI:EU:C:2011:474, para. 128; see also discussion of this point in Pekka Savola, *Internet Connectivity Providers as Involuntary Copyright Enforcers: Blocking Websites in Particular* (IPR University Center, 2015) 71.

[64] Case C-119/10 *Frisdranken Industrie Winters* [2011] ECLI:EU:C:2011:258, Opinion of AG Kokott, para. 39.

[65] Ibid.   [66] Case C-314/12 *UPC Telekabel Wien* [2014] ECLI:EU:C:2014:192, para. 53.

[67] Case C-557/07 *LSG-Gesellschaft zur Wahrnehmung von Leistungsschutzrechten* [2009] ECLI:EU:C:2009:107, para. 36.

[68] Case C-494/15 *Tommy Hilfiger Licensing and Others* [2016] ECLI:EU:C:2016:528 (emphasis mine).

to amend the E-Commerce Directive, neither with the InfoSoc Directive, nor with the Enforcement Directive. It wanted only to *complement* it.[69]

But if the provisions on injunctions against intermediaries were meant to complement the exemptions from the liability-free-zone, then the nature of the remedies *permitted* (Directive 2000/31/EC) and *prescribed* (Directive 2001/29/EC, Directive 2004/48/EC) should be the same. Certainly, the injunctions against intermediaries cover a wider range of service providers than just those covered by the three safe harbors, but in order for injunctions to fit into these very frequently applied regulatory schemes, there is no room for contradiction. If the injunctions were prescribed even in cases when they are not permitted, there would be an open conflict between the directives, which are not supposed to clash in any way.

Are there signs of such a clash? Injunctions are prescribed by requiring that rightholders "are in a position *to apply* for an injunction." This clearly refers to application before either a court or an administrative authority. It is no coincidence that the E-Commerce Directive permits measures "requiring the service provider to terminate or prevent an infringement" *only* "for a court or administrative authority." Article 8(3) of the InfoSoc Directive and Article 11(III) of the Enforcement Directive thus both fit into the exemptions of the E-Commerce Directive's safe harbors[70] like keys in the keyholes. So if the nature of keyholes in the E-Commerce Directive is to permit cooperation remedies, the keys of the InfoSoc and Enforcement Directive should be designed in exactly the same way in order to fit well into each other.[71]

Advocate General Szpunar recently remarked what could be interpreted as a confirmation of the above argument:

> The derogations in respect of the liability of intermediary providers contained in Directive 2000/31 constitute one of the factors in the balance between the different interests at stake, introduced by that directive according to recital 41 thereof. The counterpart of those derogations, in the context of that balance, is not only the absence of any complicity of intermediary providers in infringements of the law, but also their cooperation in order to avoid or prevent such infringements. They cannot escape that obligation by claiming, according to the circumstances, that the measures [to be imposed by injunctions] are either over-restrictive or ineffective.[72]

In conclusion, the injunctions against intermediaries target noninfringers and follow the goal of assistance and not of sanctions. The measures prescribed by Article 8(3) InfoSoc Directive and Article 11(III) of the Enforcement Directive are therefore

---

[69] Justice Arnold in his decision *Twentieth Century Fox Film Corp & Ors v. British Telecommunications Plc* [2011] EWHC 1981 (Ch) [152] (expressing similar view).

[70] A similar idea is presented by Thomas Dreier, "Die Umsetzung der Urheberrechtsrichtlinie 2001/29/EG in deutsches Recht" [2002] ZUM 28, 41.

[71] The CJEU seems to endorse such synchronization – see Case C-324/09 *L'Oréal and Others* [2011] ECLI:EU:C:2011:474 paras. 131–132.

[72] Case C-610/15 *Stichting Brein* [2017] ECLI:EU:C:2017:99, Opinion of AG Szpunar, para. 83.

better understood as some obligatory cooperation remedies imposing accountability without liability available before the authorities.[73]

4.3 SECONDARY LIABILITY

Union law, by prescribing the scope of different rights, profoundly regulates who the *direct infringers*, actors "using" intellectual property rights, are.[74] Secondary or accessory (tort) liability, the liability of nonactors for actors, which predominantly regulates intermediaries,[75] is mostly an issue of the Member States.[76] From existing Union law, only the anticircumvention provisions of the InfoSoc Directive and the Software Directive contain some provisions targeting nonactors to this end.[77] Otherwise, the Member States apply their national bodies of tort law or specific local provisions on negligence, accomplice, or contributory law to supplement the gap left by the Union legislator.[78] It is mostly these *domestic* doctrines that affect

---

[73] Commission, "Communication from the Commission to the European Parliament pursuant to the second subparagraph of Article 251 (2) of the EC Treaty concerning the common position of the Council on the adoption of a Directive of the European Parliament and of the Council on the harmonisation of certain aspects of copyright and related rights in the information Society" (2000) 1734 final ("However, neither Article 11 (third sentence) of the Directive, nor Article 8(3) of Directive 2001/29 link injunctions with the liability of an intermediary"); Martin Husovec, "Injunctions Against Innocent Third Parties: Case of Website Blocking" (2013) 4 JIPITEC 116, 118; Martin Husovec and Miquel Peguera, "Much Ado about Little – Privately Litigated Disconnecting Injunctions" [2015] IIC 10, 20; Christopher Czychowski and Jan Nordemann, "Grenzenloses Internet – entgrenzte Haftung?" [2013] GRUR 986, 988 (understand injunctions against intermediaries also as a kind of cooperation remedy (Hilfleistungspflicht) required from them although they did nothing (legally) wrong); Franz Hofmann, "Markenrechtliche Sperranordnungen gegen nicht verantwortliche Intermediäre" [2015] GRUR 123 (speaking about "non-liable intermediaries").

[74] If the safe harbors are synchronized with the scope of rights (Case C-119/10 *Frisdranken Industrie Winters* [2011] ECLI:EU:C:2011:837; Cases C-236/08 to C-238/08 *Google France and Google* [2010] ECLI:EU:C:2010:159), there is no problem. If the two are not synchronized, however, for instance because such a possibility does not lie with the CJEU, the safe harbors could even limit direct liability. Justice Arnold considered a possible clash of this kind in his referral to the CJEU in *L'Oreal SA v. eBay International AG* [2009] RPC 21 Chancery Division, [45(a)]; Case C-324/09 *L'Oréal and Others* [2010] ECLI:EU:C:2010:757, Opinion of AG Jääskinen (asking whether the hosting safe harbor would apply even if the intermediary were directly infringing).

[75] Case C-324/09 *L'Oréal and Others* [2010] ECLI:EU:C:2010:757, Opinion of AG Jääskinen, para. 55 (safe harbors are partial harmonization of liability).

[76] Case C-119/10 *Frisdranken Industrie Winters* [2011] ECLI:EU:C:2011:258, Opinion of AG Kokott, para. 39; Case C-324/09 *L'Oréal and Others* [2010] ECLI:EU:C:2010:757, Opinion of AG Jääskinen, para. 56 (noting that joint tortfeasorship, contributory and vicarious liability are outside of the proceedings, and hence most likely implying outside of EU law); Cases C-236/08 to C-238/08 *Google France and Google* [2009] ECLI:EU:C:2009:569, Opinion of the AG Maduro, para. 48.

[77] Martin Husovec and Miquel Peguera, "Much Ado about Little – Privately Litigated Disconnecting Injunctions" (2015) 46 IIC 10, 12; Martin Husovec, "Injunctions Against Innocent Third Parties: Case of Website Blocking" (2013) 4 JIPITEC 116, 120.

[78] Case C-324/09 *L'Oréal and Others* [2010] ECLI:EU:C:2010:757, Opinion of AG Jääskinen, para. 55 ("This case also concerns something which I will call 'secondary liability': it refers here to the possible liability of an information society service provider for infringements committed by users of the service.

Internet intermediaries. The only European provisions that the domestic courts have to take note of are the E-Commerce Directive's safe harbors concerning selected "information society service providers,"[79] very general limits of intellectual property enforcement within the Enforcement Directive and, of course, the provisions on injunctions against intermediaries.

Although secondary infringers are not defined by the Union law, injunctions, as well as other remedies prescribed by the Enforcement Directive against "infringers," arguably cover also them.[80] One could object that this is undesirable as it leaves the concept of "infringer" impossible to define on the Union level, since its content would be observable only following a reference to national law. But this is hardly a convincing objection. It assumes that direct infringements are always harmonized in the European intellectual property laws. This is simply not the case. Maybe trademark and design laws are fully harmonized on this issue, but even the harmonization of the copyright laws does not exhaust all the exclusive rights.[81] As a consequence, there might well be other exclusive rights which could be directly infringed upon, and which are not possible to determine on the Union level. The legislator surely did not want to limit the reach of the Directive only to harmonized exclusive rights and their respective direct infringements. This would omit from the scope of the Directive all nonharmonized exclusive rights of harmonized subject matter (e.g., copyright), rights to nonharmonized subject matter (e.g., utility models) and most of the secondary infringements (e.g., aiding and abetting). This is not a tenable position.

The Directive covers all the remedies irrespective of whether the subject matter or rights at stake are harmonized. This is expressly stipulated by Article 2(1) of the Directive, which states that: "the measures, procedures and remedies provided for by this Directive shall apply (. . .) to any infringement of intellectual property rights

---

As the High Court rightly notes, this type of liability for trademark infringements committed by others is not harmonized in EU trademark legislation but is a matter of national law. There is no provision in EU law requiring businesses to prevent trademark infringements by third parties or to refrain from acts or practices that might contribute to or facilitate such infringements. However, partial harmonisation of such liability, or more precisely, conditions of its absence, is provided by Articles 12, 13 and 14 of Directive 2000/31"); Case C-610/15 *Stichting Brein* [2017] ECLI:EU:C:2017:99, Opinion of AG Szpunar, para. 65; On the point of domestic doctrines, see the recent comparative works of Jaani Riordan and Christina Angelopolous (Jaani Riordan, *The Liability of Internet Intermediaries* (Oxford, 2016); Christina Angelopoulos, *European Intermediary Liability in Copyright. A Tort-Based Analysis* (Kluwer Law International, 2016)).

79 The term "information society service providers" is more narrow than the term "intermediary" used in Article 8(3) of the InfoSoc Directive and Article 11 of the Enforcement Directive, and, of course, also more narrow than "any other person [than infringer]" required in the context of the claim for information under Article 8(1) of the Enforcement Directive.

80 This also allows that injunctions against intermediaries are mutually exclusive with injunctions against infringers.

81 Thomas Dreier and Bernt Hugenholtz (eds.) *Concise European Copyright Law* (2nd ed., Wolters Kluwer 2016) 3.

as provided for by Community law and/or by the national law of the Member State concerned." The term "infringer" is thus to be understood as a person who engages in "any infringement of intellectual property rights as provided for by (. . .) the national law," including secondary infringers.[82]

Moreover, the same broad understanding of an "infringer" is also present in some other parts of the Enforcement Directive such as "infringer and/or any third party" (Article 8(3)) and "used by third parties to infringe" (Article 11). These examples show what kind of illogical results it would lead to, if we were to accept that only direct infringers are "infringers" in the sense of the Directive. It would narrow down their scope since an intermediary could no longer be asked to assist in the prevention of secondary infringements, but only of direct ones. This means, for instance, that a regular website blocking injunction against a secondary infringing website would not be possible. Perhaps this is also why the scholarship or case-law of the Member States does not appear to usually argue this way.[83] However, recently, the Dutch courts seemed unwilling to classify domestic tortious liability provided on top of copyright primary liability as a form of "infringement" in sense of Article 8(3) of the InfoSoc Directive.[84] Classifying tortious liable aiders, abettors, instigators or copyright-specific authorizers as "infringers" is not merely doctrinal issue, but has number of important consequences.

---

[82] See also Case C-681/13 *Diageo Brands* [2015] ECLI:EU:C:2015:137, para. 72 ("in accordance with Article 1 thereof, Directive 2004/48 concerns all the measures, procedures and remedies necessary to ensure the enforcement of intellectual property rights. Article 2(1) of that directive states that those measures, procedures and remedies apply to any infringement of those rights as provided for by EU law and/or by the national law of the Member State concerned").

[83] If the person who uses the services of an Internet access provider is not a user, but the targeted website in a website blocking case, the infringing acts often rely on the secondary liability of those websites. This is most likely the case even in the situation that gave rise to the *UPC Telekabel Wien* reference, but also in other national cases in the UK, such as *Twentieth Century Fox Film Corp v. British Telecommunications plc* [2011] EWHC 1981 (Ch) (the website operator is secondarily liable for joint tortfeasorship and authorization of an infringement); *Twentieth Century Fox Film Corp v. British Telecommunications plc (No 2)* [2011] EWHC 2714 (Ch); *Dramatico Entertainment Ltd v. British Sky Broadcasting Ltd* [2012] EWHC 268 (Ch) [81], [83] (the website operator is secondarily liable for joint tortfeasorship and authorization of an infringement); *Dramatico Entertainment Ltd v. British Sky Broadcasting Ltd (No 2)* [2012] EWHC 1152 (Ch); *EMI Records Ltd v. British Sky Broadcasting Ltd* [2013] EWHC 379 (Ch), [70], [74] (the website operator is secondarily liable for joint tortfeasorship and authorization of an infringement); *Football Association Premier League Ltd v. British Sky Broadcasting Ltd* [2013] EWHC 2058 (Ch) [43] (the website operator is alternatively also secondarily liable for joint tortfeasorship); *Paramount Home Entertainment International Ltd v. British Sky Broadcasting Ltd* [2013] EWHC 3479 (Ch) [35] (the website operator is alternatively also secondarily liable for joint tortfeasorship); Michel M. Walter and Dominik Goebel, "Enforcement Directive" in Michel Walter and Silke von Lewinski (eds.), *European Copyright Law: A Commentary* (OUP 2010) § 8 (as for information claims, they include both direct and secondary infringers in the scope of the term).

[84] Martin Husovec and Lisa van Dongen, "Website Blocking, Injunctions and Beyond: View on the Harmonization from the Netherlands" [2017] GRUR 9.

First of all, it opens up the principles of the Enforcement Directive also to secondary infringers. Second, it broadens, among other things, the reach of injunctions against intermediaries. Third, enforcement of any right that qualifies as "intellectual property" under the Directive, including by means of secondary liability, is consequently *constrained* by Article 3. Fourth, this opens the scope of applicability of the EU Charter, which applies to *all* the national provisions "when they are implementing Union law" (Article 51(1)). Effectively, therefore, any constitutional ceiling of *any* intellectual property enforcement is an issue of the Union. This means that although the Union law does not explicitly prescribe secondary liability, it can moderate its excessive forms. A recent judgment of the Court in a Polish preliminary reference suggests that Article 3 can have biting contours.[85]

Without the harmonization of a central part of the intermediary liability puzzle – the accessory liability, there are, in theory, at least three ways in which the CJEU generally can approach secondary liability in tort without a legislative intervention. The first is (1) to simply acknowledge that it is the law of the Member States governs the grounds for tortious secondary liability and only engage in moderation of its excessive forms through Article 3 of the Enforcement Directive and fundamental rights. The second is to engage in a judicial activism (2) by creating autonomous common criteria for accessory liability on the top of the scope of the rights. And the third is to respond by (3) incorporating ad hoc solutions of the secondary liability directly into the scope of the rights. The existing case-law does not seem to pursue a single trend but their mix. Moreover, the differences between (2) and (3) might be blurred.

The CJEU case-law contains several opinions of Advocates General remarking that secondary liability is *not* harmonized. Jääskinen, Maduro, Kokott, and Szpunar all made remarks to this extent in their opinions.[86] Lack of Union secondary liability thus appears to be a prevailing opinion. In *L'Oréal v. eBay*, even the Court explicitly held that "[i]t is therefore in the context of national law that the conditions under which such liability arises must be sought."[87]

---

[85] Case C–367/15 Stowarzyszenie *"Oławska Telewizja Kablowa* [2017] ECLI:EU:C:2017:36, para. 31; Igor Nestoruk, "Dreifacher pauschaler Schadensersatz im polnischen Urheberrecht aus verfassungsrechtlicher" [2017] GRUR Int. 12 (providing background of the case).

[86] Case C–119/10 *Frisdranken Industrie Winters* [2011] ECLI:EU:C:2011:258, Opinion of AG Kokott, para. 39; Case C–324/09 *L'Oréal and Others* [2010] ECLI:EU:C:2010:757, Opinion of AG Jääskinen, para. 56 (noting that joint tortfeasorship, contributory and vicarious liability are outside of the proceedings, and hence most likely implying outside of EU law); Cases C–236/08 to C–238/08 *Google France and Google* [2009] ECLI:EU:C:2009:569, Opinion of the AG Maduro, para. 48; Case C–610/15 *Stichting Brein* [2017] ECLI:EU:C:2017:99, Opinion of AG Szpunar, para. 65 ("If the operator in question does not itself carry out the act covered by the author's exclusive rights (for example, communication to the public), the infringement is only indirect. Given the fact that liability for that type of infringement is not harmonised at the level of EU law, express provision must be made for it under national law. It is for national courts to ascertain whether such liability exists in their domestic law").

[87] Case C–324/09 *L'Oréal and Others* [2011]ECLI:EU:C:2011:474, para. 107.

At the same time, at least in one case, the CJEU could be said to attempt to create some form of Union secondary liability doctrine.[88] In the *Donner* case,[89] arguably tried to read a test for secondary infringements into the notion of an autonomous "distribution right," when it said:

> [a] trader in such circumstances bears responsibility for any act carried out by him [. . .] or on *his behalf giving rise to a "distribution to the public" in a Member State where the goods distributed are protected by copyright.* [. . .] Any such act carried out by a third party may also be attributed to him, where he specifically targeted the public of the State of destination and *must have been aware of the actions of that third party.*[90]

The Court thus mentions two special circumstances, when acts of third party that amount to "distribution to the public" could be attributed to somebody else. These are: (1) when a third party acts "on his behalf" or (2) when he "must have been aware of the actions of that third party." This would suggest that *attribution of liability* is a mechanism of Union law that can provide some protection even beyond the actual scope of the rights. Surprisingly, there is zero scholarship analyzing this point or case-law following up on this approach. On the other hand, this path might have supporters even in some of the Member States. English judge, Arnold J, for instance, stated following in his *L'Oréal v. eBay International* ruling:

> I can conceive that it might nevertheless be argued that the Trade Marks Directive *did* approximate national laws on accessory liability in the context of infringement of national trade marks to some extent. It might also be argued that the Community Trade Mark Regulation *implicitly regulated the question of accessory liability in the context of infringement of Community trade marks to some extent.* In the present case, however, it was common ground between counsel that there was no conflict between domestic law and Community law on this issue if domestic law was properly interpreted and applied in the manner that they respectively contended for. Accordingly, it is not necessary to enquire into the effect of Community law any further.[91]

In *Daimler*, a trademark case, the CJEU faced another secondary liability situation. It was asked whether a former licensee can be considered a direct infringer with respect to advertising that was carried out by third parties to his benefit, despite his explicit protests, after the license agreement was terminated. One such advertising was previously ordered by the former licensee, while others were completely unsolicited.

---

[88] The prevalent view is that this is not regulated by EU law (Case C-119/10 *Frisdranken Industrie Winters* [2011] ECLI:EU:C:2011:258, Opinion of AG Kokott, para. 39 (referring to the domestic rules on participatory liability)); Case C-324/09 *L'Oréal and Others* [2010] ECLI:EU:C:2010:757, Opinion of AG Jääskinen, para. 56 (noting that joint tortfeasorship, contributory and vicarious liability are outside of the proceedings, and hence most likely implying outside of EU law).

[89] Case C-5/11 *Donner* [2012] ECLI:EU:C:2012:370.   [90] Ibid., para. 27 (emphasis mine).

[91] *L'Oreal SA & Ors v. EBay International AG & Ors* [2009] EWHC 1094 (Ch) [345] (emphasis mine).

The CJEU came to the conclusion that neither of the two can be viewed as a trademark use, and thus an act of direct infringement. The Court argued that "an advertiser cannot be held liable for the independent actions of other economic operators, such as those of referencing website operators with whom the advertiser has no direct or indirect dealings and who do not act by order and on behalf of that advertiser, but on their own initiative and in their own name."[92] The scope of the rights, according to the Court, regulate a person "who has direct or indirect control of the act constituting the use" as only that he or she "is effectively able to stop that use and therefore comply with that prohibition."[93] It can be therefore said that the Court negatively defined secondary liability by delineating its limits. What kind of "indirect control" would be seen as sufficient is left open.

The creation of Union notion of secondary liability by the CJEU is thus not completely impossible and might be even under way. It requires, however, preliminary references from the national courts that pose the right question in appropriate setting. The fact that no one talks about implicit doctrine of secondary liability is really no bar on judicial activism. In many countries, secondary liability is the area of judge-made law anyway. However, there is also some recent evidence suggesting that the CJEU might be in fact very reluctant to take this step. In a recent hyperlinking case, *GS Media*,[94] the Court was invited to consider a typical secondary liability situation. At least one of the governments, Slovak republic, argued that the Court should create its own secondary liability doctrine rather than inflate the notion of communication to the public. The Court did not take this path.

Instead, the Court decided to *inject* secondary liability conditions directly *into* the scope of the right to "balance out" consequences. According to the Court, hyperlinking amounts to communication to the public when neither the linked website, nor any other website published the referred work with a consent of the rightholder, on the condition that the hyperlinker had a knowledge of this. The knowledge, however, is presumed in for-profit scenarios, unless there is an evidence to the contrary.[95] The presence of knowledge in the scope of rights is doctrinally very unusual as it seems to conflate use and nonuse of works into a single exploitation standard.[96] AG Szpunar recently suggested to generalize this approach beyond regular hyperlinking.[97] Since a factual situation of accessory contribution to exploitation is seen as an act of exploitation, at least theoretically, the line drawn by domestic

---

[92] Case C-179/15 *Daimler* [2016] ECLI:EU:C:2016:134, para. 36.
[93] Ibid., para. 41.   [94] Case C-160/15 *GS Media* [2016] ECLI:EU:C:2016:644.
[95] Case C-160/15 *GS Media* [2016] ECLI:EU:C:2016:644, para. 51.
[96] Some recent yet unpublished academic projects are considering abandonment of secondary and primary liability distinction and rather to go for economic considerations – see IViR, "Reconstructing Rights: Rethinking copyright's economic rights in a time of highly dynamic technological and economic change" (2016), www.ivir.nl/projects/reconstructing-rights-rethinking-copyrights-economic-rights-in-a-time-of-highly-dynamic-technological-and-economic-change/.
[97] Case C-610/15 *Stichting Brein* [2017] ECLI:EU:C:2017:99, Opinion of AG Szpunar.

secondary liability doctrines should be moved further to helpers of helpers to dis-seminate the linked content. However, it is questionable whether, as a matter of fact, there is any room left for secondary liability at all. It might be well possible that injection of circumstances into the scope effectively "sucked" the entire room for such applicability into the scope of the exclusive right. Alternatively, one could argue that we are in fact witnessing continuous creation of autonomous Union secondary liability in disguise.

The problem of not having the central part of the jigsaw is that its nonexistence causes other pieces of the legislation – primary liability and injunctions against innocent intermediaries – to bear the burden. They are called to make up for what the legislator did not do. The harmonization of accessory liability is needed. European law needs a healthy accessory liability, whether it is in form of clauses or negligence per se rules, in order to be able to reach the infringing behavior with a full enforcement toolkit.

4.4 NEW LEGISLATIVE DEVELOPMENTS

In September 2016, the European Commission unveiled its plans for the copyright reform, including its proposal for the Directive on copyright in the Digital Single Market.[98] Although the newly proposed rules don't change existing rules on injunc-tions against intermediaries, they plan to substantially revise existing intermediary liability rules for the copyright and related rights. Article 13(1) of the Proposal reads:

> Information society service providers that store and provide to the public access to large amounts of works or other subject-matter uploaded by their users shall, in cooperation with rightholders, take measures to ensure the functioning of agree-ments concluded with rightholders for the use of their works or other subject-matter or to prevent the availability on their services of works or other subject-matter iden-tified by rightholders through the cooperation with the service providers. Those measures, such as the use of effective content recognition technologies, shall be appropriate and proportionate. The service providers shall provide rightholders with adequate information on the functioning and the deployment of the measures, as well as, when relevant, adequate reporting on the recognition and use of the works and other subject-matter.

The provision allows two readings. Either it imposes an obligation: (1) only on those with existing voluntary agreements who will be obliged to "take appropriate and proportionate measures to ensure the functioning of the agreements," including by preventing availability of works outside of the agreements, or, it imposes, in addition, (2) an obligation on everyone "to prevent the availability" of works not covered by

---

[98] Proposal for a Directive of the European Parliament and of the Council on copyright in the Dig-ital Single Market – COM(2016) 593, https://ec.europa.eu/digital-single-market/en/news/proposal-directive-european-parliament-and-council-copyright-digital-single-market.

such agreements, "including through the use of effective content identification technologies." In the former case, the Proposal would basically act as *ius cogens* regarding the content of existing licensing agreements, which would be, by the power of law, extended by a filtering obligation to nonlicensed works (probably) of the same rightholders. However, this seems very ineffective proposal. It would rest entirely on the willingness to conclude a licensing agreement at the first place. And assuming that right of communication to the public is not extended, it would make the potential agreements rather less attractive for intermediaries. Therefore, it is more likely that the Proposal advances agenda of a declaratory obligation imposed on existing licensees, and a new stand-alone stay-down obligation imposed on everyone else. Disrespecting the new stay-down obligation would not lead to a copyright violation, but sanctions imposed by the Member States. The obligation itself, unless limited to prevention permitted according to current case-law, seems to amend Article 15 of the E-Commerce Directive and the follow-up sanctions could conflict with Article 14 of the E-Commerce Directive.

At the time of writing, it is not clear whether the Proposal will stand the ground or not.[99] Reports of the Committees seems to be critical,[100] as well as most of the academic circles.[101] Putting all human rights concerns aside and assuming that it will be passed in its current form, from the perspective of this work, this begs a following question. Will it have any impact on availability of injunctions against intermediaries based on Article 8(3) InfoSoc and Article 11(III) of the Enforcement Directive? If the second reading of the proposed Article 13 is a correct one, then the Proposal will have an impact. In effect, it will legislate a copyright-specific form of stay down, an obligation to prevent reappearance of already notified works. This

---

[99] Giancarlo Frosio, "Reforming Intermediary Liability in the Platform Economy: A European Digital Single Market Strategy" (2017) 111 Northwestern University Law Review Online – forthcoming, https://ssrn.com/abstract=2912272.

[100] Draft of the Opinion of the Committee on the Internal Market and Consumer Protection for the Committee on Legal Affairs on the proposal for a directive of the European Parliament and of the Council on copyright in the Digital Single Market (2016/0280(COD); Draft Opinion of the Committee on Culture and Education for the Committee on Legal Affairs on the proposal for a regulation of the European Parliament and of the Council laying down rules on the exercise of copyright and related rights applicable to certain online transmissions of broadcasting organizations and retransmissions of television and radio programs (2016/0284(COD)).

[101] European Copyright Society, General Opinion on the EU Copyright Reform Package (2017), https://europeancopyrightsocietydotorg.files.wordpress.com/2015/12/ecs-opinion-on-eu-copyright-reform-def.pdf (against); Sophie Stalla-Bourdillon and others, "Open Letter to the European Commission – On the Importance of Preserving the Consistency and Integrity of the EU Acquis Relating to Content Monitoring within the Information Society" (2016), https://ssrn.com/abstract=2850483 (against); ALAI, "Resolution on the European proposals of 14 September 2016 to introduce fairer sharing of the value when works and other protected material are made available by electronic means" (2017), www.alai.org/en/assets/files/resolutions/170218-value-gap-en.pdf (supportive); CREATE, "Open Letter to Members of the European Parliament and the European Council" (2017), www.create.ac.uk/policy-responses/eu-copyright-reform/ (against).

legislation will then act as lex specialis with respect to application of injunctions against intermediaries.

This could have probably two effects. First, assuming that Article 13 will be passed as a full harmonization measure, it would prevent more excessive filtering measures to be imposed by means of injunctions. At the moment, looking at the CJEU case-law, this option is, however, only very hypothetical. The proposed obligation already deviates from what the CJEU accepted as "double identity" preventive measures.[102] Instead, it seems to oblige to "single identity" or even German-style "similarity" preventive measures. On the other hand, since the Proposal does not contain any specification of what has to be "prevented," one cannot rule out that the CJEU will synchronize Article 13 obligation with its "double identity" case-law. In which case, Article 13 would serve as a type of specially legislated assistance measures which instead of being available at courts, are prescribed by default by the law. In any case, as specific rules, they would limit the space for injunctions.

The second effect could arrive in case the preventive obligation expands beyond existing "double identity" cases. It is questionable then, if Article 13 could have a spill-over effect on other areas of intellectual property by watering down the boundaries of Article 3 of the Enforcement Directive, or would remain a specific regulatory response in the area of copyright and related rights. This is hard to predict. However, any legislative intervention to broaden the current scope of injunctions, whether by the Proposal or by a revision of the Enforcement Directive, needs to be scrutinized from the perspective of fundamental rights.

[102] See Chapter 7.

PART III

Accountable But Not Liable

Injunctions for Assistance

5

Right to Third-Party Information

Exponential division of labor and intensified intermediation of actions in a global and mostly anonymous environment has forced many countries to adjust their enforcement mechanisms. In particular, the need to discover and disclose information about wrongdoers has been seen vital. Some countries re-adjusted their procedural mechanisms (e.g., Jon Doe orders),[1] others created new statutory possibilities (e.g., subpoenas)[2] or simply created a new stand-alone remedy for the rightholders, such as an explicit right to information against innocent third parties.[3] The latter approach was taken, among others, by some of the Member States of the EU, which in turn inspired the Union legislator.

The right of information provided for in Article 8(1) of Directive 2004/48 is a "specific expression of the fundamental right to an effective remedy guaranteed in Article 47 of the Charter of Fundamental Rights of the European Union and thereby ensures the effective exercise of the fundamental right to property, which includes the intellectual property right protected in Article 17(2) of the Charter."[4] It enables

---

[1] Carol M. Rice, "Meet John Doe: It Is Time for Federal Civil Procedure to Recognize John Doe Parties" (1996) 57 *U. Prrr. L. REV.* 883 (United States); Michael S. Vogel, "Unmasking John Doe Defendants: The Case against Excessive Hand-Wringing over Legal Standares" (2004) 83 Or. L. Rev. 795 (United States); Julia E. Lawn, "The John Doe Injunction in Mass Protest Cases" (1998) 56 U. Toronto Fac. L. Rev. 101 (Canada); Quentin Cregan, "Roving Injunctions and John Doe Orders against Unidentifiable Defendants in IP Infringement Proceedings" (2011) 6(9) Journal of Intellectual Property Law & Practice 623 (United Kingdom).

[2] 17 U.S. Code § 512(h) (United States).

[3] One of such countries was Germany – see Christian Cychowski, "Auskunftsansprüche gegenüber Internetzugangsprovidern 'vor' dem 2. Korb und 'nach' der Enforcement-Richtlinie der EU" [2004] MMR 514, 517 (takes the view that the German transposition of this exception allows the communication of the traffic data of copyright infringers to the rightholders); Ulrich Sieber and Frank M. Höfiger, "Drittauskunftsansprüche nach § 101a UrhG gegen Internetprovider zur Verfolgung von Urheberrechtsverletzungen" [2004] MMR 575, 582; Gerald Spindler and Joachim Dorschel, "Auskunftsansprüche gegen Internet-Service-Provider" [2005] Computer und Recht 341–347.

[4] Case C–427/15 NEW WAVE CZ [2017] ECLI:EU:C:2017:18, para. 25.

the holder of an intellectual property right to identify who is infringing that right and take the necessary steps in order to protect that right.[5]

Article 8(1) of the Enforcement Directive today provides that:

> (1) Member States shall ensure that, in the context of proceedings concerning an infringement of an intellectual property right and in response to a justified and proportionate request of the claimant, the competent judicial authorities may order that information on the origin and distribution networks of the goods or services which infringe an intellectual property right be provided by the infringer and/or *any other person* who: (c) was found to be providing on a commercial scale services used in infringing activities. (emphasis mine)

As explained by Recital 21, the Union legislator felt that this claim to third-party information, albeit already present in some of the Member States, should be extended as a part of "a high level of protection" across the EU. The provision was meant to give a chance to rightholders to force not only infringers, but also any third parties, to disclose information relevant to the enforcement of their rights. The Directive did not prescribe any retention,[6] however. So any information would be provided only if it had been collected in the first place. The biggest impact of this was on the Internet intermediaries who, as third parties, often hold information about those of their users who infringe upon the IP rights of others. In particular, Internet access providers who know the identity of their subscribers were exposed to numerous litigations.

The right to information under Article 8(1) of the Enforcement Directive covers "intellectual property rights" (Article 1), but is "without prejudice to the specific provisions on the enforcement (. . .) of copyright and rights related to copyright, notably those found in (. . .) Directive 2001/29/EC and, in particular, Articles 2 to 6 and Article 8 thereof." This means that Article 8 of the InfoSoc Directive is lex specialis to the general framework of the Enforcement Directive. But since the InfoSoc Directive does not contain any provisions on the right to third-party information in the copyright context, this opens a hunt for its legal basis in *copyright law*. CJEU is inconsistent in this respect. In *Tele2*, it was discussed within the context of the injunctions against intermediaries of Article 8(3) InfoSoc Directive; in *Bonnier Audio*, in the context of the Enforcement Directive; in *Promusicae*, in the context of both of Directives.

5.1 CONDITIONS

Unlike injunctions against intermediaries, the wide reach of the Enforcement Directive's claim for third-party information was little disputed. It was immediately

---

[5] Ibid., para. 25.

[6] The opposite opinion is presented by Michel M Walter and Dominik Goebel, "Enforcement Directive" in Michel Walter and Silke von Lewinski (eds.), *European Copyright Law: A Commentary* (OUP 2010) 1275.

understood that the wording unambiguously targets "anybody" who holds information, and thus *not* just infringers.[7] According to Article 8(1), it is sufficient that a
person provides (1) services used in infringing activities (2) on a commercial scale
and, of course, (3) is still in possession of the requested information (Article 8(2)).

A person providing services used in infringing activities does not need to be an
"intermediary." It is sufficient that he engages in an activity or transactions which are
of a commercial nature. Moreover, since the Enforcement Directive is a minimal
harmonization, the Member States are free to expand it to a noncommercial context.
This is also true for the requirement that it is the "judicial authorities [that] may
order" such disclosures. The national legislators have sometimes gone substantially
beyond this requirement,[8] legislating the right to information as obligations of third
parties that are to be acted upon even without the interference of the courts.[9] This

---

7 Ibid., 1265 ("infringer" in the context of Article 8(1) of the Enforcement Directive covers both primary
   and secondary infringers, and claims for information are provided "irrespective of whether these
   persons themselves are liable for copyright infringement"); Reinhard Döring, *Die Haftung für eine
   Mitwirkung an fremden Wettbewerbsverstößen, Urheberrechts-, Marken-, Patent-, Gebrauchmuster- und
   Geschmacksmusterverletzungen* (Deutscher Anwalt Verlag 2008) 146; Annette Kur, "Rough Start Happy
   Landing" [2004] IIC 826 ("the directive expressly leaves room for application of measures and sanctions
   against persons who are not found to be infringing an IP right themselves. This concerns preliminary as
   well as permanent injunctions which may be directed against "intermediates"; the same applies to the
   right of information, and to corrective measures"); Michael Conradi, "Liability of an ISP for Allowing
   Access to File Sharing Networks" (2003) 19 Computer Law & Security Report 289, 292 (writing before
   the InfoSoc Directive was implemented in UK law, that should the directive be implemented in the
   UK, it will be possible to apply for an injunction against intermediaries, even though they escape
   their liability); Case C-557/07 *LSG-Gesellschaft zur Wahrnehmung von Leistungsschutzrechten* [2009]
   ECLI:EU:C:2009:107, para. 36.
8 Commission, "Commission Staff Working Document Analysis of the application of Directive
   2004/48/EC of the European Parliament and the Council of 29 April 2004 on the enforcement
   of intellectual property rights in the Member States Accompanying document to the Report from
   the Commission to the Council, the European Parliament and the European Social Committee on
   the application of Directive 2004/48/EC of the European Parliament and the Council of 29 April
   2004 on the enforcement of intellectual property rights" COM(2010) 779 final ("Commission Staff
   Working Document COM(2010) 779") notes: "the right to obtain information from third parties not
   directly involved in the proceedings seems to have been a novel in most Member States. (. . .) Some
   Member States seem to provide for the right of information only in cases of infringements committed
   on a commercial scale. The other Member States have moved beyond the Directive and provide
   for the right of information for all infringements." For the German, Dutch, and British pre-Directive
   situation, see Helmut Eichmann, "Die Durchsetzung des Anspruchs auf Drittauskunft" [1990] GRUR
   575–591; Michael Conradi, "Liability of an ISP for Allowing Access to File Sharing Networks" (2003)
   19 Computer Law & Security Report 289–294; Anton Ekker, "Anonimiteit en uitingsvrijheid op het
   Internet; het onthullen van identificerende gegevens door Internetproviders Verschenen" (2002) 11/12
   Mediaforum 348–351.
9 See the decision of the Austrian Supreme Court, OGH *LSG v. Tele2* (2009) 4Ob41/09x, [4.3] (coming to
   the conclusion that the CJEU does not require any court supervision, as otherwise it would have said so
   explicitly; at the same time, the court noted that such a requirement could come from constitutional
   law; it did not reach any conclusion on this point); see also critique by Alexander Peukert and
   Annette Kur, "Stellungnahme des Max-Planck-Instituts für Geistiges Eigentum, Wettbewerbs- und
   Steuerrecht zur Umsetzung der Richtlinie 2004/48/EG zur Durchsetzung der Rechte des geistigen
   Eigentums in deutsches Recht" [2006] GRUR Int 292 (the authors criticize the German proposal

makes the claim susceptible to abuse, and prompts us to ask whether disclosures of such information that lack any court oversight and/or link to commercial scale are still constitutionally acceptable.[10]

5.2 SCOPE AND LIMITATIONS

The main issue, however, became the problem of information that is protected by specific laws, such as data protection, secrecy, or protection against self-incrimination. In particular the relationship between the claim and the fundamental right to privacy and personal data has been closely scrutinized. The limitation of the remedy is primarily provided in Article 8(3) of the Enforcement Directive which reads:

> Paragraphs 1 and 2 shall apply without prejudice to other statutory provisions which: (. . .) (d) afford an opportunity for refusing to provide information which would force the person referred to in paragraph 1 to admit to his/her own participation or that of his/her close relatives in an infringement of an intellectual property right; or (e) govern the protection of confidentiality of information sources or the processing of personal data.[11]

This "without-prejudice" clause was interpreted as meaning that the data protection laws must be observed.[12] This means that the Enforcement Directive does not amend the secondary Union laws in this field.[13] So if they were to block certain personal data from being communicated, the Enforcement Directive may not override this result. A similar, but less detailed clause is included in Recital 60 of the InfoSoc

---

for extending the claim for information against innocent third parties also outside of proceedings against the infringer, turning it into an independent claim in cases of apparent infringement, thus causing serious problems. Namely, that because the claim can be granted without court supervision, it can endanger the fundamental rights of the individuals concerned, especially the fundamental right to informational self-determination); Kai Welp, *Die Auskunftspflicht von Access-Providern nach dem Urheberrechtsgesetz* (C. H. Beck 2009) 334ff. (describing the German legislative discussion of judicial control over the claims).

[10] See the opinion of the Working party 29, "Working document on data protection issues related to intellectual property rights" (2005) 8, http://ec.europa.eu/justice/policies/privacy/docs/wpdocs/2005/wp104_en.pdf ("A fair balance shall have to be found between the legitimate interests of copyright holders and individuals concerned. The criteria of the commercial advantage linked with the infringement may be decisive in this respect"); Gerald Spindler, "'Die Tür ist auf' – Europarechtliche Zulässigkeit von Auskunftsansprüchen gegenüber Providern – Urteilsanmerkung zu EuGH „Promusicae/Telefónica" [2008] GRUR 574, 576; Gerald Spindler, "Der Auskunftsanspruch gegen Verletzer und Dritte im Urheberrecht nach neuem Recht" [2008] ZUM 640, 644; Martin Husovec, *Zodpovednosť na Internete: podľa slovenského a českého práva* (CZNIC 2014) 171ff.

[11] Case C-275/06 *Promusicae* [2008] ECLI:EU:C:2008:54, Opinion of AG Kokott, para. 48 (TRIPS does not override personal data).

[12] Case C-461/10 *Bonnier Audio AB and Others* [2011] ECLI:EU:C:2011:753, Opinion of AG Jääskinen, para. 54.

[13] Andreas Kramer, *Zivilrechtlicher Auskunftsanspruch gegenüber Access Providern* (Kovač 2007) 141–142 (for German data protection law).

Directive, which says that its provisions "should be without prejudice to national or Community legal provisions in other areas, such as (. . .) data protection."[14]

Interestingly, not only national courts, but also the CJEU seems to be rather confused about where to base *limits* of third-party information regarding the personal data. This is related to a lack of clarity about the actual legal *basis* of such injunctions. In three *copyright* cases, the following lack of consistency could be observed:

- In the *Promusicae* referral, a Spanish court relies on both the InfoSoc and Enforcement Directives. The CJEU then examines both normative legal acts as a possible legal basis and for limits.[15]
- In the *Tele2* referral, an Austrian court identifies the legal basis in the InfoSoc Directive, and hence also enquires about the scope of the term "intermediary," but as to limits, it curiously invokes the Enforcement Directive.[16] The CJEU responds as asked.[17]
- In the *Bonnier Audio* referral, a Swedish court uses the Enforcement Directive both for legal basis and as a limit.[18] The CJEU responds by relying on the provisions of the Enforcement Directive.[19]

This situation does not improve the transparency of the argumentation, which is a precondition of high-quality jurisprudence. It would be advisable for the Court to fully admit lex generalis nature of the Enforcement Directive, and use it then both as a legal basis and source of limits for third-party information in the copyright field. After all, not only is the Enforcement Directive more detailed and broader than any potential use of Article 8(3) of the InfoSoc Directive, but it always provides more explicit limitations, going beyond the data protection rules themselves. This would make it possible to invoke an autonomous defense of self-incrimination or of confidentiality of sources in the copyright context, according to Article 8(3)(d)(e) of the Enforcement Directive.

In its first case dealing with Article 8 of the Enforcement Directive, *Promusicae*,[20] the CJEU had to consider the disclosure by an Internet access provider of the identity of users linked to specific dynamic IP address. The CJEU, interpreting the data protection framework,[21] arrived at the conclusion that such a disclosure may

---

[14] A similar reference is found in Article 9 of the Directive.

[15] Case C-275/06 *Promusicae* [2008] ECLI:EU:C:2008:54, paras. 58, 59; Case C-275/06 *Promusicae* [2008] ECLI:EU:C:2008:54, Opinion of AG Kokott, paras. 44, 45, 59.

[16] Case C-557/07 *LSG-Gesellschaft zur Wahrnehmung von Leistungsschutzrechten* [2009] ECLI:EU:C:2009:107, paras. 22, 24.

[17] Ibid., paras. 24, 29, 42, 46.

[18] Case C-461/10 *Bonnier Audio AB and Others* [2011] ECLI:EU:C:2011:753, Opinion of AG Jääskinen, para. 36.

[19] Case C-461/10 *Bonnier Audio AB and Others* [2012] ECLI:EU:C:2012:219, para. 55.

[20] Case C-275/06 *Promusicae* [2008] ECLI:EU:C:2008:54.

[21] Directive 2002/58/EC of the European Parliament and of the Council of 12 July 2002 concerning the processing of personal data and the protection of privacy in the electronic communications sector

be justified as it may fall within the derogation for "the protection of the rights and freedoms of others."[22] It is a choice of the Member States whether they take advantage of this; they do not have to.

Therefore, despite the fact that a right to third-party information is mandatory and aims to disclose "the identity of any third parties involved in the infringement" (Recital 21), the Court held that the remedy does *not* harmonize situations in which personal data is the subject of such requests. Similarly, neither the InfoSoc Directive nor TRIPS contains such an obligation.[23] As a consequence, it is up to the Member States whether they extend the right to cover personal data. Nonexistence of the relief does not breach Union law.[24] However, if the Member State decides to extend the right to third-party information to cover personal data, it has to assure, as a matter of Union law that the disclosure allows a fair balance to be struck between the

---

[2002] OJ L 201; Directive 95/46/EC of the European Parliament and of the Council of 24 October 1995 on the protection of individuals with regard to the processing of personal data and on the free movement of such data [1995] OJ L 281.

[22] The Court came to this conclusion by reading Article 15(1) of the Directive 2002/58/EC together with Article 13(1)(g) of the Directive 95/46/EC. The Advocate General was, however, of a different opinion, rejecting the applicability of Article 13(1)(g) – see Case C-275/06 *Promusicae* [2008] ECLI:EU:C:2008:54, Opinion of AG Kokott paras. 85–89; see also Axel Metzger, "A Primer On ACTA: What Europeans Should Fear About the Anti-Counterfeiting Trade Agreement" (2010) 2 JIPITEC 4 (noting that it was clear in the case that the problem was one of interpretation of the underlying data protection rules); Christopher Kuner, "Data Protection and Rights Protection on the Internet: The Promusicae Judgment of the European Court of Justice" [2008] European Intellectual Property Review 199; Kate Brimsted and Gavin Chesney, "The ECJ's Judgment in Promusicae: The Unintended Consequences – Music to the Ears of Copyright Owners or a Privacy Headache for the Future? A Comment" (2008) 24 Computer Law & Security Review 275–279.

[23] Case C-275/06 *Promusicae* [2005] ECLI:EU:C:2008:54, paras. 59, 60 ("Nor does the wording of Articles 15(2) and 18 of Directive 2000/31 or that of Article 8(1) and (2) of Directive 2001/29 require the Member States to lay down such an obligation. As to Articles 41, 42, and 47 of the TRIPs Agreement, relied on by Promusicae, in the light of which Community law must as far as possible be interpreted where – as in the case of the provisions relied on in the context of the present reference for a preliminary ruling – it regulates a field to which that agreement applies (. . .), while they require the effective protection of intellectual property rights and the institution of judicial remedies for their enforcement, they do not contain provisions which require those directives to be interpreted as compelling the Member States to lay down an obligation to communicate personal data in the context of civil proceedings"); the reason is that Article 8(3) of the Enforcement Directive excludes issues of data protection; and since Directive 2002/58/EC does not foresee the processing for IP enforcement as one of its exceptions in Article 5 and 6, the only possibility was to rely on the optional derogation of Article 15 (see more Xavier Groussot, "Case C-275/06, Productores de Música de España (Promusicae) v. Telefónica de España SAU, Judgment of the Court (Grand Chamber) of 28 January 2008" (2008) 45 Common Market Law Review 1745–1766; Fanny Coudert and Evi Werkers, "In the Aftermath of the Promusicae Case: How to Strike the Balance?" (2010) 18 Int J Law Info Tech 50–71; Ingmar Stein, *Der Auskunftsanspruch gegen Access-Provider nach § 101 UrhG* (Kovač 2012) 49; Andreas Kramer, *Zivilrechtlicher Auskunftsanspruch gegenüber Access Providern* (Kovač 2007) 155, 167.

[24] This is a very interesting situation. If the CJEU were of the opinion that the absence of such a remedy is a violation of the Charter, unless an interpretation of secondary Union law to this end were possible, the Court would need to interfere with the validity of the secondary law, but this could lead to the Charter losing any applicability, since there could be no Union law to implement anymore.

various fundamental rights.[25] In other words, Union law does not mandate such a disclosure mechanism, but conditionally permits it, if the proportionality between fundamental rights is respected.

The result of *Promusicae* has shown that the Union right to third-party information is very limited in its breath. Basically, whenever it targets a natural person, there is a potential risk that Union law does not give any remedy. This empties the scope of the remedy and of any disclosure of "the identity of any third parties involved in the infringement" to more or less only legal persons whose data are not protected, which is rather dysfunctional, especially in cases of copyright enforcement where most of the infringements are committed by individual users. The CJEU might have therefore recently changed its stance in *Coty Germany*.

The second, and almost identical, case was *Tele 2*.[26] The CJEU handed it down in the form of an order, mostly referencing the previous *Promusicae* case. The Eighth Chamber repeated the interpretation of the Grand Chamber and added that "the freedom which Member States retain to give priority to the right to privacy or to the right to property is qualified by a number of requirements"; those requirements being an obligation to follow the interpretation of the Directives and especially of the EU Charter with the aim of achieving a balance between various fundamental rights. In other words, the CJEU just confirmed that it is *not* willing to draw the exact lines, but also that a balancing exercise has to be undertaken by a national court, as a matter of Union law.[27]

A subsequent third case, *Bonnier Audio*, was an attempt to reconsider[28] the principles postulated in *Promusicae* and *Tele 2* in the context of now invalid Directive 2006/24.[29] This Directive obliged the Member States to institute mass-surveillance

---

[25] This decision was rendered before the Lisbon Treaty entered into force. The Court thus based this opinion on the argumentation with "fundamental rights or with the other general principles of Community law, such as the principle of proportionality" Today, this would be resolved explicitly with a reference to Article 51(1) of the EU Charter.

[26] Case C-557/07 *LSG-Gesellschaft zur Wahrnehmung von Leistungsschutzrechten* [2009] ECLI: EU:C:2009:107.

[27] It can be argued that the balancing exercise gives the Member States a broader margin of appreciation. In *Chassagnou and others v. France* App no 25088/94, 28331/95 and 28443/95 (ECHR, 29 April 1999), the ECtHR stated this as follows: "It is precisely this constant search for a balance between the fundamental rights of each individual which constitutes the foundation of a "democratic society." The balancing of individual interests that may well be contradictory is a difficult matter, and Contracting States must have a broad margin of appreciation in this respect, since the national authorities are in principle better placed than the European Court to assess whether or not there is a "pressing social need" capable of justifying interference with one of the rights guaranteed by the Convention" (emphasis mine); see more Xavier Groussot, "Case C–275/06, Productores de Música de España (Promusicae) v. Telefónica de España SAU, Judgment of the Court (Grand Chamber) of 28 January 2008" (2008) 45 Common Market Law Review 1745, 1762.

[28] Case C-461/10 *Bonnier Audio AB and Others* [2011] ECLI:EU:C:2011:753, Opinion of AG Jääskinen, para. 5.

[29] Joined Cases C-293/12 and C-594/12 *Digital Rights Ireland* [2014] ECLI:EU:C:2014:238 (invalidated the Directive for breach of right to privacy and personal data).

of European citizens for the purposes of combating terrorism. The question was whether the data obligatorily stored for the purposes of fighting terrorism under a separate and stricter regime could also be disclosed in copyright infringement proceedings. The Advocate General Jääskinen, presented the following important opinion:

> For the disclosure of personal data to be possible, European Union law requires that an obligation to retain data be provided for in national law, in order to specify the types of data to be retained, the purposes of retaining the data, the period of retention and the persons with access to such data. It would be contrary to the principles of the protection of personal data to make use of databases that exist for purposes other than those thus defined by the legislature. (. . .) copyright holders must not be favoured, by allowing them to make use of personal data which have been legally collected or retained for purposes not germane to the protection of their rights. The collection and use of such data for such purposes in compliance with European Union law concerning the protection of personal data *would require the prior adoption of detailed provisions by the national legislature*, in accordance with Article 15 of Directive 2002/58.[30]

The CJEU subsequently decided that because the disclosure of data retention information in civil proceedings falls outside of the material scope of Directive 2006/24, the situation has to be judged as in *Promusicae* and *Tele 2*. The national legislation extending the purpose of the data retention information still has to be justified in the general regime of the date protection laws.[31] The Third Chamber appeared to be satisfied with the national legal order because it allowed the court to ad hoc weigh the conflicting interests involved and thus take due account of the requirement of the principle of proportionality.

It is important to note that the very same requirements would apply even if the Union legislator were to take up the task in the future. Unlike Advocate General Kokott in *Promusicae* and arguably also Advocate General Jääskinen in *Bonier Audio*, the CJEU in its ruling did not ultimately view as problematic the fact that Swedish law did *not* explicitly permit such disclosures of personal data. The perspective of the "quality of the law" as a human rights requirement was no longer reiterated.[32]

This string of the case-law has shown that European legislation does not prescribe that the Member States must provide for an important tool for fighting online infringements committed by individuals. This seems to have resulted in a general feeling of frustration among EU institutions. From the official report of the European Commission on the application of the Enforcement Directive, it appears that

---

[30] Case C-461/10 *Bonnier Audio AB and Others* [2011] ECLI:EU:C:2011:753, Opinion of AG Jääskinen para. 60 (emphasis mine).

[31] Case C-461/10 *Bonnier Audio AB and Others* [2012] ECLI:EU:C:2012:219, paras. 45, 52.

[32] This asks whether the law was formulated with sufficient precision to enable the citizen to adjust his conduct accordingly – see Case C-461/10 *Bonnier Audio and Others* [2012] ECLI:EU:C:2012:219, paras. 60, 61; Case C-275/06 *Promusicae* [2005] ECLI:EU:C:2008:54, Opinion of AG Kokott, para. 53.

neither varying the scope of disclosures in the different Member States, nor are too strict privacy limits on the enforcement welcomed.[33] The EU Observatory's study is more explicit in formulating these concerns. It names the national data protection legislation as "a significant obstacle" to effective enforcement of intellectual property rights:

> Jurisprudence in the Member States illustrates the obstacles to obtaining injunctions against ISPs. In some Member States, *national data-protection legislation is a significant obstacle*, particularly for the initial evidence collection necessary to bring such litigation in the first place. *The permissible scope of injunctions is also potentially affected by data protection and other rules, for example, with respect to the types of technical blocking that may be required under injunction.*[34]

This language is surprising. It is true that post-Promusicae state of the framework hardly leads to any harmonization of the right to third-party information and that the need for enforcement against natural persons is, without doubt, significant. But it is wrong to think of this human right as an obstacle. In fact, the obstacle to harmonization is the absence of consensus and a lack of political will on the part of the Union legislator to regulate the question precisely, not a human rights standard, which merely serves to impose certain guarantees. It is correct that the human rights framework is restraining the courts from acting, instead of an (indecisive) legislator.

The limitation by human rights could also have further practical consequences for enforcement. For instance, the Article 29 Working Party, an expert group composed of representatives from the data protection authorities of each EU Member State, suggests that the limitation of court oversight and commercial scale of activity might be understood not only as guarantees of secondary law, but directly as safeguards required by the EU Charter.[35] This would mean that despite minimal harmonization, the EU Charter would preclude the Member States from watering down or abandoning such safeguards.

Promusicae might be, however, at least partially "dead law." In *Coty Germany*, The German Federal Supreme Court asked the CJEU whether a banking institution may refuse, by invoking banking secrecy, to provide information concerning the name and address of an account holder who allegedly engaged in a trademark infringement. The situation in this case was very similar to that in *Promusicae*, the only differences being that: (1) the identity disclosure was demanded from a bank; (2) the case involved an instance of a trademark infringement; and (3) the

---

[33] The Commission also mentions that practical problems arise in respect to retention of the relevant data by intermediaries and different confidentiality regimes in the different Member States – see Commission, "Commission Staff Working Document" COM(2010) 779, 13.

[34] European Observatory on Counterfeiting and Piracy, "Injunctions in Intellectual Property Right," http://ec.europa.eu/internal_market/iprenforcement/docs/injunctions_en.pdf (emphasis mine).

[35] See the opinion of the Working party 29, "Working Document on Data Protection Issues Related to Intellectual Property Rights" (2005) 8, http://ec.europa.eu/justice/policies/privacy/docs/wpdocs/2005/wp104_en.pdf.

EU Charter was already legally binding. If the Court had followed its *Promusicae* ruling, it would have simply answered that there is no obligation to introduce such a remedy covering personal data, but if it is introduced, it has to be proportionate.[36] The CJEU, however, took a further step and held that the national provision which generally prohibits such disclosure between individuals is incompatible with the Enforcement Directive and Article 17(2) of the EU Charter.[37]

This outcome is of importance for many countries, since in some Member States, such orders are very difficult, or even impossible, to obtain, either because of bank secrecy or stringent application of the proportionality requirement.[38] However, the most important message is the underlying shift in case-law. While *Promusicae* says such disclosure is an "option," which have to be balanced, *Coty Germany* concludes that it is a "must," which have to be balanced.[39] To summarize this, after *Coty Germany*, an obligation to introduce such disclosures exists and so it is no longer an option for a Member State as its unavailability can infringe the fundamental right to an effective remedy and the fundamental right to intellectual property.[40] This shift could even be seen as a first step toward Charter-based *positive obligations* of the area.[41]

The most frequently applied limitations[42] to the right to third-party information are the privacy (Article 7) and data protection (Article 8) *human rights standards* of the EU Charter. The previously presented string of cases confirmed that when such injunctions cover personal data, Union law is "implemented," and thus the EU

---

[36] Martin Husovec, "Intellectual Property Rights and Integration by Conflict: The Past, Present and Future" (2016) 18 Cambridge Yearbook of European Legal Studies 239, 257.

[37] Case C-580/13 *Coty Germany* [2015] ECLI:EU:C:2015:485, para. 43; Case C-580/13 *Coty Germany* [2015] ECLI:EU:C:2015:243, Opinion of AG Villalón (suggesting that such a disclosure should be accessible to rightholders, subject to a proportionality exercise with the right to data protection).

[38] European Observatory on Counterfeiting and Piracy, "Injunctions in Intellectual Property Right," http://ec.europa.eu/internal_market/iprenforcement/docs/injunctions_en.pdf; for a typical example of this, see *Bankers Trust Co v. Shapira* [1980] 1 *WLR* 1274 at 1282 (disclosure of bank documents is a severe interference); Rechtbank Amsterdam *Brein v. ING* (2013) ECLI:NL:RBAMS:2013:CA0350 (denying disclosure).

[39] Case C-580/13 *Coty Germany* [2015] ECLI:EU:C:2015:485, paras. 29, 38.

[40] Martin Husovec, "Intellectual Property Rights and Integration by Conflict: The Past, Present and Future" (2016) 18 Cambridge Yearbook of European Legal Studies 239, 257.

[41] Ibid., 256 et seq.

[42] Since an Internet access providers qualifies as an "information society service provider," an "intermediary" and also "any third party," it is are regularly subject to both safe harbors and right to information. Given that Article 12 of the E-Commerce Directive limits "the liability" for the information transmitted by Internet access providers, with an exception for injunctive relief legislated "to terminate or prevent an infringement," it was questionable whether the disclosure injunctions could be limited by the the the applicability of the safe harbors. The cases of *Promusicae*, *Tele 2*, and *Bonnier Audio* all implicitly answered this question in the negative. It is true that none of the referring courts actually posed this question, but if applicable, this would most likely have been added or rephrased by the CJEU. In the literature, very few, if any, voices presented the argument that safe harbors should bar the right to information. The Dutch Supreme Court explicitly rejected this (Hoge Raad *Lycos v. Pessers* (2005) ECLI: NL: HR 2005: AU4019).

Charter applies (Article 51(1)). It is questionable, however, if the same would also hold true when the data requested is not personal data, but subject to the exclusions of Article 8(3), such as confidentiality of sources. In my opinion, this is also to be answered in the affirmative. The CJEU has repeatedly held that derogations from Union law also fall under the scope of its implementation, to which fundamental rights apply.[43] This means that the CJEU can ultimately moderate the content of Article 8(3) limitations even if their content is not regulated by other secondary Union laws.

5.3 COSTS

Despite no guidance on the Union level, many Member States, including Germany and the United Kingdom, offer reimbursement of the compliance costs. In the United Kingdom, the compensation element already predates the Enforcement Directive in the form of "Norwich case-law" (see Section 10.2). In Germany, it was legislated with respect to access providers in § 101(9) of the German Copyright Act, according to which "the costs of judicial order are to be borne by the injured."[44] This provision is then replicated in § 19(9) of the German Trade Mark Act, § 140b(9) of the German Patent Act, § 46(9) of the German Design Act and § 24b of the German Utility Models Act. The compensatory elements were seen as an effort to balance the inconvenience to a noninfringer (*Nichtverletzer*).[45] In Finland, the rightholders have to compensate for legal and compliance costs of information disclosures. According to the preparatory materials, this obligation was imposed in order to achieve that only significant cases are pursed.[46] In France, the Council of State (the Conseil

---

[43] This would mean that what constitutes "self-incrimination" under Article 8(3)(d) is also to be answered with reference to the EU Charter. The CJEU, at a time (1991) when fundamental rights and freedoms were only part of the "general legal principles," adjudicated in case Case C-260/89 *ERT v. DEP* [1991] ECLI:EU:C:1991:254, para. 44 et sq. that the discretion of the Member State in the case of derogation from Union law also falls into the scope of his review. And therefore, that national legislation which invokes derogation must subsequently also conform to the human rights standards of the Convention (paras. 44, 45). This decision is not isolated and was later confirmed by CJEU (Case C-368/95 *Familiapress* [1997] ECLI:EU:C:1997:325). The recent decision in Case C-617/10 *Åkerberg Fransson* [2013] ECLI:EU:C:2013:280 confirms, that the doctrine of the CJEU from the times of "general legal principles" continues even today, when human right standards are now a part of the EU Charter. On the limitation by confidential information against infringers see Case C-275/06 *Promusicae* [2008] ECLI:EU:C:2008:54, Opinion of AG Kokott, fn 22: "The fourth sentence of Article 42 of TRIPS could, admittedly, in its German version, be (mis)construed as meaning that effective legal protection must provide for the discovery of confidential information, yet, on the contrary, that provision is intended to protect confidential information in judicial proceedings. This is more clearly apparent in the authentic language versions (English, French and Spanish)."

[44] § 101(9) UrhG ("Die Kosten der richterlichen Anordnung trägt der Verletzte").

[45] Thomas Dreier and Gernot Schulze, *Urheberrechtsgesetz: UrhG* (4th ed., C. H. Beck 2013) § 101 para. 15.

[46] Pekka Savola, *Internet Connectivity Providers as Involuntary Copyright Enforcers: Blocking Websites in Particular* (IPR University Center, 2015) 90.

d'Etat), ordered the government to take regulatory measures to indemnify the access providers for the costs incurred when the HADOPI Commission requires them to provide information concerning their users who are suspected of have infringed copyright law.[47] In addition, in 2013, the High Court of Paris ordered a blocking of 16 streaming websites to a number of access providers, on the condition that they pay for the implementation costs.[48]

---

[47] Conseil d'Etat, *Bouygues Télécom* (2015) Case No 383110.

[48] High Court of Paris, Tribunal de Grande Instance, *Association des producteurs de cinema (APC) et autres c. Auchan Telecom et autres* (2013) Case of 28 November – see Christina Angelopoulos, *European Intermediary Liability in Copyright: A Tort-Based Analysis* (Kluwer Law International 2017) 228–229.

6

Conditions for Injunctions Against Intermediaries

As a matter of Union law, in order to establish a course of action, the plaintiff has to prove the following elements: (1) the defendant is an "intermediary" (2) "whose service are used by a third party" (3) "to infringe an intellectual property right." The Member States may, however, deviate from these conditions.[1]

6.1 "INTERMEDIARY"

The term "intermediary" is interpreted by the CJEU case-law in a broad way, basically including anyone who "provide[s] a service *capable of being used* by a third party to infringe."[2] It does not need to be a person who acts as an agent between two parties, as the dictionary definition would suggest. It seems enough that a person provides a *service* to another party who engages in an infringement, for instance a contractor filling the cans of beverage[3] or a flea-market landlord who sublets the stalls.[4] It would therefore appear that a "service provider" would perhaps be a more appropriate description of the contents of the term. However, the term is even looser. The Court confirms that "it is not necessary [to] maintain a specific relationship with that or those persons."[5] This suggest that even being the indirect beneficiary of a service is sufficient. In any case, the term is certainly broader than the "information society service provider" used by the E-Commerce Directive, as it covers also offline or not-at-distance intermediaries, such as landlords or ordinary contractors.[6]

---

[1] See Section 6.4.
[2] Case C-557/07 *LSG-Gesellschaft zur Wahrnehmung von Leistungsschutzrechten* [2009] ECLI:EU:C:2009:107; Case C-494/15 *Tommy Hilfiger Licensing and Others* [2016] ECLI:EU:C:2016:528, para. 25.
[3] Case C-119/10 *Frisdranken Industrie Winters* [2011] ECLI:EU:C:2011:258, Opinion of AG Kokott.
[4] Case C-494/15 *Tommy Hilfiger Licensing and Others* [2016] ECLI:EU:C:2016:528.
[5] Case C-494/15 *Tommy Hilfiger Licensing and Others* [2016] ECLI:EU:C:2016:528, para. 23.
[6] Ibid; Case C-119/10 *Frisdranken Industrie Winters* [2011] ECLI:EU:C:2011:258, Opinion of AG Kokott.

The term "intermediary" is also not completely foreign to the E-Commerce Directive either. In fact, the Directive uses it several times in its text (Recitals 14, 40, 50) including it in the name of the rubric for Section 4, "Liability of intermediary service providers." In its case-law, the CJEU doesn't synchronize its usage across the InfoSoc Directive, the Enforcement Directive, and the E-Commerce Directive. The same goes for "intermediary character of services," which the CJEU repeatedly required in order to qualify for one for the E-Commerce Directive's safe harbors,[7] but has never been invoked for injunctions.

The reason for this is rather obvious. The CJEU wants the injunctions to be as broad as possible. Requiring an "intermediary character of services" would significantly narrow down their scope, since it would require that an intermediary, in the sense of Article 8(3) of the InfoSoc Directive and Article 11(III) of the Enforcement Directive, must also be passive in the sense that it has neither knowledge nor control of the infringing acts.[8] This would mean that active intermediaries couldn't be subject to these injunctions, but would have to be targeted as "infringers." Although this could provide a means to distinguish potentially secondarily infringing intermediaries – in the state of absent harmonization where there is no guarantee that such national doctrines covering active intermediaries exists – the Court naturally takes the broader reading of the provision, which encompasses also nonactive intermediaries. If the Court, however, were to strive for coherence, it would become instantly clear that injunctions cover only passive intermediaries, which are unlikely to qualify for any secondary liability.

The only common requirement between the three Directives could possibly be that they all constitute a "service." This term has its standard definition in Article 57 of the Treaty on the Functioning of the European Union (TFEU), which legislates the scope of EU competences. It provides that the "services shall be considered to be 'services' within the meaning of the Treaties where they are *normally provided for remuneration*, in so far as they are not governed by the provisions relating to freedom of movement for goods, capital and persons." A related piece of secondary Union legislation, the Services Directive,[9] also closely follows the scope of the wording of Article 57 TFEU. Its provisions, for instance, note that nonprofit making amateur sporting activities might not constitute economic activity and thus might fall outside the scope of this Directive (Recital 35). This definition also appears in the E-Commerce Directive context.[10]

---

7 Case C-291/13 *Papasavvas* [2014] ECLI:EU:C:2014:2209, para. 39 ("As is apparent from the title of Section 4 of that directive, the behaviour of the service provider referred to by those articles must be restricted to that of an 'intermediary service provider'").

8 Case C-291/13 *Papasavvas* [2014] ECLI:EU:C:2014:2209; Case C-324/09 *L'Oréal and Others* [2011] ECLI:EU:C:2011:474; Joined Cases C-236/08 to C-238/08 *Google France and Google* [2010] ECLI:EU:C:2010:159.

9 Directive 2006/123/EC of the European Parliament and of the Council of 12 December 2006 on services in the internal market [2006] OJ L 376/36.

10 See the E-Commerce Directive, Article 2(a) ("information society services": services within the meaning of Article 1(2) of Directive 98/34/EC as amended by Directive 98/48/EC).

In *Papasavvas*,[11] the CJEU interpreted this building block in the context of Internet business models. The Court referred to Recital 18 of the E-Commerce Directive to point out that some services are activities "which are not remunerated by those who receive them, such as those offering on-line information or commercial communications." This, in the opinion of the Court, "corresponds to that of the concept of 'services' within the meaning of Article 57 TFEU, which also does not require the service to be paid for by those for whom it is performed."[12]

Such argumentation, however, does not reduce the worry that nonprofit services which are nevertheless capable of being commercialized will be excluded from the scope of the term. This would not only mean that Union law would not extend its safe harbors to them, but also that it would not provide for any injunctions against them. After all, EU injunctions only target intermediaries that provide some "services." This poses an important question. Are intermediaries such as Wikipedia, which is entirely nonprofit and supported only by donations, or an operator of open and free WiFi, also providers of a "service" in this sense? Of course, national law could extend both injunctions and safe harbors beyond their Union law templates, but a narrow reading of the term could complicate the life of many intermediaries and rightholders.

In *Mc Fadden*, the Court ruled that an economic activity might be considered a service as long as there are some indirect transactions which could be interpreted as a form of consideration, such as purchase of advertised goods or services. The court confirmed this approach accepting that the open wireless in question is provided by remuneration because "the cost of that activity is incorporated into the price of those [advertised] goods or services."[13] At the same time, it was stressed that a mere economic character of an activity would not be sufficient to qualify an activity as a service; some additional circumstances have to be present.[14] Since the open wireless in question could have been construed as a form of advertising and the operator was not a private person, the court did not have to directly answer the question whether mere provision of open wireless at home would also qualify as a service. But the judgment and its language suggest a rather flexible test.[15]

For now, the CJEU has confirmed that an Internet access provider,[16] a social network,[17] and an auction platform,[18] an operator of an open wireless,[19] a landlord of

---

[11]   Case C-291/13 *Papasavvas* [2014] ECLI:EU:C:2014:2209.

[12]   Ibid., para. 29; Case 352/85 *Bond van Adverteerders and Others* [1988] EU:C:1988:196, para. 16.

[13]   Case C-484/14 *Tobias McFadden v. Sony Music* [2016] ECLI:EU:C:2016:170, Opinion AG Szpunar, para. 42.

[14]   Ibid., Opinion AG Szpunar, para. 41.

[15]   Martin Husovec, "Holey Cap! CJEU Drills (Yet) Another Hole in the E-Commerce Directive's Safe Harbors" (2017) 12(2) Journal of Intellectual Property Law & Practice, 115, 117.

[16]   Case C-557/07 *LSG-Gesellschaft zur Wahrnehmung von Leistungsschutzrechten* [2009] ECLI:EU:C: 2009:107; Case C-70/10 *Scarlet Extended* [2011] ECLI:EU:C:2011:771.

[17]   Case C-360/10 *SABAM* [2012] ECLI:EU:C:2012:85.

[18]   Case C-324/09 *L'Oréal and Others* [2011] ECLI:EU:C:2011:474.

[19]   Case C-484/14 *Tobias McFadden v. Sony Music* [2016] ECLI:EU:C:2016:689 (only indirectly).

stalls,[20] qualify as an "intermediary" for the purposes of an injunction. Further intermediaries that are likely to be covered include providers of payment or anonymizing services, domain name authorities, search engines, VPN providers, or providers of other technical infrastructure. The term is broad enough to even accommodate injunctions against electricity or other utility providers.[21]

In the case-law of the Member States, the Belgian courts were reported to include also transport carriers within the scope of the term.[22] A similar injunction was granted by the court in Milan,[23] which held that a shipping agent who contracted for the transportation of a counterfeiting machine is such an intermediary.[24] Pechan and Schneider note that carriers, customs agents, and other service providers used by the infringer to move infringing goods within the EU are generally considered intermediaries in the practice of the Member States.[25] This reading is confirmed by the report of the European Commission, which also includes transport intermediaries within the scope of the term.[26]

To conclude, although the Directive uses the term "intermediary" and the Court step by step fleshes out its contours, it is increasingly becoming clear that the underlying concept has very little to do with any intermediary role. The generous protective hand of injunctions basically extends to everyone who engages in an economic activity, in course of which, he or she is in a position to prevent third-party wrongdoing. Any definitional exercises seem to be by now a mere window-dressing for the purposes of satisfying the black-letter law.

6.2 "WHOSE SERVICES ARE USED BY A THIRD PARTY"

A person who is subject to injunctions does not only have to be an intermediary, but also his services have to be used by a third party. The CJEU interpreted the scope of this notion in its *UPC Telekabel* ruling. The Advocate General advised the CJEU that the operators of allegedly infringing websites also "use" the services of an

---

[20] Case C-494/15 *Tommy Hilfiger Licensing and Others* [2016] ECLI:EU:C:2016:528.

[21] Regardless of how unlikely, an electricity provider, for instance, could theoretically be sued, as an offline intermediary, to cut off the electricity to an infringing factory. The same point about the electricity provider, in the German context, is also presented by Thomas Sassenberg and Reto Mantz, *WLAN und Recht. Aufbau und Betrieb von Internet-Hotspots* (Erich Schmidt Verlag, 2014) 161.

[22] Belgian Court of commerce of Antwerp (Rechtbank van Koophandel Antwerpen), *Koninklijke Philips Electronics v. NV Mediterranean Shipping Company Belgium (MSC)* Case No AR 08/02290 NV, 6 May 2008 (mentioned by Lambert Pechan and Marius Schneider, "Carriers and Trade Mark Infringements: Should Carriers Care?" (2010) 5(5) Journal of Intellectual Property Law & Practice 354, 361; In Germany, BGH *Pertusin II.* (1957) I ZR 56/55, involved accountability of a transporter for injunctions against third-party goods bearing infringing marks.

[23] Lambert Pechan and Marius Schneider, "Carriers and Trade Mark Infringements: Should Carriers Care?" (2010) 5(5) Journal of Intellectual Property Law & Practice 354, 361.

[24] Ibid., 354.   [25] Ibid.

[26] Commission, "Commission Staff Working Document" COM(2010) 779, 14.

Internet access provider in the sense of Article 8(3) InfoSoc Directive.[27] He recalled that:

> The recital [59] makes it clear that intermediaries are regarded by Directive 2001/29 as the best possible addressees of measures to terminate copyright infringements, *primarily because they carry data "in a network."* The wording makes it clear that this does not necessarily mean the first transmission of the data in a network, *but also the further carrying in the network.* This is even more clearly expressed in the English and Spanish versions of the directive: *"who carries a third party's infringement of a protected work . . . in a network"* (. . .).[28]

Therefore, even where customers of a provider might not infringe rights themselves when using the website, website blocking injunctions can still be issued against the provider, as long as its services are used to channel users to infringing websites.[29] The CJEU accepted this point, arguing that even an access provider who has no affiliation or business relationship with the targeted websites is still "used" by them. The Court added that,

> given that the internet service provider is an inevitable actor in any transmission of an infringement over the internet between one of its customers and a third party, since, *in granting access to the network, it makes that transmission possible* (. . .), it must be held that an internet service provider (. . .) is an intermediary whose services are used to infringe a copyright or related right within the meaning of Article 8(3) of Directive 2001/29.[30]

According to the Court, the requirement of a business relationship "cannot be inferred from the objectives pursued by that directive, given that to admit such a requirement would reduce the legal protection afforded to the right holders."[31] The objective of the Directive is to guarantee them a high level of protection. The CJEU thus again construes the term "uses" very broadly.[32] Basically anybody who even unwittingly "carries" a third-party infringement, i.e., gets mixed up in any way with the transaction, could be asked to assist.

Rather than a causal contribution or volition, the actual position of an intermediary seems to count. This is consistent with the historical character of such remedies.[33]

---

[27] Case C-314/12 *UPC Telekabel Wien* [2013] ECLI:EU:C:2013:781, Opinion of AG Villalón, para. 59.

[28] Ibid., para. 51 (emphasis mine).

[29] Martin Husovec, "CJEU Allowed Website Blocking Injunctions with Some Reservations" (2014) 9 (8) Journal of Intellectual Property Law & Practice 63.

[30] Case C-314/12 *UPC Telekabel Wien* [2014] ECLI:EU:C:2014:192, para. 32 (emphasis mine).

[31] Ibid., para. 35; later confirmed in Case C-494/15 *Tommy Hilfiger Licensing and Others* [2016] ECLI:EU:C:2016:528, para. 23.

[32] Christina Angelopolous, "CJEU in UPC Telekabel Wien: A Totally Legal Court Order . . . to Do the Impossible" (*Kluwer Copyright Blog*, 3 April 2014), http://kluwercopyrightblog.com/2014/04/03/upc-telekabel-wien/.

[33] Martin Husovec, "Injunctions Against Innocent Third Parties: Case of Website Blocking" (2013) 4 JIPITEC 116; Recently, the Austrian Supreme Court said in its *UPC Telekabel Wien* ruling (OGH

So even an intermediary that is not a *conditio sine qua non* of an infringement (e.g., the provider of an Internet browser), could potentially appear within the radar of such injunctions. Particularly on the Internet, virtually everything that is used by someone to either reach their audience or as a tool to commit infringements can be classified as a service. Thus, the only criterion and real limit of "use" seems to be the *ability* of an online or offline service provider to put an end to an infringement;[34] which is more of a capabilities than a blameworthiness inquiry.[35]

6.3 "TO INFRINGE AN INTELLECTUAL PROPERTY RIGHT"

The person using the services to infringe must be a third party. This means that such an injunction is not available if the sole infringer is the intermediary himself (for instance as the publisher of his own information). The unanswered question is whether the word "infringe" refers to only primary or also secondary infringements. The CJEU did not confirm this explicitly yet. On the national level, on one hand, the English courts have had so far very little difficulty in accepting this.[36] On the other hand, however, in the context of the pending preliminary reference on website blocking,[37] the Dutch courts seemed unwilling to classify domestic tortious liability provided on top of copyright primary liability as a form of "infringement" in sense of Article 8(3) of the InfoSoc Directive.[38]

In my view, an infringement of a third party in sense of these provisions can be both primary and secondary. As I explained earlier in Chapter 4, notion of "infringer" should be understood as referring to anyone who violates the right that qualifies

---

(2014) 4 Ob 71/14s): "The claim that is disputed here, to prohibition the provision of the access to a particular website, has to be considered on equal terms. Because also this case, the point is to defend an exclusive right that has an in rem effect gainst an interference" ("Der hier strittige Anspruch, das Vermitteln des Zugangs zu einer bestimmten Website zu unterlassen, ist gleich zu beurteilen. Denn auch dabei geht es um die Abwehr eines Eingriffs in ein dinglich wirkendes Ausschließungsrecht").

[34] Martin Husovec, "Injunctions Against Innocent Third Parties: Case of Website Blocking" (2013) 4 JIPITEC 116, 121ff.

[35] Althaf Marsoof argues that for the purposes of Art 11(III) of the Enforcement Directive, "it is not sufficient that the ISP concerned merely carries a third party's infringement" because he "must be used for the infringement, which is much narrower language." He supports this by arguing lack of Recital 59 of the InfoSoc Directive – see Althaf Marsoof, "The Blocking Injunction – A Critical Review of Its Implementation in the United Kingdom Within the Legal Framework of the European Union" (2015) 46 IIC 632, 642. This reading is, however, following the *Tommy Hilfiger* less convincing (Case C-494/15 *Tommy Hilfiger Licensing and Others* [2016] ECLI:EU:C:2016:528, paras. 22, 23). Similarly, Advocate General Szpunar does not seem to make any major distinction on the level of their contents – see Case C-610/15 *Stichting Brein* [2017] ECLI:EU:C:2017:99, Opinion of AG Szpunar, para. 56 ("those two provisions are similar in content").

[36] If the person who uses a service of an Internet access provider is not a user, but a targeted website, such as in the website blocking cases, the infringing acts often rely on the secondary liability of those websites – see the overview of the UK case-law in Section 10.3.

[37] Case C-610/15 *Stichting Brein* [2017] (pending).

[38] Martin Husovec and Lisa van Dongen, "Website Blocking, Injunctions and Beyond: View on the Harmonization from the Netherlands" [2017] GRUR 9.

as "intellectual property." Thus secondary infringers, even if not called so under national law, or direct infringers of nonharmonized rights, are also covered by the notion. In other words, this means that diverging domestic classification of violations of accessories, either as copyright or general torts, shouldn't foreclose an opportunity for injunctions.[39] Opposite reading would lead to a further fragmentation of the availability of injunctions against intermediaries and could undermine effectiveness of the enforcement framework.

In addition, from the language of the provisions – "services [which] *are used* by a third party to infringe" – the question surfaces concerning the reach of injunctions. Is it limited to already committed infringements or also available in the form of preemptive relief,[40] i.e., in the form of an injunction to restrain wrongful acts which are threatened or imminent but have not yet commenced. This seems to be another open issue which can be of relevance, for instance, for disconnecting injunctions, whose plaintiffs may want to extend them also to other Internet access providers on the market.[41] One could argue that if cooperation remedies against third parties are concerned, there are strong policy reasons to require that they are involved only when the past has proven a need for such a measure for a future.

The wording of both provisions – "intermediaries whose services *are used*" – would suggest that preemptive injunctions are *not* prescribed. A similar reading seems to result from Recital 59 of the InfoSoc Directive, which states that "[i]n many cases such intermediaries are best placed to bring such infringing activities to an end." The CJEU, however, challenged this reading in *L'Oréal v. eBay* when it also ascribed a *preventive function* to these kind of injunctions.[42] With this background, it would not come as a surprise if this preventive function were extended not only to the future curbing of already committed infringements, but also to the prevention of imminent but not yet actual infringements of users.

In *UPC Telekabel*, however, suggests that such injunctions are not available. The Court here notes that,

> in order to obtain the issue of an injunction against an internet service provider, *the holders of a copyright or of a related right must show that some of the customers*

---

[39] Advocate General Szpunar offered similar view, although not based on the term "infringer" in Case C-610/15 *Stichting Brein* [2017] ECLI:EU:C:2017:99, Opinion of AG Szpunar, paras. 65, 84.

[40] In common law, also called *quia timet* injunctions.

[41] Martin Husovec and Miquel Peguera, "Much Ado About Little – Privately Litigated Disconnecting Injunctions" [2015] IIC 10.

[42] Both the InfoSoc and Enforcement Directives require that the measures which the Member States must take in order to conform to those directives are aimed not only at bringing to an end infringements of copyright and related rights, but also at preventing them (see to that effect the InfoSoc Directive: Case C-70/10 *Scarlet Extended* [2011] ECLI:EU:C:2011:771, para. 31; Case C-360/10 *SABAM* [2012] ECLI:EU:C:2012:85, para. 29; Case C-314/12 *UPC Telekabel Wien* [2014] ECLI:EU:C:2014:192, para. 37; and for the Enforcement Directive: Case C-324/09 *L'Oréal and Others* [2011] ECLI:EU:C:2011:474, para. 144).

of that provider actually access, on the website at issue, the protected subject-matter made available to the public without the agreement of the rightholders.[43]

However, *Tommy Hilfiger* case, implies the exact opposite. Here the Court ruled that "it must be established that [the addressee] provides a service capable of being used by one or more other persons in order to infringe one or more intellectual property rights."[44] The reference to "capable" seems to suggest that even purely preemptive injunctions could be possible.

It should be remembered, however, that national law may go beyond Union law. The German Federal Supreme Court (the BGH), for instance, accepted also preemptive injunctions against noninfringers in its decision *Internetversteigerung II*.[45] After the Court of Appeal ruling in *British Telecommunications v. One In A Million*,[46] it seems likely that the English courts would also take this route; as may the courts of other Member States.

6.4 NATIONAL IMPLEMENTATION

The European legislator left it to the Member States to provide for the whole set of requirements for injunctions against intermediaries. In Recital 59 of the InfoSoc Directive, the Union legislator left the following explanation:

> In the digital environment, in particular, the services of intermediaries may increasingly be used by third parties for infringing activities. In many cases such intermediaries are best placed to bring such infringing activities to an end. Therefore, without prejudice to any other sanctions and remedies available,[47] rightholders should have the possibility of applying for an injunction against an intermediary who carries a

---

[43] Case C-314/12 *UPC Telekabel Wien* [2014] ECLI:EU:C:2014:192, para. 36 (emphasis mine).

[44] Case C-494/15 *Tommy Hilfiger Licensing and Others* [2016] ECLI:EU:C:2016:528, para. 23.

[45] BGH *Internetversteigerung II*. (2007) I ZR 35/04; this decision was only an extension of earlier decisions of the Court of the German Empire that confirmed the availability of injunctions in general, even before the first interference materializes, as long as there is the risk it will (RG (1921) VI 473/20, RGZ 101, 335).

[46] It was suggested that Norwich Pharmacal could even give rise to the "ability to restrain dissemination of an instrument" of an infringement before it is committed – see *British Telecommunications Plc & Ors v. One In A Million Ltd & Ors* [1998] EWCA Civ 1272 ("The ability to restrain dissemination of an instrument of fraud was recognised by the Court of Appeal in *Norwich Pharmacal Co v. Customs and Excise Commissioners* (1974) AC 133. That was an action in which the plaintiffs sought discovery of the names of patent infringers. The plaintiffs submitted, by analogy to trade mark and passing-off cases, that the Customs could be ordered to give discovery of the names. (. . .) It follows that a court will intervene by way of injunction in passing-off cases in three types of case. First, where there is passing-off established or it is threatened. Second, where the defendant is a joint tortfeasor with another in passing-off either actual or threatened. Third, where the defendant has equipped himself with or intends to equip another with an instrument of fraud. This third type is probably mere *quia timet* action").

[47] This part of the text ("without prejudice to any other sanctions and remedies available") refers to remedies and sanctions available against the authors of the infringement.

third party's infringement of a protected work or other subject-matter in a network. *This possibility should be available even where the acts carried out by the interme- diary are exempted under Article 5. The conditions and modalities relating to such injunctions should be left to the national law of the Member States.*

In other words, the legislator wanted to provide for relief against intermediaries irrespective of whether they are acting in compliance with the exclusive rights. The exact "conditions and modalities" are, however, in the hands of the national legislators.[48] A similar note is found in Recital 23 of the Enforcement Directive.

There are two ways in which a reference to "conditions and modalities" can be read. First, it could be read as an expression of freedom to legislate the circle of intermediaries which might be involved. And second, it could be read as a possibility afforded to the Member States to only adjust such a tool to the national legal mechanisms, and possibly further specify its conditions, if necessary. In the former case, it is the injunctions-addressees that would differ across the Member States, in the latter case, it is only the conditions under which the prefixed addressees are subject to such injunctions. The meaning of the clause is not entirely settled yet.

On one hand, the English copyright precondition of "actual knowledge,"[49] the Austrian copyright requirement of prior cease and desist letters,[50] or German require- ment of "duties to review" could be offered as examples of such idiosyncratic national deviations. On the other hand, however, the "modalities" could cut deeper, by limiting, country by country, the scope of persons who might answer the call for such injunctions. The recent case-law developments surrounding website blocking injunctions suggest that the national courts understand the obligation as imperative in terms of players,[51] but modular, in terms of the measures and their terms.

In other words, Union law obliges to involve whoever qualifies as intermediaries, but domestic laws can decide upon the nature and preconditions of their involve- ment. However, there would be no harmonization if the Member States could simply postulate any modalities they wish. They could frustrate any efforts of Union law by imposing impossible or impracticable modalities. Therefore, in *L'Oréal v. eBay*, the CJEU postulated that the rules of the national law must "be designed in such a way that the objective pursued by the directive may be achieved."[52] Otherwise, the protection afforded by Union law would be breached, since the Member State would fail to comply with its obligation to provide for meaningful injunctions of this

---

[48] Case C-70/10 *Scarlet Extended* [2011] ECLI:EU:C:2011:771, para. 32; Case C-360/10 *SABAM* [2012] ECLI:EU:C:2012:85, para. 30.

[49] 97A Copyright, Designs, and Patents Act 1988 – see *Twentieth Century Fox Film Corp & Ors v. British Telecommunications Plc* [2011] EWHC 1981 (Ch) [121]ff.

[50] Section 81(1a) of the Austrian Copyright Act.

[51] BGH (2016) I ZR 3/14, paras. 33, 66; BGH Störerhaftung des Access-Providers (2016) I ZR 174/14, para. 22; OGH (2014) 4 Ob 71/14s, para. 3.2; *Cartier International AG & Ors v. British Sky Broadcasting Ltd & Ors* [2016] EWCA Civ 658, para. [33]ff.

[52] See Case C-324/09 *L'Oréal and Others* [2011] ECLI:EU:C:2011:474, para. 136.

kind. This serves as a moderator of domestic "modalities" that could frustrate the goals of the provision.

In delineating the edges of such a "core" obligation, the actual aim of the provision is of the foremost importance. If Article 8(3) of the InfoSoc Directive and Article 11(III) of the Enforcement Directive are remedies that "may not be made dependent on the lawfulness of the acts of intermediaries" (the Commission),[53] and "are not intended as a penalty, but are simply based on the fact that such intermediaries (. . .) are in certain cases in the best position to stop or to prevent an infringement" (the Commission),[54] then the "core" is arguably *beyond* what most of the reasonable sanctioning provisions would be capable of delivering.

In *L'Oréal v. eBay*, the binding core of an obligation to provide injunctive relief against intermediaries was derived from the doctrine of *effect utile*,[55] according to which, among several possible interpretations, the one that best guarantees the practical effect of Union law must prevail. Because the national design of such injunctions against intermediaries must achieve the objective pursued by Union law, what most likely counts is the desired result and not the doctrinal classification or mechanism used to achieve it.

Therefore the question of whether a Member State is compliant if it makes such injunctions conditional upon some form of liability in its national law cannot be automatically answered in the negative. Article 8(3) of the InfoSoc Directive and Article 11(III) of the Enforcement Directive ask for some "extra help" on top of usual the secondary liability. If that "extra help" is reached by holding intermediaries liable within very harsh national laws, the result is achieved and thus the core of the obligation satisfied. Put another way, in order to satisfy "the core" of the obligation it seems to be acceptable just to deliver the desired result, such as website blocking, regardless of whether it is achieved by considering injunctions-addressees infringers, or innocent third parties. On the other hand, one could question if harsh national laws on secondary liability,[56] with their other consequences, are still compatible

---

53 Commission, "Staff Working Document: Analysis of the application of Directive 2004/48/EC of the European Parliament and the Council of 29 April 2004 on the enforcement of intellectual property rights in the Member States – accompanying document to the Report from the Commission to the Council, the European Parliament and the European Social Committee on the application of Directive 2004/48/EC of the European Parliament and the Council of 29 April 2004 on the enforcement of intellectual property rights" COM(2010) 779 final.

54 Ibid.

55 Stefan Mayr, "Putting a Leash on the Court of Justice? Preconceptions in National Methodology *v.* Effet Utile as a Meta-Rule" (2013) 5(2) European Journal of Legal Studies 8–21.

56 When examining the practical reach of these injunctions, especially in cases such as *Scarlet Extended* or *UPC Telekabel Wien*, it becomes clear that they extend beyond most of the situations where national laws would usually be willing to find some form of secondary liability. For instance, only few countries would be ready to regard ordinary Internet access providers as secondary infringers – attributing to them the conduct of their users in a full extent.

with the general limitations of the Enforcement Directive such as proportionality or low barriers to legitimate trade (Article 3).[57]

Several documents of the European institutions make remarks on the conditions for injunctions against intermediaries. The European Commission notes that "the IPRED made a major advance by allowing rightsholders to request injunctions against intermediaries, *without any requirement* that the intermediary necessarily be complicit in or culpable for the infringement."[58] However, since the conditions imposed by national law or by jurisprudence vary from country to country, for the injunctions "to work efficiently, it could be useful to clarify that injunctions should not depend on the liability of the intermediary."[59] And that this should be no surprise, given that "injunctions against intermediaries were a new element which had to be introduced into the national laws in almost all the Member States."[60]

The report of the European Observatory on Counterfeiting and Piracy also comes to the conclusion that the conditions for injunctions against intermediaries vary widely among the Member States.[61] It suggests that:

> Articles 9 and 11 of the IPRED Directive (as well as Article 8(3) of Directive 2001/29/EC) should be interpreted consistently so as to make clear that the intermediary's liability (or the violation by the intermediary of any kind of duty) is not a pre-condition to an injunction being issued against him with respect to a third party's infringement. This appears to be the practice in the majority of Member States, and is supported by the wording of Article 9(1)(a) of the IPRED.[62]

The results of the report of the Observatory, based on a survey of local experts, is unfortunately full of misstatements about the situation in some Member States. It is therefore difficult to rely completely on the Report. Especially when the results of the Observatory are compared with the literature and case-law, one can easily

---

[57] Case C-367/15 *Stowarzyszenie "Oławska Telewizja Kablowa* [2017] ECLI:EU:C:2017:36, para. 31 (discussing a potential abusiveness of double compensation for infrignemnets caused by infringers).

[58] Commission, "Report by the Commission to the European Parliament, the Council, the European Economic and Social Committee and the Committee of the Regions on Application of Directive 2004/48/EC of the European Parliament and the Council of 29 April 2004 on the enforcement of intellectual property rights" (2010) COM 0779.

[59] Ibid.

[60] Commission, "Staff Working Document: Analysis of the application of Directive 2004/48/EC of the European Parliament and the Council of 29 April 2004 on the enforcement of intellectual property rights in the Member States – accompanying document to the Report from the Commission to the Council, the European Parliament and the European Social Committee on the application of Directive 2004/48/EC of the European Parliament and the Council of 29 April 2004 on the enforcement of intellectual property rights" COM(2010) 779 final.

[61] European Observatory on Counterfeiting and Piracy, "Injunctions in Intellectual Property Right," http://ec.europa.eu/internal_market/iprenforcement/docs/injunctions_en.pdf – the report should be taken with caution as there seem to be misstatements, at least in respect to several Member States.

[62] Ibid.

spot several obvious mistakes.[63] There either seems to be substantial disagreement among the experts about the possibility of seeking injunctions against noninfringing intermediaries or the relevant national provisions were not tested and, at the time, were only latent remedies.

In the last years, the contours of the remedy have crystalized a bit more. In *Tommy Hilfiger*, the Court already presented the following legal principles as a basis of the remedy:

> It is settled case-law that the third sentence of Article 11 of Directive 2004/48, like Article 8(3) of Directive 2001/29 to which it refers, obliges Member States to ensure that an intermediary whose services are used by a third party in order to infringe an intellectual property right may, *regardless of any liability of its own in relation to the facts at issue*, be ordered to take measures aimed at bringing those infringements to an end and measures seeking to prevent further infringements.[64]

The situation wasn't always that clear. Before *L'Oréal v. eBay*, the combination of the European provisions with several legal traditions and national laws "led to misunderstandings, and sometimes to an accidental lack of implementation."[65] Often, therefore, very little sophistication from the Member States is seen on the issue of modalities and conditions, despite the fact that the real intentions of the Union legislator did not go unnoticed.

My survey of the English and German literature shows that scholarship wasn't fully aware of the consequences. At the time of the Enforcement Directive, only few seem to have commented on the potential breadth of the measures. Among the exceptions, Spindler already back in 2002 predicted that Article 8(3) of InfoSoc is a "dynamite" and that "the reach of this inconspicuous Article is hardly foreseeable."[66] Kur in her

---

[63] Slovakia and the Czech Republic have the necessary provisions (Martin Husovec, *Zodpovednosť na internete podľa českého a slovenského práva* (CZ.NIC, 2014)), as well as Austria – all of them supposedly provide for no injunctions against intermediaries. Denmark is said to provide injunctions irrespective of liability, but some scholarship reports the opposite (Sandfeld Jakobsen, "Injunctions Against Mere Conduit of Information Protected by Copyright – A Scandinavian Perspective" [2011] IIC 151); Finland is claimed, in the document, to require infringing activity of an intermediary, but the opposite has since been reported before the courts and literature (Court of Appeal of Helsinki, *pelastakaa pedofiilit* R 07/3400, 29 May 2008; Court of Appeal of Helsinki *Elisa* S 11/3097, 15 June 2012; Court of Appeal of Helsinki *DNA*,S 12/1850, 8 February 2013; Court of Appeal of Helsinki *TeliaSonera Finland* S 12/2223, 11 February 2013; Norrgård Marcus, "Blocking Web Sites – Experiences from Finland" in Johan Axhamn (ed.), *Copyright in a Borderless Online Environment* (Norstedts Juridik, 2012); Savola Pekka and Riku Neuvonen, "KHO 2013:136 – Verkkotunnusluettelon julkistamisen katsottiin edesauttavan lapsipornon levittämistä" (2014) 112 Lakimies 114). The depiction of Sweden as requiring some form of contributory liability seems to be accurate (Sandfeld Jakobsen, "Injunctions Against Mere Conduit of Information Protected by Copyright – A Scandinavian Perspective" [2011] IIC 151, though not obsolete after Patent- och Marknadsöverdomstolen (2017) PMT 11706–15).

[64] Case C-494/15 *Tommy Hilfiger Licensing and Others* [2016] ECLI:EU:C:2016:528, para. 22 (emphasis mine).

[65] Lambert Pechan and Marius Schneider, "Carriers and Trade Mark Infringements: Should Carriers Care?" (2010) 5(5) Journal of Intellectual Property Law & Practice 354, 355.

[66] Gerald Spindler, "Europäisches Urheberrecht in der Informationsgesellschaft" [2002] GRUR 105, 119.

2004 article[67] concluded that "the directive expressly leaves room for application of measures and sanctions against persons who are *not* found to be infringing an IP right themselves."[68] And Metzger,[69] in 2010, commented that Article 8(3) of the InfoSoc Directive "allows explicitly for injunctions against non-infringing ISPs." Pechan and Schneider agreed,[70] stating that, under Union law, the claim for destruction, like an injunction against an intermediary, is *"not* restricted to the infringer."[71]

Among the Nordic authors, Jakobsen and Petersen[72] expressed doubts as to whether Union law "holds a specific legal standard precise enough to have direct effect in those EU Member States that have not enacted specific legislation to implement it," thus doubting whether any Union "core" even exists. An Icelandic author, Hjördis,[73] explains that absence of liability on the side of intermediaries is *not* in line with "the traditional view in Iceland that an injunction will only be granted to prevent certain actions that are preconceived as being delict, being illegal as such."

Two British commentators, James and Smith,[74] pondered on "an obvious tension between the UK Government's position in relation to the exposure of intermediaries and the provisions of Article 11 which explicitly state that rightholders can get injunctions against intermediaries." Most likely with a tort-law mind-set, they continue that "there must be a point where infringements by third parties through intermediaries are on such a scale that an injunction is justified against the ISP under the Directive." This again shows that the authors generally did not seem to see much room for the Member States in their implementations.

The present national case-law is gradually incorporating injunctions against intermediaries into the local remedies structure. Apart from the numerous examples in German case-law mentioned earlier and Belgian litigations that ended up in two preliminary references before the CJEU, other European courts have also gradually become more and more active. In 2012, the French Supreme Court issued an injunction[75] against Google to prevent it from suggestion keywords such as

---

[67] Annette Kur, "Rough Start Happy Landing" [2004] IIC 821, 826.

[68] Kur also notes that "already at present, national laws may allow in certain instances to direct claims for injunction etc. against non-infringers, e.g. in German law on the basis of the so-called 'Störerhaftung,' Sec. 1004 of the Civil Code (only applying under narrow conditions)" (Annette Kur, "Rough Start Happy Landing" [2004] 35 IIC 821, 826).

[69] Axel Metzger, "Primer on ACTA: What Europeans Should Fear about the Anti-Counterfeiting Trade Agreement" (2010) 1 JIPITEC 109, 114.

[70] Lambert Pechan and Marius Schneider, "Carriers and Trade Mark Infringements: Should Carriers Care?" (2010) 5(5) Journal of Intellectual Property Law & Practice 354.

[71] Ibid., 355; *Jade Engineering (Coventry) Ltd v. Antiference Window Systems Ltd* [1996] FSR 461 Chancery Division (may be directed also against an innocent person).

[72] Sandfeld Jakobsen, "Injunctions Against Mere Conduit of Information Protected by Copyright – A Scandinavian Perspective" [2011] IIC 151, 153.

[73] Halldórsdóttir Hjördis, "Enforcement of Copyright" (2004) 47 Scandinavian Studies in Law 168, 169.

[74] Will James and Joel Smith, "Is Further Legislation Really Necessary to Level the Playing Field? A UK Perspective" (2004) 20(5) Computer Law & Security Review 356, 358.

[75] Cour de cassation (2012) Case No 11–20358 – reported by Anne-Catherine Lorrain, "Supreme Court (Cour de cassation): 'Google/Keyword Suggestions'" [2013] IIC 380.

"Torrent," "Megaupload" or "Rapidshare," because as a search engine it has the ability to make copyright-infringing activities more difficult on the Internet. The legal basis for the injunction was found in the implementation of the InfoSoc Directive, L.336–2,[76] despite the fact that Google had not infringed any copyright, but only because it had provided the means to infringe copyright.[77]

In the period since 2010, website blocking injunctions against Internet access providers have been on the raise in Europe. The national courts in countries such as the United Kingdom,[78] Ireland,[79] The Netherlands,[80] Belgium,[81] Germany,[82] Austria,[83] Greece,[84] France,[85] Denmark,[86] Finland,[87] and Italy,[88] Sweden[89] were reported to have considered such injunctions.[90] Not all of them,

---

[76] L.336–2 Code de la propriété intellectuelle (French Intellectual Property Code) according to which, "In the presence of an infringement of a copyright or related right (. . .) the high court, acting where appropriate in summary proceedings, may order at the request (. . .) to prevent or stop such an attack on a copyright or a related right measures *against any person who may help remedy*" (emphasis mine).

[77] Catherine Jasserand, "France: Google Can Be Ordered to Filter Words Linking to Online Piracy Websites" (*Kluwer Copyright Blog*, 3 September 2012), http://kluwercopyrightblog.com/2012/09/03/france-google-can-be-ordered-to-filter-words-linking-to-online-piracy-websites/; Anne-Catherine Lorrain, "Supreme Court (Cour de cassation): 'Google/Keyword Suggestions'" [2013] IIC 380 ("This ruling shall not be interpreted as holding Google liable for copyright infringement. It is precisely the strength of Sec. L.336–2 to request measures from stakeholders whose infringer status is not proven but who are deemed able to prevent the infringing activity on the Internet, without presuming infringement liability").

[78] See Section 9.4.

[79] *EMI Records (Ireland) Ltd and others v. UPC Communications Ireland Ltd* [2010] IEHC.

[80] Rechtbank Amsterdam (2007) LJN BA7810 (the court of first instance); Gerechtshof Amsterdam (2008) LJN BD6223 (the court of Appeal); Rechtbank's-Gravenhage (2012) ECLI:NL:RBSGR:2012:BV0549 (the court of first instance); Gerechtshof Den Haag (2014) ECLI:NL:GHDHA:2014:88 (the court of appeal); Supreme Court, Hoge Raad (2015) ECLI:NL:HR:2015:3307 (the Supreme Court of The Netherlands); see more Martin Husovec and Lisa van Dongen, "Website Blocking, Injunctions and Beyond: View on the Harmonization from the Netherlands" [2017] GRUR (forthcoming).

[81] Belgian Court of Appeal of Antwerp, *Belgian Anti-Piracy Foundation v. Belgacom and Telenet* (2011) Case No. 2011/8314, https://edri.org/files/piratebay-decision-belgium-2011.pdf.

[82] See Section 10.3.   [83] Austrian Supreme Court, OGH (2014) 4Ob71/14s.

[84] See Editorial, "The Court of First Instance of Athens (Monomeles Protodikio Athinon): 'Security Measures Against ISPs'" [2013] IIC 468.

[85] Tribunal de Grande Instance, *Association des Producteurs de Cine´ma (APC) and others v. Auchan Telecom and others* (2013) Case No 11/60013.

[86] Danish Supreme Court, *Telenor v. IFPI Denmark* (2010) Case No. 153/2009, http://hssph.net/Sonofon_IFPI_DK_SupremeCourt_27May2010_PirateBay.pdf. Accessed 5 July 2015.

[87] Helsinki Court of Appeals, (2012) Case S 11/3097; Helsinki Court of Appeals (2013) Case S 12/1825; Helsinki Court of Appeals (2013) Case S 12/2223; The Market Court (2016) Case 243/16.

[88] AGCOM Regulations regarding Online Copyright Enforcement, 680/13/CONS 12 December 2013; Lazio Regional Administrative Tribunal, Tribunale Regionale Amministrativo (TAR) del Lazio, *FEMI and Open Media Coalition v. Autorità per le Garanzie nelle Comunicazioni (AGCOM)* (2014) Case No 2184/2014.

[89] District Court in Stockholm (2015) AB T 15142–14; Swedish Patent and Market Court of Appeal, Patent- och Marknadsöverdomstolen (2017) PMT 11706–15.

[90] For a overview – see Savola Pekka, "Proportionality of Website Blocking: Internet Connectivity Providers as Copyright Enforcers" (2014) 5(2) JIPITEC 116; Martin Husovec, "Injunctions Against

however, without any assessment of liability on the side of the Internet access providers. Especially in some Nordic countries, such injunctions were implemented as requiring "contributory" tortious legal basis,[91] which turned unsustainable in the view of recent developments.[92]

The website blocking decisions, in particular, stand out in respect to "conditions and modalities." First, the decision of the Austrian Supreme Court (OGH) in *UPC Telekabel* after the CJEU referral.[93] In this ruling, the Court seems to readily assume that Union law definitely *requires* that website blocking injunctions are available. Similarly, Justice Arnold, in his *Cartier* decision,[94] held that, because the CJEU regarded the measures from *L'Oréal v. eBay* as part of the core of the Union law obligations, the same would apply to website blocking injunctions. He thus decided to give indirect effect to Union law, and interpret the domestic provision on injunctive relief in light of Union law.[95] The German Federal Supreme Court (BGH) in its website blocking cases, admitted that Union law obliges to website blocking injunctions.[96] The Swedish appellate court[97] and the Dutch Supreme Court also consider the website blocking to be a prescribed must.[98]

The last major development is a use of Article 8(3) of the InfoSoc Directive for setting up an entire administrative system before the courts. In 2015, the Irish Commercial Court issued an injunction[99] against access providers creating, for five

---

Innocent Third Parties: Case of Website Blocking" (2013) 4 JIPITEC 116; *Twentieth Century Fox Film Corp v. British Telecommunications plc* [2011] EWHC 1981 (Ch) [102]; Althaf Marsoof, "The Blocking Injunction – A Critical Review of Its Implementation in the United Kingdom Within the Legal Framework of the European Union" (2015) 46 IIC 632, 656.

91 Sandfeld Jakobsen, "Injunctions Against Mere Conduit of Information Protected by Copyright – A Scandinavian Perspective" [2011] IIC 151.

92 Swedish Patent and Market Court of Appeal, Patent- och Marknadsöverdomstolen (2017) PMT 11706–15 (the Swedish Patent and Market Court of Appeal reverses the decision of the first instance. It finds a legal basis for the website blocking with the argument that the Union-conform interpretation requries the word "contributes" to be read in light of the Union provisions).

93 Austrian Supreme Court, OGH (2014) 4Ob71/14s.

94 *Cartier International AG & Ors v. British Sky Broadcasting Ltd & Ors* [2014] EWHC 3354 (Ch).

95 Ibid., [112]–[132].

96 In its earlier case-law the BGH implicitly assumed broad implementation leeway for the Member States (BGH *Internetversteigerung II* (2007) I ZR 35/04 – the decision, however, predates the decision of the CJEU in *L'Oréal v. eBay*); A preliminary reference to the CJEU is also possible – see Jan Nordemann, "Internetpiraterie: High Court of Justice bejaht Anspruch auf Markeninhabern auf Website-Sperrung – Eine Option auch für deutsche Rechteinhaber?" [2014] GRUR-Prax 513, 515; Matthias Leistner and Karrina Grisse, "Sperrverfügungen gegen Access-Provider im Rahmen der Störerhaftung (Teil 2)" [2015] GRUR 105, 114.

97 Nedim Malovic, "Swedish Patent and Market Court of Appeal orders block of The Pirate Bay and Swefilmer" (*IPKat*, 2017), http://ipkitten.blogspot.nl/2017/02/swedish-patent-and-market-court-of.html.

98 See more Martin Husovec and Lisa van Dongen, "Website Blocking, Injunctions and Beyond: View on the Harmonization from the Netherlands" [2017] GRUR (forthcoming).

99 *Sony Music Entertainment (Ireland) Limited v. UPC Communications Ireland Limited (No 1)* [2015] IEHC 317.

years, an entire graduated response scheme that allows disconnection of subscribers who engage in repeated infringements.[100] It concerns only non–business users and fixed broadband subscribers. It foresees that three notifications are sent to alleged infringers. Upon sending of a third notification, the plaintiffs can seek identity disclosure concerning the subscribers and also an order to terminate their access. Such applications "will not be opposed or consented to by the defendant and no costs will be sought, by or against, the defendant of the proceedings or of compliance."[101] For the administration of the scheme, the rightholders should pay 20 percent of any capital expenditure incurred by access providers, provided that it is "required to operate the scheme." However, the maximum capital expenditure cost is capped at 940,000 euros. At the same time, the amount of notifications send by rightholders may not exceed 2,500 per month.

This small preview of the case-law and of domestic approaches shows the gradual intensification of use of the injunctions. At the national level, the debate at first centered around whether the national law did enough to satisfy Union law. And although this debate will still continue for some time, the more important discussion for the years to come will concern limitations imposed on such injunctions. At the moment, it is often neglected fact that the Member States can also deviate from Union law in the opposite direction. As the Enforcement Directive puts it, "in so far as those means [are] more favourable for rightholders" (Article 2(1)), additions on the national level are allowed. So, for instance the Member State can extend such measures also to *any third party*, not only intermediaries.[102] Such national modifications, however, must be again compatible with the general limitations of the Enforcement Directive and fundamental rights. These national enforcement schemes (e.g., providing website blocking as a remedy), it should not be forgotten, are also an implementation of Article 8(3) of the InfoSoc and Article 11(III) of the Enforcement Directive.[103]

To summarize, a Member State may deviate from these Directives under certain conditions. If their own conditions provide less protection to rightholders, they must preserve a certain core that is measured by the achievable results. If they want to provide more protection to them, they still have to respect the general limitations of the Enforcement Directive. Thus the Member States are free to implement the provisions not only verbatim, but also with further additions or extensions. Given

---

[100] Gerard Kelly, "A Court-Ordered Graduated Response System in Ireland: The Beginning of the End?" (2016) 11(3) Journal of Intellectual Property Law & Practice 183–198.

[101] Ibid., 184.

[102] This was the case in the old Slovak Copyright Act, Section 56(1)(b)(c) of the Act No 618/2003 Coll. (refering to a "person who indirectly took part" in an infringing act). The provision of the new Copyright Act, Section 58(1)(b)(c) of the Act No 185/2015 Coll. now refers to "service providers."

[103] Martin Husovec and Miquel Peguera, "Much Ado About Little – Privately Litigated Disconnecting Injunctions" [2015] IIC 10, 32; The decision of the Lazio Regional Administrative Tribunal, Tribunale Regionale Amministrativo (TAR) del Lazio, *FEMI and Open Media Coalition v. Autorità per le Garanzie nelle Comunicazioni (AGCOM)* (2014) Case No 2184/2014, seems to acknowledge this.

that the Union law framework is already endlessly broad,[104] there are not many possibilities for its further broadening. Most of the countries will more probably have to deal with the question of whether their own requirements are sufficient to satisfy the Union core.

Under the newly formed Unified Patent Court, patent injunctions against intermediaries may soon become one possible exception to this entire debate of national modalities. The Agreement on a Unified Patent Court (AUPC) in its Article 63(1) AUPC does not foresee any implementation "conditions and modalities" for the Member States. So they most likely stand as autonomous conditions of international public law (not Union law), which imposes "fuller" harmonization on the Member States that Union law itself.

---

[104] Martin Husovec and Miquel Peguera, "Much Ado About Little – Privately Litigated Disconnecting Injunctions" [2015] IIC 10, 10.

7

Scope of Injunctions Against Intermediaries

The actual scope of injunctions is alfa and omega. It is closely related to the aim of the entire concept. Yet the only legislatively set normative aspiration of these injunctions can be found in the Recital 59 of the InfoSoc Directive:

> In the digital environment, in particular, the services of intermediaries may increasingly be used by third parties for infringing activities. In many cases such intermediaries are best placed to bring such infringing activities to an end.

This provision, at most, says that the reason for engaging intermediaries is more an economic one. They can, according to the law, avoid the costs of infringing activities more cheaply *in many cases*. In Section 4.2, I concluded that the nature of such engagement is one of cooperation. But how does or should this translate into the scope of injunctions?

7.1 CORRECTION AND PREVENTION

If such injunctions require positive steps to be taken, may they cure only infringements of the past, or also those of the near future? The CJEU had to deal with this question in *L'Oréal v. eBay*. As the Advocate General admitted from the outset, "the scope of injunctions against an intermediary is not [yet] defined."[1] In his opinion, however, "as this aspect [of the instrument] is added as a complementary element to the two first sentences [of Article 11 of Enforcement Directive], (. . .) these two sentences should be used in interpreting the third sentence."[2] The Advocate General then comes to the conclusion that:

---

[1] Case C-324/09 *L'Oréal and Others* [2010] ECLI:EU:C:2010:757, Opinion of AG Jääskinen, para. 173.
[2] Case C-324/09 *L'Oréal and Others* [2010] ECLI:EU:C:2010:757, Opinion of AG Jääskinen, para. 173.

The requirement of proportionality would in my opinion exclude an injunction against the intermediary *to prevent any further infringements of a trade mark*. However, I do not see anything in Directive 2004/48 which would prohibit injunctions against the intermediary requiring not only the prevention of the continuation of a specific act of infringement but also *the prevention of repetition of the same or a similar infringement in the future*, if such injunctions are available under national law. (. . .) An appropriate limit for the scope of injunctions may be that of a double requirement of identity.[3]

The Court accepted this.[4] It argued that injunctions against intermediaries also serve a prevention function, not only the removal of third-party infringements. According to the Court:

> it must be stated that, in view of the objective pursued by Directive 2004/48, which is that the Member States should ensure, especially in the information society, *effective protection of intellectual property* (see, to that effect, Case C-275/06 Promusicae [2008] ECR I-271, paragraph 43), the jurisdiction conferred, in accordance with the third sentence of Article 11 of the directive, on national courts *must allow them to order an online service provider*, such as a provider making an online marketplace available to internet users, *to take measures that contribute not only to bringing to an end infringements committed through that marketplace, but also to preventing further infringements*.[5]

Overall, the Court supported this result by three arguments based on the objectives pursued by Union law. Firstly, the objective of "effective protection" of intellectual property rights. Second, by pointing out the importance of Recital 24, which states that "the measures, procedures and remedies to be provided for should include prohibitory measures aimed at preventing further infringements of intellectual property rights." And third, an alleged obligation under the wording of Article 18 of the E-Commerce Directive according to which Member States shall ensure that "court actions available under national law (. . .) allow for the rapid adoption of measures, including interim measures, designed to terminate any alleged infringement and to prevent any further impairment of the interests involved."[6]

The obvious problem with the last argument is that the Enforcement Directive may not be affected by the E-Commerce Directive, and hence, neither can it be used as an argument in favor of certain legislative *demands* within its ambit.[7] The

---

3 Ibid., Opinion of AG Jääskinen, paras. 180, 181, 182 (emphasis mine).
4 Case C-70/10 *Scarlet Extended* [2011] ECLI:EU:C:2011:771, para. 31; Case C-360/10 *SABAM* [2012] ECLI:EU:C:2012:85, para. 29.
5 Case C-324/09 *L'Oréal and Others* [2011] ECLI:EU:C:2011:474, para. 131 (emphasis mine).
6 Case C-324/09 *L'Oréal and Others* [2011] ECLI:EU:C:2011:474, para. 133.
7 Sandfeld Jakobsen, "Injunctions Against Mere Conduit of Information Protected by Copyright – A Scandinavian Perspective" [2011] IIC 151 153 ("under this Directive, Member States are thus under no obligation to provide for such injunctions in their legal systems").

only convincing reading of this could be one of coherency of Union law. The entire argument of the Court thus rests mostly upon the language of Recital 24 and justification by a need for "effective enforcement" of intellectual property rights. Regardless of whether one deems the argumentation of the Court convincing or not, this end-position makes perfect sense. Otherwise injunctions against noninfringers would become a mere correction mechanism to clear away confirmed infringements of the past; nothing new to enforcement laws of many Member States. The preventive character of injunctions against intermediaries was confirmed also later in *Scarlet Extended, Sabam, UPC Telekabel* and *Tommy Hilfiger* cases.[8] In *Mc Fadden*, the Court even supported it with a strong "deprivation" rhetoric.[9]

The prevention still can take many forms, however. The German Federal Supreme Court (BGH), as will be explained in Chapter 9, develops the stay down obligations as a form of preventive duty after notification. This duty extends to prevention of similar infringements, irrespective of the person who infringes. In *L'Oréal v. eBay*, the Court accepted the invitation of the Advocate General to rule that preventive injunctions should cover not only one particular infringement, but also "double identity infringements" committed by the same person and against the same protected object.[10] This means that a single infringement opens the scissors of assistance not only toward the policing of one particular infringement, but also toward any infringement against the identical object by the identical person. The BGH later interpreted it as a nonexhaustive statement of the law.[11] *Tommy Hilfiger* ruling, however, suggests the opposite. The Court here says that "[b]y contrast [to obligations of general and permanent oversight], the intermediary may be forced to take measures which contribute to avoiding new infringements of the same nature by the same market-trader from taking place."[12] Given the contrasting presentation, the ruling seems to rather *confine* the extent of specific preventive obligations to these conditions.

However, what does it mean to avoid "new infringements of the same nature by the same infringer"? The double identity rules would confine specific prevention to the same object and the same infringer. The German practice confines it to a similar infringement, regardless of the infringer's identity. *Tommy Hilfiger* standard seems

---

[8] Case C-70/10 *Scarlet Extended* [2011] ECLI:EU:C:2011:771, para. 31; Case C-360/10 *SABAM* [2012] ECLI:EU:C:2012:85, para. 29; Case C-314/12 *UPC Telekabel Wien* [2013] ECLI:EU:C:2013:781, Opinion of AG Villalón, para. 40; Case C-494/15 *Tommy Hilfiger Licensing and Others* [2016] ECLI:EU:C:2016:528, para. 23; on the national level, this was discussed in *Twentieth Century Fox Film Corp v. British Telecommunications plc* [2011] EWHC 1981 (Ch) [164].

[9] Case C-484/14 *Mc Fadden* [2016] ECLI:EU:C:2016:689, para. 98.

[10] Case C-324/09 *L'Oréal and Others* [2011] ECLI:EU:C:2011:474 para. 141; Case C-324/09 *L'Oréal and Others* [2010] ECLI:EU:C:2010:757, Opinion of AG Jääskinen, para. 182.

[11] The German Federal Supreme Court is of the opinion (BGH *Kinderhochstühle im Internet II*. (2013) I ZR 216/11) that the scissors can be opened even further, since the CJEU ruling is allegedly nonexhaustive on this point.

[12] Case C-494/15 *Tommy Hilfiger Licensing and Others* [2016] ECLI:EU:C:2016:528, para. 34.

somewhere in between, however, closer to "double identity" situations. It requires the identical infringer and identical nature of the new infringement. How far such preventive obligation deviates from "double identity" depends on the interpretation of the notion of "infringement's nature." This could mean anything from any comparable infringement of any other protected object, to infringement of the same object, but irrespective of its type. At the moment, it is unclear what the Court's stance is.

7.2 GOAL OF INJUNCTIONS

An injunction is usually understood as an order requiring the person to whom it is directed to perform a particular act or to refrain from carrying out a particular act. This conventional definition of injunction addresses a person who acts against the law – an infringer – and should be stopped from doing so. Such a person acts in a way that the rights of other people prohibit. Seeking an injunction is thus nothing but the request of a rightholder to an authority (court) for the individual compliance of a particular person with the abstract letter of the law.

Injunctions against noninfringing intermediaries, however, do not target such persons. They address by-standers who *comply* with the law. The basis for this kind of injunction is thus *not* an act of disrespect toward the rights of others, but the mere existence of circumstances giving hope to rightholders, that if they are assisted by such a person, they will be better off. Put differently, such injunctions want to achieve better enforcement by seeking a help of intermediaries who can do more, but do not have to, as they did all the law required from them in order to avoid liability in tort. Assuming that their personal conduct is perfectly legal in that particular legal order, the question is whether an injunction seeking assistance from noninfringing intermediaries may take the very same form as one against intermediaries who are infringers. The CJEU deal with this issue in *L'Oréal v. eBay*, where it held the following:

> (...) it should first be stated that the use of the word "injunction" in the third sentence of Article 11 differs considerably from the use, in the first sentence thereof, of the words "injunction aimed at prohibiting the continuation of the infringement," the latter describing injunctions which may be obtained against infringers of an intellectual property right. (...) *that difference can be explained by the fact that an injunction against an infringer entails, logically, preventing that person from continuing the infringement, whilst the situation of the service provider by means of which the infringement is committed is more complex and lends itself to other kinds of injunctions.* For that reason, an "injunction" as referred to in the third sentence of Article 11 of Directive 2004/48 *cannot be equated* with an "injunction aimed at prohibiting the continuation of the infringement" as referred to in the first sentence of Article 11. (...) That implies that, in a case such as that before the referring court, which concerns possible infringements of trade marks in the context of a service

provided by the operator of an online marketplace, *the injunction obtained against that operator cannot have as its object or effect a general and permanent prohibition on the selling,*[13] *on that marketplace, of goods bearing those trade marks.*[14]

The Court then came up with two possible measures that satisfy this condition: (1) an injunction seeking the termination of an account of repeated infringer[15] and (2) an injunction obliging to increased transparency in identification of a customer-seller who can potentially infringe the rights of others.[16]

It is submitted that by the above rule, the Court wanted to prevent Article 11(III) Enforcement Directive from being used to impose *full restriction of conduct*. This is why the Court stresses that injunctions against intermediaries "cannot be equated with an injunction aimed at prohibiting the continuation of the infringement." Such a rule is very sensible. If we were to accept that an injunction against a noninfringing intermediary can restrict his full conduct, we would indirectly expand the scope of exclusive rights, since an injunction would put otherwise abstractly allowed acts under the reservation of a rightholder's consent. But an injunction should only individually prohibit what is *already* abstractly prohibited by the law and thus covered by the existing rights, their scope or associated doctrines of secondary liability. It may not go beyond.[17]

To illustrate this, consider the following example. Let's assume that an open WiFi operator whose connection was misused by a third party did not act wrongfully, that is she did not commit a tort herself, and neither can any tort be attributed to her. If she is sued based on Article 11(III) Enforcement Directive to *generally and permanently* refrain from such misuse in the future, the injunction is, in its effect, tantamount to a new exclusive right covering an individual's possibility to share his Internet connection. This is because there is no way in which an operator of WiFi can avoid the abuse, other than by not sharing its connectivity. From the perspective of the exclusivity of rights, there is no economic difference between this and a scenario in which a rightholder cannot share his connectivity because third-party communication of works is attributed to him.[18] It is the same entitlement of control

---

[13] This last part was also confirmed by Case C-70/10 *Scarlet Extended* [2011] ECLI:EU:C:2011:771, para. 36.

[14] Case C-324/09 *L'Oréal and Others* [2011] ECLI:EU:C:2011:474, paras. 128–130, 140 (emphasis mine).

[15] Ibid., para. 141.   [16] Ibid., para. 142.

[17] Austrian Supreme Court, OGH (2014) 4 Ob 140/14p (arguing that an accessory can only be prohibited from carrying out those that are wrongful: "*Dem Gehilfen kann nach allgemeinen Grundsätzen nur der konkrete Tatbeitrag untersagt werden, nicht das tatbestandsmäßige Verhalten der von ihm geförderten Person* (. . .). *Das Verbot müsste sich daher gegen das Ermöglichen eines Urheberrechtseingriffs durch dritte Personen richten, die ihrerseits als unmittelbare Täter handeln. Demgegenüber beantragt der Kläger, der Beklagten den Eingriff in das Ausschließungsrecht als solchen zu untersagen*").

[18] Attempts of this kind have already taken place – see Rosario Debilio, "Red Light for Sabam's Pricing System for Internet Access Providers: Up- and Downstream IAP Traffic Do Not Constitute Communication or Making a Work Available to the Public" (*Kluwer Copyright Blog*, 6 May 2015),

over an ability to share the connectivity, which carries protected works.[19] The only way to avoid it is by obtaining consent, a "license," to share connectivity over WiFi.

Rightholders would thereby obtain an even wider possibility to control a broad range of technologies that do not fall under the scope of the right of communication to the public which, as a rule, excludes control over mere technical infrastructure used for such communication.[20] This is why the Court warns us before injunctions for assistance that are used for a general and permanent restriction of conduct. Apart from the nature of such injunctions, that was argued earlier in this work, one can rely also on the human rights framework to support this reading.

An injunction against an intermediary should therefore always be framed as a positive obligation of assistance with a particular goal and never as a *general and permanent* prohibition of some conduct. The positive obligation still restricts, but only partially, by requiring that certain *affirmative steps* are performed to the advantage of rightholders. Put differently, the goal of an order, or its effect *should not be to prohibit conduct, but to prescribe a specific conduct*. Owing to this feature, injunctions for assistance can then be granted even beyond one committed instance of an infringement, for instance, they can cover also future works[21] or infringements of the "same nature."[22]

The case-law confirms this tendency. All the current cases before the CJEU always demanded a specific goal to be fulfilled: to filter out infringements from Internet traffic[23] or the content of a social network,[24] to block a particular

---

http://kluwercopyrightblog.com/2015/05/06/red-light-for-sabams-pricing-system-for-internet-access-providers-up-and-downstream-iap-traffic-do-not-constitute-communication-or-making-a-work-available-to-the-public/.

[19] The same is noted by the BGH in its decision BGH *Sommer unseres Lebens* (2010) I ZR 121/08, where the Court notes the provision of nonprotected wireless doesn't fall under the exclusive right ("Im Streitfall müsste das Verhalten des Beklagten – *also die Unterhaltung eines nicht ausreichend gesicherten privaten WLAN-Anschlusses* – den Tatbestand der öffentlichen Zugänglichmachung des in Rede stehenden urheberrechtlichen Werkes (§ 19a UrhG) erfüllen"). Although one can dispute whether this is convincing from the tort law perspective, as long as the consideration is about injunctions against the behavior that is considered noninfringing, the Court is perfectly right in his reluctant position to expand injunctions to assistance.

[20] See the agreed statement concerning Article 8 of the WIPO Copyright Treaty: "It is understood that the mere provision of physical facilities for enabling or making a communication does not in itself amount to communication within the meaning of this Treaty or the Berne Convention. It is further understood that nothing in Article 8 precludes a Contracting Party from applying Article 11bis(2)." Similarly Recital 27 of the InfoSoc Directive provides that "[t]he mere provision of physical facilities for enabling or making a communication does not in itself amount to communication within the meaning of this Directive."

[21] *Twentieth Century Fox Film Corporation & Anor v. Newzbin Ltd* [2010] EWHC 608 (Ch) [43] (covers also future repertoire); *Twentieth Century Fox Film Corp v. British Telecommunications plc* [2011] EWHC 1981 (Ch) [187] et seq. (breath of the orders).

[22] Case C-494/15 *Tommy Hilfiger Licensing and Others* [2016] ECLI:EU:C:2016:528, para. 34.

[23] Case C-70/10 *Scarlet Extended* [2011] ECLI:EU:C:2011:771.

[24] Case C-360/10 *SABAM* [2012] ECLI:EU:C:2012:85.

website[25] or repeatedly infringing consumers on a trading platform[26] and a physical space.[27] Even in *UPC Telekabel* where the Court allowed national courts to issue blocking orders without specifying the exact measures to be taken to satisfy them, they nevertheless always presented an intermediary with a specific "enforcement goal" – the blocking of a selected website.

In summary, unless intermediaries are sued as infringers, be it primary or secondary, the courts should not be able to order them to "refrain from their behaviour altogether." The plaintiffs may only ask them to "act to achieve something," a possible enforcement goal, because in the absence of an abstract prohibition that can be specified in the order, at least a goal is needed to direct the steps of the intermediary. If the plaintiff wants to achieve prohibition of conduct, they have to sue the intermediary as an infringer.

It should be evident that it would be more appropriate to talk about a *right to assistance* than an injunction, since the measure in itself takes only the form of an injunction rather than its nature.[28] Given the disparities among the types of orders and proceedings in the various Member States, it is natural that the Court should put the emphasis on the "object or effect" of these obligations. The goal of a right to assist depends not only on the wording of an order, but also on the subsequent manner of its enforcement. Hence the "object or effect" should be understood as referring to the broader *impact* of such obligations on the intermediary. This impact, according to the Court, should not amount to "a general and permanent prohibition" of "the continuation of the infringement."

It is not yet settled whether injunctions against intermediaries can be used, as a matter of Union law, to also cause blocking of persons who are acting lawfully. For instance, can a website blocking injunction be granted just on the basis of its user's infringing behavior, even if the targeted website isn't an infringer itself? This situation could occur when the domestic secondary liability laws are underdeveloped and they are asked to determine the infringing character of a targeted website.[29] Although the wording of the Union law does not require this explicitly, and its literal reading could theoretically support even targeting of noninfringers, the safeguards of freedom of expression would most likely render such extension of jurisdiction meaningless. This is because if the targeted website, whose sharing of information is lawful, is subject to a blocking order, then such targeting is likely to constitute a disproportional interference with the website's lawful speech.

---

[25] Case C-314/12 *UPC Telekabel Wien* [2014] ECLI:EU:C:2014:192.

[26] Case C-324/09 *L'Oréal and Others* [2011] ECLI:EU:C:2011:474.

[27] Case C-494/15 *Tommy Hilfiger Licensing and Others* [2016] ECLI:EU:C:2016:528.

[28] Case C-324/09 *L'Oréal and Others* [2011] ECLI:EU:C:2011:474, para. 134 (CJEU suggesting measures and then concluding that they might be imposed in the "form of an injunction").

[29] This is the starting point of the Dutch preliminary reference – see Martin Husovec and Lisa van Dongen, "Website Blocking, Injunctions and Beyond: View on the Harmonization from the Netherlands" [2017] GRUR (forthcoming).

7.3 ROLE OF PRELIMINARY MEASURES

Injunctions against intermediaries are also available in the form of preliminary measures based on Article 9(1)(a) of the Enforcement Directive. There is no comparable explicit provision in the InfoSoc Directive. The Union legislator, however, tried to give at least an ex post impression that preliminary injunctions are also covered by Article 8(3) of the InfoSoc Directive. In Article 9(1)(a) of the Enforcement Directive, on preliminary injunctions, it states that "injunctions against intermediaries whose services are used by a third party to infringe a copyright or a related right are covered by Directive 2001/29/EC." This should clearly refer to preliminary injunctions as well, despite the fact that such measures are not mentioned at all. As with a right to third-party information, it is interesting to see how the Union legislator is trying to invoke the legal basis of Article 8(3) of InfoSoc instead of the provisions of the Enforcement Directive that could serve as *lex generalis*.

The best example of their use is in domain name litigation before the courts,[30] where intermediaries such as domain name authorities can be obliged to prevent any resale of the domain names before the dispute is solved. In many countries, preliminary injunctions have also been used as a vehicle for website blocking or disconnection of servers.[31] Increasingly, we are seeing attempts to obtain various more complicated orders such as de-indexation or filtering in the form of preliminary relief. In fact, the *Scarlet Extended* reference came out of preliminary proceedings.[32] This should not be welcomed since the time frame of preliminary proceedings is not the correct forum for more *complicated measures*, the human rights aspect of which should be assessed in full proceedings.[33]

---

[30] This is very common in Czech republic and Slovakia – see cases reported in Martin Husovec, *Doménová čítanka* (EISi 2012).

[31] Sandfeld Jakobsen, "Injunctions Against Mere Conduit of Information Protected by Copyright – A Scandinavian Perspective" [2011] IIC 151.

[32] Case C-70/10 *Scarlet Extended* [2011] ECLI:EU:C:2011:255, Opinion of AG Villalón, para. 15.

[33] See *Ahmet Yildrimi v. Turkey* App no 3111/10 (ECHR, 18 March 2013) and the concurring opinion of the judge Pinto de Albuquerque ("If the interference with the applicant's freedom of expression on the public forum of the Internet must be assessed in terms of the negative obligations arising from Article 10 of the Convention, which already narrows the breadth of the margin of appreciation of the respondent State, *the interim and preventive nature of the contested blocking measure narrows it even further*"; emphasis mine).

8

Limits of Injunctions Against Intermediaries

One of the main consequences of the European provisions on injunctions against intermediaries is that the Member States are "not completely at liberty to design the injunctions at their own discretion."[1] In fact, the limitations of injunctions are perhaps the most decisive element that the Member States *must* have in common. The restrictions come from both primary as well as secondary Union law.[2]

In the *secondary law*, the limits of (1) Article 3 of the Enforcement Directive[3] and (2) Article 8 of the InfoSoc Directive,[4] as well as (3) Article 12–15 of the E-Commerce Directive must be observed.[5] An additional limiting factor is the *primary law* by the virtue of the Charter of Fundamental Rights of the European Union (EU Charter), which became legally binding after the Lisbon Treaty[6] entered into the force.

The case-law of the CJEU is clearly paved with considerations of the EU Charter. The Court often does not make a proper distinction between what is a "Charter

---

[1] Case C-314/12 *UPC Telekabel Wien* [2013] ECLI:EU:C:2013:781, Opinion of AG Villalón, para. 73.
[2] Case C-314/12 *UPC Telekabel Wien* [2013] ECLI:EU:C:2013:781, Opinion of AG Villalón, paras. 73, 77, 79, 80; Case C-324/09 *L'Oréal and Others* [2011] ECLI:EU:C:2011:474 paras. 138–140; Case C-324/09 *L'Oréal and Others* [2010] ECLI:EU:C:2010:757, Opinion of AG Jääskinen, para. 180; Case C-70/10 *Scarlet Extended* [2011] ECLI:EU:C:2011:771, para. 33; Case C-360/10 *SABAM* [2012] ECLI:EU:C:2012:85, para. 31.
[3] Case C-70/10 *Scarlet Extended* [2011] ECLI:EU:C:2011:771, para. 34; Case C-360/10 *SABAM* [2012] ECLI:EU:C:2012:85, para. 31; Case C-314/12 *UPC Telekabel Wien* [2013] ECLI:EU:C:2013:781, Opinion of AG Villalón, para. 75; Case C-314/12 *UPC Telekabel Wien* [2014] ECLI:EU:C:2014:192, para. 44.
[4] Case C-70/10 *Scarlet Extended* [2011] ECLI:EU:C:2011:771, para. 34; Case C-360/10 *SABAM* [2012] ECLI:EU:C:2012:85, para. 31; Case C-314/12 *UPC Telekabel Wien* [2013] ECLI:EU:C:2013:781, Opinion of AG Villalón, para. 73; Case C-314/12 *UPC Telekabel Wien* [2014] ECLI:EU:C:2014:192, para. 44.
[5] Case C-70/10 *Scarlet Extended* [2011] ECLI:EU:C:2011:771, para. 35; Case C-360/10 *SABAM* [2012] ECLI:EU:C:2012:85, para. 33; Case C-314/12 *UPC Telekabel Wien* [2013] ECLI:EU:C:2013:781, Opinion of AG Villalón, para. 75; Case C-314/12 *UPC Telekabel Wien* [2014] ECLI:EU:C:2014:192, para. 44; Case C-324/09 *L'Oréal and Others* [2011] ECLI:EU:C:2011:474 para. 139.
[6] Treaty on European Union [2012] OJ C 326/13, Art. 6.

requirement" and what is a requirement of the secondary Union legislation.[7] Very often it uses the Charter as the only framework of reference. The cases of *Scarlet Extended*, *Netlog* and *UPC Telekabel*, in particular, but also some national cases,[8] show this tendency.[9] In *Mc Fadden*, the Court was not receptive to the arguments of impact on innovation.[10]

There is no doubt that the distinction between the two levels of policy is crucial. Constitutional conformity should not be the only criterion of a good policy on intellectual property enforcement. Good policy is never measured solely by its conformity with the outer boundaries of legislative decision-making. Because not all, or even most, of what remains *within* the constitutional limits is automatically also good for the society. The CJEU, serving as both a constitutional court and a court of ordinary law, should be making much clearer distinction between the two. This could be done, for instance, by ascribing specific meaning to the existing general requirements of the secondary legislation. The debate and proportionality exercise should be framed not only in terms of human rights, but also in terms of costs and benefits for the today's and tomorrow's economic growth.

8.1 SECONDARY LAW: GENERAL LIMITATIONS

Article 3 of the Enforcement Directive directly incorporates general limitations on remedies in intellectual property enforcement.[11] According to this provision, measures, procedures and remedies used in enforcement should (1) be fair, (2) be equitable, (3) not unnecessarily complicated or costly, (4) not create barriers to legitimate trade,[12] such as unreasonable time limits or unwarranted delays,

---

7 Martin Husovec and Miquel Peguera, "Much Ado About Little – Privately Litigated Disconnecting Injunctions" [2015] IIC 10, 17.

8 A similar approach can be found in *Golden Eye (International) Ltd & Anor v. Telefónica UK Ltd* [2012] EWHC 723 (Ch) [147] (doubting whether there is any room for a discretion beyond the proportionality); *Dramatico Entertainment Ltd v. British Sky Broadcasting Ltd (No 2)* [2012] EWHC 1152 (Ch) [10]; *EMI Records Ltd v. British Sky Broadcasting Ltd* [2013] EWHC 379 (Ch), [2013] ECDR 8 [91].

9 Only Advocate General (Case C-70/10 *Scarlet Extended* [2011] ECLI:EU:C:2011:255, Opinion of AG Villalón, paras. 5, 69) makes clear that his examination mainly focuses on primary law; Case C-314/12 *UPC Telekabel Wien* [2014] ECLI:EU:C:2014:192, paras. 42, 45; Case C-314/12 *UPC Telekabel Wien* [2013] ECLI:EU:C:2013:781, Opinion of AG Villalón, para. 28; it is questionable whether the CJEU is making any distinction at all here.

10 Martin Husovec, "Holey Cap! CJEU Drills (Yet) Another Hole in the E-Commerce Directive's Safe Harbors" (2017) 12(2) Journal of Intellectual Property Law & Practice 115, 125.

11 Ansgar Ohly, "Three Principles of European IP Enforcement Law: Effectiveness, Proportionality, Dissuasiveness" in Josef Drexl (ed.) *Technology and Competition, Contributions in Honor of Hanns Ullrich* (Larcier 2009) 257; on the other hand, of the opposite opinion: Reto Hilty, "The Role of Enforcement in Delineating the Scope of IP Rights" [2015] Max Planck Institute for Innovation and Competition Research Paper No. 15-03, 16 ("In contrast, an upper limit in terms of a 'ceiling' to enforcement activities based on national law is not stipulated").

12 Case C-324/09 *L'Oréal and Others* [2011] ECLI:EU:C:2011:474, para. 140.

(5) be effective, (6) be proportionate, (7) be dissuasive, and (8) provide for safeguards against their abuse.

These principles are becoming of increasing relevance in the Union law. Although the Enforcement Directive was conceived as a form of minimal harmonization, Article 3 is becoming a fresh harmonizing force. The courts of Member States are step by step critically evaluating their own remedies and their application against the principles.[13] If the Court becomes more prescriptive, the result of this could be more harmonized remedial landscape.[14] Already today, we witness that Article 3 is a stronger moderator than its original inspiration in the TRIPS Agreement.

Similarly, the newly agreed international Agreement on a Unified Patent Court provides in Article 42 that the Court shall deal with litigation in ways which are "proportionate to the importance and complexity thereof" and also ensure "the rules, procedures and remedies provided for in this Agreement and in the Statute are used in a fair and equitable manner and do not distort competition." On the other hand, the InfoSoc Directive lacks similar overarching limits. Article 8(1) only states in the context of infringements that "the sanctions thus provided for shall be effective, proportionate and dissuasive." Nevertheless, Article 8 is increasingly interpreted by the Court as containing the same limitations as the Enforcement Directive. In the *UPC Telekabel* case, for instance, the Advocate General came, in the copyright context, to the following conclusion:

> The measure to be examined does however infringe the requirements relating to fundamental rights which, in accordance with the case-law, are to be applied to injunctions pursuant to Article 8(3) of Directive 2001/29. In this respect, the measure is neither "fair and equitable" nor "proportionate" within the meaning of Article 3 of Directive 2004/48.[15]

Since the Court was of the opposite view, we do not find confirmation of this in the actual ruling. But the willingness to interchangeably use the Enforcement Directive's limitations[16] also in the context of the copyright enforcement is also evident from some earlier rulings, such as *Scarlet Extended*,[17] *Sabam*,[18] or *Mc Fadden*.[19]

---

[13] See BGH (2016) X ZR 114/13 (applying so-called "Aufbrauchfrist" doctrine, which is a transition period given to comply with injunctions against infringers; the court discusses also its compatibility with Art 3 of the Enforcement Directive); Patents Court London, *HTC Corporation v. Nokia Corporation* [2013] EWHC 3778 (Pat) (the criteria to be applied when deciding to grant an injunction are those laid down by Article 3(2) of the Enforcement Directive).

[14] Case C–367/15 *Stowarzyszenie "Oławska Telewizja Kablowa* [2017] ECLI:EU:C:2017:36, para. 31 (discussing a potential abusiveness of double compensation for infrignemnets caused by infringers).

[15] Case C-314/12 *UPC Telekabel Wien* [2013] ECLI:EU:C:2013:781, Opinion of AG Villalón, para. 79.

[16] UK courts: *Golden Eye (International) Ltd & Anor v. Telefónica UK Ltd* [2012] EWHC 723 (Ch) [116].

[17] Case C-70/10 *Scarlet Extended* [2011] ECLI:EU:C:2011:771, para. 36.

[18] Case C-360/10 *SABAM* [2012] ECLI:EU:C:2012:85, para. 34.

[19] Case C-484/14 *Mc Fadden* [2016] ECLI:EU:C:2016:689.

Yet another reason to use the very same limitations in the copyright context is the TRIPS Agreement, which, in fact, is their original source. Article 41 requires "effective" enforcement procedures to "be applied in such a manner as to avoid the creation of barriers to legitimate trade and to provide for safeguards against their abuse," and that they are "fair and equitable" and "not be unnecessarily complicated or costly, or entail unreasonable time-limits or unwarranted delays." This means that only the requirements of proportionality and dissuasiveness are provided on top of TRIPS. Since, according to the case-law of the CJEU, provisions of the secondary Union law should be read in the light of the international treaties such as TRIPS, there is no doubt that the approach of "borrowing" limitations from the general Enforcement Directive is more than justified. It is necessary.[20]

Apart from the principles of proportionality and effectiveness, the Court does not attempt to ascribe any specific meaning to the limitations, but rather uses them as one of the factors mentioned in the reasoning.[21] Very often in the context of the balancing exercise that is carried out mostly on the bedrocks of the EU Charter provisions. While most of the analysis occurs within the balancing exercise, in some cases, the Court identifies particular principles of Article 3 that are violated. In *L'Oréal v. eBay*, the Court explained that full restraint on conduct may not be delivered by injunctions against innocent intermediaries, arguing that it creates barriers to legitimate trade.[22] In *Sabam* and *Scarlet Extended*, the Court seemed to highlight the importance of the cost and complexity of the measures.[23] In *Tommy Hilfiger*, the obstacles to legitimate trade were repeatedly reiterated.[24] In *UPC Telekabel*,[25] it demanded elementary effectiveness of the measures.

The principle of effectiveness is a good illustration point for why two levels of policy – human rights and overall cost-benefit – should be assessed separately. Today, it is not entirely clear if the content of effectiveness requirement is simply copying the proportionality test from the (human rights) balancing exercise of the EU Charter, or if it is a stand-alone requirement going beyond it. The former, however, seems to be more likely.[26] If this is the case, then the courts aren't able to reject as inadmissible certain injunctions that perfectly conform all the human rights concerned, but are still very ineffective in earning any benefits to rightholders.

---

[20] Similar Pekka Savola, *Internet Connectivity Providers as Involuntary Copyright Enforers: Blocking Websites in Particular* (IPR University Center, 2015) 69.

[21] Case C-314/12 *UPC Telekabel Wien* [2013] ECLI:EU:C:2013:781, Opinion of AG Villalón, para. 106 ("According to the Court's case-law, the complexity, costs and duration of the measure must also be weighed together with the other factors").

[22] Case C-324/09 *L'Oréal and Others* [2011] ECLI:EU:C:2011:474, para. 140.

[23] Case C-70/10 *Scarlet Extended* [2011] ECLI:EU:C:2011:771, para. 48; Case C-360/10 *SABAM* [2012] ECLI:EU:C:2012:85, para. 46.

[24] Case C-494/15 *Tommy Hilfiger Licensing and Others* [2016] ECLI:EU:C:2016:528, paras. 34, 35.

[25] Case C-314/12 *UPC Telekabel Wien* [2014] ECLI:EU:C:2014:192, para. 62.

[26] Case C-314/12 *UPC Telekabel Wien* [2014] ECLI:EU:C:2014:192, para. 45.

After all, the constitutional requirement of effectiveness is not particularly high[27], specifically in order to create a sufficient maneuvering space for the legislator. Proportionate, but ineffective (useless) measures should be, in my view, prevented in the first place as a matter of ordinary law – secondary legislation. They should not rely on the outer boundaries of legislative powers. Only in this way, can the socially wasteful enforcement practices be rejected outright. Effectiveness should thus preserve a meaning that is autonomous to the proportionality test.[28] In the literature, similarly as in the case-law, there is no settled meaning for the principle of effectiveness.[29]

8.2 SECONDARY LAW: SAFE HARBORS

The safe harbors set out in the E-Commerce Directive, while protecting interme-diaries from liability, do *not* limit the possibility of injunctive relief or claims for information available under national law. All the safe harbors, including the one that covers mere conduit services such as Internet access providers (Article 12 E-Commerce Directive), unambiguously permit injunctions to be granted. This is confirmed not only by the cases of *Sabam* and *Scarlet Extended* and by the scholarly literature (see Section 4.2), but particularly by the *UPC Telekabel* case. There the CJEU allowed as constitutionally admissible, under some circumstances,[30] website blocking injunctions issued against noninfringing access providers. Thus, it implic-itly confirmed what the Advocate General had formulated as follows:

> The liability rules for intermediaries, which are laid down in Directive 2001/31, *do not, in principle, preclude the issuing of an injunction* under Article 8(3) of Directive 2001/29 against ISPs. It is true that Article 12 of that directive contains special rules on the liability of intermediary service providers as mere conduits of information. However, under paragraph 3 of that provision, those rules do not affect the possibility for a court or administrative authority of requiring the service provider to terminate or prevent an infringement.[31]

The most recent *Mc Fadden* decision only further confirms this.[32] But there is respect in which the safe harbors *do* limit injunctions. As explained in Chapters 9

[27] Martin Husovec and Miquel Peguera, "Much Ado About Little – Privately Litigated Disconnecting Injunctions" [2015] IIC 10, 18, 33.
[28] Ibid., 18.
[29] See disucussion in Pekka Savola, *Internet Connectivity Providers as Involuntary Copyright Enforcers: Blocking Websites in Particular* (IPR University Center, 2015) 70; Kevin O'Sulivan, "Enforcing Copy-right Online: Internet Provider Obligations and the European Charter of Human Rights" (2014) 36 EIPR 577.
[30] Martin Husovec, "CJEU Allowed Website Blocking Injunctions with Some Reservations" (2014) 9 (8) Journal of Intellectual Property Law & Practice 2.
[31] Case C-314/12 *UPC Telekabel Wien* [2013] ECLI:EU:C:2013:781, Opinion of AG Villalón, para. 52 (emphasis mine).
[32] Case C-484/14 *Mc Fadden* [2016] ECLI:EU:C:2016:689.

and 10, different countries have different concepts of injunctive relief as a remedy. The civil law tradition, from the time of the Pandectists, views it as a material claim existing and exercisable also outside of court, similar to damages. Common law, on the other hand, views it as more or less procedural remedy that can be granted only by a court. Since safe harbor provisions note that they do not affect the possibility of "a court or administrative authority" to require the service provider to terminate or prevent an infringement, the reach of civil law injunctions that exist and lead to effects also out-of-court should arguably be limited.

Germany offers a great example in this respect. Its injunction-based accountability of Internet intermediaries stretches beyond the courts. This means that a claim to an injunction arises when the conditions are met, not when the court grants it. Of course, such a claim may not be enforced against a person without judicial interference. But it is enough to cause the addressee of such a claim to be bound to pay the pretrial and trial cost[33] when the injunction is subsequently issued by the court. This is particularly the case for pretrial costs based on the so-called *negotiorum gestio* doctrine.[34] Unlike ex post enforcement costs, these costs occur before the court decides on a particular injunction. Arguably, this is inconsistent with the idea of safe harbors as, according to the safe harbor legislation, no liability apart from court-imposed injunctions may be imposed on intermediaries *before* the procedure is initiated. The CJEU's decision in *Mc Fadden*, however, offers different reading. It does not *immunize* from prelitigation costs concerning such injunctions; though it might still *moderate* them in the future (see Chapter 4).

8.3 SECONDARY LAW: ILLEGAL GENERAL MONITORING

Another limitation of the E-Commerce Directive is the prohibition of a general monitoring obligation. Article 15 provides the following:

(1) Member States shall not impose a general obligation on providers, when providing the services covered by Articles 12, 13 and 14, to monitor the information which they transmit or store, nor a general obligation actively to seek facts or circumstances indicating illegal activity.

(2) Member States may establish obligations for information society service providers promptly to inform the competent public authorities of alleged illegal activities undertaken or information provided by recipients of their service or obligations to communicate to the competent authorities, at their request, information

---

33 See more Tilman Bezzenberger, "Der negatorische Beseitigungsanspruch und die Kosten der Ersatzvornahme" [2005] JZ 373; Markus Bölling, "Unterlassungsantrag und Streitgegenstand im Falle der Störerhaftung" [2013] GRUR 1092; Johannes Hewicker and others, "Der Abmahnkosten-Ersatzanspruch im Urheberrecht" [2014] NJW 2753; BGH (2012) v. ZR 136/11; BGH (2011) I ZR 145/10; OLG Karlsruhe (2012) 12 U 143/11.
34 Martin Husovec, "Holey Cap! CJEU Drills (Yet) Another Hole in the E-Commerce Directive's Safe Harbors" (2017) 12(2) Journal of Intellectual Property Law & Practice 115, 118.

enabling the identification of recipients of their service with whom they have storage agreements.[35]

Article 15 makes general monitoring illegal as long as *union* safe harbors of hosting, caching, or mere conduit apply. For any additional *national* safe harbors, such as ones for linking or search engines, or services falling outside of any of the safe harbors, Article 15 does *not* apply. But it might also be illegal to impose general monitoring on these services. The CJEU very interestingly "transplanted" the prohibition of a general monitoring obligation as a limit from Article 15 of the E-Commerce Directive *into* the Enforcement Directive itself.[36] The Court *later* in *Scarlet Extended* explained this as follows:

> In that regard, the Court has already ruled that that prohibition applies in particular to national measures which would require an intermediary provider, such as an ISP, to actively monitor all the data of each of its customers in order to prevent any future infringement of intellectual-property rights. Furthermore, such a general monitoring obligation would be incompatible with Article 3 of Directive 2004/48, which states that the measures referred to by the directive must be fair and proportionate and must not be excessively costly (see *L'Oréal and Others*, paragraph 139).[37]

By incorporating this concept *inside* the Article 3 limitations, the CJEU now explicitly recognizes that the principle of illegal general monitoring also applies even outside of the scope of safe harbors, that is in the offline context.[38] So even if the external limit of Article 15 of the E-Commerce Directive were repealed one day, the same limit could be found *within* the Enforcement Directive itself.[39] This in addition supported by the fact that the European Court of Human Rights also recognizes prohibition of general monitoring in its case-law.[40]

Recital 16 of the InfoSoc Directive and Article 2(3)(a) of the Enforcement Directive make clear that implementations of the two may *not* affect the provisions of the

---

[35] The CJEU held that 15(2) does not impose any obligation to provide for personal data – see Case C-275/06 *Promusicae* [2005] ECLI:EU:C:2008:54, para. 59.

[36] Although the starting point is still Art. 15 (Case C-324/09 *L'Oréal and Others* [2011] ECLI:EU: C:2011:474, para. 139).

[37] Case C-70/10 *Scarlet Extended* [2011] ECLI:EU:C:2011:771, para. 36.

[38] Case C-494/15 *Tommy Hilfiger Licensing and Others* [2016] ECLI:EU:C:2016:528, para. 34.

[39] BGH (2013) I ZR 216/11 (applying the same logic).

[40] In the recent case-law, the ECtHR held that an obligation of general monitoring can be exceptionally imposed by the national law in the area of hate speech, however, the law of defamation cannot extend such obligations and has to rely on notice and take-down procedure (*Delfi AS v. Estonia*, App no. 64569/09 (ECHR, 16 June 2015); *Magyar Tartalomszolgaltatok Egyesulete and Index.hu ZRT v. Hungary*, App no. 22947/13 (ECHR, 2 February 2016) *Pihl v. Sweden*, App. no. 74742/14 (ECHR, 9 March 2017)). For further commentary see Christina Angelopoulos, "MTE v. Hungary: A New ECtHR Judgment on Intermediary Liability and Freedom of Expression" (2016) 11 Journal of Intellectual Property Law & Practice 582–584; Martin Husovec, "ECtHR (Again) Accepts General Monitoring of Third Party Content as Compatible with Freedom of Expression" (2016) 11(1) Journal of Intellectual Property Law and Practice 17–20.

E-Commerce Directive and, more specifically, Articles 12 to 15 thereof. This reading was confirmed by the CJEU in its *Scarlet Extended*[41] and *Sabam*[42] ruling and does not seem to be controversial in any case. What is controversial, however, is to what extent the prohibition of general monitoring in turn limits the possibility to grant injunctions against intermediaries.

Naturally, any injunction imposed on an intermediary is by definition an "obligation." When an injunction targets past actions, such as de-registration of a domain name or removal of the infringing content, there is usually very little concern that this would amount to "monitoring." The greatest concern comes with injunctions that attempt to police *future* infringements on a particular platform. In order to carry them out, they usually require the provider to "monitor the information which they transmit or store" or to "actively (. . .) seek facts or circumstances indicating illegal activity." Although the two are worded as alternatives, it is hard to imagine any type of monitoring which would not involve the seeking of facts. Perhaps the first prong of the provision could target passive, automated measures (for instance filtering), and the second active, nonautomated measures (for instance manual review).[43]

The fact that measures such as the blocking of websites, disconnections, filtering obligations, and de-indexation or manual review of content amount to "monitoring" is probably very little disputed. What is disputed, however, is when such monitoring becomes "general," since the provision does not outlaw specific monitoring. This is confirmed by Recital 47, which states that the "Member States are prevented from imposing a monitoring obligation on service providers *only* with respect to obligations of a general nature; this does *not* concern monitoring obligations in a *specific case* and, in particular, does not affect orders by national authorities in accordance with national legislation."

The CJEU has so far rejected as illegal forms of general monitoring injunctions requiring an Internet access provider and a social network to install filtering systems that would involve the "systematic analysis of all content and the collection and identification of users' IP addresses from which unlawful content on the network is sent."[44] The Court also confirmed that a full prohibition of conduct, as opposed to partial assistance of a specific kind, imposed on intermediaries would be unacceptable. It said that an injunction against an operator of an online market place "cannot have as its object or effect a general and permanent prohibition on the selling, on that marketplace, of goods bearing those trade marks."[45]

---

[41] Case C-70/10 *Scarlet Extended* [2011] ECLI:EU:C:2011:771, para. 34.

[42] Case C-360/10 *SABAM* [2012] ECLI:EU:C:2012:85, para. 32.

[43] The latter also seems to be suggested by Case C-314/12 *UPC Telekabel Wien* [2013] ECLI:EU: C:2013:781, Opinion of AG Villalón, para. 78.

[44] Case C-70/10 *Scarlet Extended* [2011] ECLI:EU:C:2011:771, para. 40; Case C-360/10 *SABAM* [2012] ECLI:EU:C:2012:85, para. 38.

[45] Case C-324/09 *L'Oréal and Others* [2011] ECLI:EU:C:2011:474, para. 140.

On the other hand, the Court approved of website blocking measures as a legitimate type of monitoring when it followed the advice given by the Advocate General:

> It would constitute such an inadmissible measure if the court had ordered the ISP actively to seek copies of the infringing page among other domain names or to filter all the data carried in its network in order to ascertain whether they constitute transfers of specific protected film works and to block such transfers. However, such a measure is not in issue in the present case. Rather, the referring court is required to decide on the blocking of a specific website. The measure therefore does not infringe Article 15(1) of Directive 2000/31.[46]

This reasoning is not without problems, in particular because website blocking is an enforcement goal and not the exact execution thereof. So it can be carried out in many different ways, including filtering that would scan all the data carried in the network as it passes an inspection point, in order to decide whether the packet may pass or if it needs to be routed to a different destination such as an educational antipiracy website.

In *Mc Fadden*, Advocate General Szpunar recently argued that "a measure requiring the owner of an Internet connection to examine all communications transmitted through that connection" would "clearly conflict with the prohibition on imposing a general monitoring obligation."[47] In his view, "in order to constitute a monitoring obligation 'in a specific case,' such as is permitted under Article 15(1), the measure in question must be limited in terms of the subject and duration of the monitoring, and that would not be the case with a measure that entailed the examination of all communications passing through a network."[48] The Court accepts the outcome of AG's analysis, without explicitly referring to the two conditions.

In *Tommy Hilfiger*, the Court reiterated the following principles of its case-law in the offline context:

> Lastly, the Court held that injunctions must be equitable and proportionate. They must not therefore be excessively expensive and must not create barriers to legitimate trade. Nor can the intermediary be required to exercise general and permanent oversight over its customers. By contrast, the intermediary may be forced to take measures which contribute to avoiding new infringements of the same nature by the same market-trader from taking place.[49]

As far as "general and permanent oversight of customers" is equivalent of "general monitoring," the decision seems to again suggest that only specific oversight that would be acceptable is one limited to "avoiding new infringements of the same nature by the same market-trader from taking place."

---

[46] Case C-314/12 *UPC Telekabel Wien* [2013] ECLI:EU:C:2013:781, Opinion of AG Villalón, para. 78.
[47] Case C-484/14 *Mc Fadden* [2016] ECLI:EU:C:2016:170, Advocate General Szpunar, para. 132.
[48] Ibid.
[49] Case C-494/15 *Tommy Hilfiger Licensing and Others* [2016] ECLI:EU:C:2016:528, para. 34.

In summary, the CJEU still seems to be on its way of outlining what exactly constitutes an illegal general monitoring obligation.[50] In particular, the temporal character of measures is not clear. What is clear, however, is that any proactive measures attempting to prevent infringements from a particular infringer can be compatible as long as they do not extend to his other infringements that aren't of the "same nature." The proactive measures can therefore particularly impose various repeat-infringer obligations. They cannot, however, impose an obligation to simply prevent reappearance of already notified content from *anyone*. It also explains why website-centered monitoring can be permitted even if it entails some broader measures. It is because the website blocking still remains infringer specific – the infringer being the website.[51] The infringer-identity limitation thus seems to prevent the injunctions from imposing full-fledged notice–and–stay down systems, like the German one.

From the Member States, the German courts are most willing to impose various broad filtering obligations on intermediaries. First, they extended the filtering obligations of a trading platform to *similar* infringements to those which were notified.[52] Later, in a series of cases involving the cyberlocker Rapidshare, the German Federal Supreme Court (the BGH) ordered Rapidshare not only to implement word filters, but also required it to carry out some manual checks of external websites, such as search engines, which could point to infringing content on the service.[53] One of the Advocates General has already cast doubts on the compatibility of such filtering obligations with the prohibition of a general monitoring obligation.[54]

---

[50] Andreas Paulus, "Schutz des geistigen Eigentums" in Josef Isensee and Paul Kirchhof (eds.), *Handbuch des Staatsrechts der Bundesrepublik Deutschland, Band XI* (C. H. Beck 2013) § 247, para. 49–51.

[51] Martin Husovec, "CJEU Allowed Website Blocking Injunctions with Some Reservations" (2014) 9 (8) Journal of Intellectual Property Law & Practice 631, 633 (the decision is not such a vehement rejection of filtering); see also other cases applying this – *Twentieth Century Fox Film Corp v. British Telecommunications plc* [2011] EWHC 1981 (Ch) [169 et seq.] (rejecting Art. 15 defense); *Cartier International AG & Ors v. British Sky Broadcasting Ltd & Ors* [2014] EWHC 3354 (Ch) [141].

[52] BGH *Internetversteigerung I.* (2004) I ZR 304/01.

[53] BGH *Kinderhochstuehle im Internet I.* (2010) I ZR 139/08; BGH *Alone in the Dark* (2012) I ZR 18/11; BGH *File-Hosting-Dienst* (2013) I ZR 80/12; BGH *Kinderhochstühle im Internet II.* (2013) I ZR 216/11.

[54] Case C-324/09 *L'Oréal and Others* [2010] ECLI:EU:C:2010:757, Opinion of AG Jääskinen, fn 82 says: "See also three German cases, commonly known as 'Internet Auction I, II and III.' (. . .) The court held that electronic marketplace operators qualified for the exemption of liability established in Article 14 of Directive 2000/31. Yet they formulated *extensive criteria for injunctions against the operators which, as to their scope, may give rise to some issues of compatibility with Directive 2000/31.*" (emphasis mine). – In the literature: Jan Nordemann, "Internet Copyright Infringement: Remedies Against Intermediaries – The European Perspective on Host and Access Providers" (2012) 59 Journal of the Copyright Society – USA 773, 783 (arguing compatibility); Patrick Breyer, "Verkehrssicherungspflichten von Internetdiensten im Lichte der Grundrechte" [2009] MMR 14, 15 (arguing incompatibility); Sabine Sobola and Kathrin Kohl, "Haftung von Providern für fremde Inhalte" [2005] CR 443, 449 (arguing incompatibility); Arndt Berger and Ruth Janal, "Suchet und Ihr werdet finden? Eine Untersuchung zur Störerhaftung von Online-Auktionshäusern" [2004] CR 917, 922 (arguing incompatibility); Georg Nolte and Jörg Wimmers, "Wer stört? Gedanken zur Haftung von Intermediären im Internet – von praktischer Konkordanz, richtigen Anreizen und offenen Fragen" [2014] GRUR 16, 21ff. (arguing incompatibility).

8.4 PRIMARY LAW: HUMAN RIGHTS LIMITS

Because any injunction issued against intermediaries is ultimately implementing EU law, all possible conflicts with fundamental rights and freedoms will always need to be tested against the provisions of the EU Charter (Article 51(1)),[55] and not merely against the national constitutions. The EU Charter as a source of law will therefore strongly guide many Member State courts in their application of various injunctions against intermediaries. Possible differing levels of protection of fundamental rights at national and European level will sometimes need to be adjusted to the "Charter standards," regardless of whether they must be *lowered* or *increased* for these purposes.[56] This, for instance, means that should the national court want to reject an injunction against an intermediary in consideration of the right to a fair trial of an unrepresented user, it could be required to explore the compatibility of such a decision with the EU Charter provision, here Article 47, perhaps even by means of a reference for a preliminary ruling to the CJEU.[57] Such a reference could then prevent possible incompatibility with the national human rights considerations, which bar such injunctions, but are *not* shared by the CJEU, which interprets the respective provision of the EU Charter. In these cases, the national court could be forced by Union law to provide for an injunction against an intermediary despite its national human rights doubts.

Application of human rights as limits to privately litigated injunctions also pose more fundamental questions. Because intermediaries are often private individuals without any ties to the state powers, and so are the copyright holders, the question is *when* (if at all) and to *what extent* human rights prerogatives should limit the actions of individuals. Although the idea of horizontal effect of human rights is not new to the courts of most of the European countries, including the ECtHR,[58] the struggle of CJEU case-law to moderate private intellectual property disputes via human rights law has only started. The evidence that we might witness a tectonic shift in the long run is well-demonstrated in the recent *UPC Telekabel Wien*, where the CJEU held that "in order to prevent the fundamental rights recognized by EU

---

[55] See Case C-617/10 *Åkerberg Fransson* [2013] ECLI:EU:C:2013:280.

[56] In Case C-399/11 *Melloni* [2013] ECLI:EU:C:2013:107, the CJEU postulated that Art. 53 of the Charter "confirms that, where an EU legal act calls for national implementing measures, national authorities and courts remain free to apply national standards of protection of fundamental rights, *provided that the level of protection provided for by the Charter, as interpreted by the Court, and the primacy, unity and effectiveness of EU law are not thereby compromised*" (emphasis mine).

[57] A similar situation already arises in the context of the right to information and its conflict with the data protection framework – see the CJEU cases Case C-275/06 *Promusicae* [2005] ECLI:EU:C:2008:54; Case C-557/07 *LSG-Gesellschaft zur Wahrnehmung von Leistungsschutzrechten* [2009] ECLI:EU:C:2009:107; Case C-461/10 *Bonnier Audio AB and Others* [2012] ECLI:EU:C:2012:219.

[58] See Achim Seifert, "Die horizontale Wirkung von Grundrechten. Europarechtliche und rechtsvergleichende Überlegungen" (2011) 18 Europäische Zeitschrift für Wirtschaftsrecht (EuZW) 696; Jürgen Schwabe, *Die sogenannte Drittwirkung der Grundrechte* (Goldman 1971).

law from precluding the adoption of an injunction such as that at issue in the main proceedings, the national procedural rules must provide a possibility for internet users to assert their rights before the court once the implementing measures taken by the internet service provider are known."[59]

This requirement of *locus standi* for users arguably isn't compatible with the basic principle of the ECtHR case-law on positive obligations.[60] Namely, that any horizontal effect of freedom of expression based on the doctrine of "positive obligations," can only prescribe the state to act to achieve certain "human-rights-conform" situation among individuals, and not to act in the form of a specific measure.[61] And also that individuals can *not* directly invoke their human rights prerogatives against other individuals.[62] The Austrian Supreme Court applying the above CJEU's *ratio decidendi* in the follow-up proceedings, proved ready not only to provide for such a horizontal effect *indirectly*, by basing it in the contractual arrangement between the ISP and its customer,[63] but also *directly* by safe-guarding it, if needed, by an action in the law of torts.[64]

The latter approach could be change a lot, especially if applied in the context of voluntary disconnection schemes, where the state powers (through courts) are not even remotely involved. The CJEU is surely better empowered than the ECtHR to require instrument-specific positive obligations, since its relationship with the Member States is closer than that of the ECtHR. One could therefore think of

---

59 Case C-314/12 *UPC Telekabel Wien* [2014] ECLI:EU:C:2014:192, para. 57 (emphasis mine).

60 It can also be said to go beyond the ECHR case law – cf. *Akdeniz v. Turkey* App no 20877/10 (ECHR, 11 March 2014)(mere status as a user is not sufficient to be regarded as a victim under Art. 34 of the Convention).

61 See Achim Seifert, "Die horizontale Wirkung von Grundrechten. Europarechtliche und rechtsvergleichende Überlegungen" (2011) 18 Europäische Zeitschrift für Wirtschaftsrecht (EuZW) 696, 698; *VgT Verein gegen Tierfabriken v. Switzerland* App no 24699/94 (ECHR, 28 June 2001), para. 78; German cases of the German Constitutional Court, BverfG (1995) 1 BvF 1/90, 1 BvR 342/90 and 1 BvR 348/90, BverfGE 92, 26, 46 (on freedom to conduct a business according to Article 12 GG); BverfG (1990) 1 BvR 26/84, BverfGE 81, 242, 255 (on freedom to conduct a business according to Article 12 GG).

62 See Achim Seifert, "Die horizontale Wirkung von Grundrechten. Europarechtliche und rechtsvergleichende Überlegungen" (2011) 18 Europäische Zeitschrift für Wirtschaftsrecht (EuZW) 696, 698.

63 It is interesting to note that ECtHR in its *Akdeniz v. Turkey* decision (paras. 24–26) rejected the compliant of a user of services that were blocked in Turkey on copyright grounds ("the mere fact that the applicant – like the other Turkish users of the websites in question – had been indirectly affected by a blocking measure against two music-sharing websites could not suffice for him to be regarded as a 'victim' for the purposes of Article 34 of the Convention" – see *Akdeniz v. Turkey* App no 20877/10 (ECHR, 11 March 2014), cited from the English summary: Information Note on the Court's case-law No. 173); German scholarship also supports that the redress to over-blocking can be found in the contract and tort law – see Gerald Spindler, "Zivilrechtliche Sperrverfügungen gegen Access Provider nach dem EuGH-Urteil 'UPC Telekabel'" (2014) GRUR 827, 832.

64 Austrian Supreme Court, OGH *UPC Telekabel Wien* (2014) 4 Ob 71/14s; Gerald Spindler, "Zivilrechtliche Sperrverfügungen gegen Access Provider nach dem EuGH-Urteil 'UPC Telekabel'" (2014) GRUR 827, 832; Peukert suggests, in relation to the use of DRMs which could infringe upon the freedom of expression, that tort law could similarly serve to provide the indirect effect also against the rightholders – see Alexander Peukert, *Die Gemeinfreiheit: Begriff, Funktion, Dogmatik* (Mohr Siebeck 2012) 267ff.

various other positive obligations for the future, such as an obligation to supervise the orders or review them ex post.[65]

8.4.1 *Quality of the Law*

Both the CJEU[66] and the ECtHR[67] acknowledge that limitations on the exercise of rights and freedoms have to be "provided for by law." According to this doctrine and now also Article 52(1) of the EU Charter, any limitation, interference or restriction must previously be based on a legal framework which is sufficiently precise in regard to the objective it pursues. The requirement takes precedence over other considerations,[68] including proportionality, since it is based on the essence of democratic institutions, the legitimacy of the law itself.

The relevance of this criterion is twofold in the context of injunctions. First, it is an enquiry into the kind of injunctions that can still rely on a simple provision such as Article 8(3) of the InfoSoc Directive and Article 11(III) of the Enforcement Directive. And second, it is a subsequent enquiry into how such an order should be formulated.

Maintaining the sufficient quality of the law is of utmost importance for any functioning democratic society. Only law that was enacted in a democratically legitimized process could serve as a limitation on the fundamental rights of the constituents of a state. The possibility of rightholders to propose abstract obligations punishable by penalties, and then to impose them on intermediaries in proceedings before a court, based on one sentence of the law, arguably privatizes the law-making process. Because if an obligation is, in its content, as abstract as the norm of a

---

[65] In the UK, the courts are, for instance, able to install a so-called supervising solicitor to oversee the implementation of the orders – see *Media CAT Ltd v. Adams* [2011] WL 291789 Patents County Court; *Golden Eye (International) Ltd & Anor v. Telefónica UK Ltd* [2012] EWHC 723 (Ch); *Golden Eye (International) Ltd & Ors v. Telefónica UK Litd & Anor* [2012] EWCA Civ 1740.

[66] For simple "mentions" of the condition – see Joined Cases 46/87 and 227/88 *Hoechst v. Commission* [1989] ECLI:EU:C:1989:337, para. 19; Case 85/87 *Dow Benelux v. Commission* [1989] ECLI:EU:C:1989:379, para. 30 et seq.; Case C-368/95 *Familiapress* [1997] ECLI:EU:C:1997:325, para. 26; Case C-60/00 *Carpenter* [2002] ECLI:EU:C:2002:434, para. 42; and Case C-407/08 P *Knauf Gips v. Commission* [2010] ECLI:EU:C:2010:389, para. 91; for a "review" of the condition, see Joined cases C-92/09 and C-93/09 *Volker und Markus Schecke and Eifert* [2010] ECLI:EU:C:2010:662, para. 66; Case C-275/06 *Promusicae* [2008] ECLI:EU:C:2008:54, Opinion of AG Kokott, para. 53; Case C-70/10 *Scarlet Extended* [2011] ECLI:EU:C:2011:255, Opinion of AG Villalón, para. 35; Joined Cases C-293/12 and C-594/12 *Digital Rights Ireland* [2014] ECLI:EU:C:2014:238.

[67] *Leander v. Sweden* App no 9248/81 (ECHR, 26 March 1987), para. 50; *Tan v. Turkey* App no 9460/03 (ECHR, 3 July 2007), paras. 22 to 26; *Kruslin v. France* App no (ECHR, 24 April 1990), para. 30; *Coban v. Spain* App no 17060/02 (ECHR, 25 September 2006); *Sanoma Uitgevers v. the Netherlands* App no 38224/03 (ECHR, 14 September 2010), paras. 81, 82; *Margareta and Roger Andersson v. Sweden* App no 12963/87 (ECHR, 25 February 1992), para. 75; *Ahmet Yildrimi v. Turkey* App no 3111/10 (ECHR, 18 March 2013); *Contrada v. Italy (no. 3)* App no 66655/13 (ECHR, 14 April 2014).

[68] Case C-70/10 *Scarlet Extended* [2011] ECLI:EU:C:2011:255, Opinion of AG Villalón, para. 37.

legislator is required to be, an injunction is not far from a blanket grant of legislative powers to selected individuals, under the supervision of the courts.

For instance, a rightholder could, based on injunctions against innocent intermediaries, try to impose small-scale blanket data retention obligations on intermediaries.[69] There is no doubt that such retention of the personal data of users and their behavior could help them in the enforcement of their rights. But do not such obligations have an effect equal to that of the law? Can the democratic legitimacy behind *the provision* on injunctions against intermediaries still *support a court-imposed obligation* which is so universal that it achieves basically the same binding effect as a legal norm on data retention?

The Irish Court of Appeal is recently deciding whether injunctions against intermediaries could be used to create an entire graduated-response scheme that allows enforcement against the subscribers.[70] Such schemes were legislated in countries like France following an extensive political discussion.[71] Injunctions imposing complex schemes circumvent the legislative process and the public discussion is being shrunk to the court hearing of a single judge or a panel of judges.

The generality or abstractness of an obligation is thus dubious not only due to its possible disproportionality, but also from the perspective of the rule of law. Any small-scale blanket data retention would surely need to be weighed against the right to privacy of users.[72] Any obligatory graduated-response scheme should be preferably discussed in the Parliament. It is the requirement of the rule of law, which takes precedence over the proportionality debate.[73] Its goal is to prevent the granting of powers to individuals which enable them to circumvent the democratic legislative process by unilaterally imposing abstract obligations of an equal effect to the provisions of the law.

In *Scarlet Extended*, Advocate General Villalón, although not so explicit about the scope of the problem, warned that an obligation *in abstracto*, that is without the need to be connected to a particular infringement,[74] should not be "imposed on ISPs in the form of an injunction and on a legal basis" in Belgian law[75] at all, since it is "an obligation to achieve a certain result on pain of a periodic penalty

---

[69] Something similar was attempted by the plaintiff in a case before the LG Munich (2011) 17 HK O 1398/11 – see http://wiki.vorratsdatenspeicherung.de/images/Lg-muenchen_wlan_17-hk-0-1398–11–anon.pdf.

[70] Gerard Kelly, "A Court-Ordered Graduated Response System in Ireland: The Beginning of the End?" (2016) 11(3) Journal of Intellectual Property Law & Practice 183–198.

[71] Eldar Haber, "The French Revolution 2.0: Copyright and the Three Strikes Policy" (2011) 2(2) Harvard Journal of Sports & Entertainment Law 297.

[72] Joined Cases C-293/12 and C-594/12 *Digital Rights Ireland* [2014] ECLI:EU:C:2014:238.

[73] Case C-70/10 *Scarlet Extended* [2011] ECLI:EU:C:2011:255, Opinion of AG Villalón, para. 37.

[74] As interpreted by Case C-70/10 *Scarlet Extended* [2011] ECLI:EU:C:2011:255, Opinion of AG Villalón, para. 63.

[75] Case C-70/10 *Scarlet Extended* [2011] ECLI:EU:C:2011:255, Opinion of AG Villalón, para. 68.

payment,"[76] which "by its very nature, can only be general in every regard."[77] He closes his Opinion with following broader remark:

> In the light of all these conditions, it is the very existence of that "law" which, once again, is lacking, in my view, *"law" understood to be "deliberated" law, that is, democratically legitimised.* Indeed, only a law in the parliamentary sense of the term would have made it possible to examine the other conditions in Article 52(1) of the Charter. In that regard, it could be argued that Article 52(1) of the Charter incorporates an implicit requirement for a "deliberated" law, in line with the intensity of public debate. However, it is the express requirement of a law, as "prior law," which is at issue here. Since it has been established that this is lacking in the present case, it is possible to reply to the first question posed by the national court.[78]

The prohibition of *general measures* might thus embody the principle that the provision of a legal order may not serve the purpose of the subsequent creation of new laws in circumvention of the principle of the rule of law and democracy.[79] The prohibitions of complicated, permanent, or monitoring measures could be all interpreted as emulating this principle.

But the problem does not stop here. The quality of law requirement offers more. An excellent example is offered by the case of *Scarlet Extended*. The Advocate General Villalón here argued that the filtering injunctions should be rejected *without* assessing proportionality, due to the fact that the Belgian provision on injunctions *cannot serve as a legal basis* for very complicated filtering measures which seriously interfere with the right to privacy and freedom of expression. His argument is worth citing in full:

> *The "law" must therefore be sufficiently clear and foreseeable as to the meaning and nature of the applicable measures, and must define with sufficient clarity the scope and manner of exercise of the power of interference in the exercise of the rights guaranteed by the ECHR.* [. . .] From the point of view of the users of Scarlet's services

---

[76] Ibid., para. 54.

[77] Ibid., paras. 53, 66 ("The very general scope of the system to be deployed necessarily renders the scope ratione personae and the scope ratione materiae of the measure requested in the form of an injunction themselves general, just as its scope ratione temporis is general, as the national court states").

[78] His remarks (ibid., para. 113 – emphasis mine) about the deliberated law, however, get very close to our above argument.

[79] Similar point was made in: *EMI Records (Ireland) Ltd & Ors v. UPC Communications Ireland Ltd* [2010] IEHC 377 [86] ("The courts must defer, however, to the manner in which the Oireachtas [Irish legislator] circumscribes and regulates the enforcement of those rights. (. . .) *For the Court to pursue the course of granting an injunction on the basis not of law but of economic abuse or moral turpitude would lead the Court beyond the threshold of the judicial arm of government and into legislation.* It would undermine respect for the rule of law: for no one would know quite what the rule of law might be if it depended on attitudes forged through legal argument in individual cases as to what was acceptable conduct"; emphasis mine); The CJEU considered its concept of a "Community based on the rule of law" in following cases: Case 294/83 *Les Verts v. Parliament* [1986] ECLI:EU:C:1986:166, para. 23; Joined Cases C-402/05 P and C-415/05 P *Kadi and Al Barakaat International Foundation v. Council and Commission* [2008] ECLI:EU:C:2008:461, para. 281.

and of Internet users more generally, the filtering system requested is designed, irrespective of the specific manner in which it is used, to apply systematically and universally, permanently and perpetually, but its introduction is not supported by any specific guarantee as regards in particular the protection of personal data and the confidentiality of communication.[. . .] The necessary conclusion is therefore that *the national law provision at issue cannot*, in the light of Articles 7, 8 and 11 of the Charter and in particular of the requirements relating to the "quality of the law" and, more generally, the requirements of the supremacy of the law, *be an adequate legal base on which to adopt an injunction imposing a filtering and blocking system such as that requested in the main proceedings.*[80]

The Belgian provision, in this respect, was a word-for-word implementation of Article 8(3) of the InfoSoc Directive.[81] We now know that, the Court eventually rejected the filtering on the basis of the proportionality (merits) rather than quality of the law. Since the Member States are at liberty to implement certain procedural conditions, national implementations could also be more detailed than the wording in Union law.[82] Thus, they could allow, in some Member States, measures which are impossible to obtain in others. This would create a welcome pressure on the legislator to specify further the requirements for particular cases, such as disconnecting injunctions,[83] or website blocking injunctions,[84] or even decide against them, by his own inaction. Similarly, the CJEU requires the law on third-party information, which covers personal data, to be particularly detailed and foreseeable,[85] which forces the legislators to provide for explicit rules, instead of passing the hot potato to the courts.[86]

---

[80] Case C-70/10 *Scarlet Extended* [2011] ECLI:EU:C:2011:255, Opinion of AG Villalón, paras. 88–114 (emphasis mine).

[81] Article 87(1) of the Law of 30 June 1994 on Copyright and Related rights: "The President of the Court of First Instance and the President of the Commercial Court] may also issue an injunction against intermediaries whose services are used by a third party to infringe a copyright or related right."

[82] Interestingly, ECtHR Judge Pinto de Albuquerque notes that: "This framework must be established via specific legal provisions; neither the general provisions and clauses governing civil and criminal responsibility nor the e-commerce Directive constitute a valid basis for ordering Internet blocking" – see *Ahmet Yildrimi v. Turkey* App no 3111/10 (ECHR, 18 March 2013).

[83] Martin Husovec and Miquel Peguera, "Much Ado About Little – Privately Litigated Disconnecting Injunctions" [2015] IIC 10.

[84] General Comment No. 34 on Article 19 of the International Covenant on Civil and Political Rights requires in its Article 43 that any website blocking is content-specific and notes that generic bans on the operation of particular websites and systems should be deemed incompatible.

[85] Case C-275/06 *Promusicae* [2008] ECLI:EU:C:2008:54, Opinion of AG Kokott, paras. 53, 76, 95; Joined cases C-465/00, C-138/01 and C-139/01 *Österreichischer Rundfunk and Others* [2003] ECLI:EU:C:2003:294, paras. 77–81; Case C-461/10 *Bonnier Audio AB and Others* [2012] ECLI:EU:C:2012:219, Opinion of AG Jääskinen, paras. 61, 62.

[86] A similar condition was presented by the ECtHR in *K.U. v. Finland* App no 2872/02 (ECHR, 2 December 2008): "it is nonetheless the task of the legislator to provide the framework for reconciling the various claims which compete for protection in this context. Such framework was not, however, in place at the material time, with the result that Finland's positive obligation with respect to the applicant could not be discharged."

The question of the *legal basis* of the orders, however, needs to be distinguished from the subsequent *formulations of orders*, although the two are interrelated. When a court imposes an injunction on an innocent intermediary with a specific goal in mind, it must decide exactly how to express the assistance obligation. May an obligation to assistance be formulated as an open-ended order, or is measure-specific wording required? The latter would specify the exact steps and technologies to be used in order to satisfy the court, while the former would state the result that it wishes to achieve, leaving the details of implementing decision to the addressee. A possible middle ground would be to specify at least one satisfactory way of implementing the order, but at the same time give the option to the addressee to satisfy the obligation by other means, at their discretion.

The Advocates General at the CJEU persistently suggest that, as a matter of Union law, the orders should be measure-specific. Jääskinen in *L'Oréal v. eBay* demanded that the order should make be such that "the intermediary can know with certainty what is required from him"[87] and Villalón in *UPC Telekabel* very convincingly argued that "the balance between the fundamental rights must be observed *when the injunction is issued*"[88] and therefore the mere prohibition of outcome, which considers measures only in the enforcement proceedings, should not be admissible. Szpunar in *Mc Fadden* proposed the Court to hold that EU law "preclude[s] the issuing of an injunction which leaves it to the addressee thereof to decide what specific measures should be taken" and that it is the task of the "national court hearing an application for an injunction to ensure that appropriate measures do indeed exist that are consistent with the restrictions imposed by EU law."[89]

The CJEU, however, is very reluctant to accept this principle explicitly. In *UPC Telekabel*, it decided against such a proposition by saying that "the fundamental rights recognised by EU law must be interpreted as not precluding a court [a website blocking] injunction (. . .) when that injunction does *not* specify the measures which that access provider must take and when that access provider can avoid incurring coercive penalties for breach of that injunction by showing that it has taken all reasonable measures."[90] In *Mc Fadden*, the Court did not address this issue and curiously jumped directly to assessment of the measures. This implies that there must have been a disagreement among the judges of the Third Chamber as to the right approach. Implicitly, however, the court seems to have confirmed the view of the Advocate General.[91] Even if the CJEU would not require precision of such

---

[87] Case C-324/09 *L'Oréal and Others* [2010] ECLI:EU:C:2010:757, Opinion of AG Jääskinen, para. 181.

[88] Case C-314/12 *UPC Telekabel Wien* [2013] ECLI:EU:C:2013:781, Opinion of AG Villalón, para. 88.

[89] Case C-484/14 *Tobias McFadden v. Sony Music* [2016] ECLI:EU:C:2016:170, Opinion AG Szpunar, para. 124.

[90] Case C-314/12 *UPC Telekabel Wien* [2014] ECLI:EU:C:2014:192, para. 64.

[91] Martin Husovec, "Holey Cap! CJEU Drills (Yet) Another Hole in the E-Commerce Directive's Safe Harbors" (2017) 12(2) Journal of Intellectual Property Law & Practice 115, 121.

orders, does not have any bearing on the possibility of the Member States to continue with such a requirement in their national law, whether as a matter of procedural law or human rights law.[92] Even considering the *Melloni* judgment,[93] it is difficult to see how this could ever compromise the effectiveness of Union law.

8.4.2 *Legitimate Purpose*

Any attempt to limit human rights must attain a purpose which the legal order accepts as legitimate. According to Article 52(1) of the EU Charter, "limitations may be made only if they (. . .) genuinely meet objectives of general interest recognised by the Union or the need to protect the rights and freedoms of others." Enforcement of intellectual property rights is generally accepted as a way of protecting the rights of others.[94] Justification thus stems from the constitutional roots of intellectual property rights themselves. The EU Charter is unfortunately rather unsophisticated on this front.[95] It laconically states in its Article 17(2) that "intellectual property shall be protected," without specifying the purpose or social function of such protection, or even what falls under the umbrella of the term.[96] This provision obliges the Member States to respect only the laws that they have adopted,[97] but does not mandate any particular affirmative approach to copyright or other IP policy.[98]

---

92 David Wright, *Remedies* (Federation Press, 2010) 187–189 (on the common law requirement of clarity of orders due to a follow-up in a form of the contempt of the court); in Slovakia and the Czech republic this is required due to procedural laws; *Ahmet Yildrimi v. Turkey* App no 3111/10 (ECHR, 18 March 2013) (the concurring opinion of the judge Pinto de Albuquerque also formulates this requirement); *Twentieth Century Fox Film Corp v. British Telecommunications plc* [2011] EWHC 1981 (Ch) [171]ff.; *Cartier International AG & Ors v. British Sky Broadcasting Ltd & Ors* [2014] EWHC 3354 (Ch) [133]ff.

93 Case C-399/11 *Melloni* [2013] ECLI:EU:C:2013:107.

94 Case C-70/10 *Scarlet Extended* [2011] ECLI:EU:C:2011:255, Opinion of AG Villalón, para. 92; Case C-70/10 *Scarlet Extended* [2011] ECLI:EU:C:2011:771, para. 42.

95 Christopher Geiger, "Implementing Intellectual Property Provisions in Human Rights Instruments: Towards a New Social Contract for the Protection of Intangibles" in Christopher Geiger (ed.), *Research Handbook on Human Rights and Intellectual Property* (Edward Elgar 2014); Alexander Peukert, "Intellectual Property as an End in Itself?" [2011] European Intellectual Property Review 67–71; Adolf Dietz, "Verfassungsklauseln und Quasi-Verfassungsklauseln zur Rechtfertigung des Urheberrechts – gestern, heute und morgen" [2006] GRUR Int 1.

96 Adolf Dietz, "Verfassungsklauseln und Quasi-Verfassungsklauseln zur Rechtfertigung des Urheberrechts – gestern, heute und morgen" [2006] GRUR Int 1, 7–8.

97 *Balan v. Moldova* App no 19247/03 (ECHR, 29 January 2008) (per analogy).

98 As the recent UN Report in the field of cultural rights put it, "States are free to adjust copyright rules through legal processes to promote the interests of authors, the right of everyone to take part in cultural life and other human rights such as the right to education" (Farida Shaheed, Copyright policy and the right to science and culture (UN Special Report, 2014), para. 53); Slovak Constitutional Court *Tank Man* (2015) II. ÚS 647/2014–22 – see Martin Husovec, "Tank Man Hits the Constitutional Court: Copyright and Freedom of Expression" (*Hutko's Technology Law Blog*, 25 March 2015), www.husovec .eu/2015/03/tank-man-hits-constitutional-court.html.

Regardless of the tradition, however, it is accepted that once exclusive rights are legislated, even beyond the constitutional minimum, they also become equipped with guarantees of their effective protection.[99] The CJEU also follows this interpretation under the argument of effective level of protection, based on Articles 17 and 47 of the EU Charter.[100] In its *Promusicae* ruling, for instance, the Court held that the absence of a legal framework to allow for the disclosure of infringers behind their IP addresses is *not* infringing upon a right to effective remedy, and therefore the establishment of such a framework is not a "constitutional must."[101] In the last case-law of the Court, the trend seems to be changing. The Court is willing to recognize positive obligations of the state.[102]

8.4.3 *Conflicting Fundamental Rights*

The enforcement of intellectual property rights inevitably collides with other fundamental rights. Because resolving such conflicts is inherently political,[103] human rights law lays out the exact methodology for resolving them. This methodology of

---

99 "Right to Effective Remedy" (*Recht auf wirksame Durchsetzung*) is also part of the human right standard – see Case C-275/06 *Promusicae* [2005] ECLI:EU:C:2008:54, para. 61 (right to effective remedy is not infringed in the event that there is a lack of the procedure for the disclosure of personal data of infringers by the intermediaries); *K.U. v. Finland* App no 2872/02 (ECHR, 2 December 2008) ("it is nonetheless the task of the legislator to provide the framework for reconciling the various claims which compete for protection in this context. Such framework was not, however, in place at the material time, with the result that Finland's positive obligation with respect to the applicant could not be discharged"); Andreas Paulus, "Schutz des geistigen Eigentums" in Josef Isensee and Paul Kirchhof (eds.), *Handbuch des Staatsrechts der Bundesrepublik Deutschland, Band XI* (C. H. Beck 2013) § 247, para. 23; UN General Comment No. 17: The right of everyone to benefit from the protection of the moral and material interests resulting from any scientific, literary, or artistic production of which he or she is the author, para. 18; revisited First Section decision in *Delfi AS v. Estonia*, App no. 64569/09 (ECHR, 10 October 2013) ("the State's positive obligations under Article 8 may involve the adoption of measures designed to secure respect for private life allowing an injured party to bring a claim not only against the authors of defamatory comments, but also against intermediaries"); Case C-314/12 *UPC Telekabel Wien* [2013] ECLI:EU:C:2013:781, Opinion of AG Villalón, paras. 65, 99, 107 ("the rightholder must not be rendered unprotected from a website massively infringing its rights"); Case C-324/09 *L'Oréal and Others* [2011] ECLI:EU:C:2011:474 paras. 131, 142; Case C-580/13 *Coty Germany* [2015] ECLI:EU:C:2015:243, Opinion of AG Villalón, paras. 27, 31ff.; Case C-484/14 *Tobias McFadden v. Sony Music* [2016] ECLI:EU:C:2016:689, para. 98 ("would thus be to deprive the fundamental right to intellectual property of any protection").

100 Case C-275/06 *Promusicae* [2005] ECLI:EU:C:2008:54, paras. 41, 46, 57, 61; Case C-275/06 *Promusicae* [2008] ECLI:EU:C:2008:54, Opinion of AG Kokott, paras. 55, 120, 125.

101 Case C-275/06 *Promusicae* [2008] ECLI:EU:C:2008:54, Opinion of AG Kokott, paras. 120, 125; Case C-275/06 *Promusicae* [2005] ECLI:EU:C:2008:54, para. 61; It would be an interesting situation if the CJEU were hold otherwise. This would mean that the Union law that was erected was insufficient to satisfy the Charter. If invalidated, the situation would *not* be ex post regulated by the Charter anymore. It is a situation similar to that in which the entire directive is repealed due to higher union standard of human rights, which, in the absence of another general framework, leads to inapplicability of the Charter.

102 Martin Husovec, "Intellectual Property Rights and Integration by Conflict: The Past, Present and Future" (2016) 18 *Cambridge Yearbook of European Legal Studies* 239.

103 Bodo Pieroth et al., *Grundrechte. Staatsrecht II* (C. H. Beck 2014) 2.

mutual balancing then,[104] in turn lends, legitimacy to the decisions of the judicial power, including those of the decision of the courts in which they act as negative legislator. In the EU Charter, Article 52(1) explicitly states that "Subject to the principle of proportionality, limitations may be made only if they are necessary and genuinely meet objectives of general interest recognised by the Union or the need to protect the rights and freedoms of others."

There are therefore two types of conflicts. One is the balancing of several rights among themselves, and the second is weighing the (public) interests against such rights.[105] The CJEU has already had a chance to resolve conflicts[106] between the protection of intellectual property (Article 17) on the one hand, and the rights to private and family life (Article 7),[107] secrecy of communications (Article 7),[108] personal data (Article 8),[109] freedom of expression and information (Article 11),[110] freedom to conduct a business (Article 16),[111] and remotely even right to property (Article 17).[112]

Although there is insufficient space in this work to explore these conflicts fully,[113] three important conflicting fundamental rights and their occurrence in the

---

[104] Case C-275/06 *Promusicae* [2005] ECLI:EU:C:2008:54; Case C-70/10 *Scarlet Extended* [2011] ECLI:EU:C:2011:771, paras. 44, 45; Case C-360/10 *SABAM* [2012] ECLI:EU:C:2012:85, paras. 42, 43; Case C-314/12 *UPC Telekabel Wien* [2014] ECLI:EU:C:2014:192, para. 46; Case C-314/12 *UPC Telekabel Wien* [2013] ECLI:EU:C:2013:781, Opinion of AG Villalón, paras. 76, 81, 84.

[105] Case C-580/13 *Coty Germany* [2015] ECLI:EU:C:2015:243, Opinion of AG Villalón, para. 27.

[106] Sometimes, such as in *Scarlet Extended*, the Advocate General and the Court would identify and use different fundamental rights; the CJEU uses a standard opening phrase for its balancing exercise: "The protection of the right to intellectual property is indeed enshrined in Article 17(2) of the Charter of Fundamental Rights of the European Union ("the Charter"). There is, however, nothing whatsoever in the wording of that provision or in the Court's case-law to suggest that that right is inviolable and must for that reason be absolutely protected" (Case C-360/10 *SABAM* [2012] ECLI:EU:C:2012:85, para. 41; Case C-70/10 *Scarlet Extended* [2011] ECLI:EU:C:2011:771, para. 43; Case C-314/12 *UPC Telekabel Wien* [2014] ECLI:EU:C:2014:192, para. 61).

[107] Case C-275/06 *Promusicae* [2005] ECLI:EU:C:2008:54; Case C-557/07 *LSG-Gesellschaft zur Wahrnehmung von Leistungsschutzrechten* [2009] ECLI:EU:C:2009:107; Case C-461/10 *Bonnier Audio AB and Others* [2012] ECLI:EU:C:2012:219; Case C-70/10 *Scarlet Extended* [2011] ECLI:EU:C:2011:255, Opinion of AG Villalón, para. 71.

[108] Case C-70/10 *Scarlet Extended* [2011] ECLI:EU:C:2011:255, Opinion of AG Villalón, para. 71.

[109] Case C-360/10 *SABAM* [2012] ECLI:EU:C:2012:85, para. 49 (systematic analysis of conduct); Case C-70/10 *Scarlet Extended* [2011] ECLI:EU:C:2011:771, para. 50 (systematic analysis of conduct); Case C-70/10 *Scarlet Extended* [2011] ECLI:EU:C:2011:255, Opinion of AG Villalón, para. 71.

[110] Case C-70/10 *Scarlet Extended* [2011] ECLI:EU:C:2011:255, Opinion of AG Villalón, para. 71; Case C-360/10 *SABAM* [2012] ECLI:EU:C:2012:85, para. 50; Case C-314/12 *UPC Telekabel Wien* [2014] ECLI:EU:C:2014:192, paras. 47, 52, 56; Case C-314/12 *UPC Telekabel Wien* [2013] ECLI:EU:C:2013:781, Opinion of AG Villalón, paras. 86.

[111] Case C-70/10 *Scarlet Extended* [2011] ECLI:EU:C:2011:771, para. 46; Case C-360/10 *SABAM* [2012] ECLI:EU:C:2012:85, para. 44; Case C-314/12 *UPC Telekabel Wien* [2014] ECLI:EU:C:2014:192, para. 47; Case C-314/12 *UPC Telekabel Wien* [2013] ECLI:EU:C:2013:781, Opinion of AG Villalón, para. 83.

[112] Case C-70/10 *Scarlet Extended* [2011] ECLI:EU:C:2011:255, Opinion of AG Villalón, para. 71.

[113] For more extensive discussion see Pekka Savola, *Internet Connectivity Providers as Involuntary Copyright Enforers: Blocking Websites in Particular* (IPR University Center, 2015).

case-law should be at least briefly mentioned (1) the right to privacy, (2) the freedom to conduct business, and (3) the freedom of expression.

In the context of a *right to privacy*, the CJEU seems to struggle to identify its own position. On one hand, the Court's case-law in the area of state surveillance position the court in a role of guardian of privacy. However, in copyright enforcement context, the Court seems more hesitant. Although it rejected general filtering in *Scarlet* and *Sabam*,[114] and Advocate General even highlighted that "the opportunity to remain anonymous is essential if it is wished to preserve the fundamental right to a private life in cyberspace,"[115] its recent *Mc Fadden* ruling dilutes the Court's privacy message. In this case, the Court held that "a measure consisting in password-protecting an internet connection may dissuade the users of that connection from infringing copyright or related rights, provided that those users are required to reveal their identity in order to obtain the required password and may not therefore act anonymously."[116]

Second, the main counterweight on the intermediaries' side seems to be their right to conduct a business. Although it may be debatable whether this is a "right" or an "interest," in *Scarlet Extended* and *Sabam*, the Court held that too complicated and costly injunctions directly infringe upon Article 16.[117] This is because the freedom to conduct a business includes "the right for any business to be able to freely use, within the limits of its liability for its own acts, the economic, technical and financial resources available to it."[118] Therefore "an injunction (. . .) constrains its addressee in (. . .) the free use of the resources at his disposal because it obliges him to take measures which may represent a significant cost for him, have a considerable impact on the organisation of his activities or require difficult and complex technical solutions."[119] The Advocate General in *Scarlet Extended* even explicitly noted that costly injunctions have the effect of transferring wealth and cross-subsidizing the enforcement costs of rightholders.[120] This, in his opinion, was very problematic particularly because the exact costs of the measures are impossible to ascertain at the time of granting such injunctions.[121] This perception of freedom to allocate

---

[114]   On over-blocking: Case C-70/10 *Scarlet Extended* [2011] ECLI:EU:C:2011:771, para. 50; Case C-314/12 *UPC Telekabel Wien* [2014] ECLI:EU:C:2014:192, paras. 55–60.

[115]   Case C-70/10 *Scarlet Extended* [2011] ECLI:EU:C:2011:255, Opinion of AG Villalón, para. 73; Working party 29, "Recommendation 3/97: Anonymity on the Internet Adopted by the Working Party" (1997): "The ability to choose to remain anonymous is essential if individuals are to preserve the same protection for their privacy on-line as they currently enjoy offline. Anonymity is not appropriate in all circumstances"; Nicolo Zingales, "Virtues and Perils of Anonymity: Should Intermediaries Bear the Burden?" (2014) TILEC Discussion Paper No. 025.

[116]   Case C-484/14 *Mc Fadden* [2016] ECLI:EU:C:2016:689, para. 96.

[117]   Case C-70/10 *Scarlet Extended* [2011] ECLI:EU:C:2011:771, paras. 48, 49; Case C-360/10 *SABAM* [2012] ECLI:EU:C:2012:85, para. 46.

[118]   Case C-314/12 *UPC Telekabel Wien* [2014] ECLI:EU:C:2014:192, para. 49.

[119]   Case C-314/12 *UPC Telekabel Wien* [2014] ECLI:EU:C:2014:192, para. 50.

[120]   Case C-70/10 *Scarlet Extended* [2011] ECLI:EU:C:2011:255, Opinion of AG Villalón, para. 64.

[121]   Case C-70/10 *Scarlet Extended* [2011] ECLI:EU:C:2011:255, Opinion of AG Villalón, para. 52.

resources even led the CJEU to the conclusion, in its *UPC Telekabel*, ruling that the possibility to choose from several measures is in fact in favor of the provider, irrespective of the legal uncertainty that it creates for others.[122]

Under the proposal of this work – the condition of self-funding – most of the human rights considerations of the costs against service providers would be mitigated. Naturally, Article 16 would still preserve its guiding role on the obligations that limit the general freedom of intermediaries to act, but its effect would probably be less significant.

Third, both the CJEU and ECtHR now acknowledge that blocking access to lawful information is an unjustified interference with the freedom of expression and information of both the speakers of the information, as well as its potential recipients.[123] This means that if an injunction goes beyond its purpose of blocking illegal content, it over-blocks, and is no longer acceptable. Furthermore, the restriction on access is only compatible if a strict legal framework is put in place to regulate the scope of a ban and afford a guarantee of judicial review to prevent possible abuses. The CJEU in this context requires concrete positive obligations of the state.

Until now, the CJEU has failed to recognize the contextual importance of the right to a fair trial.[124] Particularly in the website blocking cases, the operators of websites that are to be blocked should arguably have the chance to defend their position.[125] If a lawsuit is only brought against the provider, the website operator is not party to the proceedings. This is even more pressing in disconnection cases, where a disconnected user is also not present.[126]

The main importance of the EU Charter is not merely the possibility to *moderate*, on a pan-European scale, what the national courts may allow,[127] but increasingly also

---

[122] Case C-314/12 *UPC Telekabel Wien* [2014] ECLI:EU:C:2014:192, para. 52.

[123] See Case C-314/12 *UPC Telekabel Wien* [2014] ECLI:EU:C:2014:192, para. 56 (stating, in the context of website blocking, that the measure "must serve to bring an end to a third party's infringement of copyright or of a related right but without thereby affecting internet users who are using the provider's services in order to lawfully access information. Failing that, the provider's interference in the freedom of information of those users would be unjustified in the light of the objective pursued"); *also Ahmet Yildrimi v. Turkey* App no 3111/10 (ECHR, 18 March 2013).

[124] The only possible attempt seen was the subsidiarity principle suggested by the Advocate General in *UPC Telekabel Wien* (Case C-314/12 *UPC Telekabel Wien* [2013] ECLI:EU:C:2013:781, Opinion of AG Villalón, para. 107); *Totalise Plc v. Motley Fool Ltd* [2002] 1 W.L.R. 1233 [25], [26] (the interests of those who are not party to the proceedings must be weighted even more); *Media CAT v. Adams*, 2011 WL 291789 [14] (on supervising solicitor).

[125] See *Ahmet Yildrimi v. Turkey* App no 3111/10 (ECHR, 18 March 2013) and the concurring opinion of the judge Pinto de Albuquerque.

[126] Martin Husovec and Miquel Peguera, "Much Ado About Little – Privately Litigated Disconnecting Injunctions" [2015] IIC 10; Althaf Marsoof, "The Blocking Injunction – A Critical Review of Its Implementation in the United Kingdom Within the Legal Framework of the European Union" (2015) 46 IIC 632–664.

[127] Case C-70/10 *Scarlet Extended* [2011] ECLI:EU:C:2011:771, para. 54; Case C-360/10 *SABAM* [2012] ECLI:EU:C:2012:85, para. 52; Case C-275/06 *Promusicae* [2005] ECLI:EU:C:2008:54, para. 68.

the ability to formulate exact *positive obligations* that the national courts or legislator have to satisfy when granting injunctions or transposing the directives.

8.4.4 *Appropriateness, Necessity, and Proportionality*

The main focus of the Court's analysis often is the proportionality, or balancing exercise. The weighing of interests is nothing unusual. It is present in most of the legal systems. However, it takes different forms. While some courts engage in a mere cost and benefit analysis of *all* interests at stake, others focus only a *selected number* of the most important interests known as fundamental rights, in order to reconcile them. Such exercise is therefore not homogenous even if it is called by the same name.

What matters is the *framing* of such balancing exercise, in particular, which interests are taken into account and with what weight. To illustrate, the *cost and benefit analysis* of password locking of open wireless will consider the cost and benefits that it imposes on everyone. On the other hand, the *fundamental rights inquiry* will only identify relevant subjects who hold "fundamental rights" at stake and measure them against each other. As a consequence, the latter proportionality exercise won't take into account some of the costs or benefits. This is understandable as the use of the latter is primarily to outlaw the extreme policies, not to properly guide the good ones. Such proportionality should lead to a range of acceptable outcomes and not a prescription of a single one. The Court's current application of balancing, which is framed as a fundamental rights inquiry,[128] seems to be gradually tightening the scrutiny and becoming more prescriptive.

The biggest loser of fundamental rights framing is what lies ahead – future innovation. Innovation doesn't fit well any of the fundamental rights. Even a right to conduct business covers a firm's ability "to freely use, within the limits of its liability for its own acts, the economic, technical and financial *resources available to it.*"[129] The emphasis on existing resources as opposed to potential resources takes "innovation capabilities" off the fundamental rights radar.

In the human rights framework, any restraints on the rights of others must be appropriate, necessary, and proportionate.[130] Article 52 of the EU Charter provides

---

[128] In Mc Fadden case, for instance, the CJEU rejected to consider the impact of password-locking measures on innovation, even thought this aspect was seen as one of the crucial arguments against the measures presented by the Advocate General Szpunar – see Martin Husovec, "Holey Cap! CJEU Drills (Yet) Another Hole in the E-Commerce Directive's Safe Harbors" (2017) 12(2) Journal of Intellectual Property Law & Practice 115–125.

[129] Case C-314/12 *UPC Telekabel Wien* [2014] ECLI:EU:C:2014:192, para. 49 (empahsis mine).

[130] Necessity and proportionality are directly mentioned in Article 52(1) of the EU Charter, whereas appropriateness was adopted by the Court (Case C-275/06 *Promusicae* [2005] ECLI:EU:C:2008:54, para. 49; Case C-275/06 *Promusicae* [2008] ECLI:EU:C:2008:54, Opinion of AG Kokott, para. 54; Case C-314/12 *UPC Telekabel Wien* [2013] ECLI:EU:C:2013:781, Opinion of AG Villalón, paras. 94–103).

an explicit framework for this exercise. The website blocking cases are a particularly illustrative example of employing this test. The Advocate General in *UPC Telekabel* tested appropriateness by asking whether a measure is "appropriate for the further-ance of the aim, that is to say, make a contribution to the attainment of the aim."[131] Although the AG then expressed doubts over the ease with which both the users and targeted website can circumvent the block, he was of the opinion that this does not prevent the measure from being issued because there might still be some effect on the behavior of certain users.[132] The quantitative assessment of the foreseeable success is, according to the AG, only one of the factors to be weighed.[133] Concluding that the measure is appropriate, the AG examined the necessity and proportionality *stricto sensu* of the limitation. He wrote:

> The measure ordered must also not go beyond what is necessary to achieve the objective, and, of several appropriate measures, recourse must be had to the least onerous. Finally, the disadvantages caused by the measure must not be dispropor-tionate to the aim pursued.[134]

Applying this to the question of website blocking, the AG suggested that this needs to be evaluated in every individual case, but that website blocking is *not* "in principle, disproportionate solely because it entails not inconsiderable costs" and "can easily be circumvented without any special technical knowledge."[135] The Court accepted this.[136]

A similar balancing exercise is also present in the case-law related to third-party information and its conflict with the right to privacy. Because any such disclosure relating to personal data is an implementation of Union law,[137] the CJEU has already postulated several requirements for such a disclosure, if implemented on the national level. Apart from strong guarantees of the quality of the law,[138] the legislator has to

---

[131] Case C-314/12 *UPC Telekabel Wien* [2013] ECLI:EU:C:2013:781, Opinion of AG Villalón, para. 99.

[132] Ibid., paras. 100–102.   [133] Ibid., para. 105.   [134] Ibid., para. 103.   [135] Ibid., para. 109.

[136] Moreover, given the *Ahmet Yildirim v. Turkey* decision, it is questionable whenever ECtHR would not require more strict safeguards. For instance, one of the judges stated, in his separate opinion, that unlimited measures in time terms are *per se* incompatible with the Convention: "By the same token, blocking orders imposed on sites and platforms which remain valid indefinitely or for long periods are tantamount to inadmissible forms of prior restraint, in other words, to pure censorship" (*Ahmet Yildrimi v. Turkey* App no 3111/10 (ECHR, 18 March 2013)).

[137] According to *Promusicae*, they are based on a derogation from Union law, Article 15(1) of Directive 2002/58 and Article 13(1) of Directive 95/46 (Case C-275/06 *Promusicae* [2005] ECLI:EU:C:2008:54, para. 53), which is still implementing Union law and thus has to be tested against the EU Charter (paras. 68, 69).

[138] Case C-461/10 *Bonnier Audio AB and Others* [2012] ECLI:EU:C:2012:219, Opinion of AG Jääskinen, paras. 61, 62 (prior national implementation has to be detailed); Case C-461/10 *Bonnier Audio AB and Others* [2012] ECLI:EU:C:2012:219, paras. 58, 59 (responding that the Swedish legislation requiring "clear evidence of an infringement of an intellectual property right," that "the information can be regarded as facilitating the investigation into an infringement" and that "the reasons for the measure outweigh the nuisance or other harm which the measure may entail for the person affected by it or for some other conflicting interest" are sufficient to comply with the EU Charter requirements).

give the courts discretion to carry out the balancing exercise in each individual case, and may not allow access to data that was collected for other purposes.[139] These obligations are positive obligations of the state that need to be observed when formulating and subsequently interpreting the laws.[140]

The proportionality is better understood as a range. To illustrate it, consider the application of the effectiveness of the measures by the Court. The CJEU's "do something" approach,[141] as aptly labeled by "Angelopoulos", requires a very low level of effectiveness. However, is such a low threshold generally prescribed as the only acceptable one? The *UPC Telekabel* decision and its low effectiveness threshold were decided in the context of the question what minimum level of effectiveness justifies the interference with the opposing fundamental rights. Therefore the decision says, in my view, that the website blocking "must be sufficiently effective to ensure genuine protection of the fundamental right at issue"[142] in order to be permissible at all. The requirement that injunctions "must have the effect of preventing unauthorized access to the protected subject-matter or, at least, of making it difficult to achieve and of seriously discouraging internet users,"[143] should be therefore read as a bare minimum. This would allow also higher thresholds as long as they would not compromise the very essence of the policy choice, as explained by *L'Oréal v. eBay* (see Section 8.1)[144] or of a fundamental right to intellectual property. The Court would thus retain the ability to moderate only the opposite extremes – too low and too high domestic thresholds, but would not be prescribing what happens in between. The level of domestic modularity would depend on how far apart the two extremes lie.

The Court's post-UPC case-law is not very clear on this point. In *McFadden*, the Court presents the efficiency as the minimum needed to prevent violation of a fundamental right under Article 17(2) of the EU Charter.[145] Advocate General Szpunar reviews the case-law by pointing to both minimum from the perspective of other rights and the right to intellectual property.[146] He then concludes the following:

---

[139] Case C-461/10 *Bonnier Audio AB and Others* [2011] ECLI:EU:C:2011:753, Opinion of AG Jääskinen, para. 60 ("It would be contrary to the principles of the protection of personal data to make use of databases that exist for purposes other than those thus defined by the legislature").

[140] Martin Husovec, "Intellectual Property Rights and Integration by Conflict: The Past, Present and Future" (2016) 18 *Cambridge Yearbook of European Legal Studies* 239–269.

[141] Christina Angelopoulos, *European Intermediary Liability in Copyright: A Tort-Based Analysis* (Kluwer Law International 2017) 227.

[142] Case C-314/12 *UPC Telekabel Wien* [2014] ECLI:EU:C:2014:192, para. 62.   [143] Ibid.

[144] Similar argument seems to be made by AG Szpunar in Case C-610/15 *Stichting Brein* [2017] ECLI:EU:C:2017:99, Opinion of AG Szpunar, paras. 81, 83 ("Acceptance of the reasoning of the defendants in the main proceedings would amount to accepting that no measure to prevent infringement of the law can be effective because new infringements will always be committed by other persons").

[145] Case C-484/14 *Mc Fadden* [2016] ECLI:EU:C:2016:689, para. 98.

[146] Case C-610/15 *Stichting Brein* [2017] ECLI:EU:C:2017:99, Opinion of AG Szpunar, paras. 77–83.

If a measure that is less restrictive for service providers and constitutes less of an intrusion upon the rights of users were now rejected on the ground that it is not sufficiently effective, internet service providers would ultimately be released de facto from their duty to cooperate in the fight against copyright infringement. (...) They cannot escape that obligation by claiming, according to the circumstances, that the measures are either over-restrictive or ineffective.[147]

If followed by the Court, the case-law could become very prescriptive. The statement suggests that the proportionality leads to only one outcome that is determined by the opposing fundamental rights. It would also suggest that situational denial of any measure against a particular provider never leads to a balance, even though there might be other providers whose actions could be of better help. Such development would be problematic because rights and measures that get attention drive the outcome of balancing.

8.5 A NEW APPROACH

In Chapter 2, I suggested that the courts should presume the effectiveness of measures, since this type of assessment should be outsourced to the plaintiffs who need to self-fund the measures they propose. If this suggestion is not followed, for instance because countries believe that their courts can estimate the real private costs and benefits of the measures, then the effectiveness really needs to preserve its meaning independent of the human rights exercise of balancing the rights. As was mentioned earlier, constitutional limits are not a good indicator of a good policy, they only indicate the outer boundaries of what is permissible policy. Constitutional proportionality should look more like a range and not an outcome. Welfare maximizing analysis should then take place within this range. The available legislative platform to fill in constitutionally permissible range is Article 3 of the Enforcement Directive.

The current case-law lacks any systematic approach to dealing with the limitations of injunctions. In addition to self-funding, it would be advisable therefore, to conceptually distinguish between three types of limits – (a) human rights limits, (b) direct costs limits, and (c) indirect cost limits; and categorize existing factors respectively.

An injunction is not socially wasteful if the rightholders obtain more benefits than the society pays for its implementation (if $E(\pi) > C^1 + C^2 + C^3 + C^4$). The requirements of (e) effectiveness, (g) dissuasiveness, (c) not excessive costliness and complexity of measures could be said to apply to the *direct costs* of rightholders (C^1), intermediaries (C^2) and of the state (C^3). These direct costs and benefits are crucial in understanding whether the requested enforcement measure is socially wasteful or welfare maximizing. Socially wasteful measures should be incompatible with these enforcement limitations.

---

[147] Case C-610/15 *Stichting Brein* [2017] ECLI:EU:C:2017:99, Opinion of AG Szpunar, para. 83.

But even if the benefits to rightholders are higher than their own costs, and those of intermediaries and the state (if $E(\pi) > C^1 + C^2 + C^3$), the measures might still exhibit high levels of other collateral *indirect costs* (C^4). These indirect costs could then be captured by the requirement that the measures should not create (d) barriers to legitimate trade, or, more specifically, not cause unreasonable time limits or unwarranted delays. In *Mc Fadden*, Advocate General Szpunar proposed to reject password locking on the basis that:

> Wi-Fi access points indisputably offer great potential for innovation. Any measures that could hinder the development of that activity should therefore be very carefully examined with reference to their potential benefits.[148]

Although the Court did not follow this part of the reasoning, the objections are important. Impact on follow-on innovation should be integral part of the assessment of any proposed measures of assistance. Any restriction that unreasonably delays innovation undermines the very goals of intellectual property – to bring society forward.

Last but not least, even if the measures proposed are welfare maximizing, they might still be incompatible with human rights. Requirements of (a) fairness, (b) equitableness, (c) proportionality, and (d) safeguards against the abuse can be seen as a part of the human rights considerations. This would mean that a proposed measure could be rejected as unfair or disproportionate only provided that such a value judgment is imposed by the EU Charter itself. The human rights assessment should be carried out first, as welfare maximizing measures that infringe upon basic rules of society, e.g., principles of rule of law, aren't acceptable, regardless of their economic benefits.

Under the proposal of this work, rightholders would need to self-fund all the direct costs of their actions ($C^1 + C^2 + C^3$). They would thus feel their weight as a private cost. Under such a system, the courts could give up any analysis of effectiveness, dissuasiveness, costliness, and complexity of the measures. This calculation would be done by those who are better placed to carry it out – the rightholders. The courts, however, would not be relieved from analyzing indirect costs (C^4) and respect for human rights. The requirements of a lack of *barriers to legitimate trade* and *human rights limitations*, would thus become central to the analysis.

8.6 COSTS

The InfoSoc Directive does not even mention the costs of enforcement. The Enforcement Directive does, but only by stressing that the enforcement measures imposed "shall not be unnecessarily costly" (Article 3). No other provision even indirectly touches upon the *implementation costs* incurred by noninfringers. This means that

---

[148] Case C-484/14 *Mc Fadden* [2016] ECLI:EU:C:2016:170, Advocate General Szpunar, para. 149.

allocation of such costs is a domestic modality,[149] which is, however, still subject to Article 3 evaluation.

On the other hand, the Directive includes an explicit provision concerning the reimbursement of *legal costs*. Article 14 stipulates that the "Member States shall ensure that reasonable and proportionate legal costs and other expenses incurred by the successful party shall, as a general rule, be borne by the unsuccessful party, unless equity does not allow this." The broadly framed term "unsuccessful party" seems to cover any defendant, including noninfringers.[150] The CJEU confirmed this in *Diageo Brands*, where it held that "[the] provision is applicable to the legal costs incurred in the context of any procedure falling within the scope of [the] directive."[151] This means that exoneration of innocent intermediaries from legal costs has to be resolved by resorting to considerations of equity and the innocent character of their behavior. Given that the primary purpose of the provision is to burden those who infringed, or falsely invoked their rights, abstaining from burdening those defendants who did nothing wrong seems more than compatible with the aim of the provision.[152] Again, the history of the Norwich jurisdiction and its considerations of equity, as described in Chapter 10, can be of much inspiration in this regard. After all, the rule that the unsuccessful party bears the costs is a very common rule of thumb applicable usually in ordinary adversarial proceedings, which the injunctions against innocent third parties are not.[153]

Moreover, as the Advocate General Villalón in *UPC Telekabel* demonstrates, a specific cost-split could even be *mandated* by the proportionality exercise.[154] In his opinion for the Court, he wrote the following:

> Should a specific measure prove to be disproportionate in that regard in view of its complexity, costs and duration, it must be considered whether proportionality can be established by a partial or full assumption of the cost burden by the rightholder.[155]

The Court eventually did not discuss this proposition in detail, but its ruling does not seem to contradict the AG's rationale. So although the reimbursement is not mandated by the Union law, if the costs of the assistance measures were to be borne by the rightholders, this could arguably increase the possibility that the measures will be granted as proportionate. On the other hand, the Union law does not prevent that the Member States allocate all the implementation costs with rightholders.

---

[149] Similarly Pekka Savola, *Internet Connectivity Providers as Involuntary Copyright Enforcers: Blocking Websites in Particular* (IPR University Center, 2015) 91.

[150] Ibid., 91; Jaani Riordan, *The Liability of Internet Intermediaries* (Oxford, 2016) 385, para. 12.41.

[151] Case C-681/13 *Diageo Brands* [2015] ECLI:EU:C:2015:137, para. 78 (holding that the provision is applicable to the legal costs incurred by the plaintiff in the context follow-on lawsuit to collect damages caused by an unjustified request for a preliminary injunction).

[152] Similar Jaani Riordan, *The Liability of Internet Intermediaries* (Oxford, 2016) 386, para. 12.41.

[153] *Totalise Plc v. Motley Fool Ltd* [2002] 1 W.L.R. 1233 [29–30].

[154] Case C-314/12 UPC *Telekabel Wien* [2013] ECLI:EU:C:2013:781, Opinion of AG Villalón, para. 106.

[155] Ibid.

Such imposition also does not seem incompatible with the Union law.[156] The EU principle of the procedural autonomy allows that the national legal order regulates the procedures pertaining to claims accorded under EU law, however, subject to principles of equivalence and effectiveness. According to this principle, "national procedures may not make the exercise of rights conferred under EU law practically impossible or excessively complicated."[157] An unsupervised shift of the costs of implementation onto rightholders under which these intermediaries can arbitrarily inflate the costs could, however, violate Article 3 of the Enforcement Directive and Article 47(1) of the EU Charter.

The costs considerations are a recurring issue on the domestic level. They form an important part of the assessment of the measures and are often considered in the policy discussions.[158] The costs predetermine the how the regulatory intervention by injunctions is received. As Riordan points out, "costs rules therefore indirectly influence whether or not claims related to internet intermediaries will be judicially determined."[159] This is because, as I have written elsewhere, "a compensation that intermediaries have to pay after imposition of such measures represents the incentive to early-comply without agents of the state getting involved through the formal procedures."[160] The only way how to avoid this effect is by prohibiting to comply voluntarily, for example based on net neutrality laws or data protection laws. However, such prohibition often isn't feasible or practicable. Therefore a great attention should be given to the issue of costs. Not only for the purpose of achieving welfare maximizing enforcement, but also to achieve its proper adjudication through the court system.

The fact that the first cases go adjudicated shouldn't be perceived as a victory of judicial oversight. If the test cases establish the cost allocation rules that create a large enough incentive for an intermediary to "early-comply," then subsequently, intermediaries will resort to private arrangements in the long run and seek more informal and less costly informal procedures. The private ordering can, moreover, reduce the level of their transparency and human rights scrutiny. The deference of

---

[156] Case C–73/16 *Puškár* [2017] ECLI:EU:C:2017:253, Opinion of AG Kokott, paras. 65–69 (AG opining that an obligatory administrative remedy causing not insignificant costs as precondition of right to effective remedy are generally acceptable as long as they pursue legitimate objectives in the general interest); Case C–317/08 *Alassini e.a.* [2010] ECLI:EU:C:2010:146 (an obligatory alternative dispute resolution does not compromise a right to effective remedy).

[157] Case C–73/16 *Puškár* [2017] ECLI:EU:C:2017:253, Opinion of AG Kokott, para. 47.

[158] In the UK, the Digital Economy Act 2010 came up with splits of 75 percent born by rightholders and 25 percent born by intermediaries – see Communications Act 2003, Section 124M; Online Infringement of Copyright (Initial Obligations) Cost Sharing Order 2010 (UK); Ofcom, "Online Infringement of Copyright and the Digital Economy Act 2010: Notice of Ofcom's Proposal to Make by Order a Code for Regulating the Initial Obligations" (2012), para. 8.8.

[159] Jaani Riordan, *The Liability of Internet Intermediaries* (Oxford, 2016) 603, para. 18.14.

[160] Martin Husovec, "Holey Cap! CJEU Drills (Yet) Another Hole in the E-Commerce Directive's Safe Harbors" (2017) 12(2) Journal of Intellectual Property Law & Practice 115, 119.

the proper allocation of costs until the moment when practice becomes costly on the aggregate, therefore can undermine the goals of balanced adjudication.

The costs are also crucial for yet another reason. They decide upon the attractiveness of injunctions against innocent intermediaries in comparison with remedies against wrongdoers. These two are clearly in competition.[161] If the law doesn't design the incentives right, enforcement against infringers might be crowded out by enforcement against innocent third parties who will ultimately cross-subsidize the enforcement efforts, regardless of their own innocence. This will not only distort the allocative goals of tort law, but also undermine its design. If comparable relief or solutions can be achieved with less litigation resistance, the winner in the contest of remedies is clear. The costs are one of the most effective ways, apart from the scope of injunctions, how to assure than a new regulatory instrument is used in the situations where addressing the wrongdoers isn't more efficient.

---

[161] Martin Husovec, "Injunctions Against Innocent Third Parties: Case of Website Blocking" (2013) 4 JIPITEC 116, 125–126.

PART IV

Legal Traditions

9

Injunctions in Civil Law

Germany

Knowing the history allows us to better evaluate presence. It helps us to demystify current doctrine and to see even the most heated debates from some healthy distance. The following section will try to do exactly that, to demystify and distance. Maybe unusually for a book about an Internet phenomenon, it starts with Romans and their view of injunctions. This is because, this is where it all started.

The two biggest legal traditions of the world, civil and common law, owe a lot to the heritage of Roman law. Although "the Roman law was not 'received' in England to the degree and in the manner that it was 'received' on the Continent,"[1] certain contrasts can be still striking. As Buckland put it, "it may be a paradox, but it seems to be the truth that there is more affinity between the Roman jurist and the common law lawyer than there is between the Roman jurist and his modern civilian successor."[2] The field of our study here, injunctions, certainly shows both a predictable continuation of the Roman tradition in the legal systems of the civil law countries, but also a surprising Roman influence in the common law of equity.[3]

9.1 ROMAN INFLUENCE

Roman legal doctrine typically differentiated between (enforcement) actions *in rem* and actions *in personam*.[4] This distinction developed from different understanding

---

[1] Edward D. Re, "The Roman Contribution to the Common Law" (1961) 29 Fordham L. Rev. 447, 448.

[2] William W. Buckland and Arnold D. McNair, *Roman Law and Common Law* (2d ed., Cambridge University Press 1952) xvi.

[3] Marion Smith, *Elements of Law, in Studying Law* (2nd ed., Vanderbilt 1955) 171, 341 ("In equity there was, of course, more borrowing than elsewhere").

[4] For discussion of the usefulness of such a distinction from the perspective of today – see William W. Buckland and Arnold D. McNair, *Roman Law and Common Law* (2nd ed., Cambridge University Press 1952) 89, and Anna Mancini, *Ancient Roman Solutions to Modern Legal Issues: The Example of Patent Law* (2nd ed., Buenos Books America 2007) 50.

of remedies, and not of the rights giving rise to them[5] (which differs significantly from the later common law style distinction between personal and real actions).[6] The most typical in rem action was *rei vindicatio*, a legal action by which a plaintiff demands that a defendant returns a thing that belongs to the plaintiff. This remedy was exclusively about the object (thing) and its return to the plaintiff's possession.[7] The plaintiff was not asserting any right against anyone.[8] In fact, the plaintiff would not even name a defendant.[9] The entire actio ultimately served the aim of *defining the right to a thing* which was claimed.[10] Because *rei vindicatio* did not focus on the defendant, it was of course also irrelevant how he obtained the thing. The objective disharmony between the legal and factual situation alone, gave rise to the action.

We can similarly describe *actio negatoria* – an action denying the right of others to a thing.[11] Actio negatoria was also understood as an in rem action.[12] According to Buckland,[13] even though in a normal in rem action, the plaintiff would assert his rights without naming a defendant, actio negatoria, in fact, did name an opposing party. This party, however, was *not* named *as a defendant*, but most likely only served the purpose of the action, namely, *defining the scope of the right* that was actually claimed. The decision of a "judge" hearing this actio in rem would still, however,

---

[5] William W. Buckland, *A Text-Book of Roman Law: From Augustus to Justinian* (Cambridge University Press 2007) 668; Yoshikazu Kawasumi, *Von der römischen action negatoria zum negatorischen Beseitigungsanspruch des BGB* (Nomos Verlag 2001) 14.

[6] Frederic W. Maitland, Alfred. H. Chaytor and William J. Whittaker, *The Forms of Action at Common Law: A Course of Lectures Paperback* (Cambridge University Press 1936) 73–78; William W. Buckland and Arnold, D. McNair, *Roman Law and Common Law* (2nd ed., Cambridge University Press 1952) 89; Lawrence Collins, *The Civil Jurisdiction and Judgments Act 1982* (Butterworths 1983) 78–79 (pointing out that "the expression 'proceedings which have as their object rights in rem or tenancies of immovable property' does not fit with any existing concepts of property law in the United Kingdom").

[7] More about who could have been addressee of such a claim – see Heinrich Siber, *Die Passivlegitimation bei der rei vindicatio als Beitrag zur Lehre von der Aktionenkonkurrenz* (Deichert 1907).

[8] William W. Buckland, *A Text-Book of Roman Law: From Augustus to Justinian* (Cambridge University Press 2007) 668; Erika Wagner, *Gesetzliche Unterlassungsansprüche im Zivilrecht: zugleich eine Untersuchung des Beseitigungsanspruchs* (Manz 2004) 17, fn. 79.

[9] Buckland (William W. Buckland, *A Text-Book of Roman Law: From Augustus to Justinian* (Cambridge University Press 2007) 670) writes that "actions in rem had general characteristics that the *intentio* alleged a right in the plaintiff and did not mention the defendant."

[10] Ibid., 671.

[11] Conrad-Baldenstein (Ulysses Conrad-Baldenstein, *Die Actio Negatoria mit besonderer Berücksichtigung der Beweislast* (Orell Füssli 1907) 29) writes that the mere objective disharmony matters ("dass der Eingriff subjektiv gewollt war oder nicht, und ob beklagter dolus oder kulpos handelte und ob durch den Schaden estanden ist, ist für das Zustandekommen der actio [negatoria] an sich gleichgültig").

[12] Erika Wagner, *Gesetzliche Unterlassungsansprüche im Zivilrecht: zugleich eine Untersuchung des Beseitigungsanspruchs* (Manz 2004) 16, fn. 75; Peter Apathy and Georg Klingenberg, *Einführung in das römische Recht* (Böhlau 1994) 12; William W. Buckland, *A Text-Book of Roman Law: From Augustus to Justinian* (Cambridge University Press 2007) 668; Yoshikazu Kawasumi, *Von der römischen action negatoria zum negatorischen Beseitigungsanspruch des BGB* (Nomos Verlag 2001) 12.

[13] William W. Buckland, *A Text-Book of Roman Law: From Augustus to Justinian* (Cambridge University Press 2007) 671.

then condemn a certain person.[14] This also explains why actio negatoria in some civil law countries even today (e.g., Austria or Switzerland) is also known as an "action for freeing a property" (*Eigentumsfreiheitsklage*).[15] Actio negatoria thus, by establishing the exact scope of the right, liberated it from foreign interference. Or as Macini puts it,[16] actio in rem asked: "what is my power over a thing" and *not*: "what is my right against a certain person."

This understanding of in rem remedy continued in civil law. Rei vindicatio, as opposed to the common law concept of conversion, did not rely on any tortuous obligation that arose in the meantime between plaintiff and defendant, but on the rightholder's exclusive legal power over the tangible object of protection (*res*).[17] Reinhold Johow, nicely summarizes this as follows:

> the real claim (*dingliche Anspruch*)[18] to property, actio in rem or action for a thing, enables, that the owner can take a possession of his thing, wherever he finds it. Which person he will face during such realisation of his right, is indifferent, because the special characteristics of that person, or his behaviour, are indifferent for the content of the real claim.[19]

It follows from the above that an action in rem would thus focus only on an *objective situation of disharmony between law and reality*, and *not* on a person and his conduct that *led* to that situation.[20] Injunctions against intermediaries that were incorporated into EU law also share this feature of Roman law. They do not ask what an intermediary *did*, but rather what, given the situation, it *can do*.

---

[14] William W. Buckland and Arnold D. McNair, *Roman Law and Common Law* (2d ed., Cambridge University Press 1952) 89.

[15] Ibid.

[16] Anna Mancini, *Ancient Roman Solutions to Modern Legal Issues: The Example of Patent Law* (2d ed., Buenos Books America 2007) 50.

[17] Heinrich Honsell, *Römisches Recht* (Springer 2010) 72; Ugo Mattei, *Basic Principles of Property Law: A Comparative Legal and Economic Introduction* (Praeger 2000) 183.

[18] The concept of *dignliche Anspruch* (claim in rem or real claim) according to William W. Buckland and Arnold D. McNair (William W. Buckland and Arnold D. McNair, *Roman Law and Common Law* (2nd ed., Cambridge University Press 1952) 89) originates from the work of Bernhard Windscheid (Bernhard Windscheid, *Lehrbuch des Pandektenrecht, I. Band* (Verlagshandlung von Julius Buddeus 1862) 89ff.); Klaus Bacher, *Die Beeinträchtigungsgefahr als Voraussetzung für Unterlassungsklagen im Wettbewerbsrecht und in anderen Gebieten des Zivilrechts* (Centaurus-Verlagsgesellschaft Pfaffenweiler 1996) 42 (discussing the Windscheid's concept of a claim – *Anspruch*); see also Franz Hofmann, *Der Unterlassungsanspruch als Rechtsbehelf* (Mohr Siebeck 2017).

[19] Reinhold Johow, *Die Vorlagen der Rektoren für die erste Kommission zur Ausarbeitung des Entwurfs eines Bürgerlichen Gesetzbuches – Sachenrecht, Teil 1, Allgemeine Bestimmungen, Besitz und Eigentum* (first published 1880, De Gruyter 1991) 285 ("Der dingliche Anspruch des Eigenthümer, der actio in rem oder Klage auf eine Sache geht darauf, daß der Eigenthümer, wo er auch seine Sache findet, in den Besitz derselben sich setze. Welcher Person er bei dieser Verwirklichung seines Rechts begegnet, ist gleichgültig, da die besonderen Eigenschaften dieser Person oder deren Handlungsweise für den Inhalt des dinglichen Anspruchs gliechgültig sind").

[20] Martin Husovec, "Injunctions Against Innocent Third Parties: Case of Website Blocking" (2013) 4 JIPITEC 116, 121.

Civil law furthered the idea of in rem actions. Although *rei vindicatio* and *actio negatoria* historically developed very differently,[21] in the time of the *Pandectists* (nineteenth century) it became generally accepted that both actions not only have the same origin, but also that they are of the same quality or basis, differing only in the type of interference they aim to protect from. Whereas rei vindicatio served to protect from losing possession, actio negatoria served to protect from *all other* types of interference.[22] The Pandectists thus made it more abstract, extending it to protection against any other interference than withdrawal from possession (§ 1004 BGB).[23] This abstraction was first found in the works of Heise[24] and Puchta[25] and was later generally accepted among Pandectists, thanks to Windscheid.[26]

According to Boháček,[27] civil law codifications that came after the period of the Pandectists and German Civil Code, e.g., Hungarian, Soviet, and Chinese, were all strongly influenced by this understanding of actio negatoria.[28] In contrast, civil law codifications preceding Pandectists, for instance French,[29] Austrian,[30] and Italian,

---

[21] Miroslav Boháček, *Actio negatoria k dějinám zápůrči žaloby* (Nákl. České Akad. Věd a Umění 1938); Heinrich Siber, *Die Passivlegitimation bei der rei vindicatio als Beitrag zur Lehre von der Aktionenkonkurrenz* (Deichert 1907); Yoshikazu Kawasumi, *Von der römischen action negatoria zum negatorischen Beseitigungsanspruch des BGB* (Nomos Verlag 2001).

[22] This categorization of other interferences is also apparent from the text of § 523 ABGB – see Erika Wagner, *Gesetzliche Unterlassungsansprüche im Zivilrecht: zugleich eine Untersuchung des Beseitigungsanspruchs* (Manz 2004) 24.

[23] Erika Wagner, *Gesetzliche Unterlassungsansprüche im Zivilrecht: zugleich eine Untersuchung des Beseitigungsanspruchs* (Manz 2004) 28.

[24] Arnold Heise, *Grundriss eines Systems des Gemeinen Civilrechts, Buch II* (Mohr u. Winter 1807) 1807.

[25] Georg Puchta, *Über die negatorienklage* (Rhein Museum 1827) 161 ("(...) der Grund der Negatoria des Eigenthum und nichts weiter ist, wie bey der Vindikation, und daß *sich beide nicht in dem Klagegrund, sondern nur durch die Verletzung unterscheiden* (...))) 165, 179; see more about the background of this work: Yoshikazu Kawasumi,*Von der römischen action negatoria zum negatorischen Beseitigungsanspruch des BGB* (Nomos Verlag 2001) 6ff.

[26] Miroslav Boháček, *Actio negatoria k dějinám zápůrči žaloby* (Nákl. České Akad. Věd a Umění 1938) 2; Yoshikazu Kawasumi,*Von der römischen action negatoria zum negatorischen Beseitigungsanspruch des BGB* (Nomos Verlag 2001) 65.

[27] Ibid., 6.

[28] Boháček mentions § 499 of the Hungarian Draft Civil Law (1914), Article 59 of the Soviet Civil Code (1922) and Article 767 of the Chinese Civil Code (1929–1930) – see Miroslav Boháček, *Actio negatoria k dějinám zápůrči žaloby* (Nákl. České Akad. Věd a Umění 1938) 3.

[29] Reinhold Johow, *Die Vorlagen der Rektoren für die erste Kommission zur Ausarbeitung des Entwurfs eines Bürgerlichen Gesetzbuches – Sachenrecht, Teil 1, Allgemeine Bestimmungen, Besitz und Eigentum* (first published 1880, De Gruyter 1991) 984; Karl S. Zachariä, *Handbuch des Französichen Civilrechts, Erste Band* (Akademische Buchhandlung von Ernst Mohr 1853) 551–552; Charles Aubry and Charles F. Rau, *Cours de Droit civil Francias* (2nd ed., Marchal und Billard 1935) 539.

[30] The provision § 523 of ABGB – see Miroslav Boháček, *Actio negatoria k dějinám zápůrči žaloby* (Nákl. České Akad. Věd a Umění 1938) 4; Antonín Randa, "Žaloba zápůrči" [1871] 10 Právník 181, 183; Antonín Randa, *Právo vlastnické dle rakouského práva v. pořádku systematickém* (Nákl. České akademie císaře Františka Josefa pro vědy, slovesnost a umění 1917) 295, 299; Heinrich Klang, *Kommentar zum ABGB* 1, 2 (Verl. Österreich 1931) 416; recently, the Austrian Supreme Court hinted, in its post-Telekabel ruling (OGH (2014) 4 Ob 71/14s), on this concept ("Der hier strittige Anspruch, das Vermitteln des

held to a more classical Roman understanding of actio negatoria (at least in their legal texts).

Another important difference, from the perspective of this work, is that rei vindicatio and actio negatoria under Roman law, unlike today, were seen as what we today would name as procedural rules for courts, and not the claims of substantial law. In this aspect, Roman actions were closer to the concept of remedies in the common law. They were primarily owed to the "courts," rather than individuals. Current doctrine in Germany,[31] Austria,[32] Slovakia and the Czech Republic,[33] however, does not share this view any more. The metamorphosis of the Roman view, according to which private law is a collection of court actions, into today's prevailing understanding in civil law countries, namely, that a court action already presupposes a material claim (subjective right), can be traced to the nineteenth century works of von Savigny and Windscheid.[34] It was seen as inappropriate that the rights of individuals would rest on a set of court actions alone.[35] As a consequence, actio negatoria was modified from a procedural entitlement to sue to a material claim that is guaranteed and exercisable also outside of the court.[36] Obligations are owed to individuals primarily, and if the courts get involved upon request, they only officially *recognize* these obligations and thereby equip them with additional legal effects.[37] This "doctrinal" feature of the system, leads to divergent consequences of remedies.

Zugangs zu einer bestimmten Website zu unterlassen, ist gleich zu beurteilen. *Denn auch dabei geht es um die Abwehr eines Eingriffs in ein dinglich wirkendes Ausschließungsrecht"*).

[31] Johow rejects this Roman view – see Reinhold Johow, *Die Vorlagen der Rektoren für die erste Kommission zur Ausarbeitung des Entwurfs eines Bürgerlichen Gesetzbuches – Sachenrecht, Teil 1, Allgemeine Bestimmungen, Besitz und Eigentum* (first published 1880, De Gruyter 1991) 982 (for actio negatoria), 886 (for rei vindicatio).

[32] Erika Wagner, *Gesetzliche Unterlassungsansprüche im Zivilrecht: zugleich eine Untersuchung des Beseitigungsanspruchs* (Manz 2004) 53–55.

[33] Štefan Luby, *Výber z diela a myšlienok* (IURA Edition 1998) 252.

[34] Friedrich Carl von Savigny, *System des heutigen Römischen Rechts: Band. 5.* (Veit 1841) 1ff.; Bernhard Windscheid, *Lehrbuch des Pandektenrecht, I. Band* (Verlagshandlung von Julius Buddeus 1862) 182; Bernhard Windscheid, *Die Actio des römischen Civilrechts, vom Standpunkte des heutigen Rechts* (Buddeus 1856); Erika Wagner, *Gesetzliche Unterlassungsansprüche im Zivilrecht: zugleich eine Untersuchung des Beseitigungsanspruchs* (Manz 2004) 52, fn. 8, 18; Yoshikazu Kawasumi, *Von der römischen action negatoria zum negatorischen Beseitigungsanspruch des BGB* (Nomos Verlag 2001) 128ff. (discussing the process of transformation in detail).

[35] Johow rejects this Roman view – see Reinhold Johow, *Die Vorlagen der Rektoren für die erste Kommission zur Ausarbeitung des Entwurfs eines Bürgerlichen Gesetzbuches – Sachenrecht, Teil 1, Allgemeine Bestimmungen, Besitz und Eigentum* (first published 1880, De Gruyter 1991) 886.

[36] See more Bernhard Windscheid, *Die Actio des römischen Civilrechts vom Standpunkte des heutigen Rechts* (Buddeus 1856); Robert Neuner, *Privatrecht und Prozeßrecht* (Bensheimer 1925) 7ff.; Klaus Bacher, *Die Beeinträchtigungsgefahr als Voraussetzung für Unterlassungsklagen im Wettbewerbsrecht und in anderen Gebieten des Zivilrechts* (Centaurus-Verlagsgesellschaft Pfaffenweiler 1996) 34ff.

[37] More about this: Franz Hofmann, *Der Unterlassungsanspruch als Rechtsbehelf* (Mohr Siebeck 2017).

In the civil law countries, Germany is the engine of legal development on the front of injunctions. Its jurisprudence closely follows and builds upon the Roman law, and also has a very rich case-law that is a result of the extensiveness of German judicial practice. Moreover, accountability for injunctions is one of the main regulating forces in the digital era.

9.2 GERMAN CIVIL CODE IN THE MAKING

German codification at the end of nineteenth century was of course strongly influenced by the results of the work of the Pandectists. The provision of § 1004 BGB is the first *legislative fusion* of rei vindicatio and actio negatoria. As was already mentioned, Pandectists accepted that both claims were in fact of the same quality and origin, but differ only in the type of interference they aim to protect from. The unity of both claims in the BGB is apparent from the text of § 1004, where actio negatoria is defined as a course of action protecting against any *other* interference than withdrawal of possession, which means any different interference than the one protected under rei vindicatio.

This negative formulation, however, also had another consequence that is important for this work.[38] Namely, because the interference in the case of actio negatoria was very abstract and only negatively formulated, it was impossible to reach exactly the same clarity as under rei vindicatio, which protects against one certain type of interference (withdrawal of possession). Hence it was possible to positively describe the addressee for rei vindicatio, but not for actio negatoria. From this perspective, the extension of addressees of injunctions under § 1004 BGB can be seen as a cumulative consequence of: (1) an extension of protected interferences *other* than withdrawal of possession in comparison with classical or Justinian Roman law, (2) abstraction of language used to imply the same quality as rei vindicatio, and (3) change from actio, a procedural remedy, to a material claim exercisable also outside of the courts.

Reinhold Johow, who authored the proposal of the BGB for the property law chapter, tried, from the very beginning,[39] to strictly separate purely in rem (*dingliche*) claims[40] on the one hand, and delictual claims on the other hand. Whereas delictual claims should require at least an act, for injunctive claims merely an *objective interference* with the property should suffice.[41] Johow explains this bipartition in the

---

[38] Boháček says that the preparatory Commission was aware of this problem (Miroslav Boháček, *Actio negatoria k dějinám zápůrči žaloby* (Nákl. České Akad. Věd a Umění 1938) 2).

[39] Walter notes that this was not entirely clear because title of the section was still "prohibition of acts" – see Andreas Walter, *Störerhaftung bei Handeln Dritter* (Peter Lang 2011) 25.

[40] Johow explictly say that actio negatoria is a second in rem action (Reinhold Johow, *Die Vorlagen der Rektoren für die erste Kommission zur Ausarbeitung des Entwurfs eines Bürgerlichen Gesetzbuches – Sachenrecht, Teil 1, Allgemeine Bestimmungen, Besitz und Eigentum* (first published 1880, De Gruyter 1991) 982).

[41] Andreas Walter, *Störerhaftung bei Handeln Dritter* (Peter Lang, 2011) 25, fn. 68; Reinhold Johow, *Die Vorlagen der Rektoren für die erste Kommission zur Ausarbeitung des Entwurfs eines Bürgerlichen*

context of rei vindicatio by the argument that because pure in rem protection would not sufficiently protect the owner, the ownership is "completed" also with other claims. These other claims, however, according to Johow, "no longer have their basis in the property law alone, but also in the special circumstances which create a tie of obligations between the owner and obliged party."[42]

Johow's proposal is also very clear on whether the behavior of the defendant needs to be wrongful. He denies this by saying that "the behaviour of the opponent, which awakened the interests on the determination of the right, can be in itself wrongful, but this is not required."[43] He even goes further to state that "which grounds need to be seen as sufficient, is determined merely from consideration of *usefulness*, while the justification of claims arising from the wrongful behaviour is deduced from the principle of the atoning justice."[44]

The first precodification proposals still described actionable disturbances of a property right as an "infringement" (*Verletzung*). This narrower term was, however, later substituted[45] with the broader term "interference" (*Beeinträchtigung*) that encompasses all "infringements," but at the same time makes clear that undesired disturbance of a property does *not* have to originate in somebody's infringing behavior. The actionable "interference" was thus tied to any factual situation of disharmony between legally granted rights and reality. For the purposes of "interference," it is therefore irrelevant if the disharmony was caused by the rightholder's own acts, acts of other people, natural causes, vis major or something else. And even though the term "interference" was not intended to be used from the very beginning, from the existing protocols one can conclude that there was certainly at least an agreement on what the term should *express*. For instance, Protocol I 4257, still using the term "infringement," notes the following considerations of the Commission:

> The term infringement earns a preference before the other suggested terms like interference, intrusion and limitation, because it prevents a misunderstanding that some direct acts of the defendant would be required, *when already the wrongful*

Gesetzbuches – Sachenrecht, Teil 1, Allgemeine Bestimmungen, Besitz und Eigentum (first published 1880, De Gruyter 1991) 984 ("zur Beseitigung des das Eigenthum beeinträchtigenden Zustandes") 991; Motive – see Benno Mugdan (ed.), *Die gesamten Materialien zum Bürgerlichen Gesetzbuch für das Deutsche Reich: Band III* (Deker's Verlag, 1899–1900) 236.

[42] Reinhold Johow, *Die Vorlagen der Rektoren für die erste Kommission zur Ausarbeitung des Entwurfs eines Bürgerlichen Gesetzbuches – Sachenrecht, Teil 1, Allgemeine Bestimmungen, Besitz und Eigentum* (first published 1880, De Gruyter 1991) 885.

[43] Reinhold Johow, *Die Vorlagen der Rektoren für die erste Kommission zur Ausarbeitung des Entwurfs eines Bürgerlichen Gesetzbuches – Sachenrecht, Teil 1, Allgemeine Bestimmungen, Besitz und Eigentum* (first published 1880, De Gruyter 1991) 992 ("Dieses Verhlaten des Gegners, welches das Interesse an der Rechtsfestellung wachruft, kann ein an sich rechtswidriges sein, aber nothwendig ist solches durchaus nicht").

[44] Ibid., 992 ("Welche Veranlassungen als genügend anzustehen seien, bestimmt sich rein aus Rücksichten der Zweckmäßigkeit, während die Rechtfertigung der aus Rechtsverletzungen entspringenden Ansprüche sich aus Grundsätzen der sühnenden Gerechtigkeit herleitet").

[45] Andreas Walter, *Störerhaftung bei Handeln Dritter* (Peter Lang 2011) 53, fn. 224.

situation per se without need of own acts, fault or intent is enough, e.g., overlapping of a building over the border.[46]

Another protocol, Protocol I 4261 shows the intended relationship with tort law:

> The claim for an injunction has solely an objective infringement of rights as a precondition. This does not suffice to establish liability for tort, unless some other circumstances step in, that will at the same time let the infringement appear as a tort.[47]

It is of course understandable that any objective status of an infringement, which the addressee of an injunction is called to prevent or remove, can usually be somehow attributed to the conduct of a person (either acts or omissions). One can argue that a right in rem is only "in the air" till *someone does something* which gives right of action.[48] It is certainly difficult to think of the usefulness of a claim for an injunction without thinking about the defendants who will have to comply with it.

The explanatory note furthermore explains[49] that actio negatoria was modeled as "an extension" of rei vindicatio, ideas of which should be analogically applicable to it.[50] And also that, similarly as with rei vindicatio, the claim can be brought against "any person, by whose will the situation that is conflicting with the content of the property is maintained."[51] Or in other words, an injunction under § 1004 BGB should be addressed against anybody whose behavior stands in way of the

---

[46] Horst H. Jakobs and Werner Schubert (ed.), *Die Beratung des Bürgerlichen Gesetzbuchs: In systematischer Zusammenstellung der unveröffentlichten Quellen* (De Gruyter 1978) 852 (emphasis mine) ("Der Ausdruck "Verletzung" verdiene den Vorzug vor den sonst vergeschlagenen Ausdrücken Störung, Eingriff, Beschränkung, weil er das Mißverständnis fern halte, daß eine unmittelbare Handlung des Beklagten erforderlich sei, während doch auch schon ein ohne eigenes Handeln sowie ohne culpa und dolus eingetretener rechtswidriger Zustand, z.B. Die Hinüberneigung ines Gebäudes über die Grenze, genüge").

[47] Ibid., 854 ("Der negatorische Anspruch habe lediglich eine objektive Rechtsverletzung zur Voraussetzung und eine solche genüge nicht zur Begründung einer Schadenersatzpflicht, wenn nicht Umstände hinzuträten, welche die Verletzung zugleich als Delikt erscheinen ließen").

[48] William W. Buckland and Arnold D. McNair, *Roman Law and Common Law* (2nd ed., Cambridge University Press 1952) 89.

[49] Motive III, 423 – see Benno Mugdan (ed.), *Die gesamten Materialien zum Bürgerlichen Gesetzbuch für das Deutsche Reich: Band III* (Deker's Verlag 1899–1900) 237 ("Der Anspruch geht auf Wiederaufhebung einer fortbestehenden Beeinträchtigung des Eigenthumers. Der Fortbestand und die Wiederaushebbarkeit der Beeinträchtigung setzen ein körperliches Verhältnis voraus. *Der Anspruch hat, analog wie bei der Vindikation, seine Richtung gegen die Person desjenigen, durch dessen Willen der mit dem Inhalte des Eigenthumes in Widerspruch stehende Zustand aufrecht erhalten wird*").

[50] See also Horst H. Jakobs and Werner Schubert (ed.), *Die Beratung des Bürgerlichen Gesetzbuchs: In systematischer Zusammenstellung der unveröffentlichten Quellen* (De Gruyter 1978) 851 ("Man müsse die Voraussetzung für die actio negatoria in analoger Weise bestimmen, wie die Prämisse für die Vindikation. Das Analogon sei freilich nicht leicht näher zu bezeichnen. Gemeinsam sei dar Erforderniß, daß eine objektive Verletzung des Eigenthums vorliegen müsse. Alsdann werde entweder die Vindikation oder der negatorsiche Anspruch platzgreifen").

[51] Benno Mugdan (ed.), *Die gesamten Materialien zum Bürgerlichen Gesetzbuch für das Deutsche Reich: Band III* (Deker's Verlag 1899–1900) 237 ("seine Richtung gegen die Person desjenigen, durch dessen Willen der mit dem Inhalte des Eigenthumes in Widerspruch stehende Zustand aufrecht erhalten wird").

legally conform situation.[52] It should be noted that the provision was from the very beginning intended to be applicable also outside of property law, to other absolute rights.[53]

In the legislative text that came into force on 1 January 1900, actio negatoria was eventually incorporated using the following language:

Section 1004: Claim for removal and injunction
(1) If the ownership is interfered with by means other than removal or retention of possession, the owner may require the disturber to remove the interference. If further interferences are to be feared, the owner may seek a prohibitory injunction.[54]

Interpretation of § 1004 BGB, even after more than hundred years, is far from settled. The deeper meaning of virtually each word is disputed. The scope of interference, legal consequence, as well as the claim-addressee are much argued about, and only the position of a rightholder seems to be without controversy.[55] The controversy is so intensive that Canaris and Larenz, the two stellar scholars of German private law, did not hesitate to name it "the darkest and most disputed chapter of private law."[56] The most significant controversies concern (1) the relationship between claims under § 1004 BGB and tort law (§ 823 BGB) and (2) the demarcation of a person accountable under § 1004 BGB. Many legal questions relevant for this thesis have their origin in these deep doctrinal problems.

Since the beginning of twentieth century, German courts have tried to identify an appropriate "attribution principle" (*Zurechnungskriterium*) under § 1004 BGB that would best delineate a person who must comply with injunctions. Although the basic principle, deriving from the Roman law, that *not the conduct*, but only the *result* needs to be wrongful, was arguably accepted,[57] the courts have always

---

[52] Andreas Walter, *Störerhaftung bei Handeln Dritter* (Peter Lang 2011) 25, 81; Benno Mugdan (ed.), *Die gesamten Materialien zum Bürgerlichen Gesetzbuch für das Deutsche Reich: Band III* (Deker's Verlag 1899–1900) 236.

[53] Motive III, 392 – see in Benno Mugdan (ed.), *Die gesamten Materialien zum Bürgerlichen Gesetzbuch für das Deutsche Reich: Band III* (Deker's Verlag 1899–1900) 218 ("Eine analoge Anwendbarkeit der Vorschriften über den Eigenthumsschutz wird allerdings in weitem Umfange zulässig sein"); this, of course, subverts some of the works that reject application of § 1004 BGB in intellectual property law due to the nonexistence of "unintended gap in the law" (planwidrige Gesetzeslücke) such as Reinhard Döring, *Die Haftung für eine Mitwirkung an fremden Wettbewerbsverstößen, Urheberrechts-, Marken-, Patent-, Gebrauchsmuster- und Geschmacksmusterverletzungen* (Deutscher Anwalt Verlag 2008) 122.

[54] In German § 1004 reads, "Beseitigungs- und Unterlassungsanspruch (1) Wird das Eigentum in anderer Weise als durch Entziehung oder Vorenthaltung des Besitzes beeinträchtigt, so kann der Eigentümer von dem Störer die Beseitigung der Beeinträchtigung verlangen. Sind weitere Beeinträchtigungen zu besorgen, so kann der Eigentümer auf Unterlassung klagen."

[55] Elke Herrmann, *Der Störer nach § 1004 BGB. Zugleich eine Untersuchung zu den Verpflichteten der §§ 907, 908 BGB* (Duncker & Humbolt 1987) 5.

[56] Karl Larenz and Claus-Wilhelm Canaris, *Lehrbuch des Schuldrechts II* (13th ed., C. H. Beck 1994) 675.

[57] BVerwG (1985) 4 C 46.82 ("Nach der Rechtsprechung des Bundesgerichtshofs knüpft die Rechtsfolge des § 1004 BGB nicht an die Rechtswidrigkeit eines Eingriffs an, sondern an einen dem Inhalt des Eigentums widersprechenden Zustand"); BGH (2003) v. ZR 175/02 ("Entscheidend ist insoweit nicht die Rechtswidrigkeit des Eingriffs, sondern der dem Inhalt des Eigentums widersprechende

struggled to connect injunctions to *concrete persons* who did not behave wrongfully. As will be shown, the attribution principle used by the highest German courts, and also their argumentation, changed over time. Although the courts often cite the so-called "maintenance formula" (*Aufrechterhaltungsformel*), originating from the BGB's explanatory note,[58] they do not really *apply* it.

In 1987, Herrmann examined the jurisprudence and came to the conclusion that there is often a significant gap between the claimed principle ("maintenance formula") and its follow-up application by the courts.[59] My work analyzed over hundred decisions handed down by the German courts from 1901 to 2016, mostly in the field of intellectual property, unfair competition, and personality rights.[60] The great majority applied or even develop the doctrine in one way or another. These cases show exactly the same trend as noted by Herrmann. The courts often do not subsume factual circumstances under the "maintenance formula." On the contrary, they often develop and apply *other* attribution principles which are actually used to decide the cases. As the following section will show, the past hundred years have been marked with significant developments on this front.

They are often caused by an objective lack of a single understanding of the very relationship between claims under § 1004 BGB (injunctions) and § 823 BGB (tort law). As will be seen, the courts, in their attempts to define a person accountable under § 1004 BGB, often refer so much to the principles of tort law, such as causality or later also duty of care, that the resulting case-law is then legitimately criticized by Picker as "a type of subsidiary tortious claim" (*Art sekundärem Deliktsanspruch*) abridged of the culpability requirement.[61] Whereas the prevailing scholarly opinion generally does not find this convergence with tort law problematic,[62] or does so only

---

Zustand"); Andreas Walter, *Störerhaftung bei Handeln Dritter* (Peter Lang 2011) 143, 144, 145; Christian Baldus, "Beseitigungs- und Unterlassungsanspruch" in Roland Rixecker and others (eds.) *Münchener Kommentar zum BGB* (6th ed., C. H. Beck 2013) § 1004 para. 198 ("Insbesondere ist regelmäßig die auf menschliches Verhalten zurückführbare Verletzung des Eigentums als rechtswidrig indiziert").

[58] "Analogically to rei vindicatio, the claim is addressed to any person, with whose will, the situation that is conflicting with the content of the property, is maintained" – see Benno Mugdan (ed.), *Die gesamten Materialien zum Bürgerlichen Gesetzbuch für das Deutsche Reich: Band III* (Deker's Verlag 1899–1900) 237 ("Der Anspruch hat, analog wie bei der Vindikation, seine Richtung gegen die Person desjenigen, durch dessen Willen der mit dem Inhalte des Eigenthumes in Widerspruch stehende Zustand aufrecht erhalten wird").

[59] Elke Herrmann, *Der Störer nach § 1004 BGB.: Zugleich eine Untersuchung zu den Verpflichteten der §§ 907, 908 BGB* (Duncker & Humblot 1987) 12, 18–19.

[60] The decisions were obtained from several sources: (1) a 2016 website search on the Web page of the German Federal Supreme Court for the term "Störerhaftung," (2) from the lists compiled by Walter [Andreas Walter, *Störerhaftung bei Handeln Dritter* (Peter Lang 2011)] and Döring [Reinhard Döring, *Die Haftung für eine Mitwirkung an fremden Wettbewerbsverstößen, Urheberrechts-, Marken-, Patent-, Gebrauchsmuster- und Geschmacksmusterverletzungen* (Deutscher Anwalt Verlag 2008)] and (3) the cases that were referenced in the decisions of (1) and (2).

[61] Eduard Picker, *Der negatorische Beseitigungsanspruch* (Mohr 1972) 31.

[62] Christian Armbrüster, "Eigentumsschutz durch den Beseitigungsanspruch nach § 1004 I 1 BGB und durch Deliktsrecht" (2003) 43 *NJW* 3087–3090; Mathias Habersack and others, *Münchener Kommentar*

to some extent,[63] Picker and his supporters attack this development as conceptually and/or historically wrong.[64] They offer a competing view that is strongly rooted in the Roman understanding of in rem actions[65] and consists of a strict separation of tortious and in rem injunctive protection.

To try to resolve this debate within the frame of this book would be naive. Too much ink has been spilled over this question by more qualified scholars in decades of German scholarship on property and intellectual property law.[66] The aim of this

---

zum BGB (6th ed., C. H. Beck 2013) § 1004 paras. 61, 78ff.; Joachim Wenzel, "Der Störer und seine verschuldensunabhängige Haftung im Nachbarrecht" [2005] NJW 241; Helmut Köhler, "'Täter' und 'Störer' im Wettbewerbs- und Markenrecht – Zur BGH-Entscheidung 'Jugendgefährdende Medien bei eBay'" GRUR [2008] 1.

[63] Herrmann discusses a scepsis concerning the use of causality criterion in the frame of § 1004 BGB, which was triggered by the work of Picker (Elke Herrmann, *Der Störer nach § 1004 BGB.: Zugleich eine Untersuchung zu den Verpflichteten der §§ 907, 908 BGB* (Duncker & Humblot 1987) 72).

[64] Eduard Picker, *Der negatorische Beseitigungsanspruch* (Mohr 1972) 61; Eduard Picker, "Der 'dingliche Anspruch'" in Helmut Koziol and Peter Rummel (ed.) *Im Dienste der Gerechtigkeit: Festschrift für Franz Bydlinski* (Springer 2002); Yoshikazu Kawasumi, *Von der römischen action negatoria zum negatorischen Beseitigungsanspruch des BGB* (Nomos Verlag 2001); Karl-Heinz Gursky, "Zur neueren Diskussion um § 1004 BGB" [1989] Juristische Rundschau 397ff.; Karl-Heinz Gursky, *Julius von Staudingers Kommentar zum Bürgerlichen Gesetzbuch – Buch 3: Sachenrecht §§ 985–1011* (13th ed., Sellier – de Gruyter 1999) § 1004 para. 93ff.

[65] Eduard Picker, "Der 'dingliche Anspruch'" in Helmut Koziol and Peter Rummel (ed.) *Im Dienste der Gerechtigkeit: Festschrift für Franz Bydlinski* (Springer 2002) 269ff.

[66] Eduard Picker, *Der negatorische Beseitigungsanspruch* (Mohr 1972); Elke Herrmann, *Der Störer nach § 1004 BGB.: Zugleich eine Untersuchung zu den Verpflichteten der §§ 907, 908 BGB* (Duncker & Humblot 1987); Yoshikazu Kawasumi, *Von der römischen action negatoria zum negatorischen Beseitigungsanspruch des BGB* (Nomos Verlag 2001); Klaus Bacher, *Die Beeinträchtigungsgefahr als Voraussetzung für Unterlassungsklagen im Wettbewerbsrecht und in anderen Gebieten des Zivilrechts* (Centaurus-Verlagsgesellschaft Pfaffenweiler 1996); Karl-Heinz Gursky, "Zur neueren Diskussion um § 1004 BGB" [1989] Juristische Rundschau 397ff.; Eduard Picker, "Der 'dingliche Anspruch'" in Helmut Koziol and Peter Rummel (ed.) *Im Dienste der Gerechtigkeit: Festschrift für Franz Bydlinski* (Springer 2002) 269; Eduard Picker, "Prävention durch negatorischen Schutz" in Luboš Tichý and Jiří Hrádek (eds.) *Prevention in Law* (Centrum Právní Komparatistiky PFUK v. Praze 2013) 61–105; Christian Armbrüster, "Eigentumsschutz durch den Beseitigungsanspruch nach § 1004 I 1 BGB und durch Deliktsrecht" (2003) 43 NJW 3087–3090; Gerhard Hohloch, *Die negatorische Ansprüche und ihre Beziehungen zum Schadensersatzrecht* (Alfred Metzner Verlag 1976); Gerold Bezzenberger, "Der negatorische Beseitigungsanspruch und die Kosten der Ersatzvornahme" [2005] Juristenzeitung 373; Rita Wetzel, *Die Zurechnung des Verhaltens Dritter bei Eigentumsstörungstatbeständen* (Mohr Siebeck 1971); Wolfgang Münzberg, *Verhalten und Erfolg als Grundlagen der Rechtswidrigkeit und Haftung* (Vittorio Klostermann 1966); Angelika Schneider, *Vom Störer zum Täter?* (Nomos 2012); Jonathan Kropp, Die Haftung von Host- und Access-Providern bei Urheberrechtsverletzungen Gebundene Ausgabe (Peter Lang 2012); Erika Wagner, *Gesetzliche Unterlassungsansprüche im Zivilrecht: zugleich eine Untersuchung des Beseitigungsanspruchs* (Manz 2004); Reinhard Döring, *Die Haftung für eine Mitwirkung an fremden Wettbewerbsverstößen, Urheberrechts-, Marken-, Patent-, Gebrauchmuster- und Geschmacksmusterverletzungen* (Deutscher Anwalt Verlag 2008); Alina Hügel, *Haftung von Inhabern privater Internetanschlüsse für fremde Urheberrechtsverletzungen* (C. H. Beck 2014); Felix Scheder-Bieschin, *Modernes Filesharing* (OlWIR Verlag 2013); Alexander Hartmann, *Unterlassungsansprüche im Internet* (C. H. Beck 2009); Leo Schapiro, *Unterlassungsansprüche gegen die Betreiber von Internet-Auktionshäusern und Internet-Meinungsforen* (Mohr 2011); Sandra Mießner, *Providerhaftung, Störerhaftung und Internetauktion* (Peter Lang 2008); Thomas Hoeren and Silviya Yankova, "The

section is therefore rather different than to engage with German doctrinal debates surrounding § 1004 BGB. The goal is to present cases that involve injunctions which were granted in situations where the tortious liability of their addressees was denied,[67] thus resulting in the phenomenon of accountability without liability. This historical exercise should help us in illuminating the principles, tendencies, and arguments that the courts considered relevant, which should, in turn, give us sufficient insight into the problems faced by the German judges today.

9.3 FROM THE CIVIL CODE TO TODAY'S PRINCIPLES

Probably the first case where § 1004 BGB came into the spotlight was the decision of the Court of the German Empire from 1900 which found a landlord to be a potential additional addressee of injunctions for interferences committed by his tenant.[68] The Court recognized that such a result can also be derived from the German "common law" predating the BGB. The test used for determining a person as a "disturber" was that he was "in a position to prevent" (*in der Lage zu hindern*) the behavior of his tenant.

In 1918, the Court of the German Empire[69] confirmed the rationale from the first case, namely, that the existence of an "interfering situation" and the "position to prevent" are the main considerations for the Court. He argued that "the action can be successful merely if it is established not only that an interfering situation exists, but also that a defendant can, with his will, achieve" the introduction of a certain measure which will prevent further interferences. Because only "then would the continuation of the interference be dependent on the decisive will of the defendant."[70] This requirement of "decisive will" (*maßgebende Wille*) was used as a test for existence of a possibility to prevent further interferences.

Liability of Internet Intermediaries – The German Perspective" [2012] IIC 501–531; Matthias Leistner, "Störerhaftung und mittelbare Schutzrechtsverletzung" GRUR-Beil. [2010] 1; Joachim Bornkamm, "E-Commerce Directive vs. IP Rights Enforcement – Legal Balance Achieved?" [2007] GRUR Int. 642–644.

[67] To identify this was not always easy. The key distinguishing principles used were: (1) in cases where damages and injunctions were claimed, only the cases with denied damages were included, provided that such a denial was not due to reasons such as lack of fault; (2) in cases where no damages were sought, in the field of unfair competition, the third parties were identified by a lack of "competitive intent" that used to be required for all the direct tortfeasors before the *Jugendgefährdende Medien bei eBay* case; for other cases (3), I have tried to determine if the court stated that the defendant infringed the right or was said to be in the position of a by-stander.

[68] RG (1900) VI. 316/00, RGZ 47, 164.   [69] RG (1918) V 228/17, RGZ 92, 22.

[70] RG (1918) V 228/17, RGZ, 92, 22 ("Da aber der Kläger mit der Klage von Beklagten verlangt, daß er die Einführung des Dränagewassers in den Graben des Klägers unterläßt, so kann die Klage nur Erfolg haben, wenn festzustellen ist, daß nicht nur eine unberechtigte Störung vorliegt, sondern daß auch der Beklagte seinen Willen verwirklichen kann, mit der Bölkenwiese aus der Genossenschaft mit dem Erfolge auszuscheiden, daß die Zuführung des Dränagewassers der Wiese in den Graben des Klägers aufhört. *Denn dann würde die Fortdauer der Störung von dem maßgebenden Willen des Beklagten abhänging sein*").

The Court of the German Empire[71] took this argument one step further in 1921, by deciding that injunctive claims can arise only against those who are also in a position "to satisfy them."[72] Due to the absence of a "position to prevent" the interference, the Court then rejected an injunction against an ex-owner who no longer exercised control over the property from which the disturbance originated. The Court, however, noted that in the event that the ex-owner acted culpably, he could be sued for damages. In deciding all three cases therefore the Court mostly focused on the position of the addressee and the options for removing an interference that are at his disposal.

The line established by the Court of German Empire (RG) was also followed by its successor, the German Federal Supreme Court (the BGH). In its first known decision from 1954,[73] the court referred to the principles of the above decisions, adding that it is a *legal* possibility to prevent further interferences that counts.[74] As a result, the Court accepted an injunction against an employer who was not liable for the acts of his employees, but was found to have a "legal possibility" to prevent further interference by means of instructions to his employees and their enforcement, if necessary.

In the following chain of decisions, the Court applied the criterion of legal possibility in the field of personality rights,[75] unfair competition,[76] trademark,[77] and copyright law.[78] The first application in the field of unfair competition came in

---

71 RG (1921) V 151/21, RGZ 103, 174.

72 RG (1921) V 151/21, RGZ 103, 174 ("Während der Hinzutritt eines Verschuldens einen Schadensersatzanspruch gibt, der sich allemal gegen den schuldigen Störer als den Täter richtet, kann der negatorische Anspruch sich gegen den, der die Störung herbeigeführt oder aufrecht erhalten hat, doch nur dann richten, wenn dieser dem aus der Störung erwachsenen negatorischen Ansprüche *auch genügen kann*. Als Störer kann daher derjenige, der die beeinträchtigende Handlung vorgenommen hat, gemäß § 1004 BGB. nur dann in Anspruch genommen werden, wenn die Fortdauer der Störung von seinem maßgebenden Willen abhängig ist (RGZ. Bd. 92 S. 26)").

73 BGH (1954) III ZR 1/53.

74 BGH (1954) III ZR 1/53 ("Störer im Sinne dieser Vorschrift ist jeder, "auf dessen Willen der beeinträchtigende Zustand zurückgeht oder von dessen Willen seine Beseitigung abhängt" (RG in JW [1936] 3454; RGZ 155, 319). Auch ein mittelbarer Zusammenhang genügt. "Er wird auch durch Handlungen eines Dritten nicht unterbrochen, und zwar auch dann nicht, wenn dieser aus eigenem Antrieb und selbstverantwortlich handelt, sofern nur seine Handlungsweise durch den 'Störer' ermöglicht worden ist und der 'Störer' *die rechtliche Möglichkeit hat, den Dritten an der Störungshandlung zu hindern*" (RGZ 134, 234)).

75 BGH (1952) I ZR 87/51 (personality rights); BGH (1960) VI ZR 27/60 (on the accountability of a husband for the comments of his mentally-ill wife made to their neighbors).

76 BGH *Constanze II.* (1954) I ZR 38/53 (on the accountability for noneditorial content distributed with a newspaper).

77 BGH *Pertusin II.* (1957) I ZR 56/55 (on the accountability of a transporter for third-party goods bearing infringing marks).

78 Reel-to-reel tape recorders litigation chain before the German Federal Supreme Court: BGH (1955) I ZR 8/54; BGH (1960) I ZR 41/58; BGH (1963) Ib ZR 23/62; BGH (1963) Ib ZR 127/62 (all four on the accountability of the sellers of recorders to use the so-called GEMA notices) and BGH *Personalausweisse* (1964) Ib ZR 4/63 (on the accountability of the sellers of recorders to ask their customers to show ID and sign the commitment to pay license fees to GEMA).

1954, when the BGH issued its *Constanze II* ruling.[79] This decision is interesting because the Court decided to apply § 1004 BGB only *after* rejecting an injunction under UWG, the German Unfair Competition Act, which is explicitly built on the conduct of a defendant.[80] The Court held the following:

> A disturber in the sense of § 1004 BGB is also anybody who, with material and personal means of his own operation, supports an autonomous third party, acting on its own, in engaging in unfair competition – even if in good faith – *if he has the legal possibility to prevent the third party from acting in disturbance.* The standing to be sued for an injunction for removal follows, according to general legal principles, from own conduct of any person, with whose will, even without fault or only indirectly, it is contributed to bringing about a state which results in an interference with a third party (. . .).[81]

In 1957, the BGH decided the more known *Pertusin II.* case[82] involving transport of goods infringing upon trademark rights. The Court accepted that although, as a rule, the freight forwarder had no general obligation to inspect the forwarded goods he qualifies as a "disturber" because the concept includes "any person that either caused a disturbance, or whose conduct gives rise to fear of an interference."[83] The Court unusually provided justification for this broad rule by saying that:

> The right owner must have a possibility to effectively protect himself against interference with his right and to proceed against anybody whose conduct leads to or can lead to an interference or disturbance thereof. When more persons participate in the disturbance, the right owner can not be expected, before invoking a defence claim, to closely examine the question of who has actual economic interests and who acted only as an auxiliary and whose activity was "decisive" or had only "subordinate" importance. The attempts made in this direction (cf., e.g., Staudinger-Berg, BGB § 1004, note 24) in order to limit the circle of a disturber may be based on

---

[79] BGH *Constanze II.* (1954) I ZR 38/53.

[80] The court is citing the Cupresa decision to support this (BGH *Cupresa* (1954) I ZR 178/52).

[81] BGH *Constanze II.* (1954) I ZR 38/53 (emphasis mine) ("Störer im Sinn des § BGB § 1004 BGB ist auch derjenige, der die unzulässige Wettbewerbshandlung eines aus eigenem Antrieb und selbstverantwortlich handelnden Dritten – sei es auch guten Glaubens – durch die sachlichen und persönlichen Mittel seines Betriebes unterstützt und die rechtliche Möglichkeit hat, den Dritten an der Störungshandlung zu hindern. Die Passivlegitimation für den Beseitigungsanspruch folgt insoweit nach allgemeinen Rechtsgrundsätzen aus dem eigenen Verhalten desjenigen, der durch seinen maßgeblichen Willen, sei es auch ohne Verschulden und nur mittelbar, an der Herbeiführung eines Zustandes mitgewirkt hat, der die Beeinträchtigung eines Dritten zur Folge hat (. . .)").

[82] BGH *Pertusin II.* (1957) I ZR 56/55.

[83] BGH *Pertusin II.* (1957) I ZR 56/55 ("Nach ständiger Rechtsprechung ist davon auszugehen, daß als Störer jeder anzusehen ist, der die Störung herbeigeführt hat oder dessen Verhalten eine Beeinträchtigung befürchten läßt. Es ist belanglos, ob der Störer die beinträchtigende Handlung aus eigenem Antrieb oder auf Veranlassung eines Dritten, z.B. auf Grund einer Anstiftung oder in Erfüllung eines Auftrages, ausgeführt hat oder auszuführen beabsichtigt (. . .)").

the consideration that it appears unreasonable to expose mere auxiliaries to the possibility of a legal action from such claim.[84]

The Court thus opined that narrowing down the scope of possible disturbers would be better carried out subsequently, by considering whether it is *unreasonable* to expose them to such a claim. The freight forwarder, the Court reasoned, however, is not such a case, because very often the right owner can effectively enforce his right only against ancillary persons like him. After rejecting any general obligation to inspect, the Court then required that a freight forwarder first receive a notice, which will then trigger his obligation to inspect the goods. As will be shown, *Pertusin's* broad starting point was eventually narrowed down by other means in the 1990s.

In the field of copyright law, the most illustrative early year's litigation chain concerned the producers of reel-to-reel tape recorders. In the 1955 *Grundig-Reporter* decision,[85] the Court opined that, even if a producer does not himself engage in the copying of copyrighted works and thus copyright infringements, he can nevertheless face injunctions under § 1004 BGB. The fact that the device was also capable of noninfringing use did not preclude the injunction.[86] The Court accepted the proposed measure of so-called GEMA notices which were meant to inform users of the devices in advertising that they needed to obtain a license from GEMA, the German collecting society for musical works, in order to be able to legally use the reel-to-reel tape recorders. The Court, simultaneously rejected as less effective and redundant an injunction that would also force a seller of these recorders to require from all of its customers a declaration of a license commitment.

Several years later, it became clear that "GEMA notices" were absolutely ineffective, leading to a success rate of less than 0.5 percent.[87] As a result, the fifth litigation involving reel-to-reel tape recorders was filed. This time, GEMA demanded that

---

[84] BGH *Pertusin II.* (1957) I ZR 56/55 ("Der Schutzrechtsinhaber muß die Möglichkeit haben, sich gegen jede Beeinträchtigung seines Rechts wirksam zu schützen und gegen jeden vorzugehen, dessen Verhalten zu einer Störung oder Beeinträchtigung seines Rechts führt oder führen kann. Wenn mehrere Personen an der Störung beteiligt sind, kann dem Schutzrechtsinhaber nicht zugemutet werden, vor Geltendmachung eines Abwehranspruches näher zu prüfen, wer etwa als der eigentlich wirtschaftlich Interessierte und wer nur als Hilfsperson tätig wird und wessen Willensbetätigung "maßgebende" oder nur "untergeordnete" Bedeutung hat. In dieser Richtung unternommene Versuche einer Einschränkung des Kreises der Störer (vgl. z. B. Staudinger-Berg, BGB § 1004 Anm. 24) dürften auf der Erwägung beruhen, es könne unbillig erscheinen, bloße Hilfspersonen der Möglichkeit einer gerichtlichen Inanspruchnahme auszusetzen").

[85] BGH (1955) I ZR 8/54.

[86] BGH (1955) I ZR 8/54 ("Der Umstand, daß die Selbstaufnahmegeräte, wie die Beklagte geltend macht, auch ohne Eingriff in Urheberrechte benutzt werden können, beispielsweise als Diktiergeräte, steht der ernsthaften Besorgnis eines urheberverletzenden Verhaltens der privaten Benutzer dieser Geräte nicht entgegen").

[87] Noted by Dietrich Reimer (Dietrich Reimer, "BGH: BGH 29.05.1964 Ib ZR 4/63 'Personalausweise'" [1965] GRUR 104, 109) who say that fewer than 5,000 private persons licensed their recording devices according to information from the respective collecting society. The number of devices in Germany at that time was estimated at one million.

producers and retailers require their customers to first show their IDs and then sign a declaration of commitment before all the purchases. The Court in *Personalausweisse*[88] accepted that the producers can be sued for an injunction, but ultimately rejected the proposed measure on the grounds of reasonableness. It argued that such a measure would strongly affect the personal sphere of a broad circle of customers and would disproportionally interfere with the right to private life and substantially disturb the "peace under the law" of those who have nothing to do with the infringements. The Court also concluded that if there was no less intrusive means of curbing the infringement problem, the plaintiff could ultimately try to prohibit the production of the goods entirely, permitting it only on the condition that a producer will pay reasonable compensation to the plaintiff.[89] Due to legislative changes, this never happened.

This decision, however, shows a marked departure[90] from the "maintenance formula." This is clear from the following part of the BGH's reasoning, which recognizes that such an injunction is potentially possible by saying that:

> As a basis for the injunction request of the plaintiff, both a preventive injunction, through the application of § 1004 BGB, as well as a so-called delictual injunction for cease and desist and for removal are possible (§§ 11, 15, 36 LUG, § 823(1) and § 823(2) BGB). They *both* require that the prohibited conduct of the defendant and the feared wrongful intrusion by the owner of a reel-to-reel tape recorder into the exclusive rights of the plaintiff constitute *adequate proximate cause*, i.e. that the conduct of the defendant is a conditio sine qua non and that the occurrence of the result, under objective assessment, does not lie beyond any probability.[91]

The Court thus strongly focused not on "legal possibility," but on *causality* and the *preinfringement conduct* of a defendant. It stressed several times that reasonableness *alone* limits what kind of measures could be requested.[92] In subsequent cases, causality became the testing principle.[93] Litigation against producers of reel-to-reel

---

[88] BGH *Personalausweisse* (1964) Ib ZR 4/63.　　[89] BGH *Personalausweisse* (1964) Ib ZR 4/63.

[90] Probably the first one, because I ZR 8/54, which was the first in this series, still uses the so-called "maintenance formula."

[91] BGH *Personalausweisse* (1964) Ib ZR 4/63 (emphasis mine) ("Als Grundlage des Unterlassungs-begehrens der Kl. kommt sowohl die vorbeugende Unterlassungsklage in entsprechender Anwendung des § 1004 BGB als auch die sog. deliktische Unterlassungs- oder Beseitigungsklage (§§ 11, 15, 36 LUG, § 823 Abs. BGB § 823 Absatz 1 und BGB § 823 Absatz 2 BGB) in Betracht (. . .). Beide setzen voraus, daß zwischen dem zu verbietenden Verhalten der Bekl. und dem zu befürchtenden rechtswidrigen Eingriff der Tonbandgerätebesitzer in die Ausschließlichkeitsrechte der Kl. ein adäquater Ursachen-zusammenhang besteht, d. h., daß das Verhalten der Bekl. eine nicht hinwegzudenkende Bedingung des Verletzungserfolgs ist und der Eintritt dieses Erfolgs bei objektiver Beurteilung auch nicht außer-halb aller Wahrscheinlichkeit liegt (. . .)").

[92] On the grounds of unreasonableness, the Court later also rejected injunctions against an importer of Yugoslavian newspapers that included untrue libelous statements (BGH *VUS* (1976) VI ZR 23/72) and a registrar of third-party certification marks that were misleading (BGH (1994) I ZR 122/92).

[93] BGH *Verkaufsfahrten II.* (1988) I ZR 36/87; BGH *Firmenrufnummer* (1989) I ZR 27/88; BGH *Schönheitschirugie* (1989) I ZR 29/88.

recorders could be seen as a forerunner of attempts to solve the infringement problem by imposing various assistance measures on the intermediaries of today.

Soon, however, the causality requirement had to be stretched to absurd dimensions. When the owner of a funeral home received unsolicited help from the city through their advertising of his services and telephone number, he requested that the city remove the unsolicited advertisement, but the city refused to do so. Despite this, the owner himself was sued by a competitor. The Court found that, because the owner of the funeral home was party to an (obligatory) contract about the provision of funeral services,[94] he causally contributed to the acts of the city. Unsolicited wrongful advertising by the city "was not beyond any probability," according to the Court.

In 1976, the Court also had to consider cross-border effects. It decided an important case, *VUS*,[95] about the possibility of issuing injunctions against an importer of Yugoslavian newspapers into Germany, which included untrue libelous statements about the plaintiff. The Court heavily relied on its previous decision in *Pertusin II*. It noted that an importer, in a similar way to wholesalers, retailers and the owners of a book shop, can qualify as a "disturber" under § 1004 BGB. The Court did not apply the "maintenance formula," but instead the criteria mentioned in *Pertusin II*, namely, that a disturber "can be any person that either causes a disturbance, or whose conduct gives rise to fear of an interference."[96] The Court explicitly points out that:

> The fact that the last mentioned persons [wholesalers, retailers and owners of a book shop], in particular, often lack the knowledge of the circumstances establishing the elements of an infringement or its wrongfulness, does preclude a claim for damages, but not injunctive relief.[97]

The plaintiff's argument that his activity is only of "subordinate" importance and that there are other ways to prevent the disputed infringement was accepted by the Court to the extent that this should be reflected when testing the *reasonableness* of the proposed measures. After establishing the possibility of injunctions, the Court concluded that general monitoring would be unreasonable, though technically possible. In this case, however, according to the Court, the defendant is obliged to check only the specific text which was brought to his attention. Therefore, also for the future, such obligation to control should concern only the notified cases. As will

---

94 BGH (1989) I ZR 27/88.   95 BGH *VUS* (1976) VI ZR 23/72.
96 BGH *Pertusin II.* (1957) I ZR 56/55 ("als Störer jeder anzusehen ist, der die Störung herbeigeführt hat oder dessen Verhalten eine Beeinträchtigung befürchten läßt").
97 BGH *VUS* (1976) VI ZR 23/72 ("Daß besonders den zuletzt genannten Personen häufig die Kenntnis der die Tatbestandsmäßigkeit und die Rechtswidrigkeit begründenden Umstände fehlt, steht zwar einem Schadensersatzanspruch, nicht aber schon dem negatorischen Unterlassungsbegehren entgegen").

be shown, the later case-law of the Court also adopts this logic of action-upon-notice for the Internet cases.

The major turning point came in 1996, when the Court in *Architektenwettbewerb* case rejected an injunction against a company which organized a contest for architectural works.[98] It argued that observance of the minimal prices is the business of architects, not the organizer of the call. Instead of rejection based on grounds of unreasonableness, however, the Court resorted to the case-law on tortious liability of the press[99] and noted:

> Here it nevertheless must be considered that, with the help of the disturbance liability, the obligation of its addressees may not be excessively extended over innocent by-standers. *Because in the event of acceptance of disturbance liability, the duty to review is unavoidably assumed, compliance with which is required to avoid a repeated claim. A disturber against whom it is claimed must therefore be able to raise an exceptional objection that, in a specific case the duty to review should not be entirely or partially expected of him,* because the disturbing situation was not readily recognizable for him.[100]

This brought a major change in to the case-law. Soon, the *exceptional objection*[101] to the duty to review (*Prüfungspflicht*), which arguably incorporated nothing but

---

[98] BGH *Architektenwettbewerb* (1996) I ZR 129/94.

[99] The Court additionally makes reference to its case-law on the liability of newspapers for third-party content (BGH *Produktinformation I.* (1993) I ZR 14/91; BGH *Beipackzettel* (1994) I ZR 51/92; BGH *Produktinformation II.* (1994) I ZR 167/92; BGH *Produktinformation III.* (1995) I ZR 227/93; BGH *Badische Rundschau* (1972) I ZR 1/71; BGH *Pressehaftung I* (1990) I ZR 127/88; BGH *Ausländischer Inserent* (1992) I ZR 166/90; BGH *Schlankheitswerbung* (1994) I ZR 316/91; BGH *Schlußverkaufswerbung II.* (1994) I ZR 147/92; BGH *Pressehaftung I.* (1990) I ZR 127/88; BGH *Pressehaftung II.* (1992) I ZR 119/90). All these cases, however, as the court itself implicitly admits, were about tort liability for unfair competition (*Pressehaftung I.* (discusses even damages), *Badische Rundschau* (discusses requirements of competitive intent)). It even refers to a tort case of the other senate from that year about a similar issue – BGH (1972) VI ZR 26/71. The same seems to be the case with *Pressehaftung II.*, *Produktinformation I.*, *Produktinformation II.*, *Produktinformation III.* (None of which mentions Störerhaftung, § 1004 BGB or its legal principles. On the contrary, some of them discuss competitive intent or a breach of good manners, which used to be a requirement for direct tortfeasorship). And even though later citations of these decisions might suggest otherwise (BGH *ambiente.de* (2001) I ZR 251/99, § 24), Prof. Eike Ullmann, who was a judge in the first senate of the BGH from 1988–1998 and 2002–2006 which decided most of these cases, notes in her 1996 article that also in cases of disturbance liability, we "should not ignore the principle that for the preservation of press privilege, liability can arise only when the breach of unfair competition is gross and recognizable without further information" (Eike Ullmann, "Einige Bemerkungen zur Meinungsfreiheit in der Wirtschaftswerbung" [1996] GRUR 948, 958).

[100] BGH *Architektenwettbewerb* (1996) I ZR 129/94 (emphasis mine) ("Hierbei ist jedoch zu beachten, daß mit Hilfe der Störerhaftung die einen Normadressaten treffende Pflicht nicht über Gebühr auf unbeteiligte Dritte erstreckt werden darf. Denn bei der Bejahung der Störerhaftung werden notgedrungen Prüfungspflichten vorausgesetzt, deren Einhaltung zur Vermeidung erneuter Inanspruchnahme geboten ist. Dem als Störer Inanspruchgenommenen muß daher ausnahmsweise der Einwand offenstehen, daß ihm im konkreten Fall eine Prüfungspflicht – etwa weil der Störungszustand für ihn nicht ohne weiteres erkennbar war – entweder überhaupt nicht oder jedenfalls nur eingeschränkt zuzumuten sei").

[101] Also applied like this in BGH *Branchen-Nomenklatur* (1997) I ZR 3/95.

limiting principles of reasonableness, was turned into a *precondition* for injunctions themselves. This metamorphosis was completed in the *Möbelklassiker* case.[102] In this copyright case, the publisher of a magazine was sued for allowing advertising of copyright-infringing pictures of knock-off furniture. Instead of considering a breach of duty to review as an exceptional corrective for injunctions on the grounds of unreasonableness, the Court transformed[103] it into a precondition.[104]

This shift has become fundamental in the today's doctrine of the Court. Very soon after *Möbelklassiker*, the Court started presenting the requirement of duty to review as a settled precondition for injunctions against a "disturber." Thus becoming a new way of testing the reasonableness. Moreover, the first senate narrowed down the term to cover only tortious nonwrongdoers.[105] The resulting cause of action became known in intellectual property circles as "disturbance lability" (*Störerhaftung*) – that is accountability for injunctions without liability in tort. In other legal circles, it continued to carry its broader meaning – that is accountability for injunctions, regardless of whether the addressee is a wrongdoer or not. It took different senates few years to realize this terminological inconsistency.[106] For the nascent Internet

---

[102] BGH *Möbelklasiker* (1998) I ZR 120/96.

[103] It is possible that the Court in this decision did not fully realize this, as the subsequent language, which refers to the possibility of an exceptional objection, clearly contradicts this principle.

[104] BGH *Möbelklasiker* (1998) I ZR 120/96 ("Die Bejahung der Störerhaftung Dritter nach § 97 Abs. 1 Satz 1 UrhG setzt deshalb wie die wettbewerbsrechtliche Störerhaftung Dritter die Verletzung von Prüfungspflichten voraus"). Also unlike in the previous copyright cases, the court does not refer to § 1004 BGB.

[105] BGH *Internetversteigerung I.* (2004) I ZR 304/01 ("derjenige, der – ohne Täter oder Teilnehmer zu sein – in irgendeiner Weise willentlich und adäquat kausal zur Verletzung eines geschützten Gutes beiträgt, als Störer für eine Schutzrechtsverletzung auf Unterlassung in Anspruch genommen werden kann"); this started in the *Meißner Dekor* case (BGH *Meißner Dekor* (2001) I ZR 22/99), where the first senate of the Court began to distinguish the accountability for injunctions of *liable* parties from those of *nonliable* parties. The term "disturber" was at first used to label anybody who is accountable for injunctions, but is not a tortfeasor (*Täter*), a co-tortfeasor (*Mittäters*) or an accessory (*Teilnehmer*); in the *Meißner Dekor*, the Court said only that such a "disturber" would not be liable for damages, but only for injunctions ("Der Störer, der – ohne Täter oder Teilnehmer zu sein – willentlich und adäquat kausal zur Verletzung eines geschützten Gutes oder zu einer verbotenen Handlung beigetragen hat, haftet dagegen lediglich auf Unterlassung und Beseitigung").

[106] The early confusion among the different senates of the German Federal Supreme Court best illustrated in the case-law relating to Google's autocomplete service (BGH *Autocomplete* VI ZR 269/12) which used the term in its original sense, i.e. also including actors/infringers – Georgios Gounalakis, "Rechtliche Grenzen der Autocomplete-Funktion von Google" [2013] NJW 2321, 2323 ("damit wird letztlich eine 'eingeschränkte Störerhaftung' nicht nur für Dritte, sondern auch für Täter und Teilnehmer konstruiert"); Mischa Dippelhofer, "Lost or found? – Die Störerhaftung der Suchmaschinenbetreiber nach dem BGH-Urteil 'Autocomplete'" [2013] MMR-Aktuell 352714 ("Obwohl der BGH Google somit als Täter einer Persönlichkeitsrechtsverletzung ansieht, prüft und bejaht er anschließend eine Haftung als Störer"); Gabriele Engels, "BGH: 'Autocomplete'-Funktion: Verantwortlichkeit eines Suchmaschinenbetreibers für persönlichkeitsrechtsverletzende Begriffsvorschläge" [2013] MMR 535 ("An dieser Stelle folgt dann die entscheidende und leider unzutreffende Weichenstellung des Senats bei der Klärung der fließenden Grenze zwischen eigenem Content und nutzergenerierten Inhalten und daran anschließend der Differenzierung der Haftungskonstellationen (Täter, Teilnehmer, Störer)"). Cases of – BGH *Posterlounge* (2015) I ZR 104/14,

case-law of the Court, the narrower version of "disturbance liability" appeared completely natural and was often treated as given.

But why did the doctrine of "disturbance liability" became used so intensively in German practice? It has something to do with underdeveloped tortious secondary liability. In German private law, accessory liability is generally based on the provision of § 830(2) BGB, which, according to the case-law, requires, as in criminal law, a double intent, i.e., the acts of an accessory as well of the main tortfeasor have to be intentional.[107] Apart from this, tortious liability can be established only for limited instances of inducement[108] and for adopting the third-party content as one's own.[109] These standards are usually very difficult to satisfy for most Internet cases.

As a consequence, the plaintiffs started using injunctions as a way to impose all their desires upon various intermediaries. Much of the subsequent case-law inevitably concerned he question of admissibility of various filtering and blocking measures. This gradually created massive pressure on the case-law itself, which began more and more to resemble the application of tort law principles of negligence. This, in turn, triggered loud voices in the literature,[110] questioning why the entire

---

para. 46; BGH (2016) VI ZR 34/15, para. 16; BGH (2015) VI ZR 340/14, para. 34 – already openly acknowledge this terminological difference.

[107] Until decisions BGH *Jugendgefährdende Medien bei eBay* (2007) I ZR 18/04 and BGH *MP3-Player-Import* (2009) Xa ZR 2/08, tortious liability for third-party infringements was dealt with under the doctrine of accessory liability. Accessory liability in German private law is generally based on the provision of § 830(2) BGB ("Instigators and accessories are equivalent to joint tortfeasors."), which, according to the case-law, requires, as in criminal law, a double intent, i.e. the acts of an accessory as well of the main tortfeasor have to be intentional (Mathias Habersack and others, *Münchener Kommentar zum BGB* (6th ed., C. H. Beck 2013) § 830(2) para. 15; Walter Erman and Peter Westermann, *Erman. Bürgerliches Gesetzbuch: Handkommentar mit AGG, EGBGB (Auszug), ErbbauRG, HausratsVO, LPartG, ProdHaftG, UKlaG, VAHRG und WEG* (11th ed., Schmidt Otto 2008) § 830(2) para. 3; Christina Eberl-Borges and others, *Julius von Staudingers Kommentar zum Bürgerlichen Gesetzbuch: Staudinger BGB – Buch 2: Recht der Schuldverhältnisse §§ 830 – 838* (Sellier – de Gruyter 2008) § 830(2) paras. 28, 38; Thomas Mehring, *Beteiligung und Rechtswidrigkeit bei § 830 I 2 BGB. Zugleich ein Beitrag zur Behandlung der Fälle von Anteilszweifeln und Opfermehrheiten* (Duncker & Humblot 2003); Christina Eberl-Borges, "§ 830 und die Gefährdungshaftung" [1996] Archiv für civilistische Praxis 196; BGH (2010) XI ZR 394/08, NJW-RR [2011] 551, 553; Hulmut Köhler, "'Täter' und 'Störer' im Wettbewerbs- und Markenrecht – Zur BGH-Entscheidung 'Jugendgefährdende Medien bei eBay'" GRUR [2008] 1.

[108] BGH *Cybersky* (2009) I ZR 57/07.

[109] Direct liability arises when intermediaries act as own-content providers. According to German courts, intermediaries are not only directly liable for content which they have created but are for the content they have adopted. The later praxis of courts is based on § 7 TMG, which distinguishes between content providers as providers of their "own contents" and intermediaries as providers of "contents of third parties." This distinction led to a court praxis according to which an intermediary can adopt the contents of third parties and become an own-content provider itself (German Federal Supreme Court, marions-kochbuch.de, 12.11.2009, Case No. I ZR 166/07; BGH (2016) VI ZR 34/15, para. 17; BGH *Posterlounge* (2015) I ZR 104/14, para. 48).

[110] Reinhard Döring, "Die Haftung für eine Mitwirkung an Wettbewerbsverstößen nach der Entscheidung des BGH 'Jugendgefährdende Medien bei eBay'" [2007] WRP 1131, 1140; Hulmut Köhler, "'Täter' und 'Störer' im Wettbewerbs- und Markenrecht – Zur BGH-Entscheidung 'Jugendgefährdende Medien bei eBay'" GRUR [2008] 1, 6; Matthias Leistner and Felix Stang, "Die

concept is limited to injunctions only, and excludes, most notably, damages. Today, the concept de facto serves two roles. While it implements injunctions against noninfringers, it also supplements proper accessory liability.

Interestingly enough, the academic disapproval soon led to the expansion of direct tortfeasorship in the field of unfair competition,[111] by the same senate, and patent law,[112] by a different senate, to cover also persons who fail to satisfy their tortious "duty of care." Further expansion of tortious duty of care to other rights was rejected.[113] In practice, this causes a curious split where patents and actions against unfair competition are fully tortiously protected against negligent acts of intermediaries with respect to third-party infringements, while other intellectual property rights enjoy only injunctive protection.

For them, the Court firmly continued to uphold its prior case-law, however, with a new a theory, according to which the "disturbance liability" only applies to absolute rights.[114] The category of absolute rights was meant to clearly delineate

---

Neuerung der wettbewerbsrechtlichen Verkehrspflichten – Ein Siegeszug der Prüfungspflichten?" WRP [2008] 533, 535; Matthias Leistner, "Störerhaftung und mittelbare Schutzrechtsverletzung" GRUR-Beil. [2010] 1, 29ff.; Hans-Jürgen Ahrens, "21 Thesen zur Störerhaftung im UWG und im Recht des Geistigen Eigentums" WRP [2007] 1281, 1285; Joachim von Ungern-Sternberg, "Die Rechtsprechung des Bundesgerichtshofs zum Urheberrecht und zu den verwandten Schutzrechten in den Jahren 2010 und 2011 (Teil II)" GRUR [2012] 321, 326; Ansgar Ohly and Olaf Sosnitza, *Gesetz gegen den unlauteren Wettbewerb* (6th ed., C. H. Beck 2014) § 8.

[111] BGH *Jugendgefährdende Medien bei eBay* (2007) I ZR 18/04; the metamorphosis of injunctions against innocent third parties into full tort liability in unfair competition law is based on the doctrinal legal principle of duty of care (*Verkehrversicherungspflichten*) which was first developed by the German courts in 1902 to delimit tortious negligent (wrongful) omissions (see Christian von Bar, *Verkehrspflichten richterliche Gefahrsteuerungsgebote im deutschen Deliktsrecht* (Heymann 1980) 3–4); RGZ 52, 373; RGZ 54, 53). The Court concludes in *Jugendgefährdende Medien bei eBay* that: "This jurisprudence from different fields of law have in common a general legal principle that everyone, who in his sphere of responsibility creates or maintains a source of risk, must take reasonable measures and arrangements, which are needed for prevention of dangers threatening third parties. Who breaches such duty of care in the unfair competition field, is a direct tortfeasor of tort of unfair competition."

[112] BGH *MP3-Player-Import* (2009) Xa ZR 2/08. (The case deals with the question of accountability of a shipping agent in the event of infringement of patent rights by third-party goods. After summarizing the case-law of the Court, the tenth senate decided to base injunctions in the tort law by establishing a direct tortfeasorship for negligent (wrongful) omissions. At the same time, however, the Court accepted principles and some outcomes which were decided in the context of the accountability of a disturber.)

[113] BGH *Sommer unseres Lebens* (2010) I ZR 121/08, para. 13 ("*Es kommt auch keine täterschaftliche Haftung des Beklagten unter dem Aspekt der Verletzung einer wettbewerbsrechtlichen Verkehrspflicht* (vgl. BGHZ 173, 188 Tz. 22 – Jugendgefährdende Schriften bei eBay) *in Betracht. Diese für das Wettbewerbsrecht entwickelte Haftungsgrundlage setzt voraus, dass die Merkmale einer täterschaftlichen Haftung nach dem jeweiligen Haftungsregime erfüllt sein müssen*"). The Court here argues that the situation in copyright law is dogmatically different from unfair competition law, but does not explain why then the same Court in patent law took exactly the same approach just a few months before, in the decision of another senate in *MP3-Player-Import*.

[114] BGH *Geschäftsführerhaftung* (2014) I ZR 242/12, para. 11; BGH *Videospiel-Konsolen II* (2013) I ZR 124/11, para. 84; BGH *Posterlounge* (2015) I ZR 104/14, para. 16; BGH *TV-Wartezimmer* (2015) I ZR 84/14, para. 17; BGH *Haftung für Hyperlink* (2015) I ZR 74/14, paras. 14, 21. This is in line with

intellectual property rights from unfair competition law. In unfair competition law, which helped to develop the case-law for years, the doctrine was explicitly abandoned and substituted with tortious liability, though with not always identical demands or prerequisites.[115] However, as a collateral effect, it also led to rejection of accountability without liability in some adjacent areas, such as anticircumvention protection of copyrighted works.[116]

In intellectual property law, therefore, accountability without liability still persists. I will explain what "obligations landscape" emerged over years from its steady application before the courts.

9.4 AGE OF INTERNET CASES

Until very recently, the Union law has had very little "shaping" effect on German case-law. The legislator felt no need to transpose Article 8(3) of the InfoSoc Directive and Article 11(III) of the Enforcement Directive, since it was believed that accountability under § 1004 BGB per analogy was sufficient to satisfy this obligation.[117] The only Union concern of German judges was rather the E-Commerce Directive than general "remedial" principles of the Enforcement Directive.[118] The German case-law applying "disturbance lability" online is very extensive. Since 2000, the case-law accumulated impressive 60 cases of the German Federal Supreme Court applying and developing its principles in the field of intellectual property rights, personality rights, and unfair competition. In order to explain the vast case-law in some more accessible way, I will divide the cases according to the resulting obligations.

The great majority of cases impose obligation only upon a notification or knowledge of some prior events. There are also few instances where the Court imposed an obligation prior to any notification (*prenotification*). Given the Union-prescribed prohibition of any obligation to monitor, envisaged by Article 15 of the E-Commerce Directive, these cases naturally exist only where this prohibition is inapplicable. For instance, the Court held that Amazon traders are obliged to perform regular surveillance of their product descriptions which can be edited by other independent traders

historical considerations – see Motive III, 392; Benno Mugdan (ed.), *Die gesamten Materialien zum Bürgerlichen Gesetzbuch für das Deutsche Reich: Band III* (Deker's Verlag 1899–1900) 218.

[115] More about this in Section 9.7.   [116] BGH *Videospiel-Konsolen II* (2013) I ZR 124/11, 84.

[117] In Germany, the Enforcement Directive was implemented by *Gesetz zur Verbesserung der Durchsetzung von Rechten des geistigen Eigentums* (VDRgEG) after the Commission initiated infringement proceedings against Germany (Case C-395/07 *Commission v. Germany* [2008] ECLI:EU:C:2008:325); Lambert Pechan and Marius Schneider, "Carriers and Trade Mark Infringements: Should Carriers Care?" (2010) 5(5) *Journal of Intellectual Property Law & Practice* 354, 355.

[118] For instance even the preliminary reference in *McFadden* was filed with explicit reference to Art 12 of the E-Commerce Directive, but without referring to Art 8(3) of the InfoSoc Directive (see more Martin Husovec, "Holey Cap! CJEU Drills (Yet) Another Hole in the E-Commerce Directive's Safe Harbors" (2017) 12(2) Journal of Intellectual Property Law & Practice 115–125).

without their knowledge.[119] The requirement of a proactive obligation is very rare and such cases often border with acting as a direct co-tortfeasor, such as user of a trademark.[120] It is the established principle that general monitoring obligation, whether offline or online, is in principle not desirable.[121]

Providers generally have to act in some way upon receiving notification or knowledge of events (*postnotification*). The obligations differ, however, greatly depending upon what kind of duties follow. There are broadly three different situations. First, the injunction-addressees have to remove or block *only* a subset of notified information, such as unambiguously wrongful content (Type A). Second, they have to remove or block not only notified, but also *similar* information in the future (Type B). And third, they have to help by providing some other duty of assistance (Type C).

Type A and Type C obligations are usually imposed on more remote infrastructure providers, such as domain name authorities or access providers. Usually they involved very softened or conditional take-down or blocking obligation which is meant to reflect the more privileged social status of the intermediary. Often, the intermediaries would be simply too distant players for regular tort law.

A typical case of a Type A obligation is *ambiente.de*.[122] It concerns an injunction solely against the domain name authority, DENIC, to cancel the registration of a domain name. After analyzing the criteria, including "duty to review," the Court came to the conclusion that DENIC has no duty to review the domain names of third parties before their registration. And even after registration, DENIC must cancel the registration only if the contested domain name has been brought to its attention and is (1) either determined to be infringing by the court or is (2) at least "unambiguously infringing," such as when a domain name is identical to a well-known mark.[123] This case-law was later confirmed on several occasions[124] and extended also to administrative contacts of the domain names.[125] It illustrates that some providers can, despite the notice, be obliged to act upon only a subset of

---

[119] BGH *Angebotsmanipulation bei Amazon* (2015) I ZR 104/14.
[120] BGH *Posterlounge* (2015) I ZR 104/14.
[121] BGH *Pertusin II.* (1957) I ZR 56/55; BGH *VUS* (1976) VI ZR 23/72; BGH. *Kinderhochstühle im Internet II.* (2013) I ZR 216/11; BGH *Auto-compelete* (2013) VI ZR 269/12 (all of these cases apply the principle without specific legislative prescription in the statute).
[122] BGH *ambiente.de* (2001) I ZR 251/99.   [123] An example given by the BGH itself.
[124] BGH *kurt-biedenkopf.de* (2004) I ZR 82/01 (even in cases of reregistration of a previously infringing registration, the domain name authority is not obliged to review them ex ante; the technical and organizational measures to implement such a duty would, according to the Court, make the registration proceedings more lengthy and expensive; as a consequence, the Court rejected an injunction that would block a previously infringing domain name from future registrations entirely). It should be noted that there is no ADR system for domain names in Germany.
[125] BGH *Basler Haar-Kosmetik* (2011) I ZR 150/09 (carte blanche power granted to the administrative contact is such a special circumstance triggering proactive duties); BGH *dlg.de* (2012) I ZR 150/11 (a high number of domain name registrations shortly after the expiration of the sun-rise period can constitute such a special circumstance, triggering the duty to review).

notifications. The Court explained the main role of these providers is to "to ease the enforcement of such rights" and "not the own responsibility of the administrative contact."[126]

Ambiente.de is also illustrative for judicial considerations at play in these cases. The Court considered that DENIC serves an important public interest, employs only a small number of people, uses an automated registration procedure, has a huge number of requests, provides a fast and inexpensive registration system and would anyway not be in a position to assess all the legal issues surrounding conflicting domain name registrations. All these arguments are of course valid, but most of them, with the notable exception of public interest and position to determine infringements, represent a *circular* logic – you are not required to do more, because you would need to change your current processes. The decision is thus better understood as emphasizing the longer-term effects of a rule on the information society. Thus serving as a moderator of excessive emphasis on short-term effects in situations where positive externalities of a service are so highly disproportionate that accepting a broad duty of care can endanger them.

Another group of providers enjoying special postnotification treatment are Internet access providers. In website blocking cases, the Court accepted[127] that an obligation to block websites concerns only websites whose "legal content is negligible in comparison to illegal one."[128] Moreover, it arises only after the rightholders spent "reasonable efforts" to enforce their rights against website operators and their Web hosting providers.[129] This includes their obligation to institute a private investigator to first uncover their real identity or even to submit a criminal complaint to secure a cooperation of the prosecutor. The Court unusually for the first time postulated an enforcement prerequisite, although it is the established principle that there is no rule of subsidiarity between enforcing against tortfeasors and "disturbers" or among "disturbers" themselves. It argued that unlike in other cases, access providers operate very socially beneficial service and the blocking itself targets a single entity, which makes the prerequisite efforts more appropriate.[130]

---

[126] Ibid., para. 56 ("Auch soweit Dritten, die sich durch den registrierten Domainnamen in ihren Rechten verletzt sehen, die rechtliche Verfolgung ihrer Interessen durch den Admin-C erleichtert wird, geht es zunächst allein darum, die Durchsetzung solcher Rechte gegenüber dem im Ausland residierenden Inhaber des Domainnamens zu erleichtern, und nicht um eine eigene Verantwortlichkeit des Admin-C").

[127] At first, lower courts rejected this: OLG Köln (2014) 6 U 192/11, GRUR [2014] 1081; OLG Hamburg (2014) 5 U 68/10, GRUR-RR [2014] 140.

[128] BGH *Störerhaftung des Access-Providers* (2016) I ZR 174/14, paras. 55, 65 ("wenn nach dem Gesamtverhältnis rechtmäßige gegenüber rechtswidrigen Inhalten nicht ins Gewicht fallen "); BGH (2016) I ZR 3/14, para. 66.

[129] BGH (2016) I ZR 3/14, para. 68, 69, 70, 73, 75; BGH *Störerhaftung des Access-Providers* (2016) I ZR 174/14, paras. 29, 82, 83, 87.

[130] BGH (2016) I ZR 3/14, paras. 68, 69.

Nevertheless, the Court assumed the website blocking injunctions are prescribed by the Union law[131] and in their absence, according to judges, the rightholders would remain unprotected.[132] Unlike in previous cases, the Court considered Union principles for granting injunctions, such as effectiveness, and their limitations, such as overblocking,[133] need to be prescribed by the law[134] or user's standing,[135] very seriously. According to the Court, the proportionality of the measures hinges on their reasonableness which is in turn evaluated by their effectiveness.

The Court accepted the CJEU's level of effectiveness. Even more interesting is its framing of the enquiry. According to the Court, effectiveness of the blocking shouldn't be measured by how it reduces infringement of rightholder's rights in aggregate, but only by how substantially it impedes access to a particular website, regardless of the substitution effects. Moreover, the private benefits of rightholders arising from such blocking don't have to be substantiated.[136] Since no website blocking was yet imposed due to lack of prior "reasonable efforts" by the plaintiffs, it remains to be seen how the Court will approach the element of costs. Deutsche Telekom, the access provider, already speculated that the costs should exceed 1 million euros.[137] The analysis, however, already shows that the Court is not very likely to replicate more nuanced cost-benefit analysis of the English courts.[138] What is nevertheless clear is that the "reasonable efforts" precondition for plaintiffs will increase the costs of website blocking in Germany. In order for blocking to be welfare maximizing in Germany, it will need to yield even higher expected benefit to cover for these extra costs.

Type B obligations are a norm in the world of hosting services. They popularized the "disturbance liability" outside of Germany. Effectively, they constitute a stay-down obligation. This means that upon receiving a notice, an intermediary is obliged not only to take-down the notified content, but also to prevent its further reappearance.

The entire saga of filtering obligations started with the *Internetversteigerung I.* judgment.[139] The case involved the liability of an auction platform and the Court drew several important conclusions. First, that the hosting safe harbor does not apply to injunctions, and second, that a disturber needs to breach a duty to review to be held accountable for injunctions under § 1004 BGB. There is no obligation to review the content of entries prior to their publication because this would disturb the

---

[131] BGH *Störerhaftung des Access-Providers* (2016) I ZR 174/14, para. 22; BGH (2016) I ZR 3/14, paras. 33, 66.

[132] BGH *Störerhaftung des Access-Providers* (2016) I ZR 174/14, para. 49.

[133] BGH (2016) I ZR 3/14, paras. 44, 51–56.   [134] Ibid., para. 60.   [135] Ibid., para. 46.

[136] BGH (2016) I ZR 174/14, paras. 47, 59.   [137] Ibid., para. 29.

[138] The court deployed nevertheless an interesting strategy where access providers are forced to unveil and argue the costs of the implementation by means of secondary burdens of proof.

[139] BGH *Internetversteigerung I.* (2004) I ZR 304/01.

business model of the platform. However, the auction platform's interest to provide a cheap and smooth service is less significant than in the case of the domain name authority. Therefore, the platform operator must block any "clear infringements" which are pointed out to him. In addition, he must take proactive steps to prevent infringements of a "similar kind" from occurring again. The Court further suggested that the platform operator can take advantage of filtering software for this purpose.

In its sequel, *Internetversteigerung II.*,[140] the Court further confirmed that an injunction against a disturber is also available in cases, where no third-party infringements have yet been committed, but are only feared. The Court ruled that a platform should implement filtering software that would flag objectively suspicious offers (e.g., due to their low price for a certain keyword) which could subsequently be reviewed manually by the employees. It observed that the limit of reasonableness would certainly be reached if there are no other keywords for the filter. The platform operator, however, should block the offers only if they constitute instances of "clear infringement."

These two auction platform cases became landmarks for several reasons. Not only did they broaden the scope of enforcement to "similar" infringements, but they also imposed the first filtering obligations, thus practically discarding as irrelevant for intermediaries most of the safe harbors. In the years to come, the main focus of the cases were these filtering obligations of platforms, such as auction platforms[141] and filesharing platforms,[142] but also re-publishers of RSS feeds,[143] blogging platforms,[144] and domain name parking companies.[145] Although the BGH was always explicit in rejecting general prenotification monitoring in its reasoning,[146] whether the safe harbors were applicable or not, the measures imposed postnotification often led to monitoring that is hard to label as specific (see Section 8.3).

In a typical scenario, an intermediary receives a notification regarding a particular infringement. He is obliged to take it down if wrongful, and further take reasonable efforts to prevent its reappearance. However, this proactive stay-down obligation is not

---

[140] BGH *Internetversteigerung II.* (2007) I ZR 35/04.

[141] BGH *Internetversteigerung I.* (2004) I ZR 304/01; BGH *Internetversteigerung II.* (2007) I ZR 35/04; BGH *Kinderhochstühle im Internet II.* (2013) I ZR 216/11; BGH *Kinderhochstuehle im Internet I.* (2010) I ZR 139/08.

[142] BGH (2013) I ZR 79/12; BGH *File-Hosting-Dienst* (2013) I ZR 80/12; BGH (2013) I ZR 79/12; BGH *Alone in the Dark* (2012) I ZR 18/11.

[143] BGH *RSS-Feed* (2012) VI ZR 144/11.

[144] BGH *Blogger* (2011) VI ZR 93/10, paras. 22, 24, 26 (the operator of a blogging platform does not have to review the content apriori, but must only act upon a notice. The notice, however, must, without need of detailed factual and legal check, enable the platform provider to establish the wrongfulness of objected content. If such notice is received, the provide must not only remove the objected content, but also take reasonable measure to prevent its reappearance).

[145] BGH *Sedo* (2010) I ZR 155/09.

[146] This was also rejected for domain name parking operators (BGH *Sedo* (2010) I ZR 155/09), online archives (BGH *Jahrhundertmörder* (2010) VI ZR 30/09), picture-sharing platforms (BGH *Preußische Gärten* (2010) V ZR 44/10) and blogging platforms (BGH *Blogger* (2011) VI ZR 93/10).

limited to identical content from identical user, but extends also to infringements of "similar kind" of the same work/sign,[147] even if infringing content reappears only in part,[148] regardless by whom they are committed.[149] One notification is thus enough to create this stay-down obligation for a particular protected subject matter.[150] The extent of "technically and commercially reasonable" measures to prevent reappearance depends on many factors, including active role and nature of the posed risk by the platform.[151]

The Court already ruled that some hosting providers may be required to (1) employ word-filtering technology for the name of the notified work, including on existing uploads,[152] (2) use better than basic fingerprinting technology that only detects identical files, such as MD5,[153] as a supplementary tool, (3) manually check external websites for the infringing links associated with the notified name of a work on services like Google, Facebook and Twitter or (4) use Web-crawlers to detect other links on own service.[154] According to the Court's argument, this last proactive measure is more reasonable than to manually review the files that were not caught by the word-filter.[155]

This shows that the Court's willingness to expand stay-down obligation is undeniable. The obligation includes not only use of automated solutions, such as filters, but also internal and external checks. These obligations are so extensive that they can even run into incompatibility with the Union law. There are two points where the extent of obligations does not seem to meet the Union standards. First, it is when the Court expanded preventive obligation beyond instances of double identity infringements, which is identical user and subject matterwise. In *Kinderhochstühle II.*, the Court notes that it did not have to limit the proactive measures to the same infringements committed by the same users, because the guidance of the CJEU in *L'Oréal and Others* was not exhaustive in this regard.[156] As I argue in Chapter 8, this is not very convincing. And second, the incompatibility might occur when the Court requires manual or automated review of external websites. This so-called market-surveillance

---

[147] BGH *Internetversteigerung I.* (2004) I ZR 304/01.   [148] BGH (2013) I ZR 79/12, para. 55.
[149] Ibid., para. 45; BGH *Alone in the Dark* (2012) I ZR 18/11 (tenor).
[150] BGH (2013) I ZR 79/12, para. 58.
[151] Ibid., para. 20; BGH *File-Hosting-Dienst* (2013) I ZR 80/12, para. 15; BGH *Kinderhochstühle im Internet II.* (2013) I ZR 216/11, para. 48.
[152] BGH *Alone in the Dark* (2012) I ZR 18/11.
[153] BGH *File-Hosting-Dienst* (2013) I ZR 80/12, para. 58; BGH (2013) I ZR 79/12, para. 46.
[154] This type of duty to research external websites first appeared in the *Basler Kosmetik* case.
[155] BGH *Alone in the Dark* (2012) I ZR 18/11, 39; BGH (2013) I ZR 79/12, para. 53.
[156] The refence is made to Case C-324/09 *L'Oréal and Others* [2011] ECLI:EU:C:2011:474, which held in para. 143 that "the measures that are described (non-exhaustively) in the preceding paragraphs, as well as any other measure which may be imposed in the form of an injunction under the third sentence of Article 11 of Directive 2004/48, must strike a fair balance between the various rights and interests mentioned above" – see BGH *Kinderhochstuehle im Internet II.* (2013) I ZR 216/11, para. 54 ("Der Gerichtshof hat in der Entscheidung betont, dass die dort angeführten Maßnahmen keine abschließende Aufzählung darstellen").

obligation (*Marktbeobachtungspflicht*)[157] is hard to square with the prohibition of general monitoring or Article 3 of the Enforcement Directive, as it forces to actively seek facts or circumstances indicating illegal activity of their own content.

One the other hand, however, the same Court seems to be willing to accept a submission or takedown interface as a substitute to these obligations. In *Kinderhochstühle im Internet I.*,[158] the Court held that the existence of the possibility to undertake content review by the plaintiff within a partner program is also to be taken into account.[159] More specifically, the Court opined that, given that a plaintiff was offered an option to *manually* search and notify infringements within an interface, "it is not obvious why the defendant should take over the review of the trade mark infringements from the plaintiff, which can be carried out with equal effort personally by the plaintiff as a right holder."[160]

However, the Court is not willing to accept just any submitter's interface as an alternative. In two cases concerning Rapidshare,[161] the Court found that restricted takedown interface, such as one which doesn't include the possibility to search for new links, but only to delete known links, and also without the possibility to obtain disclosure of identity, isn't a real alternative.

The last group of obligations, Type C, is less common. They don't involve simple removal or blocking of the content. The archetypical obligation of this kind is a password-protection obligation of an open WiFi operator.

In 2010, the Court dealt with the issue of whether a private operator of a WiFi hotspot is accountable for copyright infringements committed by unauthorized third parties and what is his obligation to prevent them.[162] As a way out for the situation where no previous misuse of the WiFi was reported, the Court approved of injunction obliging the private operator of the WiFi hotspot to secure it lege artis to the date of acquisition of the router. Mere password protection was found to be insufficient, if the password was not long enough. The Court considered that only negligible costs will be incurred by the WiFi operator, because securing it is in the operator's own interest anyway, and as long as he is a private person, no business model can be endangered. The question of how the decision applies to operators other than private individuals became disputed before the lower courts.[163]

---

[157] BGH (2013) I ZR 79/12, para. 54.

[158] BGH *Kinderhochstuehle im Internet I.* (2010) I ZR 139/08.   [159] Ibid., para. 43.

[160] Ibid., para. 43 ("Es ist schon nicht ohne Weiteres einzusehen, warum die Bekl. der Kl. eine Überprüfung von Markenverletzungen abnehmen soll, die die Kl. als Schutzrechtsinhaberin mit gleichem Aufwand selbst bewerkstelligen kann"); cf. Jan Nordemann, "Haftung von Providern im Urheberrecht – Der aktuelle Stand nach dem EuGH-Urteil v. 12. 7. 2011 – C-324/09 – L'Oréal/eBay" [2011] GRUR 977, 981 (discussion of the interface option).

[161] BGH *File-Hosting-Dienst* (2013) I ZR 80/12; BGH (2013) I ZR 79/12.

[162] BGH *Sommer unseres Lebens* (2010) I ZR 121/08.

[163] LG Frankfurt am Main (2010) 2–6 S 19/09, ZUM-RD 2011, 371 (hotels); LG Hamburg (2010) 310 O 433/10, MMR 2011, 475 (cybercafé); LG Frankfurt am Main (2013) 2–06 O 304/12, ZUM-RD 2014, 36 (holiday apartments); see comments by Reto Mantz, "Die Haftung des Betreibers eines gewerblich

Years later, this decision continues to be criticized by scholars,[164] industry associations such as Bitkom[165] and ECO,[166] as well as civil society organizations.[167] No wonder. The decision is a perfect example of an erroneous focus on the short-term benefits of enforcement measures, as opposed to the long-term goals of promoting economic progress. The decision became especially problematic after it was coupled with the pretrial reimbursement of cease and desist letters,[168] which potentially exposed all the operators of open WiFi to demands of several hundred euros per request. This risk then led to rapid over-compliance with the ruling among the general public and generally lack of free and open wireless in Germany.

Five years later, in 2015, the German legislator tried to fix the situation by passing a 2016-amendment to the German implementation of the E-Commerce Directive,[169] clarifying that operators of open wireless are also mere conduits in its sense. Moreover, a lower court in Munich, tried to review the case-law by means of preliminary

---

betriebenen WLANs und die Haftungsprivilegierung des § 8 TMG" [2013] GRUR-RR 497; Gerald Spindler, "Haftung für private WLANs im Delikts- und Urheberrecht" [2010] CR 592.

[164] Franz Hofmann, "Die Haftung des Inhabers eines privaten Internetanschlusses für Urheberrechtsverletzungen Dritter" [2014] ZUM 654, 660; Ansgar Ohly, "Urheberrecht in der digitalen Welt – Brauchen wir neue Regelungen zum Urheberrecht und dessen Durchsetzung?" in Gregor Bachmann (ed.) *Verhandlungen des 70. Deutschen Juristentages* (C. H. Beck, 2014) F 128; Thomas Sassenberg and Reto Mantz, *WLAN und Recht. Aufbau und Betrieb von Internet-Hotspots* (Erich Schmidt Verlag, 2014) 160ff.

[165] Bitkom, "Öffentliche WLAN-Zugänge fristen Nischendasein" (2015), www.bitkom.org/de/presse/8477-82493.aspx.

[166] Eco, "Gesetzliche Bestrebungen im Hinmblick auf die Haftung von Betreibern öffentlicher, lokaler Funknetze als Zugang zum Internet" (2014), www.eco.de/wp-content/blogs.dir/20140516-eco-positionspapier-wlan-und-stoererhaftung.pdf.

[167] Digitalegesselschaft, "Wlan-Störerhaftung Beseitigen" (2017), https://digitalegesellschaft.de/mitmachen/storerhaftung-beseitigen/.

[168] According to the German case-law, a rightholder has the possibility to obtain reimbursement for the cease and desist letters they have sent based on the doctrine of *negotiorum gestio* (§§ 677, 683(1), 670 BGB – see RG (1941) VI ZR 129/40, RGZ 167, 55, 58; BGH (1966) *v.* ZR 126/63; BGH *Fotowettbewerb* (1969) I ZR 3/68; BGH (1984) I ZR 45/82; BGH *Selbstauftrag* (2004) I ZR 2/03; BGH *Kosten des Patentanwalts II* (2011) I ZR 181/09; BGH *Kosten des Patentanwalts IV* (2012) I ZR 70/11; this doctrine was codified in the field of copyright law in § 97a of the German Copyright Act (UrhG)). The underlying idea is that the entitled sender of such letters saves costs to its receiver by giving him a last chance to avoid litigation by complying with the request, since any involvement in litigation will cost him more. See Markus Bölling, "Unterlassungsantrag und Streitgegenstand im Falle der Störerhaftung" [2013] GRUR 1092, 1098; Klaus Bacher, *Die Beeinträchtigungsgefahr als Voraussetzung für Unterlassungsklagen im Wettbewerbsrecht und in anderen Gebieten des Zivilrechts* (Centaurus-Verlagsgesellschaft Pfaffenweiler 1996) 70; Ansgar Ohly, "Urheberrecht in der digitalen Welt – Brauchen wir neue Regelungen zum Urheberrecht und dessen Durchsetzung?" in Gregor Bachmann (ed.) *Verhandlungen des 70. Deutschen Juristentages* (C. H. Beck, 2014) F 117; Andreas Bergmann, *Die Geschäftsführung ohne Auftrag als Subordinationsverhältnis* (Mohr Siebeck 2010) 352; the costs are to be reimbursed depending on the legal ground. If the addressee infringed the right, the first letter is already subject to reimbursement. If the addressee is only in the position of a noninfringer, the obligation to reimburse is only triggered after it does not comply with the required duties once notified of their formation.

[169] Zweites Gesetz zur Änderung des Telemediengesetzes (2016) Teil I Nr. 36, 1766.

reference before CJEU. None of two efforts seems to have resulted in much. The legislative amendment was re-purposed in the process so that it doesn't have any teeth against domestic case-law.[170] And the CJEU's holding in *McFadden* essentially gave blessing to the German practice.[171] It therefore comes as a no surprise that in the most recent decision on the matter, the German Federal Supreme Court simply carries on with its case-law.[172] In 2017, the legislator already announced its second attempt to change the law.[173]

9.5 INFORMATION DISCLOSURE

Unlike in the United Kingdom, in Germany, the information disclosure against noninfringers developed not before, but after the general accountability framework was already recognized and heavily in use. In 1990, the German legislator decided to improve the enforcement framework by creating a stand-alone claim for information.[174] The claim was building upon an older judge-made concept of accessory claim for information, which remained applicable in some limited circumstances.[175] This autonomous claim for information was incorporated in the intellectual property law, however, it remained restricted to an obligation of "infringers."[176]

The extension of the claim to noninfringers (*Nichtverletzern*) across all IP statues was undertaken only with the implementation of the Enforcement Directive into German law in 2008.[177] Some commentators criticized this as going too far or even as "foreign to the German liability system."[178] The legislator itself noted in the

---

[170] Jan Nordemann, "Nach TMG-Reform und EuGH McFadden" (2016) 11 GRUR 1097; KG Berlin (2017) 24 U 117/15 (holding that the 2016-amendment did not prevent injunctions from applying).

[171] See Martin Husovec, "Holey Cap! CJEU Drills (Yet) Another Hole in the E-Commerce Directive's Safe Harbors" (2017) 12(2) Journal of Intellectual Property Law & Practice 115, 124.

[172] BGH (2016) I ZR 220/15 (full text of the decision not available at the time of writting).

[173] Bundesministeriums für Wirtschaft und Energie, "Referentenentwurf des Bundesministeriums für Wirtschaft und Energie Entwurf eines Dritten Gesetzes zur Änderung des Telemediengesetzes" (2017), www.bmwi.de/Redaktion/DE/Downloads/E/entwurf-drittes-gesetz-zur-aenderung-des-telemediengesetzes.pdf?__blob=publicationFile&v=4.

[174] Gesetz zur Stärkung des Schutzes des geistigen Eigentums und zur Bekämpfung der Produktpiraterie (Produktpirateriegesetz), (1990) BGBl I S. 422.

[175] The concept was build around § 242 BGB – see Thomas Dreier and Gernot Schulze, *Urheberrechtsgesetz: UrhG* (4th ed., C. H. Beck 2013) § 101, para. 1; it is still in use in unfair competition law – see BGH (1994) I ZR 42/93.

[176] See Gesetz zur Stärkung des Schutzes des geistigen Eigentums und zur Bekämpfung der Produktpiraterie (Produktpirateriegesetz), (1990) BGBl I S. 422.

[177] Gesetz zur Verbesserung der Durchsetzung von Rechten des geistigen Eigentums (2008) BGBl I S. 1191; Thomas Dreier and Gernot Schulze, *Urheberrechtsgesetz: UrhG* (4th ed., C. H. Beck 2013) § 101, para. 2; Georg Benkard et al., *Patentgesetz: PatG* (11th ed., C. H. Beck 2015) § 140b, para. 1.

[178] Reinhard Ingerl and Christian Rohnke, *Markengesetz: MarkenG* (3rd ed., C. H. Beck 2010) § 19, para. 17 ("Diese Erweiterung ist gegenüber dem sonstigen Haftungssystem des MarkenG systemfremd, schwer verständlich und teilweise auch sprachlich mißglückt").

explanatory note that the scope of addressees is "quite broad."[179] Unlike "disturbers," the addressees don't even have to breach any "duty to review" in order to appear on the radar.[180] It is sufficient that the person, as required by the Enforcement Directive: (1) was found in possession of the infringing goods, (2) was found to be using the infringing services, (3) was found to be providing services used in infringing activities, or (4) was indicated by the person referred to in point (1), (2), or (3) as being involved in the production, manufacture, or distribution of the goods or the provision of the services. According to subsequent case-law, the disclosure against noninfringer does not require "commercial scale" of infringer's activity.[181]

The implementation made the disclosure generally possible even without a judicial procedure, on the condition that the case concerns either an obvious infringement or the injured already initiated a proceedings against the infringer.[182] The legislator justified this with the argument that obligatory court proceedings would not only overburden the courts, but would also be generally incompatible with German procedural law.[183] The special exception, however, was foreseen for the category of traffic data,[184] the disclosure of which was limited to a specialized court procedure.

9.6 COSTS OF COMPLIANCE

Given that injunctions against infringers and noninfringers originate from the same legal doctrine, it is seems understandable that the compliance isn't governed by two distinct types of rules of cost bearing. The rules are uniformly applicable, regardless of the position.

However, the nineteenth-century authors of the BGB openly discussed, in the context of actio negatoria and rei vindicatio, the question of the costs of compliance. The debate was closely connected with the very nature of such injunctions, since it was disputed whether actio negatoria incorporates an active obligation of everybody

---

[179] Bundesregierung, "Gesetzentwurf der Bundesregierung Entwurf eines Gesetzes zur Verbesserung der Durchsetzung von Rechten des geistigen Eigentums" (2007) Drucksache 16/5048, http:// dip21.bundestag.de/dip21/btd/16/050/1605048.pdf, p.38 ("Die Vorschrift zieht damit den Kreis der Verpflichteten – entsprechend den Vorgaben der Richtlinie – sehr weit").

[180] Reinhard Ingerl and Christian Rohnke, *Markengesetz: MarkenG* (3rd ed., C. H. Beck 2010) § 19, para. 17; Thomas Dreier and Gernot Schulze, *Urheberrechtsgesetz: UrhG* (5th ed., C. H. Beck 2015) § 101.

[181] BGH *Alles kann besser werden* (2012) I ZB 80/11; For the criticism, see Gerald Spindler et al., *Recht der elektronischen Medien* (3rd ed., C. H. Beck 2015) § 101(2) UrhG, para. 8.

[182] § 101 German Copyright Act (UrhG); § 140b German Patent Act (PatG); § 24b German Utility Model Act (GebrMG); § 46 German Design Act (GeschmMG); § 37b German Plant Varieties Act (SortSchG); § 19 German Trademark Act (MarkenG).

[183] Bundesregierung, "Gesetzentwurf der Bundesregierung Entwurf eines Gesetzes zur Verbesserung der Durchsetzung von Rechten des geistigen Eigentums" (2007) Drucksache 16/5048, http://dip21 .bundestag.de/dip21/btd/16/050/1605048.pdf, 38.

[184] Thomas Dreier and Gernot Schulze, *Urheberrechtsgesetz: UrhG* (5th ed., C. H. Beck 2015) § 101.

to keep the rights of others uninfringed at their own cost.[185] In the debate, one even finds proposals for reimbursement of the costs by the right owner.[186] Eventually, it was decided that it is the injunction addressee that should bear the cost since it was expected that this could contribute to the "simplification of the legal relationships."[187] Despite this, however, in the official explanatory note (*Motive*), one finds this extremely interesting cautionary note from the members of the committee:

> Against the reasonableness of the obligation to pay the costs (...) *the doubt can be raised and it considered to be justified only towards those who, by erecting a facility, also committed a tort.* (...) The concession of possession is, in case of rei vindicatio, even when the chattels have to be taken out and moved from its position, a minor service, which does not entail an extraordinary expenditure from the own assets of the injunction-addressee and imposition of which therefore does not stretch to a perceptible hardship, especially since the obligation to surrender is a debt collectible by the creditor and the other costs of collection, in particular the costs of separation, are to be borne by the right holder. In contrast, *an elimination of a facility, e.g. of a building that is overlapping a boundary, can cause significant costs and the obligation to pay the cost hereby turn into a pressing burden.*[188]

Without doubt, today's injunctions under § 1004 BGB have become a source of considerable financial burden to intermediaries who are required to implement various filtering technologies or take on new employees to ensure that third parties do not infringe the rights of rightholders. To review the existing case-law in the light of these historical debates would be extremely interesting. Unfortunately, I

---

[185] Yoshikazu Kawasumi, *Von der römischen action negatoria zum negatorischen Beseitigungsanspruch des BGB* (Nomos Verlag 2001) 66, 105, 106, 108, 115, 125.

[186] The proposal of Mandry – see Yoshikazu Kawasumi, *Von der römischen action negatoria zum negatorischen Beseitigungsanspruch des BGB* (Nomos Verlag 2001) 104ff.

[187] Motive III, 426 – see Benno Mugdan (ed.), *Die gesamten Materialien zum Bürgerlichen Gesetzbuch für das Deutsche Reich: Band III* (Deker's Verlag 1899–1900) 238; Yoshikazu Kawasumi, *Von der römischen action negatoria zum negatorischen Beseitigungsanspruch des BGB* (Nomos Verlag 2001) 116 (see for the discussion).

[188] Motive III, 425 – see Benno Mugdan (ed.), *Die gesamten Materialien zum Bürgerlichen Gesetzbuch für das Deutsche Reich: Band III* (Deker's Verlag 1899–1900) 237 ("Gegen die Billigkeit einer solchen Kostenpflicht (...) könnte ein Zweifel erhoben und dieselbe nur gegenüber demjenigen für gerechtfertigt erachtet werden, welcher aus einem in der Errichtung der Anlagen liegenden Delikte schadensersatzpflichtig ist. (...) Bei der Vindikation ist die Einräumung des Besitzes oder der Inhabung, selbst wenn die bewegliche Sache dabei hervorgeholt und von der Stelle bewegt werden muß, eine geringe Dienstleistung, welche besondere Aufwendungen aus dem eigenen Vermögen des Leistungspflichtigen nicht mit sich bringt und deren Auferlegung deshalb nicht zu einer fühlbaren Beschwerung gereicht, zumal die Herausgabepflicht eine Holschuld ist und die weiteren Kosten des Abholens, insbes. der Trennung, von dem Anspruchsberechtigten zu tragen sind. Die Beseitigung von Anlagen, zB. eines sich über die Grenzlinie hinüberneigenden Gebäudes, kann dagegen bedeutende Kosten verursachen und die Kostenpflicht mithin zu einer drückenden Last werden"; emphasis mine).

don't have sufficient space for such explorations in this work. I hope that other colleagues will find this interesting enough to explore this further. For the purposes of this work, it is sufficient to say that the existing practice, which leads to substantial costs for injunction-addressees (who are not liable in tort), should not be treated as self-evident or forever carved in stone.

To the contrary, the compensation of compliance costs incurred by nonwrong-doers is nothing alien even to the today's intellectual property law in Germany. All intellectual property statues stipulate that noninfringers are to be compensated for "necessary effort" (*erforderlichen Aufwendungen*)[189] required to comply with an obligation to information disclosure. Spindler notes that it is disputed whether the compensation of only specifically or also of generally incurred costs is possible.[190] In case of "traffic data," "the costs of judicial order [for disclosure] are to be born by the injured."[191] The latter cost is 200 euros per request.[192] This isn't a consequence of the Union law, but purely domestic policy decision. The compensatory elements in information claims are often explained as an effort to balance the inconvenience to a noninfringer (*Nichtverletzer*).[193] The legislator itself did explain this domestic solution by the fact that a noninfringer is requested as an uninvolved third party.[194] This reference to the hardship, inconvenience, or involvement echoes the old scholarly debate mentioned above. In the recent literature, the proposal that the costs should be reimbursed to intermediaries, although often based on rather constitutional arguments, seems to find a broad support among scholars, however, only in the context of most typical remote services – the access providers.[195]

---

[189] Art 101(2) third sentence of the German Copyright Act („Der zur Auskunft Verpflichtete kann von dem Verletzten den Ersatz der für die Auskunftserteilung erforderlichen Aufwendungen verlangen").

[190] Gerald Spindler et al., *Recht der elektronischen Medien* (3rd ed., C. H. Beck 2015) § 101 UrhG, paras. 10, 27.

[191] Art 101(9) third sentence of the German Copyright Act ("Die Kosten der richterlichen Anordnung trägt der Verletzte").

[192] Georg Benkard et al., *Patentgesetz: PatG* (11th ed., C. H. Beck 2015) § 140b, para. 28.

[193] Thomas Dreier and Gernot Schulze, *Urheberrechtsgesetz: UrhG* (4th ed., C. H. Beck 2013) § 101 para. 15.

[194] Bundesregierung, "Gesetzentwurf der Bundesregierung Entwurf eines Gesetzes zur Verbesserung der Durchsetzung von Rechten des geistigen Eigentums" (2007) Drucksache 16/5048, http://dip21 .bundestag.de/dip21/btd/16/050/1605048.pdf, 39 ("(...) weil der Dritte, solange er nicht als Störer gemäß Absatz 1 in Anspruch genommen werden kann, letztlich als Unbeteiligter in Anspruch genommen wird. (...) Da Artikel 8 zur Frage der Kosten keine Regelung enthält, kann diese Lücke durch innerstaatliches Recht geschlossen werden").

[195] Ansgar Ohly, "Urheberrecht in der digitalen Welt – Brauchen wir neue Regelungen zum Urheberrecht und dessen Durchsetzung?" in Gregor Bachmann (ed.) *Verhandlungen des 70. Deutschen Juristentages* (C. H. Beck, 2014) F 109 (arguing that imposing costs on Internet access providers is unreasonable and that they should be reimbursed); Gerhard Spindler, "Zivilrechtliche Sperrverfügungen gegen Access Provider nach dem EuGH-Urteil 'UPC Telekabel'" [2014] GRUR 826, 832 (arguing that the costs of website blocking should be compensated); Matthias Leistner and Karina Grisse, "Sperrverfügungen gegen Access-Provider im Rahmen der Störerhaftung (Teil 2)" [2015] GRUR 105, 112ff. (arguing for reimbursement of costs and conditional injunctions); Franz Hofmann,

Moreover, arguably, the obligation to bear own compliance costs under German law is not necessarily a policy choice, but rather a consequence of a factual position of intermediaries. The German courts are developing obligations only in order to illustrate how to prevent "disturbance." The choice of measures is in a responsibility zone of an injunction addressee not because she "deserves" it, but because she is most of the time the only one to implement them. If the same acts can be carried out personally by the victim, the responsibility and thus also the cost equation might change. In *Kinderhochstuehle im Internet I.*, the Court hinted at this problem, when it said "it is not obvious why the defendant should take over the review of the trade mark infringements from the plaintiff, which can be carried out with equal effort personally by the plaintiff as a right holder."[196] This was a situation when the rightholders could do same things through a technical interface.

Another unique feature of the German system is the system of pretrial costs reimbursement. It is a direct consequence of the fact that the debt (obligation) of an injunction addressee is formed *before* he applies to the court to force compliance.[197] That is at the point when the "committal danger" (*Begehungsgefahr*),[198] the risk of occurrence of an undesired act, is established.[199] Injunction-addressees are thus

---

"Markenrechtliche Sperranordnungen gegen nicht verantwortliche Intermediäre" [2015] GRUR 123, 129 (arguing in favor of court oversight for website blocking); Stefan Maaßen and Volker Schoene, "Sperrungsverfügung gegen Access-Provider wegen Urheberrechtsverletzung?" [2011] GRUR-Prax 394, 396 (arguing in favor of court oversight for website blocking); For Finish authors – see Taina Pihlajarinne, Internetvälittäjä ja tekijänoikeuden loukkaus (Lakimiesliiton Kustannus, 2012) 51–61, 140–148 (in favor of costs reimbursement); Pekka Savola, "Proportionality of Website Blocking: Internet Connectivity Providers as Copyright Enforcers" (2014) 5(2) JIPITEC 116–138 (in favour of costs reimbursement).

[196] BGH *Kinderhochstuehle im Internet I.* (2010) I ZR 139/08, para. 43.

[197] This feature is immanent in the concept of a material claim as such and is closely connected with very coining of the term by Windscheid (Klaus Bacher, *Die Beeinträchtigungsgefahr als Voraussetzung für Unterlassungsklagen im Wettbewerbsrecht und in anderen Gebieten des Zivilrechts* (Centaurus-Verlagsgesellschaft Pfaffenweiler 1996) 64; Andreas von Tuhr, *Der Allgemeine Teil des Deutschen Bürgerlichen Rechts, Band I. Allgemeine Lehren und Personenrecht* (first published 1910, Duncker & Humblot 2013) 255; also very illustrative in this regard: BGH *Stiftparfüm* (2011) I ZR 57/09).

[198] When exactly is an obligation corresponding to an injunction formed depends on when the courts qualify certain circumstances as a "committal danger" (*Begehungsgefahr*). This moment can vary, depending on the type of an intermediary. See Thomas Sassenberg and Reto Mantz, *WLAN und Recht. Aufbau und Betrieb von Internet-Hotspots* (Erich Schmidt Verlag 2014) 179 (arguing that the case-law of the German Federal Supreme Court delays the point of formation of an injunctive claim until the person potentially subject to an enforcement obligation fails to react to the first cease and desist letter within a reasonable time. The authors point to cases of BGH *Autocomplete* (2013) VI ZR 269/12; BGH *RSS-Feed* (2012) VI ZR 144/11; BGH *Alone in the Dark* (2012) I ZR 18/11 and then more explicit case-law of lower courts, such as OLG Stuttgart (2013) 4 W 78/13 ("Die Störerhaftung beginnt daher nicht bereits mit dem Zugang einer Abmahnung, sondern erst, wenn er trotz Kenntniserlangung den rechtsverletzenden Inhalt nicht löscht bzw. sperrt. Eine Löschung eines beanstandeten Lichtbilds binnen weniger Stunden nach Eingang ist ausreichend") and OLG Frankfurt/M. (2013) 11 W 39/13.

[199] According to the German doctrine, this happens in two situations: (1) when there is a danger of repeated interference (*Wiederholungsgefahr*) – ordinary injunctions, or (2) when there is a

expect to comply without court interference. One of the consequences of such a setup is that the rightholders might request compensation of the pretrial costs.[200] As was shown in Section 9.4, this can lead to voluntary broadening of the standard set by the court.

9.7 DUTY TO REVIEW

In the previous parts, I have demonstrated how the German Federal Supreme Court gradually divorced the concept of injunctions from its historical underpinnings by bringing it closer to the categories of tort law. The Court re-purposed the instrument from an enquiry about whether someone is in a "position to provide help" to a tort-tasting analysis of what is "reasonable to expect" from an actor. As was mentioned earlier, the concept today de facto serves two roles. While it implements injunctions against noninfringers, it also supplements lack of proper accessory liability.

The adjudicated obligations still preserve their abstract form. As the sixth senate of the Court put it recently, "the choice from several effectively available assistance measures have to be left to the disturber."[201] This is why use of an unrestricted and effective interface can potentially serve as a substitute to own filtering obligations. The target is "disturbance" and its prevention, not personal actions. The "disturbance" does not entitle its victim to demand particular actions from the defendant. The resulting obligation is always defined by what the requested person can in effect do about the disturbance. The lack of access to previously operated website, for instance, can lead to narrowing of the duty to a simple effort to exercise influence.[202] Impossibility of any assistance leads to nullification of an obligation.[203] Any obligation is tight not with a person, but his factual possibility to act. The duty to review is therefore an obligation to influence the outcome, not a duty to

---

danger of first interference (*Erstbegehungsgefahr*) – quia timet injunctions/preemptive injunctions – see Otto Teplitzky, *Wettbewerbsrechtliche Ansprüche und Verfahren* (Carl Heymanns Verlag 2011) 32ff., 119ff.; Klaus Bacher, *Die Beeinträchtigungsgefahr als Voraussetzung für Unterlassungsklagen im Wettbewerbsrecht und in anderen Gebieten des Zivilrechts* (Centaurus-Verlagsgesellschaft Pfaffenweiler 1996); Julius von Staudinger (ed.), *Bürgerliches Gesetzbuch* (13th ed., Sellier-deGruyter 1993) § 1004.

[200] Klaus Bacher, *Die Beeinträchtigungsgefahr als Voraussetzung für Unterlassungsklagen im Wettbewerbsrecht und in anderen Gebieten des Zivilrechts* (Centaurus-Verlagsgesellschaft Pfaffenweiler 1996) 70ff. (discussing various legal consequences).

[201] BGH (2015) VI ZR 340/14, para. 40 ("die Auswahl unter mehreren tatsächlich möglichen Abhilfemaßnahmen dem Störer überlassen bleiben muss").

[202] BGH (2015) VI ZR 340/14, para. 39, 40 ("Es ist anerkannten Rechts, dass der Unterlassungs oder Beseitigungsschuldner zur Erfüllung der ihm obliegenden Verpflichtung erforderlichenfalls auf Dritte einzuwirken hat, wenn und soweit er auf diese – rechtlich oder tatsächlich – Einfluss nehmen kann").

[203] BGH (2015) VI ZR 340/14, para. 34; RG (1921) V 151/21, RGZ 103, 174 (rejected an injunction against an ex-owner who no longer exercised control over the property from which the disturbance originated).

act in a specific way. That could also explain why if intermediaries provide an equally effective interface at its "front door," the obligations to filter can completely vanish.

While BGH would probably tend to explain this rule as an outcome of proportionality assessment, it can be explained as something more fundamental. Consider the following analogy. If a ball is blown by wind or kicked by a third party onto someone else's land, is the legal harmony restored and legal obligation satisfied only by incurring an effort in returning the ball, or also by making the property available for the ball owner to collect it directly and at his own expense? The submission interface case-law suggests that restoration of legal harmony occurs already with the handing over of the control over one's situation.

However, this flexibility comes at the cost. The injunctions are only generally worded as prohibiting the defendant to "*allow* for communication to the public" by third parties. The reasoning of the decisions then serves the goal to clarify approximately what kind of measures are seen as reasonable. The judicial discussion is never conclusive, however. This is part of its intentional efforts to capture also follow-on technological developments which could make the orders obsolete or less effective.[204] The question of whether the operator of the platform complied with the injunctions depends, according to German procedural law, on the culpable breach of such an order, something that is determined in the enforcement proceedings.[205] If there is no such culpable breach, there is also no legally enforceable consequence for the platform operator.

In addition, what makes the duty so difficult to distinguish from its tortious cousin is the general understanding of a remedy under civil law (*Anspruch*). In common law, where equitably duties arise with adjudication, the situation is, arguably, clearer. Pre-grant, there is strictly speaking no obligation to act, only a possibility to request such action. This means that prior to judicial involvement, the type of behavior that is legally owed by innocent third parties to the rightholders is only determined by one source – the tortious duties. In civil law, on the other hand, obligations stemming from "disturbance liability" exist even before the judges get involved. They are owed to rightholders in much a same way as tortious duty of care. And since, the Court makes no distinction on the side of prelitigation or postlitigation compliance costs, they are hard to distinguish.

The other distinguishing feature is that disrespecting them doesn't deliver the injured any damages, just a title to sue for an injunction. In unfair competition law, the court has already completed the full transition and the principles underlying injunctions against noninfringers, such as standards of care, have been used to build

---

[204] BGH (2013) I ZR 79/12, para. 21; BGH *Störerhaftung des Access-Providers* (2016) I ZR 174/14, para. 14; BGH (2015) VI ZR 340/14, para. 40.

[205] Section 890 of the German Civil Code of Procedure (ZPO); BVerfG (2007) NJW-RR 860, 861.

a new form of secondary tortious liability incorporating the negligence rule.[206] The newest case-law in this area thus provides an interesting case study into a question whether "duty to review" and "tortious duty of care" arise with same circumstances.

Originally, the idea of a tortious duty of care that protects the absolute rights beyond their immediate scope of protection was developed by the German courts in 1902, in order to delimit tortious negligent (wrongful) omissions.[207] As the Court reiterated in its recent ruling, tortious duty of care is much broader, encompassing also other duties such as duty to intervene or to control.[208] "The tortious duty of care in unfair competition law manifests itself as a duty to review in the context of liability of e-commerce operators for third-party infringing content."[209] The little case-law that we have since the transition, however, demonstrates that the building blocks such as causality or duty of care now attract closer scrutiny of judges than it used to be the case with duty to review.[210] In some scenarios, the German Federal Supreme Court even decided to discontinue its earlier assessment as to the content of the required duties.[211]

Most of the German scholars demand some form of negligence based secondary liability.[212] At the same time, however, they broadly support existing case-law on "disturbance liability."[213] It is not clear how the German Federal Supreme Court will react to this. German legal scholarship is unusually discursive. The law, more than elsewhere, develops out of a discussion between scholars, practitioners, and judges.[214] Unlike in many other countries, the courts actively listen the voices of the academics.

Even if the court follows its unfair competition case-law, this doesn't mean that injunctions against intermediaries will vanish from German IP law. Unless the court wants to risk overbroad duty of care, a gap in transposition of the Union law is likely to arise.[215] After tort law reclaims part of its (natural) territory, such injunctions will serve

---

[206] BGH *Haftung für Hyperlink* (2015) I ZR 74/14.

[207] RG (1902) VI 208/02, RGZ 52, 373; RG (1903) VI 349/02, RGZ 54, 53 – see Christian von Bar, *Verkehrspflichten richterliche Gefahrsteuerungsgebote im deutschen Deliktsrecht* (Heymann 1980) 3–4.

[208] BGH *Geschäftsführerhaftung* (2014) I ZR 242/12, para. 21.

[209] Ibid., para. 21.   [210] Ibid., paras. 34–37.

[211] Ibid., para. 15 (relaxing the duties of care for the executive director over her company's actions).

[212] Juristentagung, "Beschlüsse des 70. Deutschen Juristentages Hannover" (2014), www.djt.de/fileadmin/downloads/70/djt-70-Beschluesse_141202.pdf, 29 (at German congress of lawyers, 37 voted in favor and only 3 against gross-negligence based liability of active intermediaries).

[213] Ibid., 29 (at German congress of lawyers, 34 voted in favor and only 4 against the proposition that the disturbance liability should remain governed by BGH's doctrine).

[214] The German Council of Science and Humanities, "Prospects of Legal Scholarship in Germany Current Situation, Analyses, Recommendations" (October 2013) 31, www.wissenschaftsrat.de/download/archiv/2558–12_engl.pdf.

[215] Jan Nordemann, "Haftung von Providern im Urheberrecht – Der aktuelle Stand nach dem EuGH-Urteil v. 12. 7. 2011 – C-324/09 – L'Oréal/eBay" [2011] GRUR 977, 981; Christopher Czychowski and Jan Nordemann, "Grenzenloses Internet – entgrenzte Haftung?" [2013] GRUR 986, 989; Franz

more limited area of application; the area that mostly concerns remote providers. The old injunctive "duties of review," now relieved of serving partially "tortious agenda," could be again re-purposed to fill the gap, or the court can return to origins of injunctive protection under Section 1004 BGB. Alternatively, the legislator could step in.

In the German literature, one can already find voices calling for a divorce of *Störerhaftung* doctrine from the implementation of Article 8(3) of the InfoSoc Directive and of Article 11(III) of the Enforcement Directive. Most notably, Nordemann, Czychowski,[216] and Hofmann[217] argue that the *Störerhaftung* doctrine is inappropriate to give full effect to Union law. In consonance with the proposal of this work, they seek solutions that would stress the innocent character of the actions of the (remote) intermediaries and assistance character of their obligations.[218] Hofmann suggests[219] emancipating the German implementation from the *Störerhaftung* doctrine by postulating a separate claim, which would be modeled on the right to third-party information. He recommends extending the legal construct behind the provisions § 101(9) of the German Copyright Act and § 19(9) of the German Trademark Act to cover any type of assistance. This proposal is sensible because the mentioned provisions of German law already include several features advocated in this work, namely, judicial control over a claim-grant,[220] compensation of the respondent's costs and safeguards of the interests of third parties, including their human rights.

Hofmann, "Markenrechtliche Sperranordnungen gegen nicht verantwortliche Intermediäre" [2015] GRUR 123, 128.

[216] Jan Nordemann, "Haftung von Providern im Urheberrecht – Der aktuelle Stand nach dem EuGH-Urteil v. 12. 7. 2011 – C-324/09 – L'Oréal/eBay" [2011] GRUR 977, 981; Christopher Czychowski and Jan Nordemann, "Grenzenloses Internet – entgrenzte Haftung?" [2013] GRUR 986, 989.

[217] Franz Hofmann, "Markenrechtliche Sperranordnungen gegen nicht verantwortliche Intermediäre" [2015] GRUR 123, 128.

[218] Christopher Czychowski and Jan Nordemann, "Grenzenloses Internet – entgrenzte Haftung?" [2013] GRUR 986, 990 ("Auch begrifflich scheint der Rückgriff auf die deutsche 'Störer'-Haftung neben der Sache zu liegen. Die Haftung wird europarechtlich nicht wegen einer 'Störung' angeordnet, sondern wegen Hilfeleistungspflichten"); Jan Nordemann, "Haftung von Providern im Urheberrecht – Der aktuelle Stand nach dem EuGH-Urteil v. 12. 7. 2011 – C-324/09 – L'Oréal/eBay" [2011] GRUR 977, 981 ("Dieses Haftungssystem gewährt Unterlassungsansprüche gegen Internetprovider als Vermittler von Urheberrechtsverletzungen unabhängig von solchen Verantwortlichkeitserwägungen als 'Hilfeleistung eines Unschuldigen'"); Franz Hofmann, "Markenrechtliche Sperranordnungen gegen nicht verantwortliche Intermediäre" [2015] GRUR 123, 127 ("Ähnlich wie im englischen Recht ('not liable'), geht es gerade nicht um eine deliktische (Verursachungs-)Haftung wegen einer Rechtsverletzung. Kurzum: Eine 'Störung' ist nicht das Kriterium. In diesem Sinne hat auch der Zugangsprovider mit der Rechtsverletzung nichts zu tun").

[219] Franz Hofmann, "Markenrechtliche Sperranordnungen gegen nicht verantwortliche Intermediäre" [2015] GRUR 123, 128.

[220] The debate about the constitutional necessity of court oversight in Germany was especially heated in the context of the right to third-party information – see Kai Welp, *Die Auskunftspflicht von Access-Providern nach dem Urheberrechtsgesetz* (C. H. Beck 2009) 334ff. (describing the German discussion with respect to the claim for information and the judicial control that surrounded the implementation of the Enforcement Directive).

Recently, at German lawyer's congress (*Juristentagung*), great majority of specialists favored a specific legal provision for judge-supervised website blocking and more limited obligations of WiFi operators.[221]

---

[221] Juristentagung, "Beschlüsse des 70.Deutschen Juristentages Hannover" (2014), www.djt.de/fileadmin/ downloads/70/djt_70_Beschluesse_141202.pdf, pp. 29–30.

10

Injunctions in Common Law

England

The Romans also influenced common law. Immediately after 1066, common law was the sole source of law. With time, however, common law started to be too rigid and inflexible to deliver justice in some cases.[1] Since the King could still overturn the decisions, individuals started to petition him for his mercy. The office that assisted the King was called the Chancery and basically functioned as a "keeper of the King's Conscience."[2]

By the time of King Edward III, the Chancery had assumed a definite and separate character as a court. The petitions were already addressed directly to King's Lord Chancellor.[3] With this new branch of the judiciary, the influence of Roman law also increased because for several hundred years, practically all the Chancellors were "churchmen" or "ecclesiastics," who were trained in the civil law system used in ecclesiastical courts.[4] According to Bryce, "system of Equity, built up by the Chancellors, the earlier among them ecclesiastics, takes not only its name but its guiding and formative principles, and many of its positive rules, from the Roman acquitas, which was in substance identical with the Law of Nature and the ius gentium."[5] In his reading, although the Chancellors and Masters of the Rolls did not talk much about Nature or about ius gentium and referred rather to "the law of God and to Reason," "the ideas were Roman, drawn either from the Canon Law or directly from the Digest and the Institutes, and they were applied to English facts in a manner not dissimilar from that of the Roman jurists."[6]

This aspect of their education also gave them a less conformist view of the law, much needed in their task as corrective courts of justice. Naturally, a rivalry between

---

[1] David Wright, *Remedies* (Federation Press 2010) 4.
[2] Edward D. Re, "The Roman Contribution to the Common Law" (1961) 29 Fordham Law Review 447, 479 (more on the history of how this happened).
[3] Ibid., 479.
[4] Ibid., 479; Thomas E. Scrutton, *The Influence of the Roman Law on the Law of England* (Cambridge University Press 1885) 153.
[5] James Bryce, *Studies in History and Jurisprudence* (Oxford University Press 1901) 599–600.
[6] Ibid.

the court of common law and the court of equity soon developed. Although equity eventually prevailed, when Sir Francis Bacon became Lord Chancellor, he immediately made a number of gestures to the common law judges.[7] Soon, the principle would be established that equitable remedies, such as injunctions, would be applied only if the remedies of common law were inadequate.[8]

Like early Roman law, early common law provided only for compensation.[9] The notion of prevention was developed only later. The Chancellor who made his greatest practical contribution by modernizing the law through set of specific remedies such as injunctive relief,[10] claimed to have an inherent jurisdiction to do so. Until 1854, the Court of Chancery was the only court which had the power to grant injunctions.[11] After this date, the law conferred this jurisdiction also upon the common law courts.[12] The power to grant so-called common law injunctions, limited to cases of "breach of contract or other injury,"[13] exists until today,[14] but equitable injunctions are by far the most prevalent.[15]

10.1 COURT'S POWERS

In the late nineteenth century, the courts of common law and the courts of equity in the United Kingdom were fused into a single jurisdiction by the Supreme Judicature Act 1875. The Act, however, did *not* fuse the sources of law, equity, and common law, but only vested their administration in the hands of the same judges.[16] The legal principles thus remained distinct. Similarly, the Act did *not* grant any new powers to issue injunctions to the newly established High Court of Justice, but only recognized that it can exercise the existing powers of previous courts.[17]

---

7   David Wright, *Remedies* (Federation Press 2010) 4.   8   Ibid.
9   Ibid., 183–184; Edward D. Re, "The Roman Contribution to the Common Law" (1961) 29 Fordham Law Review 447, 481.
10   Edward D. Re, "The Roman Contribution to the Common Law" (1961) 29 Fordham Law Review 447, 481.
11   *Cartier International AG & Ors v. British Sky Broadcasting Ltd & Ors* [2014] EWHC 3354 (Ch) [94].
12   Section 79 provided, "In all cases of breach of contract or other injury, where the party injured is entitled to maintain and has brought an action, he may, in like case and manner as herein before provided with respect to mandamus, claim a writ of injunction against repetition or continuance of such breach of contract or injury of a like kind, arising out of the same contract, or relating to the same property or right; and he may also in the same action include a claim for damages or other redress."
13   See more *Beddow v. Beddow* [1878] 9 Ch. D. 89; with clarifications Ian Spry, *Equitable Remedies* (9th ed., Sweet & Maxwell 2013) 334.
14   Ian Spry, *Equitable Remedies* (9th ed., Sweet & Maxwell 2013) 342–345; David Wright, *Remedies* (Federation Press, 2010) 184.
15   David Wright, *Remedies* (Federation Press 2010) 184.
16   Ibid., 5; Ian Spry, *Equitable Remedies* (9th ed., Sweet & Maxwell 2013) 339; this triggered lively debate about the future of the two when some judges started assuming that common law and equity became one – see the influential critique of this "fusion fallacy" by Heydon Meagher and others, *Doctrines and Remedies* (4th ed., Butterworths 2002).
17   This was considered in the following cases: *North London Railway Co v. Great Northern Railway Co* [1883] 11 QBD 30, at 36–37 ("if no court had the power of issuing an injunction before the Judicature

Section 25(8) of the Supreme Judicature Act 1875 provided that "an injunction may be granted (. . .) by an interlocutory order in all cases in which it shall appear to the court to be *just or convenient* that such order shall be made." This Section was later replaced by other similar acts in the United Kingdom and elsewhere,[18] but the wording changed very little.[19] Today, Section 37 of the Senior Courts Act 1981 is decisive in the United Kingdom. It reads as follows:

(1) The High Court may by order (whether interlocutory or final) grant an injunction or appoint a receiver in all cases in which it appears to the court to be just and convenient to do so.

(2) Any such order may be made either unconditionally or on such terms and conditions as the court thinks just.

The formula of "just and convenient," composed of two mutually nonexclusive requirements,[20] is omnipresent in the common law countries. It is used by the courts of Ireland,[21] Australia,[22] and Canada.[23] It is used for preliminary, as well as

Act, no part of the High Court has power to issue such an injunction now"); *Gouriet v. Union of Post Office Workers* [1978] A.C. 435; *The Siskina* [1979] AC 210; *Castanho v. Brown & Root (UK) Ltd* [1981] AC 557; *British Airways Board v. Laker Airways Ltd* [1985] AC 58; *South Carolina Insurance Co Ltd v. Assurantie Maatschappij De Zeven Provincien NV* [1987] AC 24; *Pickering v. Liverpool Daily Post* [1991] 2 AC 370; *Kirklees MBC v. Wickes Building Supplies Ltd* [1993] AC 227; *Channel Tunnel Group Ltd v. Balfour Beatty Construction Ltd* [1993] AC 334; *Mercedes-Benz AG v. Leiduck* [1996] AC 284; *Fourie v. Le Roux* [2007] UKHL 1, [2007] 1 WLR 320; *Tasarruf Mevduati Sigorta Fonu v. Merrill Lynch Bank & Trust Company* [2011] UKPC 17, [2012] 1 WLR 1721; *Ust-Kamenogorsk Hydropower Plant JSC v. AES Ust-Kamenogorsk Hydropower Plant LLP* [2013] UKSC 35, [2013] 1 WLR 1889; *Australian Broadcasting Corporation v. Lenah Game Meats Pty Ltd* [2001] HCA 63 (deciding on Australian Section 11 of the Supreme Court Civil Procedure Act 1932 (Tas), which is equivalent of Section 25(8) of the English Supreme Judicature Act 1875, the court held that this section did not confer on the court power to make an order); *Holmes v. Millage* [1893] 1 Q.B. 551; *Cartier International AG & Ors v. British Sky Broadcasting Ltd & Ors* [2014] EWHC 3354 (Ch) [92], [94]; *Broadmoor Special Hospital Authority v. Robinson* [2000] QB 775 at 20.

18 The Supreme Court of Judicature Act (Ireland) 1877; the Judicature (Northern Ireland) Act 1978; the Judicature Act (New Zeland) 1908; the Supreme Court Civil Procedure Act 1932 (Tas); The Supreme Court Act 1986 (Vic); Judicature Act 2000 (Canada); Law and Equity Act 1996 (British Columbia), etc.

19 The only clarification concerned the availability of both permanent and preliminary injunctions.

20 *Beddow v. Beddow* [1878] 9 Ch. D. 89 ("in ascertaining what is "just" you must have regard to what is convenient"); also Ian Spry, *Equitable Remedies* (9th ed., Sweet & Maxwell 2013) 341.

21 *EMI Records [Ireland] Ltd v. Eircom PLC* [2009] IEHC 411 (citing the Supreme Judicature Act of 1875).

22 Section 11 of the Supreme Court Civil Procedure Act 1932 (Tas) gives the Tasmanian Supreme Court the power to issue an interlocutory injunction "in all cases in which it shall appear to the Court or judge to be just and convenient"; applied in *Australian Broadcasting Corporation v. Lenah Game Meats Pty Ltd* [2001] HCA 63.

23 *Equustek Solutions Inc. v. Jack* [2014] BCSC 1063 (on an injunction against a nonparty, another term for an innocent third party, which is not named as a defendant); Norwich Pharmacal has been adopted as part of the law in Canada by decisions: *Kenney v. Loewen* [1999], 64 BCLR (3d) 346, 1999, *Procon Mining and Tunnelling Ltd. et al. v. McNeil, Bonnar et al.* [2007] BCSC 454 and *Pierce v. Canjex Publishing Ltd.* [2011] BCSC 1503; *GEA Group AG v. Flex-N-Gate Corporation* [2009] ONCA 619

permanent injunctions. So-called *quia timet* injunctions, the injunctions granted before the completion of any wrongful acts or occurrence of their consequences,[24] can take both forms. Common law also distinguishes between mandatory and prohibitory injunctions. While a mandatory injunction commands the defendant to carry out a specific act, a prohibitory injunction restrains him from doing something. Injunctions against (innocent) intermediaries, such as identity disclosures and website blocking injunctions, are types of such mandatory injunctions, along with reverse publicity orders or freezing orders.[25]

The powers of the courts with equitable jurisdiction to grant injunctions are, subject to relevant statutory restrictions, unlimited.[26] Lord Goff expressed this in one of the House of Lords decisions as follows:

> I am reluctant to accept the proposition that the power of the court to grant injunctions is restricted to certain exclusive categories. That power is unfettered by statute; and it is impossible for us now to foresee every circumstance in which it may be thought right to make the remedy available.[27]

This does not mean that the judges are absolutely free of any restrains. The injunctions are granted only if they accord with the principles of equity, since equity is their ultimate source. Such principles embodied in numerous doctrines and practice, limit the *discretion* of judges.[28] Sir George Jessel once explained this aspect noting that: "In my opinion, having regard to these two Acts of Parliament, I have unlimited power to grant an injunction in any case where it would be right or just to do so: and what is right or just must be decided, not by the caprice of the Judge, but according to sufficient legal reasons or on settled legal principles."[29]

Even the principles, however, are not carved in stone and thus may change over time.[30] Lord Nicholls very clearly conveyed this principle – later confirmed by the

---

(establishing a right to preaction discovery of nonparties); *Glaxo Wellcome plc v. MNR* [1998] FCJ No. 874, [1998] 4 F.C. 439 (C.A.); *Alberta (Treasury Branches) v. Leahy* [2000] A.J. No. 993, 270 A.R. 1 (Q.B.), leave to appeal to SCC refused [2002] SCCA No. 235; *Isofoton SA v. Toronto Dominion Bank* [2007] 85 O.R. (3d) 780, [2007] O.J. No. 1701 (SCJ); *BMG Canada Inc. v. Doe*, 2005 FCA 193.

[24] David Wright, *Remedies* (Federation Press 2010) 188.

[25] Jaani Riordan, *The Liability of Internet Intermediaries* (Oxford, 2016) 74, para. 4.24; *Cartier International AG & Ors v. British Sky Broadcasting Ltd & Ors* [2014] EWHC 3354 (Ch) [107] (noting that publicity order against the noninfringer is a form of mandatory injunction); *Customs and Exercise Commissioners v. Barclays plc* [2007] UKHL 28.

[26] Ian Spry, *Equitable Remedies* (9th ed., Sweet & Maxwell 2013) 342.

[27] Lord Goff in House of Lords decision *South Carolina Insurance Co v. Assurantie Maatshappij De Zeven Provincien NV* [1987] A.C. 24 at 25, 44–45.

[28] Ian Spry, *Equitable Remedies* (9th ed., Sweet & Maxwell 2013) 342.

[29] *Beddow v. Beddow* [1878] 9 Ch. D. 89 at 93.

[30] Ibid., 89 ("It is to be remembered that the jurisdiction of the Court of Chancery to grant injunctions was formerly limited; it was limited by the practice of different Chancellors. The jurisdiction was never extended in modern times beyond what was warranted by the authorities; and in course of time various vexatious and inconvenient restrictions were adopted").

House of Lords[31] – in *Mercedes-Benz AG v. Leiduck* where he said that the situations in which injunctions may be granted are not "set in stone for all time."[32] To the contrary, "[a]s circumstances in the world change, so must the situations in which the courts may properly exercise their jurisdiction to grant injunctions. The exercise of the jurisdiction must be principled, but the criterion is injustice. Injustice is to be viewed and decided in the light of today's conditions and standards, not those of yester-year."[33]

The discretion of judges to issue equitable injunctions is usually said to be based on the following principles:[34] (1) an injunction must protect legal or equitable right, (2) common law remedies must be inadequate, and (3) there must be no discretionary considerations against the award. However, the principle (1) is currently in doubt and its broad construction might as well be read as its nonexistence.[35] In cases where specific legislation has been passed to provide for statutory remedies, the general equitable jurisdiction will be prevented from applying *only* if the legislator intended to exclude it, either expressly or by implication. Spry writes that "it is only very rare occasions that the conferring of special statutory remedies or the provision of penalties should be construed as abrogating or curtailing rights to injunctive and other such relief that otherwise exist on the application of general equitable principles."[36]

This is very relevant even today in two ways. The UK legislator did not see the need to implement Article 11(III) of the Enforcement Directive in the national law.[37] This forced Justice Arnold to consider whether such injunctions could be based in the equitable protective jurisdiction.[38] One of the hurdles could have been whether

---

[31] *Ashworth Hospital Authority v. MGN Ltd* [2002] HRLR 41 House of Lords [57].

[32] *Mercedes-Benz AG v. Leiduck* [1996] A.C. 284 at 308.   [33] Ibid.

[34] Ian Spry, *Equitable Remedies* (9th ed., Sweet & Maxwell 2013) 342–343, 396–407; David Wright, *Remedies* (Federation Press 2010) 190.

[35] In the Cartier decision of Arnold J (*Cartier International AG & Ors v. British Sky Broadcasting Ltd & Ors* [2014] EWHC 3354 (Ch), para. 106), the underlying equitable right is seen in a parallel equitable duty to provide assistance that is modeled on Norwich jurisdiction. However, Arnold J seems generally willing to confine to the condition of an underlying equitable right if necessary. It seems that he generally views the precondition as not applicable, at least at the case at hand (see paras. 104–106). This also corresponds to Kitchin LJ's reading of the judgment which he supported (*Cartier International AG & Ors v. British Sky Broadcasting Ltd & Ors* [2016] EWCA Civ 658 [55–56]).

[36] Ian Spry, *Equitable Remedies* (9th ed., Sweet & Maxwell 2013) 378; it must be clarified, however, that this is stated in the context of primary rights that would exist even in absence of statutory provisions.

[37] Patent Office, "The UK Implementation of the Directive on the Enforcement of Intellectual Property Rights" (2005) ("No action is required. The jurisdiction of the High Court to grant injunctions is derived from Section 37(1) of the Supreme Court Act 1981. It may do so on such terms and conditions as it thinks fit (Section 37(2))").

[38] *L'Oreal SA & Ors v. EBay International AG & Ors* [2009] EWHC 1094 (Ch) [454] (Union-conform interpretation); *Cartier International AG & Ors v. British Sky Broadcasting Ltd & Ors* [2014] EWHC 3354 (Ch) [121–132] (Union-conform interpretation).

the absence remedies in the UK Trade Mark Act forecloses equitable jurisdiction. Justice Arnold rejected this argument; and so did the Court of Appeals.[39]

The statutory curtailing of court's powers could be also relevant in the copyright context, where, in an effort to implement Article 8(3) of the InfoSoc Directive, the Parliament eventually inserted following new Sections 97A (copyright) and also 191JA (performer's right) into the Copyright, Designs, and Patents Act 1988 (CDPA):

> (1) The High Court (in Scotland, the Court of Session) shall have power to grant an injunction against a service provider, where that service provider has actual knowledge of another person using their service to infringe [copyright/a performer's right]. (2) In determining whether a service provider has actual knowledge for the purpose of this section, a court shall take into account (. . .).[40]

Looking at the transposition, the open question is whether the courts are permitted to grant injunctions against "service providers," on the basis of equity, even when some of the conditions aren't met. In my view, the answer is very likely to be "yes" because the implementation itself is a mere declaration of powers.

10.2 ASSISTING BY INFORMATION DISCLOSURE

Prior to 1973, the information disclosure could be requested only from those individuals against whom an independent cause of action could be reasonably maintained. In particular, it could not have been requested of those who are in a position of a mere witness. The reason behind the rule was that "[i]t would be intolerable if an innocent person – without any interest in a case – were to be subjected to an action in Chancery simply to get papers or information out of him. The only permissible course is to issue a subpoena for him to come as a witness or to produce the documents to the court."[41] Thus an innocent third party could be requested to

---

[39] *Cartier International AG & Ors v. British Sky Broadcasting Ltd & Ors* [2014] EWHC 3354 (Ch) [131] ("there is nothing inconsistent between granting an injunction against intermediaries under section 37(1) and the provisions of the 1994 Act, just as there is nothing inconsistent between the third sentence of Article 11 and the Trade Marks Directive"); *Cartier International AG & Ors v. British Sky Broadcasting Ltd & Ors* [2016] EWCA Civ 658 (confirming).

[40] The UK government, was at first, of the opinion that there is no need to implement Article 8(3) of the InfoSoc Directive. Only after obtaining the results of consultation did it change its mind – see Patent Office, "Consultation on UK Implementation of Directive 2001/29/EC on Copyright and Related Rights in the Information Society: Analysis of Responses and Government Conclusions" (2003), www .patent.gov.uk/about/consultations/responses/copydirect/index.htm ("On further consideration, the Government has concluded that, in order to avoid uncertainty, Article 8.3 should be specifically implemented in UK law, by way of provisions in Parts I & II of the CDPA enabling the High Court (or Court of Session in Scotland) to grant injunctions against service providers, where the latter have actual knowledge of a third party using the service to infringe rights").

[41] *Norwich Pharmacal Co v. Customs & Excise Commissioners* [1974] AC 133 at 139 (Lord Denning); Jaani Riordan, *The Liability of Internet Intermediaries* (Oxford, 2016) 72, para. 4.15.

deliver evidence, but only in a role of a witness, after the main proceedings against a wrongdoer were initiated. This case-law thus did not prevent, but only delayed the disclosure.[42]

Probably the first case which recognized the possibility to issue orders *directly* against innocent third parties was *Upmann v. Elkan*,[43] from 1871. In this case, the Chancery court decided that a forwarding agent who was unknowingly forwarding his customers' trademark-infringing case of cigars may be ordered to remove the signs from the goods and provide information about the identity of the consignors. Lord Romilly MR explained that this equitable duty arises from the misfortune of his having a dishonest correspondent. In his view, "[i]t is his duty to know this and if he receives notice that [the goods] bear a fraudulent imitation of another man's brand, he ought to ascertain this as speedily as possible after such notice, and to take the proper and necessary steps to prevent their being disposed of in that state."[44] The Court in this case did not address the issue of under what circumstances the freight forwarder could himself become liable for the tortious acts of his customer. Lord Romilly MR, however, clarified that he "does not look on [Defendants] as guilty persons." More importantly, he explained that:

> It does not, in my opinion, make any difference whether the goods are sent to a person who does not deal in the article consigned, and whose duty is simply to distribute the goods to other persons, or whether the goods are sent to him as consignee for his own purposes. *In either case they are sent to the dock to be at his disposal, and without his signature the goods cannot be disposed of.*[45]

This would suggest that the relief is not triggered by the conduct, but the possibility of an innocent third party to prevent further circulation of infringing goods. In the following case, *Orr v. Diaper*,[46] the question was whether the holder of a trademark for a type of packaging for sewing cotton could require a shipper to disclose the identity of the senders and receivers of allegedly infringing goods that the shipper was transporting. The rightholder was clear about the fact that he did not intend to include the shipper in the follow-on suit and that he did not suggest any liability on the shipper's side.[47]

The later case-law speculated about the actual holding and the context in which it was given. It was argued that the judgment is based on the assumption that the defendants weren't mere witnesses and that they could themselves have been sued.[48]

---

[42] Jaani Riordan, *The Liability of Internet Intermediaries* (Oxford, 2016) 72, para. 4.15.

[43] *Upmann v. Elkan* [1871] L.R. 12 Eq. 140, 7 Ch App 130 at 145 ("it is his duty at once to give all the information required, and to undertake that the goods shall not be removed or dealt with until the spurious brand has been removed, and to offer to give all facilities to the person injured for that purpose").

[44] *Upmann v. Elkan* [1871] L.R. 12 Eq. 140, 7 Ch App 130 at 146–147.   [45] Ibid., 146 (emphasis mine).

[46] *Orr v. Diaper* [1876] 4 Ch. D. 92.   [47] *Orr v. Diaper* [1876] 4 Ch. D. 92 at 94–95.

[48] *Norwich Pharmacal Co v. Customs & Excise Commissioners* [1974] AC 133 [61] (Viscount Dilhorne).

Furthermore, it was argued that it is the *possession* of goods that could explain both cases. According to Buckley LJ, the principle upheld in both cases is rather following:

> The man having the goods in his possession or control must not aid the infringement by letting the goods get into the hands of those who may use them or deal with them in a way which will invade the proprietor's rights. Even though by doing so he might not himself infringe the patent or trade mark, he would be in dereliction of his duty to the proprietor. This duty is one which will, if necessary, be enforced in equity by way of injunction (...) The man having possession or control may also be under a duty to give information in relation to the goods to the proprietor of the patent or mark.[49]

In 1973, the case-law was re-defined. The House of Lords handed down its famous *Norwich Pharmacal v. Customs & Excise Commissioners* decision.[50] The case involved a patent holder whose patented chemical compound was imported into the United Kingdom without his permission. He tried to discover the identity of the importers, but without success. He therefore decided to request their identity from the Customs, to whom every importer is legally obliged to report this information. The Customs were not infringers or wrongdoers themselves.[51]

Lord Kilbrandon was probably the most hesitant to rely on the former two cases as authorities. He even went as far as to say that "to erect on them a structure of principles which should guide a modern court in the administration of justice seems to me to be building on quicksands."[52] Other judges also noted several ambiguities concerning the said cases.

The House of Lords eventually unanimously accepted the possibility to demand identity disclosures from the Customs.[53] One of the common arguments relied on was that it would be illogical or irrational to limit the right to discovery only to wrongdoers[54] and in some cases it could lead to a denial of justice.[55] The main holdings often cited and closely analyzed in the case-law are embodied in the following passage written by Lord Reid:

> They [previous cases] seem to me to point to a very reasonable principle that if through no fault of his own a person gets mixed up in the tortious acts of others so as to facilitate their wrong-doing he may incur no personal liability but he comes under a duty to assist the person who has been wronged by giving him full information

---

49 Ibid., [61] (Viscount Dilhorne).   50 Ibid.
51 Ibid., [53], [91] (neither wrongdoers, nor infringers); In the follow-on lawsuit, the importer was found to be jointly liable in tort law – see *Morton Norwich Products v. Intercen* [1978] RPC 501.
52 *Norwich Pharmacal Co v. Customs & Excise Commissioners* [1974] AC 133 [106].
53 Another consideration was whether there is a statutory prohibition of such disclosure or other policy reasons to rule against it. None were found.
54 *Norwich Pharmacal Co v. Customs & Excise Commissioners* [1974] AC 133, Lord Cross [95], [97] and Lord Reid [13].
55 *Norwich Pharmacal Co v. Customs & Excise Commissioners* [1974] AC 133, Lord Reid [12], [15], [18], Lord Morris [28], [31], [37], [42], Viscount Dilhorne [87] and Lord Kilbrandon [110], [114].

and disclosing the identity of the wrongdoers. I do not think that it matters whether he became so mixed up by voluntary action on his part or because it was his duty to do what he did. It may be that if this causes him expense the person seeking the information ought to reimburse him. But justice requires that he should co-operate in righting the wrong if he unwittingly facilitated its perpetration.[56]

This "Norwich holding" is a turning point. The principle that independent action of disclosure can be sought only against the alleged wrongdoer was challenged, however, without completely erasing the witness rule. A new threshold for an independent action against an innocent third party became the extent of its "involvement" in the transactions which distinguishes it from a mere witness. As Viscount Dilhorne put it:

Someone involved in the transaction is not a mere witness. If he could be sued, even though there be no intention of suing him, he is not a mere witness. (. . .) it matters not that the involvement or participation was innocent and in ignorance of the wrongdoing. Are the Respondents to be regarded as so involved in this case? I think the answer is yes. They were not, it is true, involved of their own volition. They were involved in the performance of their statutory duty. (. . .) I do not see how it can be said that they were not involved in the importation of this chemical.[57]

Thus the consideration of involvement has a filtering function. It is meant to prevent the overburdening of innocent spectators. It most certainly isn't any test of causality, volition, knowledge, or intent. This requirement could be said to echo *Upmann v. Elkan's* "innocently mixed up with the transaction."[58]

Over the years, considerable case-law has developed[59] and *Norwich Pharmacal* has became an often cited authority in support of various orders against innocent third parties, not only in the United Kingdom, but the entire common law world. The newly adopted measures took the form of various disclosures against Internet access

---

[56] Ibid., [12].   [57] Ibid., [75].   [58] Ibid., [12], [95], [111], [115].

[59] *Interbrew SA v. Financial Times Ltd* [2002] WL 237064 Court of Appeal (on disclosure of journalistic sources in the context of breach of confidence – as to disclosure, it was found to infringe upon Art. 10 of the Convention – *Financial Times Ltd and Others v. The United Kingdom*, App no. 821/03 (ECHR, 15 December 2009)); *Jade Engineering (Coventry) Ltd v. Antiference Window Systems Ltd* [1996] FSR 461 Chancery Division; *Microsoft Corp v. Plato Technology Ltd* [1999] FSR 834 Chancery Division; *Golden Eye (International) Ltd & Anor v. Telefónica UK Ltd* [2012] EWHC 723 (Ch); *Golden Eye (International) Ltd & Ors v. Telefónica UK Litd & Anor* [2012] EWCA Civ 1740; *JSC BTA Bank v. Ablyazov & 16 Ors* [2014] EWHC 2019 (Comm); *Totalise Plc v. Motley Fool Ltd* [2002] 1 W.L.R. 1233; *L'Oreal SA v. eBay International AG* [2009] RPC 21 Chancery Division; *Samsung Electronics (UK) Ltd v. Apple Inc* [2012] EWCA Civ 1339; *CHC Software Care v. Hopkins & Wood* [1993] FSR 241 Chancery Division; *Media CAT Ltd v. Adams* [2011] WL 291789 Patents County Court; *Ashworth Hospital Authority v. MGN Ltd* [2002] HRLR 41 House of Lords; *British Steel Corporation v. Granada Television Ltd* [1981] A.C. 1096 House of Lords; *Rugby Football Union v. Viagogo Ltd* [2013] EMLR 25 Supreme Court; *British Telecommunications Plc & Ors v. One In A Million Ltd & Ors* [1998] EWCA Civ 1272.

providers,[60] discussion forums,[61] newspapers or other media,[62] trading platforms[63] and banks.[64] It was heralded as "opening a new chapter in the law"[65] and an "exceptional jurisdiction,"[66] but not necessarily one of last resort.[67] The House of Lords and later the Supreme Court clarified the decision on several other occasions.[68] In *Ashworth*, Lord Woolf CJ summarized the governing principles as follows: "The Norwich Pharmacal case clearly establishes that where a person, albeit innocently, and without incurring any personal liability, becomes involved in a wrongful act of another, that person thereby comes under a duty to assist the person injured by those acts by giving him any information which he is able to give by way of discovery that discloses the identity of the wrongdoer."[69]

The subsequent case-law continues to put a strong emphasis[70] on a requirement for an innocent third party to be mixed up in the transaction by means of "involvement."[71] Although no case is known where a lack of this precondition has led to rejection of an order,[72] the *Ashworth* decision of the House of Lords, in

[60] *Golden Eye (International) Ltd & Anor v. Telefónica UK Ltd* [2012] EWHC 723 (Ch); *Golden Eye (International) Ltd & Ors v. Telefónica UK Litd & Anor* [2012] EWCA Civ 1740.

[61] *Totalise Plc v. Motley Fool Ltd* [2002] 1 W.L.R. 1233.

[62] *Interbrew SA v. Financial Times Ltd* [2002] WL 237064 Court of Appeal; *Ashworth Hospital Authority v. MGN Ltd* [2002] HRLR 41 House of Lords; *British Steel Corporation v. Granada Television Ltd* [1981] A.C. 1096 House of Lords.

[63] *Rugby Football Union v. Viagogo Ltd* [2013] EMLR 25 Supreme Court.

[64] *Bankers Trust Co v. Shapira* [1980] 1 W.L.R. 1274 Court of Appeal.

[65] *British Steel Corp v. Granada Television Ltd* [1980] WL 264756 Court of Appeal at 1127 ("No doubt Norwich Pharmacal Co. v. Customs and Excise Commissioners [1974] A.C. 133 opened a new chapter in our law. It enables a person, who has been injured by wrongdoing, to bring an action to discover the name of the wrongdoer").

[66] *Ashworth Hospital Authority v. MGN Ltd* [2002] HRLR 41 House of Lords [57] ("The Norwich Pharmacal jurisdiction is an exceptional one and one which is only exercised by the courts when they are satisfied that it is necessary that it should be exercised").

[67] *Rugby Football Union v. Viagogo Ltd* [2013] EMLR 25 Supreme Court [16] ("The test of necessity does not require the remedy to be one of last resort"); this seems to contrast, however, with the treatment of *Norwich Pharmacal* ("this being their only practicable source of information") in the Canadian case-law, where consideration of "whether the third party is the only practicable means to obtain the relief sought" is always one of the factors (*Equustek Solutions Inc. v. Jack* [2014] BCSC 1063 [154]; *Glaxo Wellcome plc v. MNR* [1998] FCJ No. 874, [1998] 4 F.C. 439 (C.A.)); but perhaps this is only a question of different emphasis on a particular factor; even the UK courts *do* seem to look into alternatives to the proposed injunction – see *Cartier International AG & Ors v. British Sky Broadcasting Ltd & Ors* [2014] EWHC 3354 (Ch).

[68] *Ashworth Hospital Authority v. MGN Ltd* [2002] HRLR 41 House of Lords; *British Steel Corporation v. Granada Television Ltd* [1981] A.C. 1096 House of Lords; *Rugby Football Union v. Viagogo Ltd* [2013] EMLR 25 Supreme Court.

[69] *Ashworth Hospital Authority v. MGN Ltd* [2002] HRLR 41 House of Lords [26].

[70] *Ashworth Hospital Authority v. MGN Ltd* [2002] HRLR 41 House of Lords [1] (Lord Slynn: "participated" or "involved"); *Bankers Trust Co v. Shapira* [1980] 1 W.L.R. 1274 Court of Appeal at 1282 (a bank was mixed up in the third-party fraud).

[71] *JSC BTA Bank v. Ablyazov & 16 Ors* [2014] EWHC 2019 (Comm) [72] ("where the third party has become mixed up in the wrongdoing of the defendant, however innocently, he is under a duty to assist the claimant").

[72] *Golden Eye (International) Ltd & Anor v. Telefónica UK Ltd* [2012] EWHC 723 (Ch) [13] (an ISP was mixed up); *Rugby Football Union v. Viagogo Ltd* [2013] EMLR 25 Supreme Court.

particular, illustrates that it is not perceived as a mere condition on paper. The Court here held that "[a]lthough this requirement of involvement or participation on the part of the party from whom discovery is sought is not a stringent requirement, it is still a significant requirement. It distinguishes that party from a mere onlooker or witness."[73] The requirement has a certain de minimis character, which forms a precondition to any discussions about proportionality of the disclosure. According to the Court, it "provides justification for [the] intrusion" that comes with the duty of disclosure.[74] However, "[i]t is not the only protection available to the third party," since "the more general protection (. . .) derives from the fact that this is a discretionary jurisdiction which enables the court to be astute to avoid a third party who has become involved innocently in wrongdoing by another from being subjected to a requirement to give disclosure unless this is established to be a necessary and proportionate response in all the circumstances."[75] As a consequence, there is an extensive case-law discussing proportionality and safeguards applicable to the disclosure.[76]

The courts have also gradually clarified that, as long as a plaintiff pursues a legitimate aim, there is no need to follow-up with the lawsuit after the disclosures.[77] Moreover, the individual whose identity is to be disclosed, does not even necessarily need to be a wrongdoer.[78] The disclosures can also be subject to fairly strict preventive and ex post supervision from the court.[79] However, there still has to be wrongdoing carried out by *someone*.[80] This means that disclosure in absence of any third-party wrongdoing does not seem possible.[81]

---

[73] *Ashworth Hospital Authority v. MGN Ltd* [2002] HRLR 41 House of Lords [31].

[74] Ibid., [35].   [75] Ibid., [36].

[76] For an exhaustive survey of the issue – see Jaani Riordan, *The Liability of Internet Intermediaries* (Oxford, 2016) 82–112.

[77] *Media CAT Ltd v. Adams* [2011] WL 291789 Patents County Court [13]; *British Steel v. Granada Television* [1981 AC 1096 HL, Lord Fraser at 1200; *Ashworth Hospital Authority v. MGN Ltd* [2002] UKHL 29 [2001] 1 WLR 2033, Lord Woolf CJ at 41–47.

[78] *Jade Engineering (Coventry) Ltd v. Antiference Window Systems Ltd* [1996] FSR 461 Chancery Division; *CHC Software Care v. Hopkins & Wood* [1993] FSR 241 Chancery Division at 250; *British Steel Corp v. Granada Television Ltd* [1980] WL 264756 Court of Appeal at 1127 ("Mr. Irvine suggested that this was limited to cases where the injured person desired to sue the wrong-doer. I see no reason why it should be so limited. The same procedure should be available when he desires to obtain redress against the wrong-doer – or to protect himself against further wrongdoing").

[79] *Media CAT Ltd v. Adams* [2011] WL 291789 Patents County Court [124], [129]; *Golden Eye (International) Ltd & Anor v. Telefónica UK Ltd* [2012] EWHC 723 (Ch).

[80] *Ashworth Hospital Authority v. MGN Ltd* [2002] HRLR 41 House of Lords [26] ("While therefore the exercise of the jurisdiction does require that there should be wrongdoing, the wrongdoing which is required is the wrongdoing of the person whose identity the claimant is seeking to establish and not that of the person against whom the proceedings are brought"); *Warner-Lambert Company LLC v. National Health Service Commissioning Board* [2015] EWHC 2548 (obliging to disclosure in a case where eventually no infringement occured).

[81] Jaani Riordan, *The Liability of Internet Intermediaries* (Oxford, 2016) 78, para. 4.42 (also expressing doubts and pointing to the requirement of being "mixed up in third party wrongdoing") 412, para. 13.08; 475, para. 14.56.

It also became clear that *Norwich Pharmacal* can also be used against wrongdoers,[82] particularly as, before disclosure, it may not be clear if somebody is innocent or not. As a response, however, the courts held that if it transpires that the defendant is a wrongdoer, this can affect the costs split usually associated with the order. It is not difficult to understand why the House of Lords accepted information disclosure by third parties. Such disclosures can clearly stand in a way to proper enforcement of rights. The Union law with its broadly construed Article 8 of the Enforcement Directive, but also later case-law of the ECtHR[83] provided for further justification. Until today, *Norwich Pharmacal*, with its few in-built limitations, wasn't challenged in light of the Union law. However, given the generously understood notion of "involved" party in a transaction, there is hardly a practical occasion where Union law could become anyhow "disappointed of equity." And, if necessary, the witness rule could be simply further narrowed down under the pressure of the Directive.

10.3 ASSISTING BY BLOCKING WEBSITES

The Norwich jurisdiction is limited to assistance by information disclosures. It was a matter of time when the equitable duties of innocent third parties will be pushed further. Although *Upmann v. Elkan* and *Orr v. Diaper* already dealt with additional types of duties to assist – to refrain from distributing potentially infringing goods – they were confined to the situation of possession. The general principles embodied in these cases, together with the underlying justification, moreover suggested that there might be *other* equitable duties to assist in enforcement of intellectual property rights, regardless of their own wrongdoing. This impression was reinforced after the implementation of the InfoSoc and Enforcement Directives took place which explicitly postulated a possibility to seek injunctions against intermediaries whose services are used by third parties to infringe. It is therefore no wonder that the first cases coming to test the boundaries of these novel equitable duties to assist were of digital footprint. And who could be a better target than novel gatekeepers to information flows, the Internet access providers?

The premier case of this kind, based on Section 97A CDPA, was the so-called *Newzbin 2*.[84] Plaintiffs in the case, the movies studios, sought an assistance by

---

[82] Implicitly in: *Microsoft Corp v. Plato Technology Ltd* [1999] FSR 834 Chancery Division; *Jade Engineering (Coventry) Ltd v. Antiference Window Systems Ltd* [1996] FSR 461 Chancery Division; *British Steel Corporation v. Granada Television Ltd* [1981] A.C. 1096 House of Lords at 1196–1197; *Omar (Mohamed) v. Omar (Chiiko Aikawa)* [1995] 1 W.L.R. 1428 Chancery Division at 1438; *The Football Association Premier League Limited v. Wells* [2015] 3910 (Ch).

[83] *K.U. v. Finland* App no 2872/02 (ECHR, 2 December 2008).

[84] *Twentieth Century Fox Film Corp v. British Telecommunications plc* [2011] EWHC 1981 (Ch), [2012] Bus LR 1471; *Twentieth Century Fox Film Corp v. British Telecommunications plc (No 2)* [2011] EWHC 2714 (Ch), [2012] Bus LR 1525.

blocking a website, a Usenet search service – Newzbin, which was previously found to have infringed upon the copyright of others by Lord Justice Kitchin[85] on theories of direct liability, joint tortfeasorship, and copyright-specific tort of authorization. A few weeks after Kitchin's judgment, Newzbin entered into voluntary liquidation and the service ceased to operate. Soon, however, a new and very similar service, Newzbin 2, emerged. It is this service that was targeted by the website blocking injunction which was sought solely against the United Kingdom's largest Internet access provider.

Justice Arnold interpreted the statutory language in a way that permitted an obligation to block websites of third parties to be imposed on innocent intermediaries,[86] relying heavily on *L'Oréal v. eBay.* Owing to attempts to circumvent the efforts, the website blocking injunction was granted as an open-ended measure allowing out-of-court submission of new IP addresses to be blocked, without any time limitations or transparency notice requirement and at the predominant expense of the intermediaries.[87] It lacked any safeguards as to the rights of affected individuals who were not party to the litigation, such as users or website operators, and the considerations of the associated costs and effectiveness were mostly speculations.[88] The prescribed blocking technique was a combination of IP address and URL blocking. These order was then extended to other providers.[89] Each of them adjusted the wording of the blocking holdings to the technological capabilities used by the particular access provider.[90]

Justice Arnold later handled several other copyright website blocking injunctions based on Section 97A CDPA.[91] A couple of other orders were issued also by Justices

---

[85] *Twentieth Century Fox Film Corporation & Anor v. Newzbin Ltd* [2010] EWHC 608 (Ch).

[86] For the exact wording of the order see *Twentieth Century Fox Film Corporation & Ors v. British Telecommunications Plc* [2011] EWHC 2714 (Ch) [56]; It has to be noted that this decision predates the *Scarlet Extended* decision of the CJEU.

[87] Only the responsibility to identify new IP addresses was assigned to the rightholders.

[88] This repeats in the first trade mark website blocking case, where the court says that "the implementation costs are likely to increase, and it is difficult to foresee by how much" (*Cartier International AG & Ors v. British Sky Broadcasting Ltd & Ors* [2014] EWHC 3354 (Ch) [249]).

[89] *Twentieth Century Fox Film Corporation & Ors v. British Sky Broadcasting Ltd* (Unreported, 12 December 2011, Vos J); *Twentieth Century Fox Film Corporation & Ors v. Talk Talk Telecom Group plc* (Unreported, 9 February 2012, Arnold J).

[90] Jaani Riordan, *The Liability of Internet Intermediaries* (Oxford, 2016) 484, para. 14.86.

[91] *Twentieth Century Fox Film Corp v. British Telecommunications plc* [2011] EWHC 1981 (Ch), [2012] Bus LR 1471; *Twentieth Century Fox Film Corp v. British Telecommunications plc (No 2)* [2011] EWHC 2714 (Ch), [2012] Bus LR 1525; *Dramatico Entertainment Ltd v. British Sky Broadcasting Ltd* [2012] EWHC 268 (Ch), [2012] 3 CMLR 14; *Dramatico Entertainment Ltd v. British Sky Broadcasting Ltd (No 2)* [2012] EWHC 1152 (Ch); *EMI Records Ltd v. British Sky Broadcasting Ltd* [2013] EWHC 379 (Ch), [2013] ECDR 8; *Football Association Premier League Ltd v. British Sky Broadcasting Ltd* [2013] EWHC 2058 (Ch), [2013] ECDR 14; *Paramount Home Entertainment International Ltd v. British Sky Broadcasting Ltd* [2013] EWHC 3479 (Ch), [2014] ECDR 7; *1967 Ltd v. British Sky Broadcasting Ltd* [2014] EWHC 3444; *Cartier International AG & Ors v. British Sky Broadcasting Ltd & Ors* [2014] EWHC 3354 (Ch); *Cartier International Ltd & Anor v. British Telecommunications Plc & Ors* [2016] EWHC 339 (Ch); *Cartier International AG & Ors v. British Sky Broadcasting Ltd & Ors* [2016] EWCA

Henderson, Briss, and Mann.[92] In *Dramatico v. Sky*,[93] the court was considering a case against the six biggest ISPs already together and without a prior independent decision on the illegality of the website against its operator. Over time, the website blocking injunctions were fine-tuned in several respects. Following Mann J's blocking order,[94] judicial practice came to include a "discharge clause" for website operators.[95] The clause enabled the affected website operators to defend themselves against the orders at any point in time. Arnold J then, in the aftermath of the CJEU decision in *UPC Telekabel* also opened this option to Internet subscribers.[96] The orders today can be therefore challenged by affected parties. Moreover, probably in the light of the *Yildirim* case of ECtHR, they were made subject to a periodical review of two years[97] and transparency obligations requiring notification of consumers about the reasons of blocking.

Broadening of the equitable duties did not stop with copyright cases. Soon, trademark holders started demanding the same. In *Cartier*,[98] Justice Arnold considered an application for a website blocking injunction on the basis of general equitable jurisdiction. Since the UK legislator did not implement Union law in the field of industrial rights, the trademark law based application had to be considered within the framework of equity.[99] After a lengthy analysis of the current state of website blocking, Arnold J accepted the jurisdiction and exercised his discretion by granting the order. He argued that both domestic and the Union-conform interpretation warrant such a result:

Civ 658; *The Football Association Premier League Ltd v. British Telecommunications Plc & Ors* [2017] EWHC 480 (Ch).

[92] *Paramount Home Entertainment International Ltd v. British Sky Broadcasting Ltd* [2014] EWHC 937 (Ch) (Henderson J); *Twentieth Century Fox Film Corp v. Sky UK Ltd* [2015] EWHC 1082 (Ch); *Bloomsbury Publishing plc v. British Telecommunications plc* (Unreported, 19 May 2015, Mann J).

[93] *Dramatico Entertainment Ltd v. British Sky Broadcasting Ltd* [2012] EWHC 268 (Ch); [2012] 3 CMLR 14; *Dramatico Entertainment Ltd v. British Sky Broadcasting Ltd (No 2)* [2012] EWHC 1152 (Ch).

[94] *Bloomsbury Publishing plc v. British Telecommunications plc* (Unreported, 19 May 2015, Mann J) – mentioned by Justice Arnold in *Football Association Premier League Ltd v. British Sky Broadcasting Ltd* [2013] EWHC 2058 (Ch), [2013] ECDR 14 [58].

[95] Following the *UPC Telekabel* decision of the CJEU, it became questionable whether the same is not required for users – see Martin Husovec, "CJEU Allowed Website Blocking Injunctions With Some Reservations" (2014) 9 (8) Journal of Intellectual Property Law & Practice 631–634.

[96] Compare *Cartier International AG & Ors v. British Sky Broadcasting Ltd & Ors* [2014] EWHC 3354 (Ch) [263] (extending the option to challenge the block also to users as an echo of the *UPC Telekabel* ruling of the CJEU) with *Akdeniz v. Turkey* App no 20877/10 (ECHR, 11 March 2014) (mere status as a user of a website service, here Last.fm, is not sufficient to be regarded as a victim under Art. 34 of the Convention).

[97] Ibid., [265] (most likely influenced by the concurring opinion of the judge Pinto de Albuquerque in *Ahmet Yildrimi v. Turkey* App no 3111/10 (ECHR, 18 March 2013).

[98] *Cartier International AG & Ors v. British Sky Broadcasting Ltd & Ors* [2014] EWHC 3354 (Ch).

[99] Justice Arnold was already prepared to extend it against innocent intermediaries in *L'Oreal SA v. eBay International AG* [2009] RPC 21 Chancery Division, where he considered a filtering obligation.

An analogy may be drawn with the equitable protective duty described by Buckley LJ in Norwich Pharmacal Co v. Customs & Excise Commissioners [1974] AC 133 (...) Although this principle is inapplicable to the circumstances of the present case, *it is not a long step from this to conclude that, once an ISP becomes aware*[100] *that its services are being used by third parties to infringe an intellectual property right, then it becomes subject to a duty to take proportionate measures to prevent or reduce such infringements even though it is not itself liable for infringement.* (...) I conclude that, even if the Court would not have power to grant a website blocking injunction in a trade mark case upon a purely domestic interpretation of section 37(1), section 37(1) can and should be interpreted in compliance with the third sentence of Article 11 by virtue of the Marleasing principle. If it were otherwise, the UK would be in breach of its obligations under the Directive.[101]

For the common law jurisdiction, this is revolutionary. It is "Norwich no. 2." Although it might be disputed whether Union law really mandates website blocking injunctions (see Section 6.4), the crucial point is that of equitable jurisdiction. *Cartier* essentially *generalizes* equitable duties of innocent third parties beyond mere provision of information. It is true that *Upmann v. Elkan* and *Orr v. Diaper* already suggested some further duties, but their limited applicability is incomparable with the breadth of an equitable duty to take precautions upon obtaining knowledge, now accommodated in interpretation of Section 37(1). Justice Arnold, sitting at the High Court, considered that jurisdiction to grant injunctions is warranted by its domestic interpretation, but also follows from Union-conform construction of the jurisdiction.[102] In his view, following threshold conditions need to be met before any discussion of appropriateness of the injunction: (1) the ISPs must be intermediaries within the meaning of the Union law (2) the users and/or the operators of the website must be infringing the claimant's rights, (3) they must use the ISPs' services to infringe and (4) the ISPs must have actual knowledge of infringing activity.[103] While the first three follow from the explicit wording of Article 11(III) of the Enforcement Directive, the fourth was interpreted to originate from Article 15 of the E-Commerce Directive.[104]

Lord Justice Kitchin, sitting at the Court of Appeal, agreed with Arnold J's analysis. He pointed out that an analogy with *Norwich Pharmacal* supports that access providers are under an equitable duty to assist.[105] Moreover, as shown in *Samsung v. Apple*, the Court of Appeal already recognized that the jurisdiction can be exercised in the new ways.[106] After reviewing the case-law of the CJEU, it opined that:

---

[100] This part seems to refer to an analogical requirement of Sections 97A and 191JA CDPA.
[101] *Cartier International AG & Ors v. British Sky Broadcasting Ltd & Ors* [2014] EWHC 3354 (Ch) [106], [132] (emphasis mine).
[102] Ibid., [94–111].   [103] Ibid., [139–141].
[104] *Cartier International AG & Ors v. British Sky Broadcasting Ltd & Ors* [2016] EWCA Civ 658 [81]; *Cartier International AG & Ors v. British Sky Broadcasting Ltd & Ors* [2014] EWHC 3354 (Ch) [141].
[105] *Cartier International AG & Ors v. British Sky Broadcasting Ltd & Ors* [2016] EWCA Civ 658 [55].
[106] Ibid.

It seems to me to be clear from this guidance that Article 11 does indeed provide a principled basis for extending the practice of the court in relation to the grant of injunctions to encompass, where appropriate, the services of an intermediary, such as one of the ISPs, which have been used by a third party to infringe a registered trade mark. There is no dispute that the ISPs are intermediaries within the meaning of Article 11 and accordingly, subject to the threshold conditions to which I shall shortly come, I believe that this court *must* now recognise pursuant to general equitable principles that this is one of those new categories of case in which the court may grant an injunction when it is satisfied that it is just and convenient to do so.[107]

Lord Justice Briggs was probably most clear on whether this decision would be possible in absence of external pressure by the Union law. He openly remarked what I observed earlier, namely, that "the courts could and probably would have developed this jurisdiction regardless of the requirement in the two Directives."[108] In a way, it is surprising that before the Court of Appeal, only the consistency of the costs of compliance became the subject of the heated debate. Justice Kitchin very quickly sided with Justice Arnold that the applicable *threshold conditions* constraining the exercise of the jurisdiction should be construed in light of the Union law.[109]

However, one might wonder why that should be the case. Norwich's requirement of "involvement," as the only threshold condition, could have been easily further developed. It would easily accommodate any Union-prescribed injunctions against intermediaries. By confining themselves to Union threshold conditions, the courts seem to for instance imply that there is no such thing as a general equitable duty of assistance by those who don't qualify as "intermediaries." Moreover, *Cartier* jurisdiction could now be used to circumvent that of *Norwich*. When intermediaries lack "involvement," though they are "intermediaries whose services are used by a third party to infringe," the plaintiffs can still request disclosures. Although when it comes to the "mere" threshold conditions, this worry seems rather theoretical, it might be more significant when it comes to "Cartier-strategy" to circumvent Norwich costs-splits in information disclosure cases.

Meeting all of the four threshold conditions is naturally not sufficient to obtain an order. Justice Arnold developed a set of principles, drawn from Article 3 of the Enforcement Directive, that guide the grant of any application. At length, he considered all the criteria whose application undeniably improved the practice of blocking over years. The overarching principle, taking aside all human rights considerations, was summarized by the judge as follows:

(. . .) the key question on proportionality is *whether the likely costs burden on the ISPs is justified by the likely efficacy of the blocking measures and the consequent*

---

[107] Ibid., [65] (emphasis mine).   [108] Ibid., [205].   [109] Ibid., [80].

benefit to Richemont having regard to the alternative measures which are available to Richemont and to the substitutability of the Target Websites.[110]

This is a powerful framing of the proportionality exercise that is, however, partially weakened by the reference to alternative measures. I have previously argued that as long as human rights are respected and all necessary checks are secured, website blocking, as any other type of enforcement EMWENT measure against innocent third parties, if prescribed, should be granted only in situations where costs are offset by expected benefits. This framing gives, under the condition of reimbursement, rightholders a right of choice to pursue enforcement strategies that they consider most effective for their business. Any attempts to impose subsidiarity are in my view unnecessary when the law sets incentives right, in particular to distinguish the seeking of help from infringers and noninfringers. The courts accepting the "subsidiarity dance," such as the German Federal Supreme Court, are inevitably harming the rightholders more than if they would prescribe reimbursement of compliance. They impose their own view of an effective enforcement strategy, which may or may not be optimal and even inflate the costs.

Although Justice Arnold considered alternative measures, such as targeting search engines, Web hosts, or payment processors, none of them was seen as really an option.[111] Lord Justice Kitchin broadly agreed with this assessment. In light of the assessment, however, it is hard to see what would satisfy the court. This is because one can always only speculate about effectiveness and can never really assign expected benefits to the particular enforcement strategies in order to rank them. For much the same reason as determining the benefits is not realistic, so is consideration of their ranking. Moreover, what works for a single rightholder, might not be the best strategy for the other. In my view, the courts should consider subsidiarity only in relationship to the fundamental rights.

10.4 COSTS OF COMPLIANCE

Following *Norwich Pharmacal,* it became established case-law that the usual cost-split for information disclosures is that the plaintiff has to pay the *reasonable compliance costs* incurred by the innocent third party.[112] However, some additional circumstances may arise under which it is appropriate to depart from this rule and order the party to bear its own costs or even to pay some or all of the plaintiff's costs.[113]

---

[110] *Cartier International AG & Ors v. British Sky Broadcasting Ltd & Ors* [2014] EWHC 3354 (Ch) [260] (emphasis mine).

[111] *Cartier International AG & Ors v. British Sky Broadcasting Ltd & Ors* [2014] EWHC 3354 (Ch) [197–217].

[112] *JSC BTA Bank v. Ablyazov & 16 Ors* [2014] EWHC 2019 (Comm) [70] (emphasis mine).

[113] Ibid., [70], [77–81] (holding this if an innocent third party turns out to be a wrongdoer upon disclosure).

This is justified since "applications against an innocent party involved in the tortious act of others (. . .) are not ordinary adversarial proceedings where the general rule is that the unsuccessful party should pay the costs of the successful party but are more akin to proceedings for pre-action disclosure."[114]

Let us recall that, in *Norwich Pharmacal*, Lord Reid held that "it *may* be that if this causes him expense the person seeking the information ought to reimburse him,"[115] but at the same time that "if the Respondents have any doubts in any future case about the propriety of making disclosures they are well entitled to require the matter to be submitted to the Court *at the expense* of the person seeking the disclosure."[116] Lord Cross, on the other hand, opined that "the full costs of the respondent of the application and any expense incurred in providing the information would *have to* be borne by the applicant."[117] This strong pro-compensation holding is somewhat in contrast with the earlier lower ruling in *Upmann v. Elkan*, where the court did not order the defendants to pay the costs of the plaintiff, but let them bear their own proceedings costs, although it was noted that "the readiness with which the information[118] was given by Messrs. Elkan [the freight forwarder] is a principal reason why [he is] not charge[d] (. . .) with costs."[119]

Only very recently, Justice Flaux identified in *JSC BTA Bank v. Ablyazov & 16 Ors* the following two situations, where *compliance costs* would be lowered or rejected under the *Norwich* rule: (1) where the defendant is knowingly implicated in wrongdoing and (2) where the defendant had frustrated the whole process by a failure to engage.[120] Interestingly, in an earlier case, the Court of Appeal in *Totalise plc v. The Motley Fool Ltd* explicitly considered scenarios, upon submission of one of the parties, where this usual compensation rule should *never* be abandoned. The Court held that: "[t]here may be cases where the circumstances require a different order, but we do not believe they include cases where (1) the party required to make the disclosure had a genuine doubt that the person seeking the disclosure was entitled to it; (2) the party was under an appropriate legal obligation not to reveal the information, or where the legal position was not clear, or the party had a reasonable doubt as to the obligations; or (3) the party could be subject to proceedings if disclosure was voluntary; or (4) the party would or might suffer damage by voluntarily giving the disclosure; or (5) the disclosure would or might infringe a legitimate interest of another."[121] Given that the criteria originate in party's submission, they should be considered nonexhaustive.[122]

---

[114]　*Totalise Plc v. Motley Fool Ltd* [2002] 1 W.L.R. 1233 [29–30].

[115]　*Norwich Pharmacal Co v. Customs & Excise Commissioners* [1974] AC 133 [12] (emphasis mine).

[116]　Ibid., 133 [18].　　[117]　Ibid., [100].

[118]　They provided information seven days after the suit was filed.

[119]　*Upmann v. Elkan* [1871] L.R. 12 Eq. 140, 7 Ch App 130 at 148.

[120]　*JSC BTA Bank v. Ablyazov & 16 Ors* [2014] EWHC 2019 (Comm) [83], [85].

[121]　*Totalise Plc v. Motley Fool Ltd* [2002] 1 W.L.R. 1233 [30].

[122]　Jaani Riordan, *The Liability of Internet Intermediaries* (Oxford, 2016) 609, para. 18.42.

This shows that compensation for hardship is part of the very *justification* of obligations imposed on innocent third parties. Equity may, in the name of justice, ask such persons to assist rightholders despite their own innocence, but has to offer something in return to compensate for the inconvenience caused. Therefore, equity itself *dictates* existence of a specific contradictory circumstance in order to be able to remove this feature from the system.

Despite this, the Norwich line of case-law wasn't taken as a guidance in the first website blocking cases. In *Newzbin 2*, Arnold J considered a case where the only defendant was a large ISP that was already equipped with an appropriate blocking system. He considered the costs of an order to be moderate.[123] In the first decision, Arnold J, also referencing Norwich practice, noted that this cost-split is not fixed forever.[124] The defendants immediately took the opportunity to argue that their situation was analogous to the Norwich line of jurisprudence. In his second judgment, Arnold J replied that "although Article 8(3) does confer a legal right to an injunction on rightholders, it remains the case that the intermediary has not committed any legal wrong."[125]

In other words, although the two orders differ by content, they have in common the rationale of imposing an obligation of assistance on an innocent third party that did not commit any wrong. Quite unusually therefore, the Court let the intermediary bear the *full* costs of complying with the measures and only partially ordered the reimbursement of its procedural costs. Under the soon established copyright practice, the costs were allocated as follows. The rightholders would bear the costs of preparing the application, going to the court (around 16,300 EUR per website) and the postgrant monitoring costs (around 4,200 EUR per website per year).[126] The cost of implementing and updating the blocks as well as some of the litigation costs would be born by intermediaries.[127] These costs vary largely, depending on the size and in-house technology of an access provider. The implementation can cost, however, between mid-three to mid-four figure sums per

---

[123] *Twentieth Century Fox Film Corp & Ors v. British Telecommunications Plc* [2011] EWHC 1981 (Ch) [177]; *Twentieth Century Fox Film Corporation & Ors v. British Telecommunications Plc* [2011] EWHC 2714 (Ch) [4] (TalkTalk protested against this point, claiming that it does not possess an equivalent system, the Court held that this does not affect the order against the current defendant).

[124] *Twentieth Century Fox Film Corp & Ors v. British Telecommunications Plc* [2011] EWHC 1981 (Ch) [189] ("Furthermore, although I cannot prejudge later arguments in this case, it is not inevitable that future applicants will recover all their costs even if successful: compare the practice in respect of Norwich Pharmacal orders, as to which see Totalise plc v. Motley Fool Ltd [2001] EWCA Civ 1897, [2002] 1 WLR 1233").

[125] *Twentieth Century Fox Film Corporation & Ors v. British Telecommunications Plc* [2011] EWHC 2714 (Ch) [19], [30].

[126] See for summary: *Cartier International AG & Ors v. British Sky Broadcasting Ltd & Ors* [2016] EWCA Civ 658 [18–19].

[127] Arnold J only ordered access providers to pay litigation costs only where they have raised points in opposition to the orders being granted and lost.

block/update, or in a low five to six figure sum a year for administering all the blocks.[128]

Justice Arnold supported this cost allocation with the following two arguments: (1) the defendant is a commercial enterprise which indirectly benefits from infringing use of its subscribers and (2) it seems implicit in the Union law that the cost is imposed on the intermediary.[129] However, he did not completely "rule out the possibility of ordering the rightholder to pay some or all of the implementation costs in an appropriate case."[130]

These arguments are, however, hardly conclusive. First of all, from a domestic doctrinal perspective, the fact that the mechanism is a remedy under Article 8(3) does not change anything about the "Norwich character" of the measures. Such measures still lead to imposition of the costs upon an innocent third party. In *Ashworth*, the House of Lords made it clear that reimbursement of the costs is one of the important reasons why third parties can be burdened at all. It was stated that "in exercising its discretion the court will take into account the fact that innocent third parties can be indemnified for their costs while at the same time recognising that this does not mean there is no inconvenience to third parties as a result of becoming embroiled in proceedings through no fault on their part."[131] The fact that these measures are based on Section 97A CDPA does not change this, especially because, strictly speaking, this statutory provision does not grant any new powers to the court, but only recognizes existing ones (see Section 10.1). Similarly the Union law origin of the statutory provision is irrelevant, as long as the domestic condition of the cost-split is not against the Union law.

The second reason why this argument is not conclusive is the statement that complying with a measure is a cost of doing business. If this were true, than banks, shippers, and forwarding agents, should also *not* receive reimbursement for their compliance under Norwich orders.[132] Despite this, the House of Lords has confirmed numerous times that this is necessary in order to justify the imposition of obligations upon innocent third parties. It is therefore not clear why website blocking cases, which led to the imposition of not negligible costs should be treated differently. Especially since the scope of assistance required of innocent parties is broader than mere disclosure. It is baffling, but costs were *never* appealed in the copyright website blocking cases.[133] Perhaps the industry underestimated the extent to which the tool will soon be utilized.

---

[128] For summary, see *Cartier International AG & Ors v. British Sky Broadcasting Ltd & Ors* [2016] EWCA Civ 658 [18–19]; in *Newzbin 2*, BT forecasted its costs at around 5830 EUR per block and 120 EUR per update – see [135].

[129] *Twentieth Century Fox Film Corporation & Ors v. British Telecommunications Plc* [2011] EWHC 2714 (Ch) [32].

[130] Ibid.   [131] *Ashworth Hospital Authority v. MGN Ltd* [2002] HRLR 41 House of Lords [35–36].

[132] Similar Jaani Riordan, *The Liability of Internet Intermediaries* (Oxford, 2016) 615, para. 18.74.

[133] *Cartier International AG & Ors v. British Sky Broadcasting Ltd & Ors* [2016] EWCA Civ 658 [133].

After the application in *Cartier*, however, the costs became the hot topic. Arnold J decided to continue with its copyright cost-splits.[134] His two main arguments were essentially the same. The access providers now suddenly demanded that rightholders cover litigation expenses, and implementation costs. As implementation costs, they identified both marginal costs of compliance, as well as contribution to "the capital costs of the technical systems which they need for that purpose."[135] Kitchin LJ made three additional points to support Arnold J's costs-splits: (1) the Union law requires the injunctions against intermediaries are possible, (2) these injunctions are price for immunities that intermediaries enjoy under the E-Commerce Directive and (3) Norwich case-law is not a source of jurisdiction, but only an analogy.[136] He also stressed, that in his reading of Arnold J's decision, particularly future of cumulative costs of the practice "should be kept under review in future applications."[137] This suggests that once the practice becomes very intensive, there might be a tipping point for the judges after which the costs-splits might be changed in order to improve its governance. However, as I explained in Section 2.4, this might come too late.

The arguments presented by Kitchin LJ are also hardly conclusive, and to some extent, even misleading. First of all, the Union law does not prescribe that injunctions are made possible without any costs to rightholders. To the contrary, on purpose, it leaves conditions and modalities to the domestic laws. The fact that the most domestic laws that reach the CJEU until now didn't include reimbursement of compliance, says nothing about compatibility of such compliance with the Union law. Some other jurisdictions also condition information disclosures upon reimbursement of the costs and the compatibility of this, in absence of an explicit Union reference, was never challenged to undermine the right to information. Second, costs of injunctions can hardly be construed as the cost of immunities. Not only are the safe harbors rather the restatement of the law than real liability exclusions,[138] injunctions against intermediaries also target market players who don't qualify under any of the

---

[134] *Cartier International AG & Ors v. British Sky Broadcasting Ltd & Ors* [2014] EWHC 3354 (Ch) [240], [249] ("I adhere to the view that, for the reasons I gave in 20C Fox v. BT (No 2) at [53], the rightholders should pay the costs of an unopposed application. I also adhere to the view that, for the reasons I gave in 20C Fox v. BT (No 2) at [32], the ISPs should generally bear the costs of implementation as part of the costs of carrying on business in this sector. Indeed, it seems to me that my reasoning is supported by the subsequent judgment of the CJEU in UPC v. Constantin at [50]. Nevertheless, as I said in 20C Fox v. BT (No 2) at [33], I do not rule out the possibility of ordering the rightholder to pay some or all of the implementation costs in an appropriate case. Equally, I consider that it makes sense for the rightholders to bear the costs of monitoring and the ISPs to bear the costs of implementation of updates, subject to the same caveat").

[135] *Cartier International AG & Ors v. British Sky Broadcasting Ltd & Ors* [2016] EWCA Civ 658 [141].

[136] Ibid., [143, 163].   [137] Ibid., [167].

[138] Case C-324/09 *L'Oréal and Others* [2010] ECLI:EU:C:2010:757, Opinion of AG Jääskinen, paras. 136, 150 (noting that it is more a clarification or a restatement and therefore does not need to be interpreted restrictively).

safe harbors, such as domain name authorities,[139] search engines,[140] or even offline intermediaries.[141] And third, as far as English law is concerned, although Norwich isn't the basis of injunctions, it demonstrates a more general principle restraining the exercise of equitable protective jurisdiction. Namely, innocent third parties can be asked to assist in enforcement of rights of others, but justice requires that they are compensated in return.

The issue of costs is likely to be heard by the Supreme Court. Lord Justice Briggs dissented on this point with Justices Kitchin and Jackson. His criticism is grounded in the following arguments: (1) injunctions against intermediaries are nothing that the equitable jurisdiction couldn't and wouldn't achieve on its own – the Union origin is thus irrelevant,[142] (2) the Union law does not prevent the reimbursement of the costs,[143] (3) *Norwich* and *Bankers Trust* case-law embodies a more general principle constraining the exercise of equitable jurisdiction applicable to those who owe equitable obligations[144] and (4) that "cost of doing business" argument is hardly convincing because the logic equally works under the *Norwich* disclosures.[145] This, in Justice Briggs' view points to the following principle: "compliance by an innocent party with an equitable duty to assist the victim of a wrongdoing should generally be at the victim's expense."[146] The compensation, however, in his reading should not only extend to "the specific cost incurred by the respondent ISP in complying with that order, but not the cost of designing and installing the software with which to do so whenever ordered."[147] According to the judge, this capital or equipment cost should be considered "a cost of carrying on the business of an ISP within jurisdictions where the power to grant such an injunction exists."[148]

It should be clarified that the access providers sought a proportionate contribution to the cost of re-designing *existing* systems which were in place even before the first copyright blocking injunctions were requested. This is also the fact that led Justice Arnold to conclude in *Newzbin 2* that compliance costs are moderate. Had the systems for filtering not existed, the applications could have been more likely conditioned upon compensation of the setup costs. Although Justice Briggs rejects ex post compensation for improvement of the systems, his opinion does not seem to dismiss compensation of their first-ever deployment. Moreover, the caveat about capital investments seems illogical from the economic standpoint. Investments into systems can make blocking cheaper and smoother for rightholders. If access providers

---

[139] See probably still pending case (unless it was settled): *Cartier International AG v. Nominet UK*, Claim No HC13 B04781 (4 November 2013, High Court of Justice, Chancery Division), http://domainincite .com/docs/Cartier%20defence.pdf.

[140] Anne-Catherine Lorrain, "Supreme Court (Cour de cassation): 'Google/Keyword Suggestions'" [2013] IIC 380.

[141] See Case C-494/15 *Tommy Hilfiger Licensing and Others* [2016] ECLI:EU:C:2016:528.

[142] *Cartier International AG & Ors v. British Sky Broadcasting Ltd & Ors* [2016] EWCA Civ 658 [205].

[143] Ibid., [199].   [144] Ibid., [202–206].   [145] Ibid., [207].

[146] Ibid., [210].   [147] Ibid., [211].   [148] Ibid., [207].

are not incentivized to improve – but for the cases when this is aligned with their self-interest, this is helpful to no one.

10.5 EQUITABLE DUTY

The English courts imposing positive (mandatory) injunctions on innocent third parties automatically create an equitable duty to act,[149] which is then enforced by an injunction. It is not entirely clear at which point the obligation arises and what the consequence of incompliance are.

In *Customs and Exercise Commissioners v. Barclays*,[150] the House of Lords recently considered a nature of an equitable duty. Lord Bingham of Cornhill recalled that he knows of "no instance in which a non-consensual court order, without more, has been held to give rise to a duty of care owed to the party obtaining the order."[151] In his view, one would have to ask then "whether a similar duty is owed by the subject of a search order, or a Norwich Pharmacal order, or a witness summons, in any case where economic loss is a foreseeable consequence of breach."[152] This, according to the judge, would seem to involve a "radical innovation."[153] The "duty of compliance" should be clearly distinct from any possible "tortious duty of care."[154]

Therefore, any reference to "duty" in *Upmann v. Elkan*,[155] *Norwich*[156] and *Cartier*[157] thus needs to be strongly distinguished from any tortious duty of care. This also applies to famous statement of Lord Buckley LJ in *Norwich Pharmacal* where, relying on *Upmann v. Elkan*, he famously noted that an innocent third party upon obtaining knowledge will be "subject to a duty, an equitable duty, not to allow those goods to pass out of his possession or control" in order "not aid the infringement."[158] And even though "by doing so he might not himself infringe the patent or trade mark, he would be in dereliction of his duty to the proprietor," which "if necessary, [can] be enforced in equity by way of injunction."[159]

In *Cartier*, Justice Arnold derived from the above holding that it would "not [be] a long step from this to conclude that, once an ISP becomes aware that its services are being used by third parties to infringe an intellectual property right, then it

---

[149] David Wright, *Remedies* (Federation Press 2010) 191 (arguing that Norwich Pharmacal creates a new equitable duty).
[150] *Customs and Exercise Commissioners v. Barclays plc* [2007] UKHL 28.
[151] Ibid., [19].   [152] Ibid.   [153] Ibid.   [154] Ibid.
[155] *Upmann v. Elkan* [1871] L.R. 12 Eq. 140, 7 Ch App 130, at. 145 ("it is his duty at once to give all the information required, and to undertake that the goods shall not be removed or dealt with until the spurious brand has been removed, and to offer to give all facilities to the person injured for that purpose").
[156] *Norwich Pharmacal Co v. Customs & Excise Commissioners* [1974] AC 133.
[157] *Cartier International AG & Ors v. British Sky Broadcasting Ltd & Ors* [2014] EWHC 3354 (Ch).
[158] *Norwich Pharmacal Co v. Customs & Excise Commissioners* [1974] AC 133 (Buckley LJ).
[159] Ibid.

becomes subject to a duty to take proportionate measures to prevent or reduce such infringements even though it is not itself liable for infringement."[160]

This statement could be read to suggest that duty arises with circumstances even *prior* to the grant. Lord Justice Kitchin in Cartier's Court of Appeal decision stressed that although he agrees with the above statement, only "subject to the qualification that the duty is more precisely characterised (. . .) as a duty to take these steps to assist the person wronged *when requested to do so.*"[161] This suggests that a request is part of the circumstances. It doesn't answer from which point the duty exists. Not acting upon an equitable duty only allows the plaintiff to petition the court to impose its content and therefore comes with limited consequences. In particular, it does not automatically lead to a tort of any kind, as that would require co-existence of a different (tortious) duty of care to carry out those very same acts. As Lord Reid also very importantly noted in *Norwich Pharmacal*, "if the Respondents have any doubts in any future case about the propriety of making disclosures they are *well entitled to require the matter to be submitted to the Court* at the expense of the person seeking the disclosure."[162] Depending on the circumstances, however, it might cause the defendant to lose some reimbursement of the costs.[163]

Although tortious duties of care are distinct, they are sometimes invoked as a supplementary cause of action. In the 1980s, rightholders initiated a test litigation against producers of tape recorders. The case became known as *Amstrad Consumer Electronics v. British Phonographic Industry*[164] and was eventually heard in the House of Lords. Among several alleged causes of action under tort law such as joint tortfeasorship, contributory liability, and negligence, the plaintiffs also attempted to construe a novel *equitable* duty of care,[165] which could serve as the basis for an injunction that was requested. This, according to the plaintiffs, should restrain the producers of tape recorders from supplying their machines without taking precautions to reasonably ensure that copyright would not be infringed by their use. This novel duty in equity was allegedly founded on the famous passage by Buckley LJ in the judgment of *Norwich Pharmacal* that was quoted above. In that passage, Buckley LJ was explaining the reason why the shippers in *Orr v. Diaper* had been exposed to the risk of an injunction restraining them from continuing to ship the goods, and why the forwarding agents in *Upmann v. Elkan* had been restrained in control of the goods.

---

[160] *Cartier International AG & Ors v. British Sky Broadcasting Ltd & Ors* [2014] EWHC 3354 (Ch) [106].

[161] *Cartier International AG & Ors v. British Sky Broadcasting Ltd & Ors* [2016] EWCA Civ 658 [52] (emphasis mine).

[162] *Norwich Pharmacal Co. & Others v. Customs and Excise Commissioners* [1974] AC 133 [18] (emphasis mine).

[163] Jaani Riordan, *The Liability of Internet Intermediaries* (Oxford, 2016) 96–97.

[164] *CBS Songs Ltd v. Amstrad Consumer Electronics Plc* [1988] WL 624207 House of Lords.

[165] Lord Justice Kitchin in Cartier confusingly referes only to "common law duty" in this context – see *Cartier International AG & Ors v. British Sky Broadcasting Ltd & Ors* [2016] EWCA Civ 658 [54].

Slade LJ, sitting on the Court of Appeal, dismissed this attempt, arguing that the two earlier cases were both about spurious imitations and so were, in themselves, "infringing."[166] This was different, said the judge, from the case of tape recorders, production, and dissemination of which is entirely legal. He squarely rejected any duty in equity, arguing that:

> If the alleged duty in equity existed in the present case, it seems to me that a similar duty would have existed in each of the line of cases beginning with *Townsend v. Haworth*. This, it would appear, was never even suggested by any of the members of this court responsible for those decisions. The suggestion, with due respect to the argument, is, in my opinion, ill-founded.[167]

In a subsequent appeal to the House of Lords, the lawyers for the defendant argued that existence of such a wide equitable duty would render irrelevant the checks and balances of the common law in relation to negligence and vicarious liability.[168] Probably confident of the argument, they openly invited the House of Lords to say that no duty of that width exists at law or in equity. The House of Lords, however, did *not* accept the invitation. It merely rejected the injunction in general, whether based on tort of negligence, or equitable duty enforceable by injunctions. It held:

> In these proceedings the court is being asked to forbid the sale to the public of all or some selected types of tape recorder or to ensure that advertisements for tape recorders shall be censored by the court on behalf of copyright owners. *The court has no power to make such orders and judges are not qualified to decide whether a restraint should be placed on the manufacture of electronic equipment or on the contents of advertising.* No one is to blame for the present situation. Copyright law could not envisage and now cannot cope with mass-production techniques and inventions which create a vast market for the works of a copyright owner but also provide opportunities for his rights to be infringed. *Parliament could place limitations on the manufacture or sale of certain types of tape recorder and could prescribe notices and warnings to be included in advertisements.* Parliament might take the view that any such restraints and prescriptions would constitute an unwarrantable interference with the development of the electronic industry and be ineffective.[169]

Amstrad could have become *Cartier* of today. The House of Lords wasn't willing to take the step. In the light of the today's developments, however, the ruling could hardly have been the same. After CJEU's ruling in *L'Oréal v. eBay* that clarified state of Union law, it became clear that even innocent actors can be subject

---

[166] *Amstrad Consumer Electronics Plc v. British Phonographic Industry Ltd* [1986] FSR 159 Court of Appeal.

[167] Ibid., 214–215 (emphasis mine).

[168] *CBS Songs Ltd v. Amstrad Consumer Electronics Plc* [1988] WL 624207 House of Lords at 1040.

[169] *CBS Songs Ltd v. Amstrad Consumer Electronics Plc* [1988] WL 624207 House of Lords at 1060 (emphasis mine).

to some of such injunctions. Moreover, after *Tommy Hilfiger*,[170] there is no doubt anymore that also offline intermediaries can be subject to such obligations. That being said, the order to prohibit entire distribution of tape recorders wouldn't be granted even today. It would constitute a disproportionate measure that is moreover incompatible with the very rationale of providing "mere" assistance. As explained in Chapter 7, injunctions against innocent intermediaries cannot have as their object or effect a general and permanent prohibition of conduct, such as selling of goods.[171] They can only seek positive steps of assistance. The second plea in *Amstrad*, namely, the request to "not advertise their equipment in such a way as to encourage copying," on the other hand, could have been more arguable. However, it would have likely failed due to lack of elementary effectiveness.

According to the case-law discussed above, the duty to assist seems to arise with the relevant circumstances, however, is legally enforceable only following its grant. Its existence before judicial assessment can be only potential because its exact form has to be qualified by the judge who presides over the assessment of its proportionality. This would confirm general claim that a remedy in common law is "a right born of the order or judgment of a court."[172] After the court super-imposes the obligation on the innocent defendant, which abrogates web of other obligations, his refusal to comply will be typically only punished by contempt of the court and not by liability in tort.[173] Punishing incompliance *after* the grant by damages owed to the plaintiff would transform the initially granted obligation. Although the literature says that the compliance with this duty in the pre-grant phase is said to be entirely *voluntary*,[174] this is, however, not to say that it might be entirely without consequences.

---

[170] Case C-494/15 *Tommy Hilfiger Licensing and Others* [2016] ECLI:EU:C:2016:528.

[171] See Section 7.2.

[172] Peter Birks, "Rights, wrongs, and remedies" (2000) 20(1) Oxford Journal of Legal Studies 1, 15.

[173] Jaani Riordan, *The Liability of Internet Intermediaries* (Oxford, 2016) 73, paras. 4.22 and 74, para. 4.26; *Customs and Exercise Commissioners v. Barclays plc* [2007] UKHL 28 at 17 ("First, as already shown, the Mareva jurisdiction has developed as one exercised by court order enforceable only by the court's power to punish those who break its orders. The documentation issued by the court does not hint at the existence of any other remedy. This regime makes perfect sense on the assumption that the only duty owed by a notified party is to the court").

[174] Jaani Riordan, *The Liability of Internet Intermediaries* (Oxford, 2016) 73, para. 4.22.

PART V

Outlook and Conclusions

11

Global Context

11.1 INTERNATIONAL PUBLIC LAW AND ITS SHIFTS

This book takes as a starting point that in most of the countries, innocent third parties aren't regularly burdened with extensive IPR enforcement obligations. It also assumes, without knowing all the laws of the world, that the European position is somewhat unique in how it treats innocent intermediaries. To support this assumption, the look into international law provides a worldwide baseline.[1]

The TRIPS Agreement was the first multilateral international agreement to regulate the enforcement of intellectual property rights in detail. Before TRIPS, multilateral international treaties such as the Berne or Paris Conventions were limited to general obligations to provide for *some* legal remedies, with the notable exception of seizures.[2] Otherwise the question of remedies was left entirely up to national law. The sources of international public law, apart from obviously setting international standards, are also important for a different reason: the European "highest court," the Court of Justice of the European Union (CJEU), usually attempts to interpret Union law in their light.[3]

---

[1] In addition, the lack of similar tools seems to be found in recent research in other countries, such as Japan (Tatsuhiro Ueno and Ryû Kojima, "Indirect Infringement and Provisions Restricting Rights in Copyright Law" in Symposium "Koko ga hen da yo nihon-ho" – "Is Japanese Law a Strange Law?" (2008), www.zjapanr.de/index.php/zjapanr/article/viewFile/384/405, 236) and China (Jie Wang, *Regulating Hosting ISPs' Responsibilities for Copyright Infringement The Freedom to Operate in the US, EU and China* (PhD Thesis 2016)).

[2] Article 9, Article 10, Article 10bis and Article 10ter(1) of the Paris Convention; Article 16 of the Bern Convention; Article 8 of the Lisbon Agreement – see more Daniel Gervais, *The TRIPS Agreement: Drafting History and Analysis* (Sweet & Maxwell 2012) 287; Martin D. Woodward, "TRIPS and NAFTA Chapter 17: How Will Trade-Related Multilateral Agreements Affect International Copyright" (1996) 31 *Texas International Law* 269, 271.

[3] Case C-275/06 *Promusicae* [2008] ECLI:EU:C:2008:54, para. 60 ("As to Articles 41, 42 and 47 of the TRIPs Agreement, relied on by Promusicae, in the light of which Community law must as far as possible be interpreted where – as in the case of the provisions relied on in the context of the present

Article 44 of TRIPS requires the Member States to provide for powers "to order a party to desist from an infringement." An infringement, naturally, can be "desisted" from only by somebody who is already an infringer.[4] Similarly, Article 47 foresees the possibility to "order the infringer to inform the right holder." Neither the provision on injunctive relief, nor the provision on the right to information thus address remedies against innocent third parties.[5]

This is less clear in the case of Article 46, which provides that judicial authorities must have the authority to order that goods are "disposed of outside the channels of commerce." The provision is silent on the requirements for the person who is to be ordered carry out such a removal. The second sentence, extending the relief to cover material and implements, could also support a reading that the defendant might also be an innocent third party, such as the owner of materials or implements.[6] Furthermore, Article 50, regulating *preliminary injunctions*, also allows several interpretations. It avoids the term "infringer" and, correspondingly, any qualities of a defendant. However, this could be explained by the fact that preliminary injunctions are also available in cases where the infringement is imminent,[7] but has not yet been committed.[8] Strictly speaking, a person endangering a right is not yet an infringer. So it is natural to refrain from using the term.

In conclusion, although TRIPS does not generally provide for permanent injunctions and claims for information against innocent third parties, some uncertainty is present in the case of a right to recall (Article 46) and less so in the case of

---

reference for a preliminary ruling – it regulates a field to which that agreement applies (. . .), while they require the effective protection of intellectual property rights and the institution of judicial remedies for their enforcement, they do *not* contain provisions which require those directives to be interpreted as compelling the Member States to lay down an obligation to communicate personal data in the context of civil proceedings").

[4] The TRIPS Agreement does not define who an infringer is or what an infringement of intellectual property right is. It does, however, define what it understands by the term "intellectual property right" in its Art. 1(2).

[5] Carlos Correa, *Trade Related Aspects of Intellectual Property Rights: A Commentary on the TRIPS Agreement* (OUP 2007) 429 (noting that information maybe be imposed on an "infringer," but not generally on a "defendant"); Jan Busche, Peter-Tobias Stoll and Andreas Wiebe (eds.), *TRIPs – Internationales und europäisches Recht des geistigen Eigentums* (2nd ed., Heymanns 2012) 642 (noting that information maybe be imposed on an "infringer"); Gerald Spindler, "'Die Tür ist auf' – Europarechtliche Zulässigkeit von Auskunftsansprüchen gegenüber Providern – Urteilsanmerkung zu EuGH 'Promusicae/Telefónica'" (2008) 7 *GRUR* 574, 576 (noting that Article 47 of TRIPS does not cover third parties or providers, but only infringers); Case C-275/06 *Promusicae* [2008] ECLI:EU:C:2007:454, Opinion of AG Kokott, para. 48 (TRIPS only targets infringers); Case C-275/06 *Promusicae* [2008] ECLI:EU:C:2008:54, para. 60 (confirmed the AG opinion, but without differentiating if the reason is in data protection law or noninfringing position of the addressee).

[6] Daniel Gervais, *The TRIPS Agreement: Drafting History and Analysis* (Sweet & Maxwell 2012) 300 (implicitly when giving an example of third parties whose interests are to be taken into account).

[7] Jan Busche, Peter-Tobias Stoll and Andreas Wiebe (eds.), *TRIPs – Internationales und europäisches Recht des geistigen Eigentums* (2nd ed., Heymanns 2012) 653 (arguing that Article 50(1) of TRIPS also covers preliminary injunctions against threatened infringements because of the contextual reading, together with Article 50(3), which talks about imminent infringement).

[8] Ibid., 654 (arguing against the possibility to issue a preliminary injunction against a third party who did not infringe because of the contextual reading of Article 50(1) with Article 43(1)).

preliminary injunctions (Article 50).[9] The TRIPS Agreement does *not* contain any specific provisions targeted at intermediaries. In its general provisions, however, it requires that signatories ensure that enforcement procedures, stipulated "in the Agreement,"[10] are effective, and also avoid the creation of barriers to legitimate trade, provide safeguards against their abuse, are fair and equitable, are not unnecessarily complicated or costly, and do not entail unreasonable time limits or unwarranted delays (Article 41(1)(2)). These requirements, according to the WTO panel, also constitute stand-alone obligations.[11]

An attempt to include injunctions against innocent third parties in the multilateral international treaty was carried out in the Anti-Counterfeiting Trade Agreement (ACTA). An earlier draft of ACTA contained a provision which was identical to the European provisions on injunctions against intermediaries. Article 2.X.2, in its draft from April 2010,[12] stated that "the Parties [may] shall ensure that rightholders are in a position to apply for an injunction against [infringing] intermediaries whose services are used by a third party to infringe an intellectual property right," with terms in brackets being under consideration. The provision has proved, however, too controversial. Surprisingly, not because of the concerns of the Internet service providers, but of health activists who were worried about access to medicines.[13] This language was eventually dropped in September 2010,[14] but replaced by a "shall-provision" requiring that the judicial authorities have the authority to issue, "where appropriate, [an order] to a third party over whom the relevant judicial authority exercises jurisdiction, to prevent infringing goods from entering into the channels of commerce." Although ACTA eventually failed, this language now reappears in some other bilateral trade agreements with the EU.

The members of the World Trade Organization are free to negotiate additional international agreements that would supplement the TRIPS standards.[15] In recent

---

9   "Commission Staff Working Document COM(2010) 779," 13 ("However, an important addition to TRIPS is that such injunctions shall also be available against intermediaries whose services are used by a third party to infringe an intellectual property right").

10   *United States v. China*, Dispute DS362 (WTO Panel, 26 January 2009) at 114 et seq. ("In the Panel's view, the general obligation in Article 41.1 confirms that Article 61 contains obligations, as one of the specific provisions on enforcement procedures in Part III").

11   *United States v. European Communities*, Dispute DS174 (WTO Panel, 15 March 2005) 30 ("The Panel considers that Article 41.1 imposes an obligation. The language of that provision is expressed in terms of what Members "shall" ensure and is not hortatory. The substance of the provision adds qualitative elements to the procedures specified in Part III through use of terms such as "effective," "expeditious" and "deterrent" and is not redundant"); cf. Case C-275/06 *Promusicae* [2008] ECLI:EU:C:2008:54, para. 60.

12   See http://sites.google.com/site/iipenforcement/acta.

13   Editorial, "International Experts Find that Pending Anti-Counterfeiting Trade Agreement Threatens Public Interests" (Naked Law, 23 June 2010), www.wcl.american.edu/pijip/go/acta-communique.

14   Brook Baker, "ACTA: Risks of Third Party Enforcement for Access to Medicines" [2010] PIJIP Research Paper no. 1.

15   This freedom can, however, be restricted by EU law – see Case C-466/12 *Svensson and Others* [2014] ECLI:EU:C:2014:76, para. 40 ("Since the objective of Directive 2001/29 would inevitably be undermined if the concept of communication to the public were construed as including a wider range

years, these so-called TRIPS-plus agreements became a very popular way of further strengthening the enforcement mechanisms included in TRIPS. One of the most notable agreements of this kind is the Comprehensive Economic and Trade Agreement (CETA), which the EU recently concluded with Canada.[16] On the enforcement side, CETA includes (1) a set of minimal safe harbor provisions for some intermediaries in the field of copyright law and related rights (Article 20.11), as well as specific detailed provisions for (2) claims for information (Article 20.36), (3) preliminary injunctions (Article 20.37), and (4) permanent injunctions (Article 20.39). Since all of the provisions are strongly modeled on the EU Enforcement Directive, explicit relief against innocent third parties is present in numerous places.

First of all, *preliminary injunctions* must be, "where appropriate, [provided also] against a third party over whom the relevant judicial authority exercises jurisdiction" (Article 20.37). A similar rule applies to *permanent injunctions* in civil judicial proceedings. Judicial authorities, according to Article 20.39, must have the authority to issue an order, "where appropriate, to a third party over whom the relevant judicial authority exercises jurisdiction, to prevent infringing goods from entering into the channels of commerce." *Claims for information*, on the other hand, are still limited only to infringers or alleged infringers (Article 20.36). Last but not least, none of the *safe harbors for intermediaries* "affect[s] the possibility of a court or administrative authority, in accordance with Parties' legal systems, of requiring the service provider to terminate or prevent an infringement" (Article 20.11(5)).

In summary, this basically means that, where appropriate, third parties such as intermediaries, might be permanently ordered to "prevent infringing goods from entering into the channels of commerce" and, preliminarily, to broadly "prevent an infringement." None of the copyright safe harbors may limit this. Both of the provisions are "shall-rules." And even though Article 20.11 requires that such injunctions applied against the safe harbors–compliant intermediaries are provided "in accordance with Parties' legal systems," this is of little importance, given that Article 20.39 *prescribes* exactly this kind of injunction for all "civil judicial proceedings concerning the enforcement of intellectual property rights," though only "where appropriate." In other words, as a principle, such injunctions must be available against intermediaries, but the margin of appreciation of the signatories is rather broad.

Yet another significant bilateral agreement of the EU concerns South Korea.[17] Section C of Chapter 10 of this agreement includes an entire section of Union

16 European Commission, "Comprehensive Economic and Trade Agreement between Canada, of the one part, and the European Union and its Member States, of the other part" (2016), http://data .consilium.europa.eu/doc/document/ST-10973–2016-INIT/en/pdf.

17 Free Trade Agreement between the European Union and its Member States, of the one part, and the Republic of Korea, of the other part [2011] OJ L 127/6.

law legislation, including identically worded provisions on preliminary and permanent injunctions against "intermediaries"[18] (Article 10.46 and 10.48), the right to information against "any other person who was found to be providing on a commercial scale services used in infringing activities" (Article 10.45) and the European system of safe harbors for online services (Article 10.62 to 10.66).[19] A very similar system of provisions is also found in the recent bilateral trade agreements with Colombia, Peru,[20] and Singapore.[21] The EU is thus keen on exporting the enforcement tool abroad and all pending free trade negotiations are a possible vehicle for this effort.

11.2 NEW GLOBAL MOVEMENT?

If things are slowly shifting on the international stage, very likely, things are already brewing at the national level around the globe.

In the United States, any measures going beyond the DMCA safe harbors are referred to as "DMCA plus" measures. At the moment, the use of those tools is perceived as completely voluntary. Urban, Schofield, and Karaganis explore the use of such tools, such as content identification technologies or trusted submitters programs, in the area of hosting platforms.[22] Bridy explores practices of also more distant providers, such as access providers,[23] domain name authorities or registrars,[24] payment intermediaries;[25] only some of which aren't subject to safe harbors.

---

[18] The explanatory notes 69 and 70 of the Agreement say that "For the purposes of this paragraph, the scope of 'intermediary' is determined in each Party's legislation, but shall include those who deliver or distribute infringing goods, and also where appropriate, include online service providers" (Free Trade Agreement between the European Union and its Member States, of the one part, and the Republic of Korea, of the other part [2011] OJ L 127/6).

[19] Curiously, the Agreement also provides for rules on aiding and abetting but they are limited to criminal enforcement (Free Trade Agreement between the European Union and its Member States, of the one part, and the Republic of Korea, of the other part [2011] OJ L 127/6, Article 10.57).

[20] See Article 239 (right to information), Article 240 (preliminary injunctions), Article 242 (injunctions), Article 250–254 (safe harbors) of the Trade Agreement between the European Union and its Member States, of the one part, and Colombia and Peru, of the other part [2011] OJ L 354/3.

[21] Article 11.42 ("where appropriate, against a third party over whom the relevant judicial authority exercises jurisdiction, an injunction aimed at prohibiting the continuation of the infringement") and Article 11.47 (safe harbors) of the EU–Singapore Free Trade; see http://trade.ec.europa.eu/doclib/press/index.cfm?id=961.

[22] Jennifer Urban, Joe Karaganis and Brianna Schofield, "Notice and Takedown in Everyday Practice" (2016) UC Berkeley Public Law Research Paper No. 2755628, https://ssrn.com/abstract=2755628.

[23] Annemarie Bridy, "Graduated Response American Style: 'Six Strikes' Measured Against Five Norms" (2012) 23(1) Fordham Intellectual Property, Media & Entertainment Law Journal, 1–66; Annemarie Bridy, "ACTA and the Specter of Graduated Response" (2011) 26(3) American University International Law Review 558–577, https://ssrn.com/abstract=1619006.

[24] Annemarie Bridy, "Carpe Omnia: Civil Forfeiture in the War on Drugs and the War on Piracy" (2014) 46 Arizona State Law Journal 683–727; Annemarie Bridy, "Notice and Takedown in the Domain Name System: ICANN's Ambivalent Drift into Online Content Regulation" (2017) Washington and Lee Law Review (forthcoming), https://ssrn.com/abstract=2920805.

[25] Annemarie Bridy, "Internet Payment Blockades" (2015) 67(5) Florida Law Review 1523–1568.

In the United States, the copyright laws don't explicitly provide for a broad possibility to obtain injunctive relief against noninfringers. Under the Digital Millennium Copyright Act,[26] injunctions are granted against infringers[27] and "such relief is not granted where the addressee of the injunction has not violated the plaintiff's copyrights and is not likely to do so in the future."[28] The DMCA also includes Section 512j, which spells out rules that shall apply "in the case of any application for an injunction (. . .) against a service provider that" is covered by a safe harbor. This provision, it is argued, was historically enacted to limit injunctions insofar as they are available under "existing principles of law."[29] It thus acts as a sort of injunctions-specific safe harbor. Similarly as the European carve-outs; it does not confer a legal basis for such injunctions.

The US Copyright Act, unlike the EU law, does not know an independent cause of action for injunction against intermediaries that don't engage in infringements.[30] An attempt to change the status quo was a so-called SOPA/PIPA legislation which sought to extend enforcement to more distant intermediaries.[31] Due to failure to enact this legislation, the rightholders increasingly turn their attention to the existing law. In this respect, two separate debates seem to be under way. The debate regarding (1) the scope of jurisdiction available under the All Writs Act and (2) the scope of procedural rules of the Federal Rules of Civil Procedure. While the first tries to construe an independent cause of action for an injunction, the second construes its effects by attempting to extend the binding power of already granted orders to also nonparties.

The All Writs Act provides that "[t]he Supreme Court and all courts established by Act of Congress may issue all writs necessary or appropriate in aid of their respective

---

[26] Digital Millennium Copyright Act (1998) Pub. L. 105–304.

[27] Annemarie Bridy, "Three Notice Failures in Copyright Law" (2016) 96 *Boston University Law Review* 777, 828.

[28] *Societe Civile Succession Richard Guino v. Int'l Found. for Anticancer Drug Discovery*, 460 F. Supp. 2d 1105, 1110 (D. Ariz. 2006).

[29] Lukas Feiler, "Website Blocking Injunctions under EU and U.S. Copyright Law – Slow Death of the Global Internet or Emergence of the Rule of National Copyright Law?" (2012) TTLF Working Papers No. 13, 31; The Motion Picture Association of America was advised by one of its lawyers that "when one examines the structure and legislative history" of Sections 502 and 512(j) of the Copyright Act, "it appears substantially more likely than not that a court would require a copyright owner to establish the ISP's liability for copyright infringement before the ISP can be ordered to site-block" – see Kenneth L. Doroshow, "Finding of Copyright Infringement Liability as a Prerequisite for a Section 512(j) Injunction," www.scribd.com/document/273059624/mpaa-memo.

[30] Lukas Feiler, "Website Blocking Injunctions under EU and U.S. Copyright Law – Slow Death of the Global Internet or Emergence of the Rule of National Copyright Law?" (2012) TTLF Working Papers No. 13, 31.

[31] Michael Carrier, "SOPA, PIPA, ACTA, TPP: An Alphabet Soup of Innovation-Stifling Copyright Legislation and Agreements" (2013) 11(2) Northwestern Journal of Technology and Intellectual Property 1–31; Annemarie Bridy, "Three Notice Failures in Copyright Law" (2016) 96 Boston University Law Review 777, 826–831.

jurisdictions and agreeable to the usages and principles of law."[32] Its original form was part of the Judiciary Act of 1789, which established the judiciary of the United States. According to the Supreme Court, "[t]he All Writs Act is a residual source of authority to issue writs that are not otherwise covered by statute."[33] This means that the specific legislation can abrogate its jurisdiction,[34] similarly as under English law statutes can limit equitable jurisdiction. Bridy argues that "[a]nyone reading the All Writs Act cases in tandem with the provisions of the Copyright Act governing injunctions would be hard-pressed to conclude that the All Writs Act is a legitimate basis for the injunctions issued in the cases discussed above."[35] She points out that the courts have for instance already declined to grant injunctions over innocent purchasers of infringing books, although such recall could remedy the situation.[36] The jurisdiction is used extensively, however, for prospective assistance in the area of the state surveillance.[37]

In the last years, the courts are also increasingly asked to use procedural tools to force intermediaries to do more than required by the DMCA. Bridy documents the cases.[38] Unlike the All Writs Act jurisdiction, the injunction here takes a form of a nonparty order that only extends and supports an underlying injunction granted against an infringer. Under Rule 65 of the Federal Rules of Civil Procedure, a "[court] order binds only the following who receive actual notice of it by personal service or otherwise: (A) the parties; (B) the parties' officers, agents, servants, employees, and attorneys; and (C) other persons who are in active concert or participation with anyone described in (. . .) (A) or (B)."[39] A nonparty "in active concert or participation with" a defendant can be involved in such a way either pre-grant or postgrant. In both cases, the evidence of such conduct is necessary.[40]

Although the Seventh Circuit held in *Blockowicz v. Williams* that "the fact that [an intermediary] is technologically capable of removing [content] does not render its failure to do so aiding and abetting" in the context of the contempt,[41] the lower

---

[32] 28 U.S.C. § 1651 (2012).

[33] *Pa. Bureau of Corr. v. U.S. Marshals Serv.*, 474 U.S. 34, 43 (1985).

[34] Annemarie Bridy, "Three Notice Failures in Copyright Law" (2016) 96 Boston University Law Review 777, 827, 828.

[35] Ibid., 777, 828.

[36] Ibid. (pointing to Societe Civile Succession Richard Guino v. Int'l Found. for Anticancer Drug Discovery, 460 F. Supp. 2d 1105, 1110 (D. Ariz. 2006)).

[37] Steven R. Morrison, "Breaking iPhones Under CALEA and the All Writs Act: Why the Government Was (Mostly) Right" (2016) Cardozo Law Review (forthcoming), https://ssrn.com/abstract=2808773.

[38] Annemarie Bridy, "Three Notice Failures in Copyright Law" (2016) 96 Boston University Law Review 777, 826–831.

[39] Federal Rules of Civil Procedure (United States).

[40] Annemarie Bridy, "Three Notice Failures in Copyright Law" (2016) 96 Boston University Law Review 777, 819, 818–825.

[41] *Blockowicz v. Williams*, 630 F.3d 563, 568 (7th Cir. 2010).

courts continue to try to expand the concept.[42] Some orders are limited to Section 65(D)(2)(c) and its explicit limitation of "other persons who are in active concert or participation,"[43] others go even beyond. For instance, in *CloudFlare* case,[44] Section 65 is relied on to extend the effect of already granted injunctions against infringers to CloudFlare, an intermediary offering performance service to websites.[45]

Although the proper construction of Section 65 is still open, it is very unlikely that even the broadest construction of extended effects could led to as far-reaching consequences as the European concept of injunctions against intermediaries. On other hand, the domestic interpretation of the All Writs Act in the context of the English developments in equitable jurisdiction could bring a change that is more fundamental, unless prevented by the statute – the US Copyright Act, as argued by Bridy.

Another country of changes is *Australia*. Following unsuccessful attempts to hold access providers jointly liable for Internet piracy,[46] the rightholders turned to the legislator. The parliament adopted the Copyright Amendment (Online Infringement) Act 2015 with effect from 27 June 2015. The act created a novel Section 115A – "injunctions against carriage service providers providing access to online locations outside Australia." According to the provision, the Federal Court of Australia may, on application by the owner of a copyright, grant a website blocking injunction if the Court is satisfied that (1) a carriage service provider provides access to an online location outside Australia; and (2) the online location infringes, or facilitates an infringement of, the copyright; and (3) the primary purpose of the online location is to infringe, or to facilitate the infringement of, copyright (whether or not in Australia).[47] Such injunctions will then require the carriage service provider to "take reasonable steps

[42] See, for the extensive discussion, Annemarie Bridy, "Three Notice Failures in Copyright Law" (2016) 96 Boston University Law Review 777, 819; EFF, "Amicus Brief of Google Inc., Facebook, Inc., Tumblr, Inc., Twitter, Inc., and Yahoo, Inc. in Paramount Pictures et al v. John Does, and Jane Does, United States District Court Southern District of New York, Case No. 1:15-cv-05819-PAC" (2015), www .eff.org/files/2015/08/10/32–1.pdf, p. 3.

[43] N.Y. v. *Operation Rescue Nat'l*, 80 F.3d 64, 70 (2d Cir. 1996); *United States v. Regan*, 858 F.2d 115, 120 (2d Cir. 1988) ("[A] court generally may not issue an order against a nonparty"); *Zenith Radio Corp. v. Hazeltine Research, Inc.*, 395 U.S. 100, 112 (1969) ("[A] nonparty with notice cannot be held in contempt until shown to be in concert or participation"); *Microsystems Software, Inc. v. Scandinavia Online AB*, 226 F.3d 35, 43 (1st Cir. 2000) ("[A]ctive concert" requires a "close alliance with the enjoined defendant").

[44] EFF, "Amicus Brief of Google Inc., Facebook, Inc., Tumblr, Inc., Twitter, Inc., and Yahoo, Inc. in Paramount Pictures et al v. John Does, and Jane Does, United States District Court Southern District of New York, Case No. 1:15-cv-05819-PAC" (2015), www.eff.org/files/2015/08/10/32–1.pdf.

[45] Devlin Hartline, "CloudFlare's Desperate New Strategy to Protect Pirate Sites" (2016), http://cpip .gmu.edu/2016/08/17/cloudflares-desperate-new-strategy-to-protect-pirate-sites/.

[46] *Roadshow Films Pty Ltd v. iiNet Ltd* [2012] HCA 16 (20 April 2012); see also Kylie Pappalardo, "Duty and Control in Intermediary Copyright Liability: An Australian Perspective" (2014) IP Theory 9–27.

[47] An Act relating to copyright and the protection of certain performances, and for other purposes (Copyright Act 1968), as amended by Copyright Amendment (Online Infringement) Bill 2015, Section 115A.

to disable access to the online location." According to Section 115A(9), "[t]he carriage service provider is not liable for any costs in relation to the proceedings unless the provider enters an appearance and takes part in the proceedings." The Revised Explanatory Memorandum concerning the provision states:

> The Bill contains a standalone injunction power which operates as a no-fault remedy. It would not affect existing laws on infringement, copyright exceptions or limitations, authorisation liability or any of the safe harbour conditions. Further, the Court granting an injunction would not create a presumption that the CSP has infringed copyright nor authorised the infringement of copyright.[48]

In the first case applying the provision, the court also stresses this aspect.[49] Therefore, "[i]t is not necessary for the applicant to establish any element of knowledge or intention on the part of a CSP for the applicant to obtain relief against it under s 115A."[50] The relief thus consists of an injunction requiring it "to take reasonable steps to disable access to the online location." It is left open to the court "to grant its injunction conditionally or by the imposition of terms requiring the applicant, for example, to indemnify (in whole or part) a CSP against whom the injunction is sought, or to provide security for a CSP's costs of complying with an injunction."[51]

The examples of the domestic situation in the United States and Australia, as well as efforts surrounding ACTA and SOPA/PIPA show that injunctions against innocent intermediaries are entering the global arena. Until today, however, none of the legal systems seems to have, or at least use, as far-reaching instruments as the EU.

---

[48] Parliament of Australia, "The Parliament of the Commonwealth of Australia, House of Representatives: Copyright Amendment (Online Infringement) Bill 2015 Explanatory Memorandum" (2015), www.aph.gov.au/Parliamentary_Business/Bills_Legislation/Bills_Search_Results/Result?bId=r5446, p. 6–7.
[49] *Roadshow Films Pty Ltd v. Telstra Corporation Ltd* [2016] FCA 1503 (15 December 2016) [30].
[50] Ibid., [32].   [51] Ibid., [33].

12

Conclusions

The legislator would be ill-advised to constantly try to draw a line in sand between the features of legitimate and illegitimate services. The storm of innovation will constantly blur any such boundaries. The law-makers should not try to be technology prophets, but rather clever incentive-setters. If we get the incentives right, we get the intermediary liability and optimal enforcement right.

Before any policy change is undertaken, as a first step, we should also realize that any 100 percent enforcement is likely to be harmful to the society.[1] Attempting to "cure" every single infringement can be as bad as "curing" none. It leads to superoptimal enforcement. An infringing ecosystem often extends beyond services that technically "carry" infringements, so the problem cannot be solved by simply targeting the operator who is in the spotlight. Enforcement should always be a concert of business and enforcement decisions.[2] One without another will do little to change the ecosystem. Since the courts control only the latter and even that upon request, they should never try to solve the enforcement problem on their own.

The analysis points us toward several useful principles. First of all, we should divide the intermediaries into two kinds, *proximate* and *remote*, according to who can be exposed to notice-based liability without destroying the stability/benefits of the infrastructure (see Section 2.1). It is a choice of tools, tortious liability or entitlement to assistance, in the light of their social utility and consequences. The distinction between a proximate and remote service is based on answering the general question of whether the providers of the infrastructure at stake *ought* to be listed among

---

[1] Case C-610/15 *Stichting Brein* [2017] ECLI:EU:C:2017:99, Opinion of AG Szpunar, para. 80 ("according to the case-law of the Court, it is not necessary that intellectual property should be absolutely protected, that is to say, that the proposed measure should result in a complete cessation of copyright infringements").

[2] For an overview of the scholarship – see Brett Danaher, Michael D. Smith and Rahul Telang, "Government-sanctioned and market-based anti-piracy measures can both mitigate economic harm from piracy" (2012) 62(3) Journal of Industrial Economics 541–553.

potential tortfeasors or not. Excluding remote services from potential liability only means that, as a matter of policy, we need to solve problems which arose through other means then liability in tort.

The reader will recall my suggestion that the problem of traffic jams after car accidents should not be solved by imposing liability on the drivers, but rather remedied by promotion of self-driving technologies in cars which could reduce "traffic waves" after the accident is cleared. The principle is the same.

12.1 TWO TRADITIONS, ONE INNOVATION

The civil law and common law systems present two distinct approaches to the legal engagement of innocent third parties in the civil enforcement of rights. Whereas civil law of Germany proved ready as early as the 1900s to hold by-standers accountable for some general help, common law of England hesitated for several decades and the obligations imposed were developed only gradually. It is the stage of the twenty-first century and the era of Internet enforcement that convinced the English courts of a need to expand equitable protective jurisdiction over innocent third parties to more general types of assistance. Owing to the EU, and its legislative intervention, the scope of the two systems seems to be slowly converging, although with some idiosyncrasies caused by doctrine, long-standing case-law, or statutory language.

The uniting idea of these injunctions in both systems is a consideration of the avoidance of a denial of justice. The possibility to prevent injustice, as opposed to the blameworthiness of the conduct, seems to be at the heart of the case-law and still persistently guides it. The systems developed their own filtering mechanisms how to prevent excessive burdening of innocent spectators. However, they seem to do so on entirely different levels. In both systems, there are thresholds allowing to trigger the jurisdiction. Originally, the person who is "mixed up with the transaction," in common law, and "a person whose will maintains the situation," in civil law, could be compelled to assist. This was gradually expanded to the extent that "involvement," in common law, and "a position to prevent" – at first, later "volitional and causal contribution," in civil law of Germany, never truly posed any serious obstacles to legal actions. The main enquiry in both systems center around reasonableness, now dubbed as proportionality of the consequences of such assistance. This confirms the wisdom of the nineteenth-century drafters of the German Civil Code who opined that the main consideration is that of "usefulness" (see Section 9.2).

Despite the obvious differences in legal traditions and sources of law, injunctions against noninfringers were mainly developed through the judiciary in both England and Germany. English courts applying ancient principles of equitable protective jurisdiction, the German courts applying actio negatoria, did both draw upon some legislative texts. The today's principles applied in the case-law, however, were almost entirely invented by the courts.

One important difference between two systems is how they contextualize the legal tool. The civil law system of Germany never felt the need to distinguish noninfringers from infringers by offering them a different name or a treatment. The term "disturber" simply referred to everyone who is responsible to answer a call for an injunction, regardless of whether he is wrongdoer or not. Although the first senate of the Court gradually narrowed the meaning for much of the intellectual property case-law, attempting to cover only noninfringers, the other senates of the Court don't follow this distinction. This naturally means that also in terms of their treatment by the law, whether in the field of cost or scope of injunctions, there was very little effort to differentiate. Common law, on the other hand, from the very beginning treated these types of obligations very cautiously, usually awarding reimbursement as compensation for any inconvenience, stressing "innocence" of parties and limited nature of their required assistance.

Only very recently, have the website blocking injunctions started to change this historical principle. However, the Supreme Court of the United Kingdom might still restore the old principles. The difference in treatment can be also seen in the extent of obligation, where common law injunctions would only oblige the addressee to perform a specific positive steps of assistance, and never took the form of generally worded prohibitory orders seeking a result – extensively used in Germany.

In both systems, accountability for help stands nearby tort law. While in English jurisdiction it clearly complements tortious liability, in German practice, unfortunately, it seems to serve as both partial substitute for underdeveloped accessory liability and its complement. Given that accountability for injunctions and liability in tort both set expected standards of behavior, though drawing on different foundations, this isn't so surprising. Their closeness is deeply rooted in the understanding of remedies as law's responses to someone's wrongs that need to be undone.

Practically speaking, for the addressee, the nature of his or her obligation, doesn't not matter as much as its content. Whether a stay-down obligation is forced upon intermediaries by means of duties to assist or as a precondition of their own legal behavior, matters less than what that duty demands to do. In either case, to continue with its business, they have to comply with it. And although the sanctioning mechanism for noncompliance can be very different, noncompliance with assistance can be also punished more severely than a decision to disrespect one's own standard of care in tort law. In other words, from the prescriptive perspective, the two can be largely equivalent.

What distinguishes them as regulatory tools, however, is that the injunctions against intermediaries allow for more surgical intervention by the state. Surgical in sense of ability to be targeted. Unlike tort law, where the decision about standards of care necessarily triggers an entire package of obligations, injunctions governed by courts allow for targeted responses that are better supervised in their implementation. However, exactly because these injunctions don't use a weight of damages to force private parties to arrive at a socially optimal levels of care, they pose new challenges for their cost and benefit analysis.

From the two analyzed national systems, it is the German one that seems to be more confused about the regulatory role of injunctions against noninfringers. On one hand, it tries to impose assistance, on the other, it does not want to specify it up-front. It does not impose liability for damages, but exposes to pretrial enforcement costs. Even though the courts are essential in governing the system, German law pushes private parties to "early-comply" without the judicial analysis. In contrast, the English systems develops the regulatory mechanisms as a court-supervised targeted public intervention where the court is in charge of assessing and forming its costs and benefits. This model is more complementary to tort law. However, its weakness remains in the cost allocation.

12.2 THE EUROPEAN UNION: TO REFORM OR RETHINK?

The analysis of the historical development of injunctions against innocent third parties undeniably gives certain legitimacy to measures based on Article 8(3) of the InfoSoc Directive and Article 11(III) of the Enforcement Directive. It shows that it is the common legal heritage of both common and civil law to engage innocent by-standers in the enforcement of the rights of others. In this sense, these injunctions against intermediaries cannot be rejected as simply "thoughtless inventions" of Union law. On the contrary, the fact that any assistance is based on the legal and factual possibility of preventing the wrongs of others, rather than any blameworthiness of actions, is remarkably universal given the other disparities of the two institutional systems.

But history alone should not guide our choices. The practice of injunctions against intermediaries under Union law and its application in the Member States has revealed also their numerous flaws. Union law "obliges Member States to ensure that an intermediary whose services are used by a third party in order to infringe an intellectual property right may, regardless of any liability of its own in relation to the facts at issue, be ordered to take measures aimed at bringing those infringements to an end and measures seeking to prevent further infringements."[3] The implementation and use of this instrument, as was shown, greatly differs across the Member States.

I have argued in Chapter 2 that *proximate* services like YouTube, Dropbox, or search engines should be primarily regulated by a well-designed statutory negligence rule in tort law. Its exact design wasn't subject of this work. The courts issuing injunctions against these provides should be therefore reserved when imposing any additional duties of assistance in order to prevent undermining tortious framework. Although the current Union law doesn't support or allow stay-down obligation, it might support other orders such as de-indexing, de-gradation of services (see Sections 8.3 and 10.4). These orders might be still sought by rightholders against proximate services. However, if the compensation element is employed in general, including for *proximate* services, the rightholders would always evaluate whether

---

[3] Case C-494/15 *Tommy Hilfiger Licensing and Others* [2016] ECLI:EU:C:2016:528, para. 22.

the marginal benefits from imposing other assistance measures, such as de-indexing, is worth the costs. And unless the Court of Justice of the European Union or the legislator allows for a German-style switch to notice and stay down at some point, the impact of measures on notice and takedown system will be quite limited.

For *remote services* such as access providers or payment intermediaries, which are too distant from the infringements of third parties, tort law should play only a marginal role. The primary role could be then played by accountability for assistance, which can be claimed either before the courts or negotiated in voluntary agreements. As a distinct regulatory tool that isn't grounded in own wrongfulness of actions, it removes the pressure from liability doctrines which can be substituted by more targeted right to assistance, if appropriate. Judges thus don't face a binary choice between rejecting all the help to rightholders and overburdening the infrastructure by opening the floodgates.

Currently, Article 12 of the E-Commerce Directive, the safe harbor for mere conduit services, embodies a principle that no tortious liability may be imposed on an intermediary, even after notice is received. This provision could be extended to cover other remote services, such as the activities of domain name registration authorities or payment intermediaries. Again, as with the extension of the hosting safe harbor, Union law, at least at the moment, does not generally oppose such a step to be taken on the national level. It should be noted, however, that an extended safe harbor is not strictly necessary. The same effect could be achieved if the courts interpreting domestic tort law came to the conclusion that remote service providers are generally not liable for third-party infringements, be it due to considerations of legal causality, duty of care, or reasonableness.

My suggested changes can often be implemented at the level of judicial practice. There is little need to reform, but rather a great need to rethink the Union law. Under the proposal of this work, intermediaries should be accountable for help on the following conditions: (1) rightholders pay the full direct observable costs of the proposed measures (self-financing) incurred by themselves, intermediaries, and the state ($C^1 + C^2 + C^3$); (2) the courts should moderate for indirect costs that are not as easily observable and measurable, such as impediments to innovation, under the heading of barriers to legitimate trade (C^4); and (3) the courts should also continue to moderate the measures from the human rights perspective. A national implementation, making all these aspects more clear, could for instance take the following explicit form:

Assistance from intermediaries

1   Rightholders should be in a position to apply for specific assistance in the enforcement of their rights from intermediaries whose services are used by a third party to infringe an intellectual property right.

2   The court shall grant the requested assistance in the form of an injunction on the condition that the proposed measure is compliant with the Charter of

Fundamental Rights of the European Union and does not lead to unreasonable barriers to legitimate trade and future innovation.

3   The applicant shall pay the application and implementation costs of the requested assistance. If intermediary requests to reimburse what doesn't seem to correspond to efficiently spent costs, the court can limit such compensation upon request. Intermediaries shall not be required to bear any pretrial costs.

Unlike the existing Article 8(3) of the InfoSoc Directive and Article 11(III) of the Enforcement Directive, the proposed wording *clarifies* that any measures requested may only take the form of specific positive steps of assistance. This, in common law terms, means mandatory injunctions. The undesirable civil law practice of generally worded prohibitory injunctions can be avoided by following the CJEU's requirement to avoid the granting of measures that have as their "object or effect a general and permanent prohibition" of "the continuation of the infringement" (see Section 7.1). This is necessary in order to disjoin assistance by innocent intermediaries from the other forms of injunctions. Otherwise, injunctive relief could easily be misused for the hidden creation of de facto new exclusive rights. The case-law of the CJEU supports such a distinction (see Section 7.2).

The element of self-funding forces the rightholders to internalize the direct costs of intermediaries and thus motivates them to take them into account in their calculations *before* they apply for any measures of assistance. This assures that rightholders apply for assistance only if the expected derived benefit is higher than the overall direct costs. This design choice acts as "information-free screening device" that has number of positive side-effects.[4] First, it reduces the attractiveness of assistance as a substitute for remedies against wrongdoers and thus diminishes competition of regulatory tools. Second, it eases the negotiations between intermediaries and rightholders by promoting voluntary agreements. And third, it removes the anticompetitive effects of such injunctions because their addressees are compensated based on their own situation; the bigger platforms are thus not being given competitive advantage as in the system with own financing. The idea of self-funding is compatible both the Enforcement and InfoSoc Directives (see Section 8.6), and can also find support in the equitable jurisdiction of the common law courts (see Section 11.5) and legislation or early debates in some civil law countries (see Chapter 10). The requirement that pretrial costs are not to be reimbursed just extends this logic.

As can be seen, under the proposal, the courts are still not be completely relieved of moderating the issuance of such injunctions. They would preserve the role of (1) *human rights* and (2) *innovation guardians*.

The first role (1) is rather familiar. It requires the courts to evaluate the proposed measures against the standards of the applicable human rights law. This is an exercise

---

4   Aleksandra Boutin, "Screening for Good Patent Pools through Price Caps on Individual Licenses" (2016) 8(3) American Economic Journal: Microeconomics 64–94 (explaining a information-free screening device for patent pools).

that the courts already do very often today, either under the title of proportionality or reasonableness. As explained in Section 8.4, the restraints imposed by the EU Charter should be seen as an unavoidable fence around the playing field that trumps any considerations of welfare maximization. This is why this consideration should always come first. Among other things, it also saves court's resources from assessing the second step. In the legal exercise, it is in particular recommended that the courts pay close attention to the quality of the law arguments as well as the set of safeguards against possible abuse. General monitoring, in line with CJEU's case-law, should be viewed as unacceptable disproportionate interference (see Section 8.3).

The second role (2) is less familiar. It would require the court to analyze the structure and effects of the indirect costs that will inevitably be imposed on the other members of society (C^4). "Unreasonable barriers to legitimate trade" would thus serve as an all-embracing concept which protects against excessive collateral social costs. It could, in particular, accommodate considerations of dynamic efficiency and the insights of innovation economics. So a court facing an application to oblige an intermediary to password protect his open WiFi, would consider how the issuance of such assistance might influence follow-on innovation. The judge, in this situation, will be always well-advised to limit his measures in time, since his analysis might quickly become obsolete. Since applications for assistance are only seldom proceedings against the innovator himself,[5] the court should also consult third parties whose innovations might be negatively affected before the next review of the measures, and incorporate discharge clauses for innovators (see Section 8.4).

This proposal by no means solves all the problems of Internet enforcement. The impact of voluntary agreements on innovation and human rights, for instance, still remains largely unexplored in the literature, as are certain competition law issues with voluntary enforcement agreements. It does not address how to calibrate the negligence rule applicable to proximate providers. The proposals of this work can, however, contribute to a better understanding of the enforcement landscape, and also help to crystallize existing trends within distinctive economic and social categories, where they can then be better discussed individually.

The *application scheme* of the solution would then look as follows:

1 Are the proposed measures admissible with regard to human rights?
2 Are the proposed measures admissible with regard to their effects on trade and innovation?
3 Does the intermediary already have to act upon notice in order to avoid liability?
   a If the answer is *yes* (proximate service), then granted assistance should not undermine tort law solutions. The assistance is granted under the condition of self-funding.
   b If the answer is *no* (remote service), the proposed form of assistance is granted under the condition of self-funding.

---

[5] Martin Husovec, "Injunctions Against Innocent Third Parties: Case of Website Blocking" (2013) 4 JIPITEC 116, 127.

12.3 REGULATING SELF-REGULATION: THE PROBLEM OF
VOLUNTARY AGREEMENTS

As noted in Chapter 2, voluntary agreements, at least from an economic perspective, certainly have many advantages. The resulting policy is more informed by the interests of the rightholders and intermediaries, since the parties can better re-organize their mutual affairs according to their interests. However, voluntary agreements are not without issues. On the contrary, they open very significant societal questions, especially concerning the role that the human rights ought to play in shaping the new highly privatized information society. To large extent, these issues go beyond the scope of this work. However, since this area of debate is very important, I wish to make several observations with the hope that they could attract some more future work also from my colleagues.

Today, voluntary agreements, often dubbed "self-regulation" or "co-regulation," can be found in two basic forms: (1) the policy of the intermediaries and (2) enforcement agreements between intermediaries and the rightholders. *The policies* of the intermediaries are various terms and conditions of services, and also the actual practice surrounding them. An example are the terms and conditions of using Twitter and its practice, which gives meaning to the provisions. *Enforcement agreements*, on the other hand, are jointly cooperated enforcement practices, which are either formalized or left at the level of mutual courtesy. They vary from robust one-website solutions, such as YouTube's ContentID, to informal government-pressured solutions, such as Google's change of search algorithm for repeated violators, and formalized industry-wide agreements, such as "Memorandum of Understanding on the sale of counterfeit goods via the internet" (EU),[6] "Charters for the Fight Against the Sale of Counterfeit Goods on the Internet" (France), or "IACC Payment Processor Initiative & Portal Program" (United States),[7] "Copyright Alert System" (United States),[8] "Digital Trading Standards Group" (United Kingdom),[9] and "User Generated Content Principles."[10]

The European Intellectual Property Office (OHIM) and International Chamber of Commerce recently did the first mapping exercises concerning these agreements.[11]

---

[6] See http://ec.europa.eu/internal_market/iprenforcement/memoranda/counterfeiting/index_en.htm (dedicated section); http://ec.europa.eu/internal_market/iprenforcement/docs/memorandum_04052011 _en.pdf (Memorandum of Understanding). http://ec.europa.eu/internal_market/iprenforcement/docs/ mou_meeting_summary_20141003_en.pdf (summary of the MoU meeting).

[7] See www.iacc.org/rogueblock.html.

[8] See www.copyrightinformation.org/the-copyright-alert-system/what-is-a-copyright-alert/.

[9] See www.jicwebs.org/agreed-principles/digital-trading-standards-group-good-practice-principles.

[10] See www.ugcprinciples.com/.

[11] International Chamber of Commerce, "Roles and Responsibilities of Intermediaries" (2015), www .iccwbo.org/Advocacy-Codes-and-Rules/BASCAP/International-engagement-and-Advocacy/Roles-and-Responsibilities-of-Intermediaries/; European Union Intellectual Property Office, "Study on Voluntary Collaboration Practices in Addressing Online Infringements of Trade Mark Rights, Design Rights, Copyright and Rights Related to Copyright" (2016), https://euipo.europa.eu/tunnel-web/ secure/webdav/guest/document_library/observatory/documents/Research%20and%20sudies/study_ voluntary_collaboration_practices_en.pdf.

OHIM's study also includes some legal analysis. By far the most complex report, however, was so far carried out by the Institute for Information Law (IViR) which looked at the human rights dimension of such agreements.[12] In the scholarship, Bridy is a forerunner in this by extensively mapping the US situation.[13] Elkin-Koren and Perel explore voluntary stay-down schemes.[14]

Economically speaking, if rightholders and intermediaries are able to agree upon the enforcement measures, this ought to be the best situation. They can even dissolve such agreements if they don't turn out to be as beneficial as expected.[15] But where an agreement aligns the interests of rightholders and intermediaries, it does not necessarily reflects those of other individuals, in particular other businesses or users. Consider the two following examples.

First, an industry agreement between payment processors and rightholders to block all peer-to-peer services from payment processing, and second, a unilateral decision by a dominant player, such as Google or Facebook, to block particular content from its platform as a result of rightholders' pressure or as its own business decision. In both cases, the players involved are private individuals. And although in both cases, competition law might step in in some circumstances,[16] it will not necessarily remedy the situation.

On the other hand, voluntary enforcement arrangements can also advance fundamental rights. Consider the Dutch scheme regarding the access provider's disclosure

---

[12] IViR, "Study of Fundamental Rights Limitations for Online Enforcement Through Selfregulation" (2016), www.ivir.nl/publicaties/download/1796.

[13] Annemarie Bridy, "Graduated Response American Style: 'Six Strikes' Measured Against Five Norms" (2012) 23(1) Fordham Intellectual Property, Media & Entertainment Law Journal, 1–66; Annemarie Bridy, "ACTA and the Specter of Graduated Response" (2011) 26(3) American University International Law Review 558–577, https://ssrn.com/abstract=1619006; Annemarie Bridy, "Carpe Omnia: Civil Forfeiture in the War on Drugs and the War on Piracy" (2014) 46 Arizona State Law Journal 683–727; Annemarie Bridy, "Internet Payment Blockades" (2015) 67(5) *Florida Law Review* 1523–1568; Annemarie Bridy, "Notice and Takedown in the Domain Name System: ICANN's Ambivalent Drift into Online Content Regulation" (2017) Washington and Lee Law Review (forthcoming), https://ssrn.com/abstract=2920805.

[14] Maayan Perel and Niva Elkin-Koren, "Accountability in Algorithmic Copyright Enforcement" (2016) Stanford Technology Law Review – forthcoming; Maayan Perel and Niva Elkin-Koren, "Black Box Tinkering: Beyond Transparency in Algorithmic Enforcement" (2016) Florida Law Review – forthcoming.

[15] The Copyright Alert System was announced to be terminated in its current form partly for not being effective enough – see EFF, "It's the End of the Copyright Alert System (as We Know It)" (2017), www.eff.org/deeplinks/2017/02/its-end-copyright-alert-system-we-know-it.

[16] Recently the German Competition Authority expressed concerns that a self-regulatory initiative of the industry, under which certain services will be black-listed on certain websites, could be against competition law – see Editorial, "Kartellamt stoppt Initiative gegen Piraterie" (Handelsblatt, 21 April 2015), www.handelsblatt.com/unternehmen/it-medien/urheberrechtsverletzungen-im-netz-kartellamt-stoppt-initiative-gegen-piraterie/11668680.html; in this respect it is important to consider Case C-68/12 *Slovenská sporiteľňa* [2013] ECLI:EU:C:2013:71, paras. 18–20 (three Slovak banks decided, by common agreement, to terminate in a coordinated manner the contracts they had concluded with Akcenta, a competitor, which was allegedly operating illegally on the relevant Slovak market. The Court found for a violation of the competition law).

of identity of alleged infringers.[17] The Dutch ISP XS4all set up a procedure which allows anonymous contact between its subscriber and the affected rightholders. The subscriber thus gets an opportunity to take responsibility or inform the access provider that he or she will solve it together with the rightholder. If that doesn't happen, then XS4all asks for help of an independent advisory committee to assist in deciding the disclosure request. The subscriber has again possibility to present his view before his identity is disclosed.

This example shows that the relationship between human rights and voluntary agreements should not be seen only in the negative light. However, what is the role that human rights law can play in shaping these agreements? Human rights primarily bind the state and its bodies (vertical effect). Over time, however, they have begun to have some effect among individuals themselves (horizontal effect). This was necessary, in particular to prevent the increased privatization of the state functions from becoming a back-door to the human rights obligations of the state. In the case-law of the ECtHR, this horizontal effect is covered under the rubric of "positive obligations,"[18] which complement the negative undertakings of the states.[19] A state could thus be compelled to enact specific legislation to fully observe its obligations under the Convention. However, the positive obligations cannot go as far as negative undertakings. Voluntary agreements are thus by definition less scrutinized than acts of states.

This is also relevant in the field of voluntary enforcement of intellectual property rights. The acts of intermediaries, whether based on an agreement or unilateral conduct, can in some cases lead to a responsibility of the state for the resulting outcomes. In the same way that the state would be responsible for violating the right to life if it under-protects with its police force or lacks a functioning justice system that would appropriately punish killings among its citizens.[20] Individuals responding

---

[17] Arnout Veenman, "Xs4all introduceert nieuwe klachtenprocedure" (2007), www.ispam.nl/archives/513/xs4all–introduceert–nieuwe–klachtenprocedure.

[18] See overview Jean-François Akandji-Kombe, *Positive Obligations under the European Convention on Human Rights: A Guide to the Implementation of the European Convention on Human Rights* (Council of Europe 2007), www.echr.coe.int/LibraryDocs/DG2/HRHAND/DG2-EN-HRHAND-07%282007%29.pdf.

[19] *Marckx v. Belgium* App no 6833/74 (ECHR, 13 June 1979), para. 13; *Young, James and Webster v. the United Kingdom* App no 7601/76 and 7806/77 (ECHR, 13 August 1981), para. 49; *VgT Verein gegen Tierfabriken v. Switzerland* App no 24699/94 (ECHR, 28 June 2001), para. 45; in the context of freedom of expression, reference to "duties and responsibilities" in Article 10 of the Convention is a springboard for such positive obligations, as United Nations, General Comment on Freedom of Expression No. 34 (2011) explains in para. 21 they may "relate either to respect of the rights or reputations of others or to the protection of national security or of public order (ordre public) or of public health or morals."

[20] In *VgT Verein gegen Tierfabriken v. Switzerland* App no 24699/94 (ECHR, 28 June 2001), the state was found to be responsible for the actions of a broadcaster because it refused to broadcast the advertising of another individual who was arguing that it only applied the law of Switzerland which prohibited political advertising (para. 47).

to incentives created by the legal system, or lack thereof, thus bring the resulting outcomes within the scope of human rights law as a responsibility of the state.

Intermediaries responding to the demands of right holders could therefore lead to a responsibility of the state.[21] For instance, if liability is imposed on intermediaries too quickly to allow any defense by the users, or there is a lack of legislation curtailing the blocking of websites in response to the private requests of the rightholders, the resulting systematic overblocking of legitimate content could be ascribed to the state. As a consequence, the state could be called to enact specific legislation in order to solve the problem. These positive obligations are slowly on the rise, and will surely be of great significance in the future.[22] With the increasing complexity of social interactions and various enforcement mechanisms, these obligations form a citizen's constitution of safeguards against the arbitrariness of intermediaries and rightholders. Many existing policies, such as data protection's right to explanation, or net neutrality laws, can moreover serve as a springboard to effective human rights remedies in the ordinary law.[23] In general, it seems that human rights need some lower platform to make a proper difference in this area.

A perhaps more workable human rights supervision could be achieved if the voluntary enforcement agreements are nudged toward a standard-setting process. The Court of Justice of the European Union recently held that if private standards are "attached" to the Union law, they become subject to Union law, and its interpretative powers.[24] This means that the resulting technical and organizational norms would also become directly subject to the EU Charter. If the Enforcement Directive and E-Commerce Directive would create a framework that foresees enforcement standardization by designated organizations with particular legal effects, e.g., presumption of compliance with the safe harbors or impossibility to impose more excessive forms of assistance, such standards could become "attached" to Union law as well. Moreover, such standards would benefit a lot from more open discussions in the established standard-setting bodies that are better equipped to deal with the problems such as accountability, public interest, and representativeness.

---

[21] In a recent decision about the liability of Internet platforms, the European Court of Human Rights seemed to gravely underestimate the power of incentives – see *Delfi AS v. Estonia*, App no. 64569/09 (ECHR, 16 June 2015).

[22] Recommendation CM/Rec (2012) 3 of the Committee of Ministers to Member States on the protection of human rights with regard to search engines (adopted by the Committee of Ministers on 4 April 2012 at the 1139th meeting of the Ministers' Deputies) stating that "self- and co-regulatory regimes should not hinder individuals' freedom of expression and right to seek, receive and impart information, ideas and content through any media" (emphasis mine).

[23] Overblocking of website could be construed as a violation of net neutrality. And arbitrariness of filtering technonlogies can be scrutinized by means of right to explanation regarding the fully automated decision making present in the data protection framework (see more about the right: Bryce Goodman and Seth Flaxman, "European Union Regulations on Algorithmic Decision-Making and a 'Right to Explanation'" (2016), https://arxiv.org/abs/1606.08813).

[24] Case C–613/14 *James Elliott Construction* [2016] ECLI:EU:C:2016:821, para. 40.

To conclude, standardization regulation, competition law and human rights law surely need to play a more important role in shaping the enforcement agreements occurring on the market. Further research must be undertaken to investigate the extent to which existing frameworks are sufficient to cope with the novel problems posed by shifting the enforcement from the courts to the realm of private agreements. These agreements are desirable, but they should also produce "legitimate law." They shouldn't be ignored already because they constitute a direct by-product of injunctions against intermediaries.

Table of Legislation

Treaty on European Union [2012] OJ C 326/13

Charter of Fundamental Rights of the European Union [2012] OJ C 326

Directive 2000/31/EC of the European Parliament and of the Council of 8 June 2000 on certain legal aspects of information society services, in particular electronic commerce, in the Internal Market ("Directive on electronic commerce") [2000] OJ L 178

Directive 2001/29/EC of the European Parliament and of the Council of 22 May 2001 on the harmonisation of certain aspects of copyright and related rights in the information society [2001] OJ L 167

Directive 98/71/EC of the European Parliament and of the Council of 13 October 1998 on the legal protection of designs [1998] OJ L 289

Directive 2004/48/EC of the European Parliament and of the Council of 29 April 2004 on the enforcement of intellectual property rights [2004] OJ L 157

Directive 95/46/EC of the European Parliament and of the Council of 24 October 1995 on the protection of individuals with regard to the processing of personal data and on the free movement of such data [1995] OJ L 281

Directive 2002/58/EC of the European Parliament and of the Council of 12 July 2002 concerning the processing of personal data and the protection of privacy in the electronic communications sector [2002] OJ L 201

Regulation (EC) No 864/2007 of the European Parliament and of the Council of 11 July 2007 on the law applicable to noncontractual obligations (Rome II) [2007] L 199/40

Directive 2006/123/EC of the European Parliament and of the Council of 12 December 2006 on services in the internal market [2006] OJ L 376/36

Regulation (EC) No 733/2002 of the European Parliament and of the Council of 22 April 2002 on the implementation of the .eu Top Level Domain [2002] OJ L 113

Agreement on a Unified Patent Court. Brussels, 19 February 2013

Free trade Agreement between the European Union and its Member States, of the one part, and the Republic of Korea, of the other part [2011] OJ L 127/6

Trade Agreement between the European Union and its Member States, of the one part, and Colombia and Peru, of the other part [2011] OJ L 354/3

The European Convention on Human Rights

The Agreement on Trade-Related Aspects of Intellectual Property Rights (TRIPS)

The Paris Convention for the Protection of Industrial Property

Berne Convention for the Protection of Literary and Artistic Works

The WIPO Copyright Treaty (WCT)

The Common Law Procedure Act 1854 (United Kingdom)

The Supreme Judicature Act 1875 (United Kingdom)

The Supreme Court of Judicature Act 1877 (Ireland)

The Judicature Act 1978 (Northern Ireland)

The Judicature Act 1908 (New Zeland)

Copyright Amendment (Online Infringement) Bill 2015 (Australia)

The Supreme Court Civil Procedure Act 1932 (Tasmania)

The Supreme Court Act 1986 (Victoria)

The Judicature Act 2000 (Canada)

The Law and Equity Act 1996 (British Columbia)

The Copyright, Designs, and Patents Act 1988 (United Kingdom)

The E-Commerce Act (E-Commerce Gesetz) of 21 December 2001 (Austria)

Law of 30 June 1994 on Copyright and Related rights (Belgium)

The Civil Code (Bürgerliches Gesetzbuch) of 18 August 1896 (Germany)

The Copyright Act of 1965 (Germany)

The Trade Mark Act of 1994 (Germany)

The Design Act of 2004 (Germany)

The Utility Model Act of 1986 (Germany)

The Federal Constitution of the Swiss Confederation of 18 April 1999 (Switzerland)

Act No. 40/1964 Coll. Civil Code (Slovakia)

Act No 618/2003 Coll. Copyright Act (Slovakia)

Act No 185/2015 Coll. Copyright Act (Slovakia)

Act No. 89/2012 Coll. Civil Code (Czech Republic)

The Intellectual Property Code of 1992 (France)

Tort Law of the People's Republic of China of 26 December 2009 (China)

Ryan Haight Online Pharmacy Consumer Protection Act of 2008 (United States)

Federal Rules of Civil Procedure (United States)

47 US Code § 230 (United States)

17 US Code § 512 (United States)

17 US Code § 1203 (United States)

15 US Code § 1114 (United States)

31 US Code § 5365 (United States)

Table of Cases

AUSTRALIA

Roadshow Films Pty Ltd & Ors v. iiNet Ltd [2012] HCA 16
Australian Broadcasting Corporation v. Lenah Game Meats Pty Ltd [2001] HCA 63
Roadshow Films Pty Ltd v. Telstra Corporation Ltd [2016] FCA 1503

AUSTRIA

OGH LSG v. Tele2 (2009) 4Ob41/09x
OGH (2014) 4 Ob 71/14s
VfGH (2011) U 466/11–18

BELGIUM

Rechtbank van Koophandel Antwerpen, Koninklijke Philips Electronics v. NV
    Mediterranean Shipping Company Belgium (2008) Case No AR 08/02290 NV.
Belgian Court of Appeal of Antwerp, Belgian Anti-Piracy Foundation v. Belgacom
    and Telenet (2011) Case No. 2011/8314

CANADA

Glaxo Wellcome plc v. MNR [1998] FCJ No. 874, [1998] 4 F.C. 439 (C.A.)
Kenney v. Loewen [1999], 64 BCLR (3d) 346, 1999
Alberta (Treasury Branches) v. Leahy [2000] A.J. No. 993, 270 A.R. 1 (Q.B.)
BMG Canada Inc. v. Doe, [2005] FCA 193
Isofoton S.A. v. Toronto Dominion Bank [2007] 85 O.R. (3d) 780, [2007] O.J. No.
    1701 (SCJ)
Procon Mining and Tunnelling Ltd. et al. v. McNeil, Bonnar et al. [2007] BCSC
    454
GEA Group AG v. Flex-N-Gate Corporation [2009] ONCA 619

Pierce v. Canjex Publishing Ltd. [2011] BCSC 1503
Equustek Solutions Inc. v. Google Inc. [2015] BCCA 265

COURT OF JUSTICE OF THE EUROPEAN UNION

Case 294/83 Les Verts v. Parliament [1986] ECLI:EU:C:1986:166
Case 352/85 Bond van Adverteerders and Others [1988] EU:C:1988:196
Joined Cases 46/87 and 227/88 Hoechst v. Commission [1989]
    ECLI:EU:C:1989:337
Case 85/87 Dow Benelux v. Commission [1989] ECLI:EU:C:1989:379
Case C-260/89 ERT v. DEP [1991] ECLI:EU:C:1991:254
Case C-368/95 Familiapress [1997] ECLI:EU:C:1997:325
Case C-397/01 to C-403/01 Pfeiffer and Others [2001] ECLI:EU:C:2004:584
Case C-60/00 Carpenter [2002] ECLI:EU:C:2002:434
Joined cases C-465/00, C-138/01 and C-139/01 Österreichischer Rundfunk and
    Others [2003] ECLI:EU:C:2003:294
Case C-395/07 Commission v. Germany [2008] ECLI:EU:C:2008:325
Case C-275/06 Promusicae [2008] ECLI:EU:C:2008:54
Case C-275/06 Promusicae [2008] ECLI:EU:C:2007:454, Opinion of AG Kokott
Joined Cases C-402/05 P and C-415/05 P Kadi and Al Barakaat International
    Foundation v. Council and Commission [2008] ECLI:EU:C:2008:461
Case C-557/07 LSG-Gesellschaft zur Wahrnehmung von Leistungsschutzrechten
    [2009] ECLI:EU:C:2009:107
Cases C-236/08 to C-238/08 Google France and Google [2009]
    ECLI:EU:C:2009:569, Opinion of the AG Maduro
Cases C-236/08 to C-238/08 Google France and Google [2010]
    ECLI:EU:C:2010:159
Case C-400/10 PPU-MCB [2010] ECLI:EU:C:2010:582
Case C-279/09 DEB [2010] ECLI:EU:C:2010:811
Case C-407/08 P Knauf Gips v. Commission [2010] ECLI:EU:C:2010:389
Joined cases C-92/09 and C-93/09 Volker und Markus Schecke and Eifert [2010]
    ECLI:EU:C:2010:662
Case C-324/09 L'Oréal and Others [2010] ECLI:EU:C:2010:757, Opinion of AG
    Jääskinen
Case C-324/09 L'Oréal and Others [2011] ECLI:EU:C:2011:474
Case C-119/10 Frisdranken Industrie Winters [2011] ECLI:EU:C:2011:258, Opinion
    of AG Kokott
Case C-119/10 Frisdranken Industrie Winters [2011] ECLI:EU:C:2011:837
Joined Cases C-411/10 and C-493/10 N. S. and Others [2011] ECLI:EU:C:2011:865
Case C-70/10 Scarlet Extended [2011] ECLI:EU:C:2011:255, Opinion of AG
    Villalón
Case C-70/10 Scarlet Extended [2011] ECLI:EU:C:2011:771

Case C-461/10 Bonnier Audio AB and Others [2011] ECLI:EU:C:2011:753, Opinion
of AG Jääskinen

Case C-461/10 Bonnier Audio AB and Others [2012] ECLI:EU:C:2012:219

Case C-5/11 Donner [2012] ECLI:EU:C:2012:370

Case C-360/10 SABAM [2012] ECLI:EU:C:2012:85

Case C-617/10 Åkerberg Fransson [2013] ECLI:EU:C:2013:280

Case C-314/12 UPC Telekabel Wien [2013] ECLI:EU:C:2013:781, Opinion of AG
Villalón

Case C-399/11 Melloni [2013] ECLI:EU:C:2013:107

Case C-68/12 Slovenská sporiteľňa [2013] ECLI:EU:C:2013:71

Joined Cases C-293/12 and C-594/12 Digital Rights Ireland [2014]
ECLI:EU:C:2014:238

Case C-466/12 Svensson and Others [2014] ECLI:EU:C:2014:76

Case C-348/13 BestWater International [2014] ECLI:EU:C:2014:2315

Case C-291/13 Papasavvas [2014] ECLI:EU:C:2014:2209

Case C-314/12 UPC Telekabel Wien [2014] ECLI:EU:C:2014:192

Opinion 2/13 of the Court [2014] ECLI:EU:C:2014:2454

Case C-146/13 Spain v. Parliament and Council [2015] ECLI:EU:C:2015:298

Case C-580/13 Coty Germany [2015] ECLI:EU:C:2015:243, Opinion of AG Villalón

Case C-580/13 Coty Germany [2015] ECLI:EU:C:2015:485

Case C-681/13 Diageo Brands [2015] ECLI:EU:C:2015:471, Opinion of AG Szpunar

Case C-681/13 Diageo Brands [2015] ECLI:EU:C:2015:137

Case C-494/15 Tommy Hilfiger Licensing and Others [2016] ECLI:EU:C:2016:528

Case C-484/14 Mc Fadden [2016] ECLI:EU:C:2016:689

Case C-484/14 Mc Fadden [2016] ECLI:EU:C:2016:170, Advocate General Szpunar

Case C-610/15 Stichting Brein [2017] ECLI:EU:C:2017:99, Opinion of AG Szpunar

Case C-427/15 NEW WAVE CZ [2017] ECLI:EU:C:2017:18

Case C-73/16 Puškár [2017] ECLI:EU:C:2017:253, Opinion of AG Kokott

DENMARK

Supreme Court, Telenor v. IFPI Denmark, Case No. 153/2009 (27 May 2010)

THE EUROPEAN COURT OF HUMAN RIGHTS

Marckx v. Belgium App no 6833/74 (ECHR, 13 June 1979)

Young, James, and Webster v. the United Kingdom App no 7601/76 and 7806/77
(ECHR, 13 August 1981)

Leander v. Sweden App no 9248/81 (ECHR, 26 March 1987)

Kruslin v. France App no (ECHR, 24 April 1990)

Chassagnou and others v. France App no 25088/94, 28331/95 and 28443/95 (ECHR,
29 April 1999)

Margareta and Roger Andersson v. Sweden App no 12963/87 (ECHR, 25 February 1992)

VgT Verein gegen Tierfabriken v. Switzerland App no 24699/94 (ECHR, 28 June 2001)

Coban v. Spain App no 17060/02 (ECHR, 25 September 2006)

Tan v. Turkey App no 9460/03 (ECHR, 3 July 2007)

K.U. v. Finland App no 2872/02 (ECHR, 2 December 2008)

Balan v. Moldova App no 19247/03 (ECHR, 29 January 2008)

Financial Times Ltd and Others v. The United Kingdom, App no. 821/03 (ECHR, 15 December 2009)

Sanoma Uitgevers v. the Netherlands App no 38224/03 (ECHR, 14 September 2010)

MSS v. Belgium and Greece App no 30696/09 (ECHR, 21 January 2011)

Delfi AS v. Estonia App no 64569/09 (ECHR, 10 October 2013)

Ahmet Yildrimi v. Turkey App no 3111/10 (ECHR, 18 March 2013)

Akdeniz v. Turkey App no 20877/10 (ECHR, 11 March 2014)

Contrada v. Italy (no. 3) App no 66655/13 (ECHR, 14 April 2014)

Delfi AS v. Estonia, App no. 64569/09 (ECHR, 16 June 2015)

Magyar Tartalomszolgaltatok Egyesulete and Index.hu ZRT v. Hungary, App no. 22947/13 (ECHR, 2 February 2016)

Pihl v. Sweden, App no. 74742/14 (ECHR, 9 March 2017)

FINLAND

Helsinki Court of Appeals (2008) Case R 07/3400

Helsinki Court of Appeals (2012) Case S 11/3097

Helsinki Court of Appeals (2013) Case S 12/1825

Helsinki Court of Appeals (2013) Case S 12/2223

The Market Court (2016) Case 243/16

FRENCH

Conseil Constitutionnel (2009) Case No 2009–58 DC

Cour de Cassation (2012) Case No 11–20358

Tribunal de Grande Instance, Association des Producteurs de Cine´ma (APC) and others v. Auchan Telecom and others (2013) Case No 11/60013

GERMANY

RG (1900) VI 316/00, RGZ 47, 164

RG (1902) VI 208/02, RGZ 52, 373

RG (1903) VI 349/02, RGZ 54, 53

RG (1918) V 228/17, RGZ 92, 22

RG (1918) V 228/17, RGZ, 92, 22

RG (1921) V 151/21, RGZ 103, 174
RG (1921) VI 473/20, RGZ 101, 335
RG (1937) V 74/37
RG (1941) VI ZR 129/40, RGZ 167, 55
BGH (1952) I ZR 87/51
BGH (1954) III ZR 1/53
BGH Constanze II. (1954) I ZR 38/53
BGH Cupresa (1954) I ZR 178/52
BGH Grundig-Reporter (1955) I ZR 8/54
BGH Pertusin II. (1957) I ZR 56/55
BGH (1960) VI ZR 27/60
BGH Werbung für Tonbandgeräte (1960) I ZR 41/58
BGH (1960) I ZR 30/58
BGH (1963) Ib ZR 23/62
BGH (1963) Ib ZR 127/62
BGH Personalausweise (1965) Ib ZR 4/63
BGH (1965) Ib ZR 33/64
BGH (1966) V ZR 126/63
BGH (1967) Ib ZR 22/65
BGH Fotowettbewerb (1969) I ZR 3/68
BGH Badische Rundschau (1972) I ZR 1/71
BGH (1972) VI ZR 26/71
BGH (1972) V ZR 149/71
BGH VUS (1976) VI ZR 23/72
BGH (1984) I ZR 45/82
BGH Sporthosen (1985) I ZR 86/83
BGH Verkaufsfahrten II. (1988) I ZR 36/87
BGH Benzinwerbung (1988) I ZR 170/86
BGH Firmenrufnummer (1989) I ZR 27/88
BGH Schönheitschirugie (1989) I ZR 29/88
BGH (1990) I ZR 299/88
BGH Pressehaftung I (1990) I ZR 127/88
BGH Honoraranfrage (1991) I ZR 227/89
BGH Pressehaftung II. (1992) I ZR 119/90
BGH Produktinformation I. (1993) I ZR 14/91
BGH Betonerhaltung (1994) I ZR 122/92
BGH Beipackzettel (1994) I ZR 51/92
BGH Produktinformation II. (1994) I ZR 167/92
BGH Schlankheitswerbung (1994) I ZR 316/91
BGH Schlußverkaufswerbung II. (1994) I ZR 147/92
BGH (1994) I ZR 321/91
BGH (1994) I ZR 12/92

BGH (1994) I ZR 139/92
BGH (1994) I ZR 40/92
BGH (1995) I ZR 8/54
BGH (1995) I ZR 133/93
BGH Produktinformation III. (1995) I ZR 227/93
BGH Architektenwettbewerb (1996) I ZR 129/94
BGH (1996) I ZR 184/94
BGH (1996) I ZR 130/94
BGH Branchen-Nomenklatur (1997) I ZR 3/95
BGH (1997) I ZR 36/95
BGH Möbelklasiker (1998) I ZR 120/96
BGH (1998) I ZR 179/96
BGH (1999) I ZR 49/97
BGH (1999) I ZR 121/97
BGH (2000) I ZR 167/98
BGH (2000) I ZR 67/98
BGH (2000) I ZR 269/97
BGH (2001) V ZR 389/99
BGH Meißner Dekor (2001) I ZR 22/99
BGH ambiente.de (2001) I ZR 251/99
BGH (2001) I ZR 314/98
BGH (2001) I ZR 153/99
BGH (2001) I ZR 136/99
BGH (2001) I ZR 281/99
BGH (2003) I ZR 292/00
BGH (2003) V ZR 175/02
BGH (2003) V ZR 37/02
BGH (2003) I ZR 259/00
BGH kurt-biedenkopf.de (2004) I ZR 82/01
BGH Internetversteigerung I. (2004) I ZR 304/01
BGH Selbstauftrag (2004) I ZR 2/03
BGH Schöner Wetten (2004) I ZR 317/01
BGH (2004) I ZR 303/01
BGH (2004) I ZR 156/02
BGH (2004) v. ZR 230/03
BGH (2005) I ZR 119/02
BGH (2005) I ZR 201/02
BGH (2006) I ZR 124/03
BGH (2006) I ZR 249/03
BGH Katzenfreund (2007) VI ZR 101/06
BGH Internetversteigerung II. (2007) I ZR 35/04
BGH Jugendgefährdende Medien bei eBay (2007) I ZR 18/04

BGH Internetversteigerung III. (2007) I ZR 73/05
BGH MP3-Player-Import (2009) Xa ZR 2/08
BGH marions-kochbuch.de (2009) I ZR 166/07
BGH Cybersky (2009) I ZR 57/07
BGH pcb (2009) I ZR 139/07
BGH Halzband (2009) I ZR 114/06
BGH Spickmich.de (2009) VI ZR 196/08
BGH focus.de (2009) VI ZR 210/08
BGH (2009) I ZR 109/06
BGH Kinderhochstuehle im Internet I. (2010) I ZR 139/08
BGH Jahrhundertmörder (2010) VI ZR 30/09
BGH Sommer unseres Lebens (2010) I ZR 121/08
BGH Sedo (2010) I ZR 155/09
BGH Preußische Gärten (2010) V ZR 44/10
BGH (2010) I ZR 191/08
BGH (2010) VI ZR 30/09
BGH (2010) VI ZR 34/09
BGH Basler Haar-Kosmetik (2011) I ZR 150/09
BGH Kosten des Patentanwalts II (2011) I ZR 181/09
BGH (2011) I ZR 145/10
BGH (2011) I ZR 131/10
BGH Automobil-Onlinebörse (2011) I ZR 159/10
BGH Blogger (2011) VI ZR 93/10
BGH Stiftparfüm (2011) I ZR 57/09
BGH dlg.de (2012) I ZR 150/11
BGH RSS-Feed (2012) VI ZR 144/11
BGH Morpheus (2012) I ZR 74/12
BGH (2012) V ZR 136/11
BGH (2012) I ZR 235/10
BGH (2012) I ZR 54/11
BGH (2012) VI 341/10
BGH Alles kann besser werden (2012) I ZB 80/11
BGH Alone in the Dark (2012) I ZR 18/11
BGH Kosten des Patentanwalts IV (2012) I ZR 70/11
BGH Autocomplete (2013) VI ZR 269/12
BGH File-Hosting-Dienst (2013) I ZR 80/12
BGH Kinderhochstühle im Internet II. (2013) I ZR 216/11
BGH (2013) I ZR 79/12
BGH BearShare (2014) I ZR 169/12
BGH Videospiel-Konsolen II (2014) I ZR 124/11
BGH Geschäftsführerhaftung (2014) I ZR 242/12
BGH (2015) I ZR 3/14

BGH Störerhaftung des Access-Providers (2015) I ZR 174/14
BGH Posterlounge (2015) I ZR 104/14
BGH (2015) VI ZR 340/14
BGH Haftung für Hyperlink (2015) I ZR 74/14
BGH TV-Wartezimmer (2015) I ZR 84/14
BGH WLAN Verschlüsselung (2016) I ZR 220/15
BGH Silver Linings Playbook (2016) I ZR 86/15
BGH Herstellerpreisempfehlung bei Amazon (2016) I ZR 110/15
BGH Angebotsmanipulation bei Amazon (2016) I ZR 140/14
BGH (2016) VI ZR 34/15
BGH (2016) I ZR 220/15
BVerfG (1990) 1 BvR 26/84, BVerfGE 81, 242, 255
BVerfG (1995) 1 BvF 1/90, 1 BvR 342/90, 1 BvR 348/90, BVerfGE 92, 26, 46
BVerwG (1985) 4 C 46.82
LG Frankfurt am Main (2010) 2–6 S 19/09, ZUM-RD 2011, 371
LG Hamburg (2010) 310 O 433/10, MMR 2011, 475
LG Munich (2011) 17 HK O 1398/11
OLG Karlsruhe (2012) 12 U 143/11
OLG Stuttgart (2013) 4 W 78/13
LG Frankfurt am Main (2013) 2–06 O 304/12, ZUM-RD 2014, 36
OLG Frankfurt/M. (2013) 11 W 39/13
OLG Köln (2014) 6 U 192/11, GRUR [2014] 1081
OLG Hamburg (2014) 5 U 68/10, GRUR-RR [2014] 140
LG Hamburg (2015) 310 S 23/14
KG Berlin (2017) 24 U 117/15

IRELAND

EMI Records (Ireland) Ltd v. Eircom Ltd [2005] IEHC 233
EMI Records (Ireland) Ltd v. Eircom Ltd [2009] IEHC 411
EMI Records & Ors v. Eircom Ltd [2010] IEHC 108
EMI Records [Ireland] Ltd & Ors v. UPC Communications Ireland Ltd [2010]
    IEHC 377
EMI Records (Ireland) Ltd v. Data Protection Commissioner [2012] IEHC 264
Ryanair Ltd v. Unister GMBH [2013] IESC 14
Sony Music Entertainment (Ireland) Limited v. UPC Communicaitons Ireland
    Limited (No 1) [2015] IEHC 317

ITALY

Tribunale di Milano, Reti Televisive Italiane S.p.A. (RTI) v. Yahoo! Italia S.r.l.
    (Yahoo!) et al. (2011) Case No. 3821/11

Corte d'Appello di Milano, Reti Televisive Italiane S.p.A. (RTI) v. Yahoo! Italia
  S.r.l. (Yahoo!) et al. (2015) Case No. 3821/2011
Tribunale Regionale Amministrativo (TAR) del Lazio, FEMI, and Open Media
  Coalition v. Autorità per le Garanzie nelle Comunicazioni (AGCOM) (2014)
  Case No 2184/2014

NETHERLANDS

Rechtbank Amsterdam (2007) LJN BA7810
Gerechtshof Amsterdam (2008) LJN BD6223
Rechtbank 's-Gravenhage (2012) ECLI:NL:RBSGR:2012:BV0549
Rechtbank Amsterdam, *Brein v. ING* (2013) ECLI:NL:RBAMS:2013:CA0350
Gerechtshof Den Haag (2014) ECLI:NL:GHDHA:2014:88
Hoge Raad (2015) ECLI:NL:HR:2015:3307

SLOVAKIA

Slovak Constitutional Court Tank Man (2015) II. ÚS 647/2014–22

SPAIN

Spanish Constitutional Court Melloni (2014) Case No. STC 26/2014
Audiencia Provincial Barcelona Promusicae v. X (2013) 470/2013

SWEDEN

Swedish Patent and Market Court of Appeal, Patent- och Marknadsöverdomstolen
  (2017) PMT 11706–15

UNITED KINGDOM

Upmann v. Elkan [1871] 7 Ch App 130
Orr v. Diaper [1876] 4 Ch. D. 92
Beddow v. Beddow [1878] 9 Ch. D. 89
North London Railway Co v. Great Northern Railway Co [1883] 11 QBD 30
Holmes v. Millage [1893] 1 Q.B. 551
Norwich Pharmacal Co. & Others v. Customs and Excise Commissioners [1974]
  AC 133
Gouriet v. Union of Post Office Workers [1978] A.C. 435
Morton Norwich Products v. Intercen [1978] RPC 501
The Siskina [1979] AC 210
Bankers Trust Co v. Shapira [1980] 1 W.L.R. 1274 Court of Appeal
British Steel Corporation v. Granada Television Ltd [1981] A.C. 1096 House of
  Lords 1183

Castanho v. Brown & Root (UK) Ltd [1981] AC 557

British Airways Board v. Laker Airways Ltd [1985] AC 58

Amstrad Consumer Electronics Plc v. British Phonographic Industry Ltd [1986] FSR 159 Court of Appeal

South Carolina Insurance Co Ltd v. Assurantie Maatschappij De Zeven Provincien NV [1987] AC 24

CBS Songs Ltd v. Amstrad Consumer Electronics Plc [1988] WL 624207 House of Lords

Pickering v. Liverpool Daily Post [1991] 2 AC 370

Kirklees MBC v. Wickes Building Supplies Ltd [1993] AC 227

Channel Tunnel Group Ltd v. Balfour Beatty Construction Ltd [1993] AC 334

CHC Software Care v. Hopkins & Wood [1993] FSR 241 Chancery Division

Mercedes-Benz AG v. Leiduck [1996] AC 284

Jade Engineering (Coventry) Ltd v. Antiference Window Systems Ltd [1996] FSR 461 Chancery Division

British Telecommunications Plc & Ors v. One In A Million Ltd & Ors [1998] EWCA Civ 1272

Glaxo Wellcome plc v. MNR [1998] FCJ No. 874, [1998] 4 F.C. 439 (C.A.)

Microsoft Corp v. Plato Technology Ltd [1999] FSR 834 Chancery Division

Broadmoor Special Hospital Authority v. Robinson [2000] QB 775

Australian Broadcasting Corporation v. Lenah Game Meats Pty Ltd [2001] HCA 63

Ashworth Hospital Authority v. MGN Ltd [2002] HRLR 41 House of Lords

Interbrew SA v. Financial Times Ltd [2002] WL 237064 Court of Appeal

Totalise Plc v. Motley Fool Ltd [2002] 1 W.L.R. 1233

Fourie v. Le Roux [2007] UKHL 1, [2007] 1 WLR 320

Customs and Exercise Commissioners v. Barclays plc [2007] UKHL 28

L'Oreal SA & Ors v. EBay International AG & Ors [2009] EWHC 1094 (Ch)

Metropolitan International Schools Ltd. (t/a Skillstrain and/or Train2game) v. Designtechnica Corp (t/a Digital Trends) & Ors [2009] EWHC 1765 (QB)

Mulvaney & Ors v. The Sporting Exchange Ltd trading as Betfair [2009] IEHC 133

Kaschke v. Gray & Anor [2010] EWHC 690 (QB)

Media CAT Ltd v. Adams [2011] WL 291789 Patents County Court

Twentieth Century Fox Film Corp v. British Telecommunications plc [2011] EWHC 1981 (Ch), [2012] Bus LR 1471

Twentieth Century Fox Film Corp v. British Telecommunications plc (No 2) [2011] EWHC 2714 (Ch), [2012] Bus LR 1525

Tasarruf Mevduati Sigorta Fonu v. Merrill Lynch Bank & Trust Company [2011] UKPC 17, [2012] 1 WLR 1721

Samsung Electronics (UK) Ltd v. Apple Inc [2012] EWCA Civ 1339

Dramatico Entertainment Ltd v. British Sky Broadcasting Ltd [2012] EWHC 268 (Ch), [2012] 3 CMLR 14

Dramatico Entertainment Ltd v. British Sky Broadcasting Ltd (No 2) [2012] EWHC 1152 (Ch)

Golden Eye (International) Ltd & Anor v. Telefónica UK Ltd [2012] EWHC 723 (Ch)

Golden Eye (International) Ltd & Ors v. Telefónica UK Litd & Anor [2012] EWCA Civ 1740

Samsung Electronics (UK) Ltd v. Apple Inc [2012] EWCA Civ 1339

Tamiz v. Google Inc Google UK Ltd [2012] EWHC 449 (QB)

Ust-Kamenogorsk Hydropower Plant JSC v. AES Ust-Kamenogorsk Hydropower Plant LLP [2013] UKSC 35, [2013] 1 WLR 1889

Rugby Football Union v. Viagogo Ltd [2013] EMLR 25 Supreme Court

EMI Records Ltd v. British Sky Broadcasting Ltd [2013] EWHC 379 (Ch), [2013] ECDR 8

Football Association Premier League Ltd v. British Sky Broadcasting Ltd [2013] EWHC 2058 (Ch), [2013] ECDR 14

Paramount Home Entertainment International Ltd v. British Sky Broadcasting Ltd [2013] EWHC 3479 (Ch), [2014] ECDR 7

JSC BTA Bank v. Ablyazov & 16 Ors [2014] EWHC 2019

Cartier International AG & Ors v. British Sky Broadcasting Ltd & Ors [2014] EWHC 3354 (Ch)

Warner-Lambert Company LLC v. National Health Service Commissioning Board [2015] EWHC 2548

The Football Association Premier League Limited v. Wells [2015] 3910 (Ch)

Cartier International AG & Ors v. British Sky Broadcasting Ltd & Ors [2016] EWCA Civ 658

Cartier International Ltd & Anor v. British Telecommunications Plc & Ors [2016] EWHC 339

The Football Association Premier League Ltd v. British Telecommunications Plc & Ors [2017] EWHC 480 (Ch)

UNITED STATES

Zenith Radio Corp. v. Hazeltine Research, Inc., 395 US 100, 112 (1969)

Spur Industries, Inc. v. Del E. Webb Dev. Co., 494 P.2d 700 (Ariz. 1972)

Pa. Bureau of Corr. v. US Marshals Serv., 474 US 34, 43 (1985)

United States v. Regan, 858 F.2d 115, 120 (2d Cir. 1988)

N.Y.v. Operation Rescue Nat'l, 80 F.3d 64, 70 (2d Cir. 1996)

Lockheed Martin Corp. v. Network Solutions, Inc., 985 F.Supp. 949 (C.D. Cal. 1997)

Microsystems Software, Inc. v. Scandinavia Online AB, 226 F.3d 35, 43 (1st Cir. 2000)

Lockheed Martin Corp. v. Network Solutions, Inc. 141 F. Supp. 2d 648 (N.D. Tex. 2001)

A&M Records, Inc. v. Napster, Inc., 239 F.3d 1004 (2001)

A&M Records, Inc. v. Napster, Inc., No. C 99-05183, 2001 US Dist. LEXIS 2169 (N.D. Cal. 5 March 2001)

Ellison v. Robertson, 357 F.3d 1072, 1076 (9th Cir. 2004)

MGM Studios, Inc. v. Grokster, Ltd., 545 US 913 (2005)

Societe Civile Succession Richard Guino v. Int'l Found. for Anticancer Drug Discovery, 460 F. Supp. 2d 1105, 1110 (D. Ariz. 2006)

Perfect 10, Inc. v. Visa Int'l Serv. Ass'n, 494 F.3d 788, 798 (9th Cir. 2007)

Perfect 10, Inc. v. CCBill LLC, 481 F.3d 751, 758 (9th Cir. 2007)

Rescuecom Corp. v. Google Inc., 562 F.3d 123 (2d Cir. 2009)

Blockowicz v. Williams, 630 F.3d 563, 568 (7th Cir. 2010)

Viacom International Inc et. Seq. v. Youtube, 718 F. Supp. 2d 514 (SDNY 2010)

Kelly-Brown v. Winfrey, 717 F.3d 295 (2d. Cir. 2013)

WORLD TRADE ORGANIZATION

United States v. European Communities, Dispute DS174 (WTO Panel, 15 March 2005)

United States v. China, Dispute DS362 (WTO Panel, 26 January 2009)

References

BOOKS AND BOOK CHAPTERS

Akandji-Kombe J, *Positive Obligations under the European Convention on Human Rights: A Guide to the Implementation of the European Convention on Human Rights*(Council of Europe 2007)

Angelopoulos Ch, *European Intermediary Liability in Copyright: A Tort-Based Analysis* (Kluwer Law International 2016)

Apathy P and Klingenberg G, *Einführung in das römische Recht* (Böhlau 1994)

Aubry Ch and Rau C, *Cours de Droit civil Francias* (2nd ed., Marchal und Billard 1935)

Bacher K, *Die Beeinträchtigungsgefahr als Voraussetzung für Unterlassungsklagen im Wettbewerbsrecht und in anderen Gebieten des Zivilrechts* (1996)

Baldus Ch, "Beseitigungs- und Unterlassungsanspruch" in Roland Rixecker and others (eds.) *Münchener Kommentar zum BGB* (6th ed., C. H. Beck 2013)

Ben-Shahar O, "Causation and Foresee-ability" in *Encyclopedia of Law and Economics* (vol. 2, Springer 2001)

Boháček M, *Actio negatoria k dějinám zápůrči žaloby* (Nákl. České Akad. Věd a Umění 1938)

Bryce J, *Studies in History and Jurisprudence* (Oxford University Press 1901)

Buckland W, *A Text-Book of Roman Law: From Augustus to Justinian* (Cambridge University Press 2007)

Buckland W and McNair A, *Roman Law and Common Law* (2nd ed., Cambridge University Press 1952)

Busche J, Stoll P-T, and Wiebe A (eds.), *TRIPs – Internationales und europäisches Recht des geistigen Eigentums* (2nd ed., Heymanns 2012)

Calabresi G, *The Costs of Accidents* (Yale University Press 1970)

Campbell J, *Lives of the Lord Chancellors and Keepers of the Great Seal of England, from the Earliest Times till the Reign of Queen Victoria* (7th ed., Baron 1885)

Collins L, *The Civil Jurisdiction and Judgments Act 1982* (Butterworths 1983)

Conrad-Baldenstein U, *Die Actio Negatoria mit besonderer Berücksichtigung der Beweislast* (Orell Füssli 1907)

Cooter R, *The Falcon's Gyre: Legal Foundations of Economic Innovation and Growth – Book 1* (Berkeley Law Books 2014) http://scholarship.law.berkeley.edu/books/1

Cooter R and Porat A, *Getting Incentives Right: Improving Torts, Contracts and Restitution* (Princeton University Press 2014)

Correa C, *Trade Related Aspects of Intellectual Property Rights: A Commentary on the TRIPS Agreement* (Oxford University Press 2007)

Döring R, *Die Haftung für eine Mitwirkung an fremden Wettbewerbsverstößen, Urheberrechts-, Marken-, Patent-, Gebrauchmuster- und Geschmacksmusterverletzungen* (Deutscher Anwalt Verlag 2008)

Dreier T and Hugenholtz B (eds.) *Concise European Copyright Law* (2nd ed., Wolters Kluwer 2016)

Dreier T and Schulze G, *Urheberrechtsgesetz: UrhG* (4th ed., C. H.Beck 2013)

Eberl-Borges Ch, et al., *Julius von Staudingers Kommentar zum Bürgerlichen Gesetzbuch: Staudinger BGB – Buch 2: Recht der Schuldverhältnisse §§ 830-838* (Sellier/de Gruyter 2008)

Elkin-Koren N and Salzberger E, *The Law and Economics of Intellectual Property in the Digital Age: The Limits of Analysis* (Routledge 2013)

Erman W and Westermann P, *Erman. Bürgerliches Gesetzbuch: Handkommentar mit AGG, EGBGB (Auszug), ErbbauRG, HausratsVO, LPartG, ProdHaftG, UKlaG, VAHRG und WEG* (11th ed., Schmidt Otto 2008)

Geiger Ch, "Implementing Intellectual Property Provisions in Human Rights Instruments: Towards a New Social Contract for the Protection of Intangibles" in Christopher Geiger (ed.), *Research Handbook on Human Rights and Intellectual Property* (Edward Elgar 2014)

Gervais D, *The TRIPS Agreement: Drafting History and Analysis* (Sweet & Maxwell 2012)

Grabenwarter Ch and Vranes E, *Kooperation der Gerichte im europäischen Verfassungsverbund – Grundfragen und neuste Entwicklungen* (Manzsche Verlags- und Universitätsbuchhandlung 2013)

Gursky K, *Julius von Staudingers Kommentar zum Bürgerlichen Gesetzbuch – Buch 3: Sachenrecht §§ 985–1011* (13th ed., Sellier/de Gruyter 1999)

Habersack M, et al., *Münchener Kommentar zum BGB* (6th ed., C. H. Beck 2013)

Hartmann A, *Unterlassungsansprüche im Internet* (C. H. Beck 2009)

Heise A, *Grundriss eines Systems des Gemeinen Civilrechts, Buch II* (Mohr u. Winter 1807)

Helpman E, *The Mystery of Economic Growth* (Belknap 2004)

Helpman E and Trajtenberg M, "A Time to Sow and a Time to Reap. Growth Based on General Purpose Technologies in Elhanan Helpman" in *General Purpose Technologies and Economic Growth* (MIT Press 1998)

Herrmann E, *Der Störer nach § 1004 BGB. Zugleich eine Untersuchung zu den Verpflichteten der §§ 907, 908 BGB* (Duncker & Humbolt 1987)

Hofmann F, *Der Unterlassungsanspruch als Rechtsbehelf* (Mohr Siebeck 2017)

Hohloch G, *Die negatorische Ansprüche und ihre Beziehungen zum Schadensersatzrecht* (Alfred Metzner Verlag 1976)

Holznagel D, *Notice and Takedown Verfahren als Teil der Providerhaftung* (Mohr Siebeck 2013)

Holmes O, *The Common Law* (Little, Brown 1881)

Honsell H, *Römisches Recht* (Springer 2010)

Hügel A, *Haftung von Inhabern privater Internetanschlüsse für fremde Urheberrechtsverletzungen* (C. H. Beck 2014)

Husovec M, *Doménová čítanka* (EISi 2012)

Husovec M, *Zodpovednosť na Internete: podľa slovenského a českého práva* (CZNIC 2014)

Jakobs H and Schubert W (eds.), *Die Beratung des Bürgerlichen Gesetzbuchs: In systematischer Zusammenstellung der unveröffentlichten Quellen* (De Gruyter 1978)

Johow R, *Die Vorlagen der Rektoren für die erste Kommission zur Ausarbeitung des Entwurfs eines Bürgerlichen Gesetzbuches – Sachenrecht, Teil 1, Allgemeine Bestimmungen, Besitz und Eigentum* (first published 1880, De Gruyter 1991)

Kawasumi Y, *Von der römischen action negatoria zum negatorischen Beseitigungsanspruch des BGB* (Nomos Verlag 2001)

Kerr I and Cameron I, "NYMITY, P2P & ISPS: Lessons from BMG Canada Inc. v. John Doe" in Katherine J. Strandburg and Daniela Stan Raicu (eds.), *Privacy and Technologies of Identity: A Cross-Disciplinary Conversation* (Springer 2005)

Klang H, *Kommentar zum ABGB 1, 2* (Verl. Österreich 1931)

Koziol H, "Providerhaftung nach ECG und MedienG" in Walter Berka, Christopher Grabenwarter, and Michael Holoubek (eds.) *Persönlichkeitsschutz in elektronischen Massenmedien* (Manz Verlag 2012)

Kramer A, *Zivilrechtlicher Auskunftsanspruch gegenüber Access Providern* (Kovač 2007)

Kropp J, *Die Haftung von Host- und Access-Providern bei Urheberrechtsverletzungen Gebundene Ausgabe* (Peter Lang 2012)

Landes W and Posner R, *The Economic Structure of Tort Law* (Harvard University Press 1987)

Larenz K and Canaris C, *Lehrbuch des Schuldrechts II* (13th ed., C. H. Beck 1994)
Methodenlehre der Rechtswissenschaft (3rd ed., Springer 2008)

Luby Š, *Výber z diela a myšlienok* (IURA Edition 1998)

Maitland F, Chaytor A, and Whittaker W, *The Forms of Action at Common Law: A Course of Lectures Paperback* (Cambridge University Press 1936)

Mancini A, *Ancient Roman Solutions to Modern Legal Issues: The Example of Patent Law* (2nd ed., Buenos Books America 2007)

Marcus N, "Blocking Web Sites – Experiences from Finland" in Johan Axhamn (ed.), *Copyright in a Borderless Online Environment* (Norstedts Juridik 2012)

Mattei U, *Basic Principles of Property Law: A Comparative Legal and Economic Introduction* (Praeger 2000)

Meagher H, et al., *Doctrines and Remedies* (4th ed., Butterworths 2002)

Mehring T, *Beteiligung und Rechtswidrigkeit bei § 830 I 2 BGB. Zugleich ein Beitrag zur Behandlung der Fälle von Anteilszweifeln und Opfermehrheiten* (Duncker & Humblot 2003)

Menell P, "Intellectual Property: General Theories" in *Encyclopedia of Law & Economics: Volume II* (Springer 2000)

Mießner S, *Providerhaftung, Störerhaftung und Internetauktion* (Peter Lang 2008)

Mugdan B (ed.), *Die gesamten Materialien zum Bürgerlichen Gesetzbuch für das Deutsche Reich: Band III* (Deker's Verlag 1899–1900)

Münzberg W, *Verhalten und Erfolg als Grundlagen der Rechtswidrigkeit und Haftung* (Vittorio Klostermann 1966)

Mylly T, "Constitutional Perspective" in Justine Pilla (ed.) *The Unitary EU Patent System* (Oxford University Press 2014)

Neuner R, *Privatrecht und Prozeßrecht* (Bensheimer 1925)

OECD, *The Role of Internet Intermediaries in Advancing Public Policy Objectives* (OECD Publishing 2011)

Ohly A, "Three Principles of European IP Enforcement Law: Effectiveness, Proportionality, Dissuasiveness" in J Drexl (ed.) *Technology and Competition, Contributions in Honor of Hanns Ullrich* (Larcier 2009)
"Urheberrecht in der digitalen Welt – Brauchen wir neue Regelungen zum Urheberrecht und dessen Durchsetzung?" in G Bachmann (ed.) *Verhandlungen des 70. Deutschen Juristentages* (C. H. Beck 2014)

Ohly A and Sosnitza O, *Gesetz gegen den unlauteren Wettbewerb* (6th ed., C. H. Beck 2014)

Olson M, *The Logic of Collective Action: Public Goods and the Theory of Groups* (Harvard University Press 1974)

Paulus A, "Schutz des geistigen Eigentums" in Josef Isensee and Paul Kirchhof (eds.), *Handbuch des Staatsrechts der Bundesrepublik Deutschland, Band XI* (C. H. Beck 2013)

Peguera M, *La exclusión de responsabilidad de los intermediarios en Internet* (Editorial Comares 2007)

Peukert A, *Die Gemeinfreiheit: Begriff, Funktion, Dogmatik* (Mohr Siebeck 2012)

Picker E, "Der 'dingliche Anspruch'" in Helmut Koziol and Peter Rummel (eds.) *Im Dienste der Gerechtigkeit: Festschrift für Franz Bydlinski* (Springer 2002)

  Der negatorische Beseitigungsanspruch (Mohr 1972)

  "Prävention durch negatorischen Schutz" in Luboš Tichý and Jiří Hrádek (eds.) *Prevention in Law* (Centrum Právní Komparatistiky PFUK v. Praze 2013)

Pieroth B, et al., *Grundrechte. Staatsrecht II* (C. H. Beck 2014)

Pigou A, *The Economics of Welfare* (first published 1920, Macmillan 1932)

Pihlajarinne T, *Internetvälittäjä ja tekijänoikeuden loukkaus* (Lakimiesliiton Kustannus 2012)

Pollock F and Maitland W, *The History of English Law* (2nd ed., Cambridge University Press 1893)

Posner R, *An Introduction to Economic Analysis of Law* (Aspen 1982)

  Economic Analysis of Law (Aspen 2003)

  The Economics of Justice (Harvard University Press 1981)

Puchta G, *Über die negatorienklage* (Rhein Museum 1827)

Randa A, *Právo vlastnické dle rakouského práva v. pořádku systematickém* (Nákl. České Akademie Císaře Františka Josefa pro vědy, slovesnost a umění 1917)

Rawls J, *A Theory of Justice* (Harvard University Press 1971)

Riordan J, *The Liability of Internet Intermediaries* (Oxford University Press 2016)

Sassenberg T and Mantz R, *WLAN und Recht. Aufbau und Betrieb von Internet-Hotspots* (Erich Schmidt Verlag 2014)

Savola P, *Internet Connectivity Providers as Involuntary Copyright Enforcers: Blocking Websites in Particular* (IPR University Center 2015)

Schäfer H, "Tor Law: General" in *Encyclopedia of Law and Economics: Volume II* (Springer 2001)

Schäfer H, et al., *The Economic Analysis of Civil Law* (Edward Elgar 2004)

Schapiro L, *Unterlassungsansprüche gegen die Betreiber von Internet-Auktionshäusern und Internet-Meinungsforen* (Mohr 2011)

Scheder-Bieschin F, *Modernes Filesharing* (OlWIR Verlag 2013)

Schmidt E and Cohen J, *The New Digital Age: Reshaping the Future of People, Nations and Business* (Knopf 2013)

Schneider A, *Vom Störer zum Täter?* (Nomos 2012)

Schwabe J, *Die sogennante Drittwirkung der Grundrechte* (Goldman 1971)

Shavell S, *Economic Analysis of Accident Law* (Harvard University Press 1987)

Siber H, *Die Passivlegitimation bei der rei vindicatio als Beitrag zur Lehre von der Aktionenkonkurrenz* (Deichert 1907)

Sliwka Ch, *Herausgabeansprüche als Teil des zivilrechtlichen Eigentumsrechts? die rei vindicatio und funktionsäquivalente Ansprüche des Eigentümers gegen den Besitzer im französischen, englischen und deutschen Recht* (Logos 2012)

Smith A, *An Inquiry into the Nature and Causes of the Wealth of Nations* (first published 1776, David Campbell 1991)

Smith M, *Elements of Law, in Studying Law* (2nd ed., Vanderbilt 1955)

Spindler G, et al., *Teledienstegesetz* (C. H. Beck 2004)

Spry I, *Equitable Remedies: Injunctions and Specific Performance* (5th ed., Sweet & Maxwell 1997)

> *Equitable Remedies: Injunctions and Specific Performance* (9th ed., Sweet & Maxwell 2013)

Stein I, *Der Auskunftsanspruch gegen Access-Provider nach § 101 UrhG* (Kovač 2012)

Teplitzky O, *Wettbewerbsrechtliche Ansprüche und Verfahren* (Carl Heymanns Verlag 2011)

Tuhr A, *Der Allgemeine Teil des Deutschen Bürgerlichen Rechts, Band I. Allgemeine Lehren und Personenrecht* (first published 1910, Duncker & Humblot 2013)

Ufer F, *Die Haftung der Internet Provider nach dem Telemediengesetz* (Kovač 2007)

van Boom W, "Compensating and Preventing Damage: Is There Any Future Left for Tort Law?" in Hugo Tiberg (ed.), *Festskrift till Bill W. Dufwa – Essays on Tort, Insurance Law and Society in Honour of Bill W. Dufwa: Volume I* (Jure Förlag 2006)

van Schewick B, *Architecture & Innovation: The Role of the End-to-End Arguments in the Original Internet* (MIT Press 2010)

von Bar Ch, *Verkehrspflichten richterliche Gefahrsteuerungsgebote im deutschen Deliktsrecht* (Heymann 1980)

von Savigny F, *System des heutigen Römischen Rechts: Band 5* (Veit 1841)

von Staudinger J (ed.), *Bürgerliches Gesetzbuch* (13th ed., Sellier-deGruyter 1993)

Wagner E, *Gesetzliche Unterlassungsansprüche im Zivilrecht: zugleich eine Untersuchung des Beseitigungsanspruchs* (Manz 2004)

Walter A, *Störerhaftung bei Handeln Dritter* (Peter Lang 2011)

Walter M and Goebel D, "Enforcement Directive" in M Walter and S von Lewinski (eds.), *European Copyright Law: A Commentary* (Oxford University Press 2010)

Wang J, *Regulating Hosting ISPs' Responsibilities for Copyright Infringement: The Freedom to Operate in the US, EU and China* (PhD Thesis 2016)

Welp K, *Die Auskunftspflicht von Access-Providern nach dem Urheberrechtsgesetz* (C. H. Beck 2009)

Wenzel K, et al., *Das Recht der Wort- und Bildberichterstattung: Handbuch des Äußerungsrechts* (5th ed., Otto Schmidt 2003)

Wetzel R, *Die Zurechnung des Verhaltens Dritter bei Eigentumsstörungstatbeständen* (Mohr Siebeck 1971)

Windscheid B, *Die Actio des römischen Civilrechts vom Standpunkte des heutigen Rechts* (Buddeus 1856)

> *Lehrbuch des Pandektenrecht, I. Band* (Verlagshandlung von Julius Buddeus 1862)

Wright D, *Remedies* (Federation Press 2010)

Zachariä K, *Handbuch des Französichen Civilrechts, Erste Band* (Akademische Buchhandlung von Ernst Mohr 1853)

Zippelius R, *Juristische Methodenlehre* (11th ed., C. H. Beck 2012)

ARTICLES

Ahrens H, "21 Thesen zur Störerhaftung im UWG und im Recht des Geistigen Eigentums" WRP [2007] 1281

Angelopoulos Ch, "Are Blocking Injunctions against ISPs Allowed in Europe? Copyright Enforcement in the Post-Telekabel Legal Landscape" [2014] *GRUR International* 1089

> "Filtering the Internet for Copyright Content in Europe" [2009] IRIS Plus 5

Ardia D, "Free Speech Savior or Shield for Scoundrels: an Empirical Study of Intermediary Immunity Under Section 230 of the Communications Decency Act" (2010) 43 *Loyola of LA Law Review* 373

Armbrüster Ch, "Eigentumsschutz durch den Beseitigungsanspruch nach § 1004 I 1 BGB und durch Deliktsrecht" (2003) 43 *Neue Juristische Wochenschrift* 3087

Baker B, "ACTA: Risks of Third Party Enforcement for Access to Medicines" [2010] PIJIP, Research Paper no. 1

Barry J, et al., "Coasean Keep-Away: Voluntary Transaction Costs" (2014) 14–149 San Diego Legal Studies Paper 60

Bechtold S and Tucker C, "Trademarks, Triggers, and Online Search" (2014) 11(4) *Journal of Empirical Legal Studies* 718

Berger A and Janal R, "Suchet und Ihr werdet finden? Eine Untersuchung zur Störerhaftung von Online-Auktionshäusern" [2004]CR 917

Bezzenberger G, "Der negatorische Beseitigungsanspruch und die Kosten der Ersatzvornahme" [2005] Juristenzeitung 373

Bezzenberger T, "Der negatorische Beseitigungsanspruch und die Kosten der Ersatzvornahme" [2005] JZ 373

Blake T, et al., "Consumer Heterogeneity and Paid Search Effectiveness: A Large Scale Field Experiment" [2014] Working paper http://faculty.haas.berkeley.edu/stadelis/Tadelis.pdf

Blevins J, "Uncertainty as Enforcement Mechanism: The New Expansion of Secondary Copyright Liability to Internet Platforms" (2013) 34 *Cardozo Law Review* 1821

Bölling M, "Unterlassungsantrag und Streitgegenstand im Falle der Störerhaftung" [2013] *GRUR* 1092

Bornkamm J, "E-Commerce Directive vs. IP Rights Enforcement – Legal Balance Achieved?" [2007] *GRUR International* 642

Boutin A, "Screening for Good Patent Pools through Price Caps on Individual Licenses" (2016) 8(3) *American Economic Journal: Microeconomics* 64

Brabyn J, "Protection Against Judicially Compelled Disclosure of the Identity of News Gatherers' Confidential Sources in Common Law Jurisdictions" (2006) 69 *The Modern Law Review* 895

Bradford S, "Shooting the Messenger: The Liability of Crowdfunding Intermediaries for the Fraud of Others" (2015) 83 *University of Cincinnati Law Review* 371

Breshnahan T and Greenstein S, "The Economic Contribution of Information Technology: Towards Comparative and User Studies" (2001) 11(1) *Journal of Evolutionary Economics* 95

Breshnahan T and Trajtenberg M, "General Purpose Technologies: Engines of Growth" (1995) 65(1) *Journal of Econometrics* 83

Breyer P, "Verkehrssicherungspflichten von Internetdiensten im Lichte der Grundrechte" [2009] MMR 14

Bridy A, "ACTA and the Specter of Graduated Response" (2011) 26(3) *American University International Law Review* 558–577

"Carpe Omnia: Civil Forfeiture in the War on Drugs and the War on Piracy" (2014) 46 *Arizona State Law Journal* 683–727

"Graduated Response American Style: 'Six Strikes' Measured Against Five Norms" (2012) 23(1) *Fordham Intellectual Property, Media & Entertainment Law Journal* 1–66

"Graduated Response and the Turn to Private Ordering in Online Copyright Enforcement" (2010) 89 *Oregon Law Review* 81

"Internet Payment Blockades" (2015) 67(5) *Florida Law Review* 1523–1568

"Notice and Takedown in the Domain Name System: ICANN's Ambivalent Drift into Online Content Regulation" (forthcoming) *Washington and Lee Law Review* https://ssrn.com/abstract=2920805

"Three Notice Failures in Copyright Law" (2016) 96 *Boston University Law Review* 777–832

Brimsted K and Chesney G, "The ECJ's Judgment in Promusicae: The Unintended Consequences – Music to the Ears of Copyright Owners or a Privacy Headache for the Future? A Comment" (2008) 24 *Computer Law & Security Review* 275–279

Calabresi G, "Concerning Cause and the Law of Torts: An Essay for Harry Kalven" (1975) 43 *University of Chicago Law Review* 69

Calabresi G and Hirschoff J, "Toward a Test for Strict Liability in Torts" (1972) 81 *Yale Law Journal* 1055

Calabresi G and Melamed D, "Property Rules, Liability Rules, and Inalienability: One View of the Cathedral" (1972) 85 *Harvard Law Review* 1089

Carrier M, "SOPA, PIPA, ACTA, TPP: An Alphabet Soup of Innovation-Stifling Copyright Legislation and Agreements" (2013) 11(2) *Northwestern Journal of Technology and Intellectual Property* 1

Castets-Renard C, "Le renouveau de la responsabilité délictuelle des intermédiaires de l'internet" [2012] Recueil Dalloz 827

Chesbrough H and Teece D, "When Is Virtual Virtuous? Organizing for Innovation" (1996) 74 *Harvard Business Review* 128

Cheung A and Pun K, "Comparative Study on the Liability for Trademark Infringement of Online Auction Providers" (2009) 31(11) *European Intellectual Property Review* 559

Ciolino D and Donelon E, "Questioning Strict Liability in Copyright" (2001–2002) 54 *Rutgers Law Review* 351

Coase R, "Adam Smith's View of Man" (1976) 19 *Journal of Law and Economics* 529

Coase R, "The Federal Communications Commission" (1959) 2 *Journal of Law and Economics* 1

Coase R, "The Problem of Social Cost" (1960) 3 *Journal of Law and Economics* 1

Conradi M, "Liability of an ISP for Allowing Access to File Sharing Networks" (2003) 19 *Computer Law & Security Report* 289

Cooter R, "The Cost of Coase" (1982) 11 *The Journal of Legal Studies* 1

"Liberty, Efficiency, and Law" (1972) 50 *Law and Contemporary Problems* 141

"Torts as the Union of Liberty and Efficiency: An Essay on Causation" (1987) 63 *Chicago Kent Law Review* 523

Cooter R, et al., "Liability Rules, Limited Information, and the Role of Precedent" (1979) 10(1) *The Bell Journal of Economics* 366

Coudert F and Werkers E, "In The Aftermath of the Promusicae Case: How to Strike the Balance?" (2010) 18 *International Journal of Law and Information Technology* 50

Crabit E, "La directive sur le commerce électronique. Le projet 'Méditerranée'" (2000) 4 *Revue du Droit de l'Union Européenne* 749

Craswell R, "Kaplow and Shavell on the Substance of Fairness" (2003) 32 *Journal of Legal Studies* 245–276

Cregan Q, "Roving Injunctions and John Doe Orders Against Unidentifiable Defendants in IP Infringement Proceedings" (2011) 6(9) *Journal of Intellectual Property Law & Practice* 623

Czychowski Ch, "Auskunftsansprüche gegenüber Internetzugangsprovidern 'vor' dem 2. Korb und 'nach' der Enforcement-Richtlinie der EU" [2004] MMR 514

Czychowski Ch and Nordemann J, "Grenzenloses Internet – entgrenzte Haftung?" [2013] GRUR 986

Danaher B, et al., "The Effect of Piracy Website Blocking on Consumer Behavior" (SSRN, 2015) http://ssrn.com/abstract=2612063

Danaher B, et al., "Government-Sanctioned and Market-Based Anti-piracy Measures Can Both Mitigate Economic Harm from Piracy" (2017) 60(2) ACM 68

Danaher B, et al., "The Effect of Graduated Response Anti-piracy Laws on Music Sales: Evidence from an Event Study in France" (2014) 62(3) *Journal of Industrial Economics* 541

Dietz A, "Verfassungsklauseln und Quasi-Verfassungsklauseln zur Rechtfertigung des Urheberrechts – gestern, heute und morgen" [2006] *GRUR International* 1

Dootson P and Suzor N, "The Game of Clones and the Australia Tax: Divergent Views about Copyright Business Models and the Willingness of Australian Consumers to Infringe" (2015) 38(1) *University of New South Wales Law Journal* 206

Döring R, "Die Haftung für eine Mitwirkung an Wettbewerbsverstößen nach der Entscheidung des BGH 'Jugendgefährdende Medien bei eBay'" [2007] WRP 1131

Dreier T, "Die Umsetzung der Urheberrechtsrichtlinie 2001/29/EG in deutsches Recht" [2002] ZUM 28

Drexl J, "The European Unitary Patent System: On the 'Unconstitutional' Misuse of Conflict-of-Law Rules" [2015] Max Planck Institute for Innovation & Competition Research Paper No. 15

Dworkin R, "What Is Equality? Part 2: Equality of Resources" (1981) 10 *Philosophy & Public Affairs* 283

Eberl-Borges Ch, "§ 830 und die Gefährdungshaftung" [1996] Archiv für civilistische Praxis 196

Editorial, "After Åkerberg Fransson and Melloni" (2013) 9 *European Constitutional Law Review* 170

Editorial, "The Court of First Instance of Athens (Monomeles Protodikio Athinon): 'Security Measures Against ISPs'" [2013] IIC 468

Eichmann H, "Die Durchsetzung des Anspruchs auf Drittauskunft" [1990] *GRUR* 575

Einhorn M, "Copyright, Prevention, and Rational Governance: File-Sharing and Napster" (2001) 24 *Columbia Journal of Law & the Arts* 449

Ekker A, "Anonimiteit en uitingsvrijheid op het Internet; het onthullen van identificerende gegevens door Internetproviders Verschenen" (2002) 11/12 *Mediaforum* 348

Elkin-Koren N, "Copyright Law and Social Dialogue on the Information Superhighway: The Case Against Copyright Liability of Bulletin Board Operators" (1995) 13 *Cardozo Arts & Entertainment Law Journal* 345

Engels G, "BGH: 'Autocomplete'-Funktion: Verantwortlichkeit eines Suchmaschinenbetreibers für persönlichkeitsverletzende Begriffsvorschläge" [2013] MMR 535

Faria N, et al., "The Early Spread and Epidemic Ignition of HIV-1 in Human Populations" (2014) 346 *Science* 56

Feiler L, "Website Blocking Injunctions under EU and US Copyright Law – Slow Death of the Global Internet or Emergence of the Rule of National Copyright Law?" (2012) TTLF Working Papers No. 13

Freytag S, "Verantwortlichkeit für rechtswidrige Inhalte nach der E-Commerce-Richtlinie" [2000] CR 600

Frischmann B and Lemley M, "Spillovers" (2007) 107 *Columbia Law Review* 257

Gasser U and Schulz W, "Governance of Online Intermediaries: Observations from a Series of National Case Studies" [2015] Berkman Center Research Publication No. 2015-5 7 http://ssrn.com/abstract=2566364

Gilles S, "Negligence, Strict Liability, and the Cheapest Cost-Avoider" (1992) 78 *Virginia Law Review* 1291

"Rule-Based Negligence and the Regulation of Activity Levels" (1992) 21 *The Journal of Legal Studies* 319

Ginsburg J, "Separating the Sony Sheep from the Grokster Goats: Reckoning the Future Business Plans of Copyright-Dependent Technology Entrepreneurs" (2008) 50 *Arizona Law Review* 577

Glatstein B, "Tertiary Copyright Liability" (2004) 71 *The University of Chicago Law Review* 1605

Goold P, "Corrective Justice and Copyright Infringement" (2013) 16 *Vanderbilt Journal of Entertainment and Technology Law* 251

Gounalakis G, "Rechtliche Grenzen der Autocomplete-Funktion von Google" [2013] NJW 2321

Green J, "On the Optimal Structure of Liability Laws" (1976) 7(2) *The Bell Journal of Economics* 553

Groussot X, "Case C–275/06, Productores de Música de España (Promusicae) v. Telefónica de España SAU, Judgment of the Court (Grand Chamber) of 28 January 2008" (2008) 45 *Common Market Law Review* 1745

Gursky K, "Zur neueren Diskussion um § 1004 BGB" [1989] Juristische Rundschau 397

Güth W, et al., "An Experimental Analysis of Ultimatum Bargaining" (1982) 3 *Journal of Economic Behavior & Organization* 367

Haber E, "The French Revolution 2.0: Copyright and the Three Strikes Policy" (2011) 2(2) *Harvard Journal of Sports & Entertainment Law* 297

Halldórsdóttir H, "Enforcement of Copyright" (2004) 47 *Scandinavian Studies in Law* 168

Hamdani A, "Who's Liable for Cyberwrongs" (2002) 87 *Cornell Law Review* 901

Harper J, "Against ISP Liability" (2005) 28 REG. 30

Haskel D, "A Good Value Chain Gone Bad: Indirect Copyright Liability in Perfect 10 v. Visa" (2008) 23 *Berkeley Technology Law Journal* 405

Heald P, "How Notice-and-Takedown Regimes Create Markets for Music on YouTube: An Empirical Study" (2014) Working Paper, http://ssrn.com/abstract=2416519

Heidinger R, "Die zivilrechtliche Inanspruchnahme von Access-Providern auf Sperre urheberrechtsverletzender Webseiten" [2011] ÖBl 153

Henry P and Luo H, "WiFi: What's Next?" [2002] IEEE Telecommunications Magazine 66

Hewicker J, et al., "Der Abmahnkosten-Ersatzanspruch im Urheberrecht" [2014] NJW 2753

Hindelang S, "Circumventing Primacy of EU Law and the CJEU's Judicial Monopoly by Resorting to Dispute Resolution Mechanisms Provided for in Inter-se Treaties? The Case of Intra-EU Investment Arbitration" (2012) 39 *Legal Issues of Economic Integration* 179

Hoeren T and Yankova S, "The Liability of Internet Intermediaries – The German Perspective" [2012] IIC 501

Hoffman E and Spitzer M, "The Coase Theorem: Some Experimental Tests" (1982) 25 *Journal of Law and Economics* 75

Hofmann F, "Die Haftung des Inhabers eines privaten Internetanschlusses für Urheberrechtsverletzungen Dritter" [2014] ZUM 654

"Markenrechtliche Sperranordnungen gegen nicht verantwortliche Intermediäre" [2015] GRUR 123

Husovec M, "Accountable, Not Liable: Injunctions Against Intermediaries" (2016) TILEC Discussion Paper No. 2016–012

"CJEU Allowed Website Blocking Injunctions With Some Reservations" (2014) 9 (8) *Journal of Intellectual Property Law & Practice* 631

"Injunctions Against Innocent Third Parties: Case of Website Blocking" (2013) 4 *JIPITEC* 116

"Intellectual Property Rights and Integration by Conflict: The Past, Present and Future" (2016) 18 *Cambridge Yearbook of European Legal Studies* 239

Husovec M and Peguera M, "Privately Litigated Disconnecting Injunctions" [2015] IIC 10

Husovec M and van Dongen L, "Website Blocking, Injunctions and Beyond: View on the Harmonization from the Netherlands" [2017] *GRUR* 9

Hylton K, "Missing Markets Theory of Tort Law" (1996) 90 *Northwestern University Law Review* 977

Jaeger T, "Shielding the Unitary Patent from the ECJ: A Rash and Futile Exercise" [2013] IIC 389

Jakobsen S, "Injunctions Against Mere Conduit of Information Protected by Copyright – A Scandinavian Perspective" (2011) IIC 151

Jakobsen S, "Mobile Commerce and ISP Liability in the EU" (2011) 1 *International Journal Law Information Technology* 46

James W and Smith J, "Is Further Legislation Really Necessary to Level the Playing Field? A UK Perspective" (2004) 20(5) *Computer Law & Security Review* 356

Jones Ch, "Sources of US Economic Growth in a World of Ideas" (2002) 92(1) *American Economic Review* 220

Kahneman D, et al., "Experimental Tests of the Endowment Effect and the Coase Theorem" (1990) 98 *Journal of Political Economy* 1325

Kaplow L, "Optimal Deterrence, Uninformed Individuals, and Acquiring Information about Whether Acts Are Subject to Sanctions" (1990) 6 *Journal of Law, Economics, & Organization* 93

Kaplow L and Shavell S, "Why the Legal System is Less Efficient than the Income Tax in Redistributing Income" (1994) 23 *Journal of Legal Studies* 667

Kelly G, "A Court-Ordered Graduated Response System in Ireland: The Beginning of the End?" (2016) 11(3) *Journal of Intellectual Property Law and Practice* 183

Kim J, "Strict Liability versus Negligence When the Injurer's Activity Involves Positive Externalities" (2006) 22 *European Journal of Law and Economics* 96

Kitz V, "§ 101 a UrhG: Für eine Rückkehr zur Dogmatik" [2005] *ZUM* 298, 301

Köhler H, "'Täter' und 'Störer' im Wettbewerbs- und Markenrecht – Zur BGH-Entscheidung 'Jugendgefährdende Medien bei eBay'" [2008] *GRUR* 1

Kraakman R, "Gatekeepers: The Anatomy of a Third-Party Enforcement Strategy" (1986) 2 *Journal of Law, Economics & Organization* 53

Kuczerawy A, "Intermediary Liability & Freedom of Expression: Recent Developments in the EU Notice & Action Initiative" (2014) ICRI Research Paper No. 21

Kulk S, "Filtering for Copyright Enforcement in Europe after the Sabam Cases" [2012] EIPR 791

Kuner Ch, "Data Protection and Rights Protection on the Internet: The Promusicae Judgment of the European Court of Justice" [2008] European Intellectual Property Review 199

Kur A, "The Enforcement Directive: Rough Start, Happy Landing?" [2004] IIC 821, 822

"'Freeze Plus' Melts the Ice – Observations on the European Design Directive" [1999] IIC 620

"Rough Start Happy Landing" [2004] IIC 821

Ladeur K and Gostomzyk T, "Der Schutz von Persönlichkeitsrechten gegen Meinungsäußerungen in Blogs" [2012] NJW 710

Laffranque J, "Who Has the Last Word on the Protection of Human Rights in Europe?" (2012) 1 *Juridica International* 117

Landes W and Lichtman D, "Indirect Liability for Copyright Infringement: An Economic Perspective" (2003) 16 *Harvard Journal of Law and Technology* 395

Larusdottir J, "Liability of Intermediaries for Copyright Infringement" (Stockholm Institute for Scandianvian Law paper 2010) 476

Lauinger T, et al., "Clickonomics: Determining the Effect of Anti-Piracy Measures for One-Click Hosting" (20th Annual Network and Distributed System Security Symposium, San Diego, CA, February 2013)

Lawn J, "The John Doe Injunction in Mass Protest Cases" (1998) 56 *University of Toronto Faculty Law Review* 101

Lehra W and McKnight L, "Wireless Internet Access: 3G vs. WiFi?" (2003) 27 *Telecommunications Policy* 351

Leistner M, "Störerhaftung und mittelbare Schutzrechtsverletzung" [2010] GRUR 1

Leistner M and Grisse K, "Sperrverfügungen gegen Access-Provider im Rahmen der Störerhaftung (Teil 2)" [2015] *GRUR* 105

Leistner M and Stang F, "Die Neuerung der wettbewerbsrechtlichen Verkehrspflichten – Ein Siegeszug der Prüfungspflichten?" [2008] WRP 533

Lemley M, "Faith-Based Intellectual Property" [2015] Stanford Public Law Working Paper No. 2587297

"IP in a World Without Scarcity" [2014] Stanford Public Law Working Paper No. 2413974, http://ssrn.com/abstract=2413974

"Property, Intellectual Property, and Free Riding" (2005) 83 *Texas Law Review* 1031

"Rationalizing Internet Safe Harbors" (2007) 6 *Journal of Telecommunications and High Technology Law* 101

Lemley M and Reese A, "Reducing Digital Copyright Infringement Without Restricting Innovation" (2004) 56 *Stanford Law Review* 1345

Lemley M and Weiser P, "Should Property or Liability Rules Govern Information" (2007) 85 *Texas Law Review* 783

Levinsohn J, "Protecting Copyright at the Expense of Internet Anonymity: The Constitutionality of Forced Identity Disclosure under 512(h) of the Digital Millennium Copyright Act" (2004) 23 *Temple Environmental Law & Technology Journal* 243

Litman J, "DNS Wars: Trademarks and the Internet Domain Name System" (2000) 4 *Journal of Small & Emerging Business Law* 149

Lorrain A, "Supreme Court (Cour de cassation): 'Google/Keyword Suggestions'" [2013] IIC 380

Lynch T, "Good Samaritan or Defamation Defender? Amending the Communications Decency Act to Correct the Misnomer of Section 230 Without Expanding ISP Liability" (2008) 19 *Syracuse Science and Technology Law Reporter* 1

Maaßen S and Schoene V, "Sperrungsverfügung gegen Access-Provider wegen Urheberrechtsverletzung?" [2011] *GRUR-Prax* 2011 394

MacCarthy M, "What Payment Intermediaries Are Doing about Online Liability and Why It Matters" (2010) 25 *Berkeley Technology Law Journal* 1037

Malaga M, "The European Patent with Unitary Effect: Incentive to Dominate?" [2014] *IIC* 621

Mallory A, "Ninth Circuit Unmasks Anonymous Internet Users and Lowers the Bar for Disclosure of Online Speakers" (2012) 7 *Washington Journal of Law of Technology & Arts* 75

Mann R, "Contracts – Only with Consent" (2004) 152 *University of Pennsylvania Law Review* 1873

Mann R and Belzley S, "The Promise of Internet Intermediary Liability" (2005) 47 *William & Mary Law Review* 239

Mantz R, "Die Haftung des Betreibers eines gewerblich betriebenen WLANs und die Haftungsprivilegierung des § 8 TMG" [2013] *GRUR-RR* 497

Massaguer J, "La responsabilidad de los prestadores de servicios en línea por las infracciones al derecho de autor y los derechos conexos en el ámbito digital. El Tratado de la OMPI sobre Derecho de Autor (WTC) y el Tratado de la OMPI sobre Interpretación o Ejecución y Fonogramas (WPPT)" (2003) 13 *Revista de Propiedad Intelectual* 11

Mayr S, "Putting a Leash on the Court of Justice? Preconceptions in National Methodology *v.* Effet Utile as a Meta-Rule" (2013) 5(2) *European Journal of Legal Studies* 8

Meale D, "NewzBin2: The First Section 97A Injunction against an ISP" (2011) 6 *Journal of Intellectual Property Law & Practice* 854

Medema S, "Legal Fiction: The Place of The Coase Theorem in Law and Economics" (1999) 15 *Economics and Philosophy* 209

Menell P, "Indirect Copyright Liability and Technological Innovation" [2009] UC Berkeley Public Law Research Paper No. 1415804

Merges R, "Of Property Rules, Coase, and Intellectual Property" (1994) 94 *Columbia Law Review* 2655

Metzger A, "A Primer on ACTA: What Europeans Should Fear About the Anti-Counterfeiting Trade Agreement" (2010) 2 *JIPITEC* 4

Milgrom P, et al., "The Case for Unlicensed Spectrum" (2011) http://ssrn.com/abstract= 1948257

Morrison S, "Breaking iPhones Under CALEA and the All Writs Act: Why the Government Was (Mostly) Right" (forthcoming) *Cardozo Law Review*, https://ssrn.com/ abstract=2808773

Nestoruk I, "Dreifacher pauschaler Schadensersatz im polnischen Urheberrecht aus verfassungsrechtlicher" [2017] *GRUR International* 12

Nimmer D, "Repeat Infringers" (2005) 52 *Journal of the Copyright Society of the USA* 167

Nolte G and Wimmers J, "Wer stört? Gedanken zur Haftung von Intermediären im Internet – von praktischer Konkordanz, richtigen Anreizen und offenen Fragen" [2014] *GRUR* 16

Nordemann J, "Haftung von Providern im Urheberrecht – Der aktuelle Stand nach dem EuGH-Urteil v. 12.7.2011-C-324/09 – L'Oréal/eBay" [2011] *GRUR* 977
  "Internet Copyright Infringement: Remedies Against Intermediaries – The European Perspective on Host and Access Providers" (2012) 59 *Journal of the Copyright Society USA* 773
  "Internetpiraterie: High Court of Justice bejaht Anspruch von Markeninhabern auf Website-Sperrung – Eine Option auch für deutsche Rechteinhaber?" [2014] *GRUR-Prax* 513
  "Nach TMG-Reform und EuGH McFadden" (2016) 11 *GRUR* 1097

Nowak M, et al., "Fairness versus Reason in the Ultimatum Game" (2000) 283 *Science* 289

O'Sulivan K, "Enforcing Copyright Online: Internet Provider Obligations and the European Charter of Human Rights" (2014) 36 *European Intellectual Property Review* 577

Pechan L and Schneider M, "Carriers and Trade Mark Infringements: Should Carriers Care?" (2010) 5(5) *Journal of Intellectual Property Law & Practice* 354

Peguera M, "The DMCA Safe Harbors and Their European Counterparts: A Comparative Analysis of Some Common Problems" (2009) 32 *Columbia Journal of Law & the Arts* 481
  "Internet Service Providers' Liability in Spain: Recent Case Law and Future Perspectives" (2010) 1 *JIPITEC* 151

Pekka S, "Proportionality of Website Blocking: Internet Connectivity Providers as Copyright Enforcers" (2014) 5(2) *JIPITEC* 116

Pekka S and Neuvonen R, "KHO 2013:136 – Verkkotunnusluettelon julkistamisen katsottiin edesauttavan lapsipornon levittämistä" (2014) 112 *Lakimies* 114

Perel M and Elkin-Koren N, "Accountability in Algorithmic Enforcement: Lessons from Copyright Enforcement by Online Intermediaries" [2015] Working paper, http://ssrn .com/abstract=2607910

"Black Box Tinkering: Beyond Transparency in Algorithmic Enforcement" (forthcoming) *Florida Law Review*

Peukert A, "Intellectual Property as an End in Itself?" [2011] European Intellectual Property Review 67

Peukert A and Kur A, "Stellungnahme des Max-Planck-Instituts für Geistiges Eigentum, Wettbewerbs- und Steuerrecht zur Umsetzung der Richtlinie 2004/48/EG zur Durchsetzung der Rechte des geistigen Eigentums in deutsches Recht" [2006] *GRUR International* 292

Poort J, et al., "Baywatch: Two Approaches to Measure the Effects of Blocking Access to The Pirate Bay" (2014) 38 *Telecommunications Policy* 383

Posner R, "A Theory of Negligence" (1972) 1 *The Journal of Legal Studies* 29

"Guido Calabresi's 'The Costs of Accidents': A Reassessment" (2005) 64 *Maryland Law Review* 12

Prentice R, "Locating That Indistinct and Virtually Nonexistent Line Between Primary and Secondary Liability under Section 10(b)" (1997) 75 *North Carolina Law Review* 691

Randa A, "Žaloba zápůrči" (1871) 10 *Právník* 181

Re E, "The Roman Contribution to the Common Law" (1961) 29 *Fordham Law Review* 447

Reimer D, "BGH: BGH 29.05.1964 Ib ZR 4/63 'Personalausweise'" [1965] *GRUR* 104

Reinbothe J, "Die EG-Richtlinie zum Urheberrecht in der Informationsgesellschaft" [2001] *GRUR International* 733

Rice C, "Meet John Doe: It Is Time for Federal Civil Procedure to Recognize John Doe Parties" (1996) 57 *University of Pittsburgh Law Review* 883

Roessing T, "The Dispute over Filtering 'Indecent' Images in Wikipedia" (2013) 2 *Masaryk University Journal of Law and Technology* 303

Rühmkorf A, "The Liability of Online Auction Portals: Toward a Uniform Approach?" (2010) 14(4) *Journal of Internet Law* 3

Sanchirico W, "Deconstructing the New Efficiency Rationale" (2001) 86 *Cornell Law Review* 1003

Savola P, "Proportionality of Website Blocking: Internet Connectivity Providers as Copyright Enforcers" (2014) 5 *JIPITEC* 116

Schlag P, "Appreciative Comment on Coase's the Problem of Social Cost: A View from the Left" [1986] *Wisconsin Law Review* 919

Schruers M, "The History and Economics of ISP Liability for Third Party Content" (2002) 88 *Virginia Law Review* 260

Schwab S, "Coase Defends Coase: Why Lawyers Listen and Economists Do Not" (1989) 87 *Michigan Law Review* 1171

Scott M, "Safe Harbors under the Digital Millennium Copyright Act" (2005) 99 *New York University Journal of Legislation and Public Policy* 115

Seifert A, "Die horizontale Wirkung von Grundrechten. Europarechtliche und rechtsvergleichende Überlegungen" (2011) 18 *Europäische Zeitschrift für Wirtschaftsrecht (EuZW)* 696

Seltzer W, "Free Speech Unmoored in Copyright's Safe Harbor: Chilling Effects of the DMCA on the First Amendment" (2010) 24 *Harvard Journal of Law & Technology* 171

Seng D, "The State of the Discordant Union: An Empirical Analysis of the State of DMCA Takedown Notices" (2014) 18 *Virginia Journal of Law and Technology* 369

Shavell S, "Liability and the Incentive to Obtain Information about Risk" (1992) 21(2) *The Journal of Legal Studies* 259

Sieber U and Michael F, "Drittauskunftsansprüche nach § 101a UrhG gegen Internetprovider zur Verfolgung von Urheberrechtsverletzungen" [2004] MMR 575

Sithigh D, "The Fragmentation of Intermediary Liability in the UK" (2013) 8 *Journal of Intellectual Property Law & Practice* 522

Sobola S and Kohl K, "Haftung von Providern für fremde Inhalte" [2005] CR 443

Spindler G, "Der Auskunftsanspruch gegen Verletzer und Dritte im Urheberrecht nach neuem Recht" [2008] ZUM 640

"'Die Tür ist auf' – Europarechtliche Zulässigkeit von Auskunftsansprüchen gegenüber Providern – Urteilsanmerkung zu EuGH 'Promusicae/Telefónica'" (2008) 7 *GRUR* 574

"Europäisches Urheberrecht in der Informationsgesellschaft" [2002] *GRUR* 105

"Haftung für private WLANs im Delikts- und Urheberrecht" [2010] CR 592

"Zivilrechtliche Sperrverfügungen gegen Access Provider nach dem EuGH-Urteil 'UPC Telekabel'" [2014] *GRUR* 826

Spindler G and Dorschel J, "Auskunftsansprüche gegen Internet-Service-Provider" [2005] Computer und Recht 341

"Vereinbarkeit der geplanten Auskunftsansprüche gegen Internet-Provider mit EU-Recht" [2006] CR 341

Stadler T, "Sperrungsverfügung gegen Access-Provider" [2002] MMR 343

Thaler R, "Anomalies: The Ultimatum Game" (1988) 2 *The Journal of Economic Perspectives* 195

Trotter H, "The Proper Legal Regime for 'Cyberspace'" (1994) 55 *University of Pittsburgh Law Review* 993

Ullmann E, "Einige Bemerkungen zur Meinungsfreiheit in der Wirtschaftswerbung" [1996] *GRUR* 948

Ungern-Sternberg J, "Die Rechtsprechung des EuGH und des BGH zum Urheberrecht und zu den verwandten Schutzrechten im Jahre 2014" [2015] *GRUR* 205

Urban J, Karaganis J, and Schofield B, "Notice and Takedown in Everyday Practice" (2016) UC Berkeley Public Law Research Paper No. 2755628, https://ssrn.com/abstract=2755628

Urban J and Quilter L, "Efficient Process or 'Chilling Effects'? Takedown Notices Under Section 512 of the Digital Millennium Copyright Act" (2006) 22 *Santa Clara Computer and High Technology Law Journal* 621

Vogel M, "Unmasking John Doe Defendants: The Case against Excessive Hand-Wringing over Legal Standares" (2004) 83 *Or. L. Rev.* 795

Weiß W, "Grundrechtssutz durch den EuGH: Tendenzen seit Lissabon. Europäische Zeitschrift für Wirtschaftsrecht" [2013] *EuZW* 289

Wenzel J, "Der Störer und seine verschuldensunabhängige Haftung im Nachbarrecht" [2005] NJW 241

Woodward M, "TRIPS and NAFTA Chapter 17: How Will Trade-Related Multilateral Agreements Affect International Copyright?" (1996) 31 *Texas International Law* 269

Zingales N, "Virtues and Perils of Anonymity: Should Intermediaries Bear the Burden?" (2014) TILEC Discussion Paper No. 025

Zittrain J, "The Generative Internet" (2006) 119 *Harvard Law Review* 1974

OTHER

Aguiar L, et al., "Online Copyright Enforcement, Consumer Behavior, and Market Structure" (European Commission, 2015), https://ec.europa.eu/jrc/sites/default/files/JRC93492_Online_Copyright.pdf

Anderson N, "Why the Feds Smashed Megaupload" (*Ars Technica*, 19 January 2012), http://arstechnica.com/tech-policy/2012/01/why-the-feds-smashed-megaupload/

Angelopolous Ch, "CJEU in UPC Telekabel Wien: A Totally Legal Court Order . . . to Do the Impossible" (*Kluwer Copyright Blog*, 3 April 2014), http://kluwercopyrightblog.com/2014/04/03/upc-telekabel-wien/
    "On Online Platforms and the Commission's New Proposal for a Directive on Copyright in the Digital Single Market" (2017), https://juliareda.eu/wp-content/uploads/2017/03/angelopoulos_platforms_copyright_study.pdf

Baker E, "The Official Twitch Blog Important: Changes to Audio in VODS" (*The Official Twitch Blog*, 6 August 2014), http://blog.twitch.tv/2014/08/3136/

Bitkom, "Öffentliche WLAN-Zugänge fristen Nischendasein" (2015), www.bitkom.org/de/presse/8477_82493.aspx

Bundesministerium für Wirtschaft und Energie (BMWi), "Entwurf eines Zweiten Gesetzes zur Änderung des Telemediengesetzes (Zweites Telemedienänderungsgesetz – 2. TMG ÄndG)" (2015), www.bmwi.de/BMWi/Redaktion/PDF/S-T/telemedienaenderungsgesetz,property=pdf,bereich=bmwi2012,sprache=de,rwb=true.pdf

Commission, "Communication from the Commission to the Council, the European Parliament, the Economic and Social Committee and the Committee of the Regions – Creating a Safer Information Society by Improving the Security of Information Infrastructures and Combating Computer-Related Crime – eEurope 2002," (2000).
    "Communication from the Commission to the European Parliament Pursuant to the Second Subparagraph of Article 251 (2) of the EC Treaty Concerning the Common Position of the Council on the Adoption of a Directive of the European Parliament and of the Council on the Harmonisation of Certain Aspects of Copyright and Related Rights in the Information Society," (2000)
    "Communication from the Commission to the European Parliament Pursuant to the Second Subparagraph of Article 251 (2) of the EC Treaty Concerning the Council Common Position on the Proposal for a Directive on Certain Legal Aspects of Information Society Services, in Particular Electronic Commerce, in the Internal Market" (2000)
    "Proposal for a Directive of the European Parliament and of the Council on Measures and Procedures to Ensure the Enforcement of Intellectual Property Rights" (2003)
    "Report by the Commission to the European Parliament, the Council, the European Economic and Social Committee and the Committee of the Regions on Application of Directive 2004/48/EC of the European Parliament and the Council of 29 April 2004 on the Enforcement of Intellectual Property Rights" (2010)
    "Report from the Commission to the European Parliament, the Council and the European Economic and Social Committee – First Report on the Application of Directive 2000/31/EC of the European Parliament and of the Council of 8 June 2000 on Certain Legal Aspects of Information Society Services, in Particular Electronic Commerce, in the Internal Market (Directive on Electronic Commerce)" (2003)
    "Staff Working Document: Analysis of the Application of Directive 2004/48/EC of the European Parliament and the Council of 29 April 2004 on the Enforcement of Intellectual Property Rights in the Member States – Accompanying Document to the Report from

the Commission to the Council, the European Parliament and the European Social Committee on the Application of Directive 2004/48/EC of the European Parliament and the Council of 29 April 2004 on the Enforcement of Intellectual Property Rights" (2010)

Committee on Legal Affairs and the Internal Market, "Recommendation for Second Reading on the Council Common Position for Adopting a European Parliament and Council Directive on the Harmonisation of Certain Aspects of Copyright and Related Rights in the Information Society" (9512/1/2000 – C5–0520/2000)

"Report on the Proposal for a Directive of the European Parliament and of the Council on Measures and Procedures to Ensure the Enforcement of Intellectual Property Rights" (2003, 46 – C5–0055/2003–2003/0024(COD))

Council of the European Union, "Common Position Adopted by the Council with a View to the Adoption of a Directive of the European Parliament and of the Council on the Harmonisation of Certain Aspects of Copyright and Related Rights in the Information Society" (1997)

Debilio R, "Red Light for Sabam's Pricing System for Internet Access Providers: Up- and Downstream IAP Traffic Do Not Constitute Communication or Making a Work Available to the Public" (*Kluwer Copyright Blog*, 6 May 2015), http://kluwercopyrightblog.com/2015/05/06/red-light-for-sabams-pricing-system-for-internet-access-providers-up-and-downstream-iap-traffic-do-not-constitute-communication-or-making-a-work-available-to-the-public/

Declaration by the Committee of Ministers on Internet governance principles; the Declaration of the Committee of Ministers on the protection of freedom of expression and freedom of assembly and association with regard to privately operated Internet platforms and online service providers

Declaration by the Committee of Ministers on the protection of freedom of expression and information and freedom of assembly and association with regard to Internet domain names and name strings

Declaration of the Committee of Ministers on the Digital Agenda for Europe, the Declaration of the Committee of Ministers on network neutrality

Declaration of the Committee of Ministers on the management of Internet Protocol address resources in the public interest

Declaration on a European policy for new information technologies adopted by the Committee of Ministers on 7 May 1999

Declaration on freedom of communication on the Internet adopted by the Committee of Ministers on 28 May 2003; Recommendation No. R (2001) 8 of the Committee of Ministers on self-regulation concerning cyber content

Deutsche Telekom, "Comments on the ERG Consultation Document on 'Wholesale Broadband Access via Cable'" (2004), http://berec.europa.eu/doc/publications/consult_add_cable_netw_chapter/dt.pdf

Deutscher Bundestag 4. Wahlperiode, "Entwurf eines Gesetzes über Urheberrecht und verwandte Schutzrechte (Urheberrechtsgesetz)" (14 May 1965), http://dipbt.bundestag.de/doc/btd/04/034/0403401.pdf

Doroshow K, "Finding of Copyright Infringement Liability as a Prerequisite for a Section 512(j) Injunction" (2016), www.scribd.com/document/273059624/mpaa-memo

Drexl J, "Copyright, Competition and Development" (WIPO Report by the Max Planck Institute for Intellectual Property and Competition Law 2013), www.wipo.int/export/sites/www/ip-competition/en/studies/copyright_competition_development.pdf

Duarte D, "Video Monetization, YouTube, and Multi-Channel Networks 101" (*Dlrepoter*, 3 April 2014), http://dlreporter.com/2014/04/03/video-monetization-youtube-and-multi-channel-partnerships-101/

Editorial, "Authorities Call for Wifi to Be Open after Deadly Italy Quake" (*Famagusta Gazette*, 29 May 2012), http://famagusta-gazette.com/authorities-call-for-wifi-to-be-open-after-deadly-italy-quake-p15591-69.htm

Editorial, "International Experts Find That Pending Anti-Counterfeiting Trade Agreement Threatens Public Interests" (*Naked Law*, 23 June 2010), www.wcl.american.edu/pijip/go/acta-communique

Editorial, "Kartellamt stoppt Initiative gegen Piraterie" (Handelsblatt, 21 April 2015), www.handelsblatt.com/unternehmen/it-medien/urheberrechtsverletzungen-im-netz-kartellamt-stoppt-initiative-gegen-piraterie/11668680.html

Editorial, "MySpace Implements Video Filtering System to Block Unauthorized Use of Copyrighted Content" (*Audible Magic*, 12 February 2007), https://archive.today/RXbp

Editorial, "Wer hat sie verraten? Googles Youtube-Daten!" FAZ (Frankfurt, 5 November 2014), www.faz.net/aktuell/feuilleton/debatten/youtubes-daten-gefaehrden-islamkritiker-13247806-p3.html

Editorial, "YouTube Handed Out $1 Billion in Ad Money Thanks to Content ID" (*Softpedia*, 14 October 2014), http://news.softpedia.com/news/YouTube-Handed-Out-1-Billion-In-Ad-Money-Thanks-to-Content-ID-462088.shtml

Edwards L, "Role and Responsibility of Internet Intermediaries in the Field of Copyright and Related Rights" (WIPO report, 2009), www.wipo.int/export/sites/www/copyright/en/doc/role_and_responsibility_of_the_internet_intermediaries_final.pdf

EISi, "Third Party Intervention Submission by European Information Society Institute (EISi) In re Delfi AS v. Estonia" (*EISi*, 2014), www.eisionline.org/images/EISi-Delfi-Intervention.pdf

European Commission, "A Digital Single Market for Europe: Commission Sets Out 16 Initiatives to Make It Happen, http://europa.eu/rapid/press-release_IP-15-4919_en.htm

"Electronic Commerce: Commission Proposes Legal Framework" (press release, 18 November 1998), http://europa.eu/rapid/press-release_IP-98-999_en.htm?locale=en

"Memorandum of Understanding" (May 2011), http://ec.europa.eu/internal_market/iprenforcement/docs/memorandum_04052011_en.pdf

"Public Hearing on Directive 2004/48/EC and the Challenges Posed by the Digital Environment" (report, 7 June 2011), http://ec.europa.eu/internal_market/iprenforcement/docs/conference20110607/hearing-report_en.pdf

European Observatory on Counterfeiting and Piracy, "Injunctions in Intellectual Property Right," http://ec.europa.eu/internal_market/iprenforcement/docs/injunctions_en.pdf

Friedman J, "Sponsors of SOPA Act Pulled in 4 Times as Much in Contributions from Hollywood as from Silicon Valley" (*Map Law*, 1 May 2009), http://maplight.org/content/72896

Geist M, "The Liberal Roundtable on the Digital Economy: My Comments" (*Geist Blog*, 11 February 2010), www.michaelgeist.ca/content/view/4787/125/

German Council of Science and Humanities, "Prospects of Legal Scholarship in Germany Current Situation, Analyses, Recommendations" (October 2013), www.wissenschaftsrat.de/download/archiv/2558-12_engl.pdf

Goldman E, "Stanford Technology Law Review Symposium on Secondary IP Liability" (*Technology & Marketing Law Blog*, 8 March 2011), http://blog.ericgoldman.org/archives/2011/03/stanford_techno.htm

Google, "Testimony of Katherine Oyama, Sr. Copyright Policy Counsel, Google Inc. House Judiciary Subcommittee on Courts, Intellectual Property, and the Internet Hearing on 'Section 512 of Title 17'" (13 March 2014), http://judiciary.house.gov/_cache/files/be93d452–945a-4fff-83ec-b3f51de782b3/031314-testimony-oyama.pdf

Hansen E and Bowman L, "Court: Napster Filters Must Be Foolproof" (*Cnet News*, 12 July 2001) http://news.cnet.com/Court-Napster-filters-must-be-foolproof/2100–1023_3–269837.html

Husovec M, "Tank Man Hits the Constitutional Court: Copyright and Freedom of Expression" (*Huťko's Technology Law Blog*, 25 March 2015), www.husovec.eu/2015/03/tank-man-hits-constitutional-court.html

IFPI, "Digital Music Report 2015" (2015), www.ifpi.org/downloads/Digital-Music-Report-2015.pdf

"Police Dawn Raid Stops Allofmp3.com Pirate Vouchers Scheme" (*Enforcement Bulletin*, 2007), www.ifpi.org/content/library/enforcement-bulletin-34.pdf

Jasserand C, "France: Google Can Be Ordered to Filter Words Linking to Online Piracy Websites" (*Kluwer Copyright Blog*, 3 September 2012), http://kluwercopyrightblog.com/2012/09/03/france-google-can-be-ordered-to-filter-words-linking-to-online-piracy-websites/

JWFocus, "The Future of Online Video: Multi-Channel Video Strategy" (JW Focus: Entertainment, 1 March 2014)

Kur A, "UDRP: A Study" (Max-Planck-Institute for Foreign and International Patent, Copyright and Competition Law Munich, 2010)

Lehman B and Brown R, "Intellectual Property and National Information Infrastructure" (Report of the Working Group on Intellectual Property Rights, 1995), www.uspto.gov/web/offices/com/doc/ipnii/ipnii.pdf

Linari A, et al., "Typo-Squatting: The 'Curse' of Popularity" (*Nominet.org*, 2009), http://blog.nominet.org.uk/tech/wp-content/uploads/2009/06/full-paper-websci09.pdf

Litan R and Rivlin A, "Beyond the Dot.coms" (Brookings 2001), www.brookings.edu/research/books/2001/beyond-dotcoms

Machlup F, "An Economic Review of the Patent System" (Study of Commission on Judiciary, Subcommittee on Patents, Trademarks, and Copyrights, 1958)

Marcel R and Hilmar S, "Funkstille auf dem Bürgersteig" (*Der Spiegel*, 1 July 2013)

Miller C, "The Review Site Yelp Draws Some Outcries of Its Own" (New York Times, 3 March 2009)

"Yelp Will Let Businesses Respond to Web Reviews" (New York Times, 10 April 2009)

Moody G, "Danish Court Orders Spanish Site Blocked because It Uses Trademarked English Word 'Home' as Part of Its Name" (*Techdirt*, 2012), www.techdirt.com/articles/20121228/09275521510/danish-court-orders-spanish-site-blocked-because-it-uses-trademarked-english-word-home-as-part-its-name.shtml

Mullin J, "Music Publishers Finally Pull the Trigger, Sue an ISP over Piracy" (*Ars Technica*, 28 November 2014), http://arstechnica.com/tech-policy/2014/11/music-publishers-finally-pull-the-trigger-sue-an-isp-over-piracy/

Net Names, "Behind the Cyberlocker Door: A Report on How Shadowy Cyberlocker Businesses Use Credit Card Companies to Make Milions" (*Net Names*, 2014), www2.itif.org/2014-netnames-profitability.pdf

Novak V, "SOPA and PIPA Spur Lobbying Spike" (*Open Secrets*, 26 January 2012), www.opensecrets.org/news/2012/01/sopa-and-pipa-create-lobbying-spike/

Ofcom, "Site Blocking to Reduce Online Copyright Infringement: A Review of Sections 17 and 18 of the Digital Economy Act" (*Ofcom*, 2010), http://stakeholders.ofcom.org.uk/binaries/internet/site-blocking.pdf

OSCE, "Joint Declaration on Freedom of Expression and the Internet" (2011)

Pappalardo K, "A Tort Law Framework for Copyright Authorisation" (Thomas More School of Law, Australian Catholic University [PhD thesis] 2015)

Patent Office, "Consultation on UK Implementation of Directive 2001/29/EC on Copyright and Related Rights in the Information Society: Analysis of Responses and Government Conclusions" (2003), www.patent.gov.uk/about/consultations/responses/copydirect/index.htm

"The UK Implementation of the Directive on the Enforcement of Intellectual Property Rights" (2005)

Principles of European Tort Law (PETL)

Principles, Definitions and Model Rules of European Private Law Draft Common Frame of Reference (DCFR)

Purnell N, "FireChat Messaging App Gains Users during Hong Kong Protests" (*Blogs WSJ*, 2014), http://blogs.wsj.com/digits/2014/09/29/firechat-messaging-app-gains-users-during-hong-kong-protests/

Recommendation 1332 (1997) of the Parliamentary Assembly on the scientific and technical aspects of the new information and communications technologies

Recommendation CM/Rec (2007) 16 of the Committee of Ministers on measures to promote the public service value of the Internet

Recommendation CM/Rec (2008) 6 of the Committee of Ministers on measures to promote the respect for freedom of expression and information with regard to Internet filters

Recommendation CM/Rec (2011) 8 of the Committee of Ministers to Member States on the protection and promotion of the universality, integrity, and openness of the Internet

Recommendation CM/Rec (2012) 3 of the Committee of Ministers to Member States on the protection of human rights with regard to search engines (adopted by the Committee of Ministers on 4 April 2012 at the 1139th meeting of the Ministers' Deputies)

Recommendation CM/Rec (2012) 4 of the Committee of Ministers to Member States on the protection of human rights with regard to social networking services

Recommendation No. R (99) 14 of the Committee of Ministers on universal community service concerning new communication and information services

Recommendation No. R (99) 5 for the protection of privacy on the Internet

Resolution 1120 (1997) of the Parliamentary Assembly on the impact of the new communication and information technologies on democracy

Shaheed F, "Copyright Policy and the Right to Science and Culture" (UN Special Report, 2014)

Spangler T, "Despite YouTube's Emmy, Google Still Has a Long Way to Go" (*Variety*, 24 October 2013) http://variety.com/2013/biz/news/despite-youtubes-emmy-google-still-has-a-long-way-to-go-1200756170/

Tassi P, "The Injustice of the YouTube Content ID Crackdown Reveals Google's Dark Side" (*Forbes*, 19 December 2013), www.forbes.com/sites/insertcoin/2013/12/19/the-injustice-of-the-youtube-content-id-crackdown-reveals-googles-dark-side/

Ueno T and Kojima R, "Indirect Infringement and Provisions Restricting Rights in Copyright Law" in Symposium "Koko ga hen da yo nihon-ho" – "Is Japanese Law a Strange Law?" (2008), www.zjapanr.de/index.php/zjapanr/article/viewFile/384/405

United Nations, General Comment on Freedom of Expression No. 34 (2011)

US Department of Commerce, *DMCA Notice-and-Takedown Processes: List of Good, Bad, and Situational Practices* (USPTO, 7 April 2015), www.uspto.gov/about-us/news-updates/us-commerce-department-announces-digital-millennium-copyright-act

US Fire Administration, "Technical Report Series, I-35W Bridge Collapse and Response" (2007), http://berec.europa.eu/doc/publications/consult_add_cable_netw_chapter/dt.pdf

Vargas P, "Argentine Supreme Court Decides Landmark Intermediary Liability Case" (*Stanford CIS Blog*, 5 November 2014), https://cyberlaw.stanford.edu/blog/2014/11/argentine-supreme-court-decides-landmark-intermediary-liability-case

Vermeer D, "Vrije internettoegang ook in Nederland onder vuur" (*Bits of Freedom*, 4 January 2011), www.bof.nl/2011/01/04/vrije-internettoegang-ook-in-nederland-onder-vuur/

Vuopala A, "Assessment of the Orphan Works Issue and Costs for Rights Clearance" (European Commission 2010), www.ace-film.eu/wp-content/uploads/2010/09/Copyright_anna_report-1.pdf

WAN-IFRA, "Online Comment Moderation: Emerging Best Practicies" (2013), www.wan-ifra.org/reports/

Weatherley M, "Safe Harbour Provisions and Online Service Providers" (2015), discussion paper

Witt D, "Copyright Match on Vimeo" (*Vimeo*, 23 May 2014), http://vimeo.com/blog/post:626

Wolfensberger K, "Rapidshare wohl am Ende" (*Netzwoche*, 26 February 2014), www.netzwoche.ch/de-CH/News/2014/02/26/Rapidshare-wohl-am-Ende.aspx

Working Party 29, "Working Document on Data Protection Issues Related to Intellectual Property Rights" (2005), http://ec.europa.eu/justice/policies/privacy/docs/wpdocs/2005/wp104_en.pdf

Index

access providers, 6, 7, 19, 22, 28, 29, 31, 34, 62, 76, 79, 85, 86, 93, 100, 116, 167, 177, 193, 195, 204, 205, 217, 220, 226

accessory liability, xvi, 10, 13, 14, 64, 65, 66, 67, 68, 69, 70, 92, 96, 110, 181

accountable but not liable, 8, 10, 14, 223, 226

actio negatoria, 146, 147, 148, 149, 150, 152, 153, 175, 223

actual knowledge, 43, 44, 52, 53, 95

adopted content, 56

Alone in the Dark, 170, 171

alternative dispute resolution, 21, 32, 34, 35, 167

ambiente.de, 21, 167, 168

Amstrad, 207, 208, 209

anonymity, 132

Anspruch, 147, 154, 180

Australia, 186, 220, 221

Austria, 51, 77, 91, 100, 108, 123, 147, 148, 149

balancing exercise, 4, 81, 115, 131, 134, 135, 137
 framing, 134, 169, 200

barriers to trade, 5, 31, 97, 113, 115, 138, 215, 226

Belgium, 100

BGB
 § 1004 BGB, 148, 150, 152, 153, 154, 156, 158, 159, 161, 166, 169, 176

Bonnier Audio, 76, 79, 81

Calabresi, 23, 24, 25, 26

Calabresi and Melamed, 32

Canada, 31, 33, 75, 186, 216

Canaris, 153

Cartier v. Sky, 101, 198, 199, 206, 208

causality, 19, 20, 91, 154, 160, 161, 181, 192, 226

CETA, 216

Charter of the Fundamental Rights of the European Union, 49, 54, 83, 84, 112, 115, 122, 131, 133, 138, 228, 232
 horizontal effect of human rights, 123, 231
 interpretation, 81
 scope of application, 67, 122, 124, 129, 134

cheapest cost avoider, 24

Coase theorem, 22, 23, 34

common law
 mere witness rule, 12, 189, 190, 192, 194, 195
 mixed up with the transaction, 11, 14, 91, 192, 193, 223
 preemption of equitable jurisdiction, 188, 219

communication to the public, 51, 57, 69, 71, 109, 180, 215

competition law, 37

confidentiality, 78, 79, 83, 85

constructive knowledge, 17, 53

contempt of the court, 129, 209, 219, 220

ContentID, 229

co-regulation, 34, 229, 230, 233

Coty Germany, 81, 83, 84

court supervision, 77, 194
 costs, 27
 human rights, 232

Cyprus, 56

Czech Republic, 98, 111, 129, 149

data protection, 78, 79, 80, 83, 84, 140, 232

Deep Packet Inspection, 31

defamation, 118, 161

de-indexing, 225, 226

Delfi v. Estonia, 55

Denmark, 100

Digital Millenium Copyright Act, 17, 53, 217, 218, 219

digital single market, 70
dingliche Anspruch, 147
Directive 2002/58/EC, 80, 82, 135
disconnection from Internet, 8, 102, 111, 119, 123, 133
domain names, 18, 21, 28, 111, 167, 217
Donner, 68
double identity obligation, 53, 72, 106, 107, 171
duty of care, 20, 53, 154, 165, 168, 180, 181, 206, 207, 226
duty to review, 162, 163, 167, 169, 175, 179, 180, 181

E-Commerce Directive, 42, 45, 47, 48, 50, 51, 53, 56, 57, 59, 60, 63, 65, 71, 88, 105, 112, 116, 117, 118, 119, 166, 198, 204, 226, 232
  Article 12, 17, 18, 57, 59, 112, 116, 226
  Article 14, 43, 51, 57, 58, 71
effectiveness, 3, 4, 7, 8, 25, 27, 28, 30, 93, 105, 114, 115, 116, 129, 136, 137, 138, 159, 169, 196, 200, 209
  effective remedy, 75, 83, 84, 130
  minimum required by Union law, 96
Eigentumsfreiheitsklage, 147
Enforcement Directive
  Article 11(III), 8, 12, 18, 41, 48, 166, 182, 188, 198, 225
  Article 14, 139
  Article 3, 67, 72, 114, 115, 172, 199
  Article 8, 75, 76, 77, 78
entitlements, 24, 25
equitable duty, 190, 198, 199, 205, 206, 207, 208

filtering, 33, 46, 55, 71, 72, 111, 119, 120, 121, 126, 127, 132, 164, 169, 170, 171, 176, 179, 192, 205, 223
Finland, 100
France, 85, 100, 125
freedom of expression, 54, 110, 123, 126, 131, 132, 133
freedom to conduct business, 132, 134
Frisdranken, 62, 64
full restriction of conduct, 108, 109

GEMA notices, 159
general monitoring, 42, 43, 44, 46, 117, 118, 119, 120, 121, 161, 167, 172, 228
German attribution principle, 153
German expansion of injunctions, 150
Google France, 54, 88
Greece, 100

harmonization
  by Article 3 Enforcement Directive, 67, 114
  by fundamental rights, 134, 137
  by judicial activism, 67
  Union accessory liability, 67
hate speech, 55

human rights
  freedom of expression, 54, 110, 123, 126, 132, 133
  freedom to conduct business, 132, 134
  right to intellectual property, 75, 84, 129, 136
  hyperlink, 51, 69

implementation costs, 27, 28, 34, 86, 138, 139, 203, 204, 227
  capital expenditure, 7, 102, 204, 205
in personam action, 145
in rem action, 146, 148, 155
independent supervision
  human rights, 31
information society service, 47, 65, 87
InfoSoc Directive
  Article 8(3), 8, 12, 18, 41, 45, 50, 60, 166, 182, 189, 195, 202, 203, 225, 227
injunctions
  time limitation, 28, 30, 196
innocent third party, 9, 11, 12, 13, 14, 41, 213, 214
innovation, 5, 6, 27, 30, 31, 36, 46, 55, 134, 226, 227
  before CJEU, 113
  follow-on innovation, 138, 228
  in balancing exercise, 134
  legal innovation, 206, 223
intent, 17, 152, 192
  competitive intent, 162
  double intent, 164
interference with property, 151
intermediary
  capable of being used, 87
  electricity provider, 90
  flea-market landlord, 87
  intermediary character, 88
  normally provided for remuneration, 88
  services, 88, 89
  transport intermediaries, 90
Internetversteigerung I, 163, 169
Internetversteigerung II, 94, 170
Ireland, 12, 100, 186
Italy, 5, 100

Johow, 147, 150, 151
Jugendgefährdende Medien bei eBay, 156, 164

Kinderhochstuehle im Internet I, 170, 178

L'Oréal v. eBay, 61, 93, 95, 96, 98, 101, 104, 106, 107, 115
Larenz, 153
legitimate aim, 129, 194
litigation costs, 27, 59, 202

margin of appreciation, 81, 111, 134, 137, 216
marions-kochbuch.de, 56

Mc Fadden, 59, 60, 89, 106, 113, 116, 117, 120, 128, 132, 138
Melloni, 122, 129

negligence, 13, 14, 17, 25, 29, 64, 70, 164, 181, 207, 208, 225, 228
net neutrality, 140, 232
Norwich Pharmacal, 94, 186, 191, 192, 193, 195, 198, 200, 201, 206, 207
notice
  notice and takedown, 18, 226
  submission interface, 172, 178, 179, 180

objective infringement, 152
online market place, 119, 121, 193
Orr v. Diaper, 190, 195, 198, 207
overblocking, 123, 132, 169, 232

Pandectists, 117, 148, 150
Papasavvas, 56, 89
patent law, 41, 48, 103, 165, 191, 206
payment intermediaries, 17, 19, 22, 34, 37, 90, 193, 200, 217, 226
Pertusin II, 158, 161
Portugal, 51
position to prevent, 90, 156, 157, 223
preliminary injunctions, 41, 111, 214, 216
prescribed by the law, 169
pretrial costs, 30, 59, 60, 117, 178, 179, 225, 227
prevention of wrongdoing
  choice of tools, 21
  scope, 72, 93, 106, 171
procedural autonomy, 140
Promusicae, 76, 79, 81, 82, 83, 84, 130
proximate services, 16, 17, 29, 35, 53, 225, 228

reel-to-reel tape recorders, 159, 160
rei vindicatio, 146, 147, 148, 149, 150, 151, 152, 175
Reichsgericht, 156, 157
remote services, 16, 17, 21, 23, 29, 33, 177, 223, 226
repeat infringers, 18, 19, 102, 108, 121, 229
right to intellectual property, 75, 84, 129, 136
rule of law, 126

Sabam, 115, 119, 132
safe harbors, 42, 43, 44, 50, 55, 117, 118, 205, 218, 226
  carve out for injunctions, 57, 59
  direct infringement, 57
  horizontal nature, 60
  hosting, 52, 53, 54, 56, 169, 170
  information location tools, 51
  mere conduit, 52, 59, 226
  national, 89

notion of liability, 58, 59
own content, 56
passivity of a provider, 44, 54, 55
Scarlet Extended, 111, 115, 118, 125, 126, 132
search engines, 16, 19, 51, 90, 118, 121, 200, 205, 225, 232
self-incrimination, 79
Slovak Republic, 98, 111, 149
social networks, 52, 89, 109, 119
Sommer unseres Lebens, 4, 109, 172
SOPA/PIPA, 218, 221
Spain, 7, 8, 51
Spry, 188
standardization, 232, 233
stay-down obligation, 18, 71, 106, 121, 169, 170, 171, 224, 225, 226
strict liability, 14, 55
subsidiarity of enforcement, 133, 168, 200
surveillance, 81, 132, 166, 219
  market-surveillance obligation, 172
Sweden, 100

tape recorders, 207, 208, 209
Tele2, 62, 76, 79
The Netherlands, 100
Tommy Hilfiger, 62, 94, 98, 106, 115, 120, 209
  Tommy Hilfiger standard, 106
trademark law, 11, 18, 32, 83, 197
  trademark use, 69, 167
TRIPS, 80, 114, 115, 213, 214, 215
Twentieth Century Fox v. BT, 196

unambiguously wrongful content, 167
unfair competition, 154, 156, 157, 162, 165, 166, 180, 181
UPC Telekabel Wien, 62, 90, 93, 101, 106, 110, 113, 114, 115, 116, 122, 128, 135, 136, 139, 197
Upmann v. Elkan, 11, 190, 195, 198, 201, 206

voluntary agreements, 22, 36, 226, 227, 231
  as alternative, 30
  Digital Single Market proposal, 70
  human rights, 228, 229, 231
  incentive to negotiate, 36
  negotiation impediments, 33, 35
VPN providers, 90

website blocking, 3, 22, 31, 66, 92, 95, 96, 100, 101, 102, 111, 116, 120, 121, 127, 128, 133, 135, 168, 169, 177, 183, 187, 196, 197, 198, 200, 203, 220, 224
WiFi hotspot, 4, 5, 23, 27, 30, 36, 52, 89, 108, 109, 172, 173, 183, 228
Windscheid, 148

Cambridge Intellectual Property and Information Law

Titles in the series (formerly known as *Cambridge Studies in Intellectual Property Rights*)

Brad Sherman and Lionel Bently
The Making of Modern Intellectual Property Law

Irini A. Stamatoudi
Copyright and Multimedia Products: A Comparative Analysis

Pascal Kamina
Film Copyright in the European Union

Huw Beverly-Smith
The Commercial Appropriation of Personality

Mark J. Davison
The Legal Protection of Databases

Robert Burrell and Allison Coleman
Copyright Exceptions: The Digital Impact

Huw Beverly-Smith, Ansgar Ohly and Agnès Lucas-Schloetter
Privacy, Property and Personality: Civil Law Perspectives on Commercial Appropriation

Catherine Seville
The Internationalisation of Copyright Law: Books, Buccaneers and the Black Flag in the Nineteenth Century

Philip Leith
Software and Patents in Europe

Geertrui Van Overwalle
Gene Patents and Clearing Models

Lionel Bently, Jennifer Davis and Jane C. Ginsburg
Trade Marks and Brands: An Interdisciplinary Critique

Jonathan Curci
The Protection of Biodiversity and Traditional Knowledge in International Law of Intellectual Property

Lionel Bently, Jennifer Davis and Jane C. Ginsburg
Copyright and Piracy: An Interdisciplinary Critique

Megan Richardson and Julian Thomas
Framing Intellectual Property: Legal Constructions of Creativity and Appropriation 1840–1940

Dev Gangjee
Relocating the Law of Geographical Indications

Andrew Kenyon, Megan Richardson and Ng-Loy Wee-Loon
The Law of Reputation and Brands in the Asia Pacific Region

Annabelle Lever
New Frontiers in the Philosophy of Intellectual Property

Sigrid Sterckx and Julian Cockbain
Exclusions from Patentability: How the European Patent Office is Eroding Boundaries

Sebastian Haunss
Conflicts in the Knowledge Society: The Contentious Politics of Intellectual Property

Helena R. Howe and Jonathan Griffiths
Concepts of Property in Intellectual Property Law

Rochelle Cooper Dreyfuss and Jane C. Ginsburg
Intellectual Property at the Edge: The Contested Contours of IP

Normann Witzleb, David Lindsay, Moira Paterson and Sharon Rodrick
Emerging Challenges in Privacy Law: Comparative Perspectives

Paul Bernal
Internet Privacy Rights: Rights to Protect Autonomy

Peter Drahos
Intellectual Property, Indigenous People and Their Knowledge

Susy Frankel and Daniel Gervais
The Evolution and Equilibrium of Copyright in the Digital Age

Edited by Kathy Bowrey and Michael Handler
Law and Creativity in the Age of the Entertainment Franchise

Sean Bottomley
The British Patent System and the Industrial Revolution 1700–1852: From Privileges to Property

Susy Frankel
Test Tubes for Global Intellectual Property Issues: Small Market Economies

Jan Oster
Media Freedom as a Fundamental Right

Sara Bannerman
International Copyright and Access to Knowledge

Andrew T. Kenyon
Comparative Defamation and Privacy Law

Pascal Kamina
Film Copyright in the European Union, Second Edition

Tim W. Dornis
Trademark and Unfair Competition Conflicts

Ge Chen
Copyright and International Negotiations: An Engine of Free Expression in China?

David Tan
The Commercial Appropriation of Fame: A Cultural Critique of the Right of Publicity and Passing Off

Jay Sanderson
Plants, People and Practices: The Nature and History of the UPOV Convention

Daniel Benoliel
Patent Intensity and Economic Growth

Jeffrey A. Maine and Xuan-Thao Nguyen
The Intellectual Property Holding Company: Tax Use and Abuse from Victoria's Secret to Apple

Megan Richardson
The Right to Privacy: Origins and Influence of a Nineteenth Century Idea

Martin Husovec
Injunctions Against Intermediaries in the European Union: Accountable But Not Liable?

For EU product safety concerns, contact us at Calle de José Abascal, 56–1°,
28003 Madrid, Spain or eugpsr@cambridge.org.

www.ingramcontent.com/pod-product-compliance
Ingram Content Group UK Ltd.
Pitfield, Milton Keynes, MK11 3LW, UK
UKHW020337140625
459647UK00018B/2183